'This groundbreaking book offers an evidence-informed model that n
the research base, but also empowers educators, strength
and helping to create a new generation of motivat

Jonathan Do

'At a time when attainment data is being used to n
literacy learning, this book provides critical insights ve
known or suspected: that effective literacy education gnition and
desire, on individuals and communities in collaboratio out access to culturally sustainable texts and social interactions.'

Navan Govender, Lecturer in Applied Language and Literacy Studies, University of Strathclyde, UK

'This book provides a well-researched framework to help children engage deeply with reading and writing and enjoy the experience. It offers educators advice on how to take action that has long lasting impact because the learning matters to the learners.'

Alyson Simpson, The Sydney School of Education and Social Work, University of Sydney, Australia

'This research-informed framework is essential reading for policymakers, educators and teachers seeking to nurture children's reading and writing for pleasure. It highlights the importance of agency, identity and supporting spontaneous, child-led interactions around texts to foster meaningful connections between young readers and writers. As a funder supporting literacy and oracy programmes in London, we recognise the Framework's value in shaping effective practice and helping to align policy, education and community initiatives to create lasting opportunities for volitional reading and writing'.

The Mercers' Company, as Trustee of The Mercers' Charitable Foundation and The St Paul's Schools' Foundation

'We've got to work smartly to head off the crisis and enable more children to experience the enormous benefits of reading for pleasure. *Reading and Writing for Pleasure: An Evidence-Informed Framework for Practice* is the blueprint for any reading and literacy organisations, libraries, and schools who want to know how to get more children reading (and writing) for fun.'

Cassie Chadderton, CEO, World Book Day

'This is a noteworthy evidence-informed text. It challenges and encourages educators at home, in the literacy community, in policy and educational settings to engage with understanding the socio-emotional contexts of young peoples' identities as volitional readers and writers. The research reveals ways to enhance children's agency in literacy through relational pedagogy, social interactions and the use of reflective language.'

Janet Douglas Gardner, Associate Teaching Professor, London Metropolitan University, UK

'The Reading and Writing for Pleasure Framework is a must read for researchers, teachers and educators. It throws a much-needed spotlight on cultivating a love for reading and writing, emphasising the importance of engaging socially as readers and writers. It also highlights the value of local knowledge and the impact of flexibly responding to local needs. Communities, talk and relationships are seen to be key.'

Jo Tregenza, Reader in Education, University of Sussex, UK

READING AND WRITING FOR PLEASURE

Reading and writing for pleasure represent issues of global concern and interest in policy, research and practice, underpinned by evidence illustrating their importance for young people's academic, social and emotional experiences and outcomes. In the face of a sustained decline in children's enjoyment in both reading and writing, this highly significant book presents findings from a three-year study of research and practice that nurtures young people's engagement as readers and writers.

The book offers a rich understanding of the study, highlighting the commonalities and synergies identified from the research literature and diverse practice contexts. It introduces a new and powerful Reading and Writing Framework for Practice for schools and charitable literacy programmes. The authors offer practical strategies and recommendations throughout for practitioners, researchers and policy makers who wish to advance this agenda in their own contexts. Areas covered include:

- The nature of reading and writing for pleasure
- Literate identities
- Motivating readers and writers
- Social interactions
- Role models and connected communities
- Future research, practice and policy

This field-defining text is a key resource for all those committed to halting the decline in young people's engagement as volitional readers and writers.

Teresa Cremin is Professor of Education and co-director of The Open University's Literacy and Social Justice Centre. Her research focuses on volitional reading and writing, teachers' and children's literate identities and practices and creative pedagogies.

Helen Hendry is Senior Lecturer in Education (Primary) at The Open University and co-director of the Literacy and Social Justice Centre. Her research centres on early years' pedagogy, reading for pleasure and teacher professional development.

Liz Chamberlain is Emerita Professor and past co-director of The Open University's Children's Research Centre. Her research explores the knowledge intersection between practice, learners and practitioners through the lens of literacy education.

Samantha Jayne Hulston is a Research Associate at The Open University. Her research focuses on young children's embodied engagement with stories and the role of teachers in supporting children's playful exploration of texts.

READING AND WRITING FOR PLEASURE

An Evidence-Informed Framework for Practice

Teresa Cremin, Helen Hendry, Liz Chamberlain and Samantha Jayne Hulston

Routledge
Taylor & Francis Group
LONDON AND NEW YORK

Cover image: © Onyinye Iwu

First published 2026
by Routledge
4 Park Square, Milton Park, Abingdon, Oxon OX14 4RN

and by Routledge
605 Third Avenue, New York, NY 10158

Routledge is an imprint of the Taylor & Francis Group, an informa business

British Library Cataloguing-in-Publication Data
A catalogue record for this book is available from the British Library

ISBN: 978-1-032-87427-2 (hbk)
ISBN: 978-1-032-87426-5 (pbk)
ISBN: 978-1-003-53260-6 (ebk)

DOI: 10.4324/9781003532606

Typeset in Optima
by Taylor & Francis Books

For Product Safety Concerns and Information please contact our EU representative:
GPSR@taylorandfrancis.com
Taylor & Francis
Verlag GmbH, Kaufingerstraße 24, 80331 München, Germany

MIX
Paper | Supporting responsible forestry
FSC® C013056
www.fsc.org

Printed and bound in Great Britain by
TJ Books, Padstow, Cornwall

CONTENTS

ILLUSTRATIONS

Figures

Tables

Boxes

ACKNOWLEDGEMENTS

The authors would like to thank the Mercers' Company whose young people and education programmes committee had the foresight to identify the focus of the Literacy Special Initiative as reading and writing for pleasure and who funded the work (2020–2023). In particular, we appreciated the thoughtful contributions made by Gerard Darby, Helen Stonelake and Charlotte Nugent, and the Mercers' Company's flexibility and generosity in supporting this initiative, especially during and in the aftermath of the COVID-19 pandemic. In addition, we would like to thank Dr Sarah Jane Mukherjee, Dr Becky Coles and Dr Alison Twiner who worked with us so assiduously as Research Associates in the early years of this work. Finally, we want to acknowledge the time and talent shared by the education leads of the six London-based literacy programmes that were funded by the Literacy Special Initiative, namely Katie Bareham from Doorstep Library, Jude Williams from Literacy Pirates, Rob Smith from Ministry of Stories, the Primary Shakespeare Company team, Cassie Chadderton from World Book Day, and Jasmine Tucker and the National Literacy Trust team, who with Emma Braithwaite from the Reading Agency, led Get Islington Reading. Their individual and collective openness to learning, commitment to address social inequalities and improve their programmes to enrich young people's engagement as readers and writers is inspirational. Finally, we'd like to thank all the practitioners, librarians, creatives, volunteers and the children and young people involved. We learned a great deal from each of you.

INTRODUCTION

Exploring reading, writing and pleasure

Introduction

This book derives from an original three-year research project commissioned by the Mercers' Company as part of their Literacy Special Initiative: Reading and Writing for Pleasure (2020–2023) and funded by the Charity of Sir Richard Whittington. Following a competitive process of application and review, the Mercers' Company chose to support the work of six charitable literacy programmes in London, focused on developing children's reading and/or writing for pleasure in areas of disadvantage. The Open University (OU) team, as research partners, were required to develop an accompanying piece of research which, rather than evaluating any individual programme's work, sought to review the extant research literature, learn about the approaches they deployed and explore any synergies therein, as well as help build the programmes' capacity through collaboration.

Within the Special Initiative, all the organisations worked on their own specific and highly diverse programmes aimed at enriching children's pleasure in reading and/or writing, predominantly with primary aged children. Their partners included teachers, parents and carers, creatives, librarians and volunteers. In this opening chapter, the nature of the research project is outlined and an overview of each of the programmes is offered. The programmes were led by Doorstep Library, Literacy Pirates, Ministry of Stories, Primary Shakespeare Company, World Book Day and the National Literacy Trust together with the Reading Agency, who jointly led 'Get Islington Reading'.

The research study comprised a significant literature review of global reading and writing for pleasure research over the last 20-plus years and an empirical study of the approaches to volitional reading and writing taken by six charitable literacy programmes in London. In this introductory chapter, after introducing the research project and the programmes involved, the concepts of reading, writing and pleasure are scrutinised and problematised, then research which investigates young people's views and experiences as readers and writers is examined. Due to the relatively scant attention

DOI: 10.4324/9781003532606-1

paid to the concept of writing for pleasure by research communities, policy makers and educators globally, consideration of reading for pleasure is inevitably foregrounded, although existing studies and potential parallels are examined.

The research project

During the three-year research project (2020–2023), the OU team was tasked with 'identifying the approaches and methodologies that seem to be effective in inspiring and encouraging children and young people to read and to write for pleasure'. The team mapped this into strands:

- Strand 1: To review and synthesise existing research literature (in the field of reading and writing for pleasure).
- Strand 2: To collect and analyse research data from the six participating London-based literacy programmes.
- Strand 3: To examine if and in what ways the research literature and the empirical data from the programmes might be connected.

The two reviews of existing international literature focused mainly on peer-reviewed research related to volitional reading and choosing to write for children and young people, between the ages of 5 and 13 years old. One review attended to reading for pleasure, the other to writing for pleasure. Following their completion, the OU team identified themes within, and synergies across these two reviews in relation to identifying approaches capable of supporting volitional reading and writing.

To understand the different facets of the programmes and their ways of working, the team developed an 'Activity Theory' informed methodology and collected data from the literacy programmes through interviews and focus groups with staff, creatives, volunteers, teachers and children, as well as session observations and programme documentation. A rigorous process of cross-team qualitative thematic analysis enabled common elements of their approaches to developing reading and writing for pleasure across the literacy programmes to be identified. These findings were compared with the synergistic themes from the existing research literature and combined to create the Framework for Practice.

The Reading and Writing for Pleasure Framework for Practice

The Reading and Writing for Pleasure Framework for Practice was designed to enable practitioners from a wide range of contexts to reflect upon and develop the ways in which they can best support children and young people to become engaged readers and writers in diverse and sometimes challenging circumstances. The Framework reveals the synergised findings from the empirical study of the programmes, and the key themes from the combined reviews of international literature (see Figure I.1). The outer layer or underpinning elements highlight the importance of shared values across organisations and programmes related to reading and writing for pleasure, and key organisational characteristics that were seen to support this work, such as nurturing partnerships and attending to legacy. The Framework suggests that environments that foster children's reading and writing for pleasure simultaneously enable the

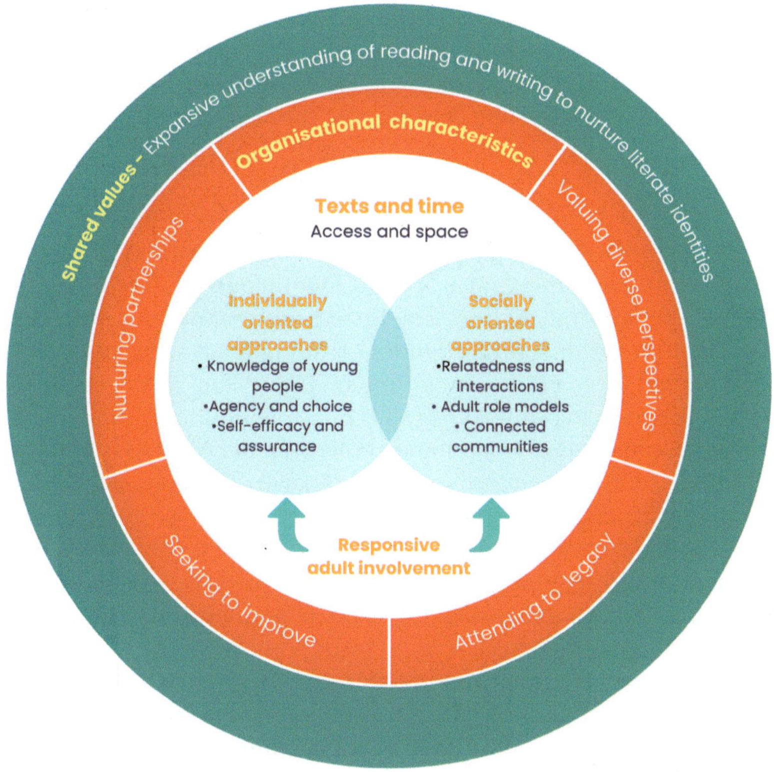

FIGURE I.1 The Reading and Writing for Pleasure Framework for Practice

development of positive literate identities. In these environments, adults see their roles as developing readers and writers rather than 'doing reading and writing' and hold expansive understandings of what counts as being a reader and/or writer. By prioritising relaxed encounters around engaging texts that reflect children's lives and interests, adults are able to foster positive attitudes and confidence in reading and writing. They make use of individually and socially oriented approaches to enable children's affective, social and relational engagement in reading and writing and enhance their sense of self as readers and writers. Furthermore, the adults participate themselves as role models, and, building on their knowledge of the children, attune their practice responsively, building literacy communities connected by these shared endeavours. Please see Chapters 12 and 13 for more detail.

The funded programmes

As part of the Mercers' Literacy Special Initiative, the programmes set out to engage children and young people in reading and writing in a number of ways. Sometimes this involved extending the charity's main work to new areas of London, or in some cases new programmes developed with the funding. The following resume of each of the programmes involved seeks to provide additional context, highlighting their range and diversity.

Doorstep Library aims to help overcome the barriers faced by some of London's most under-resourced communities and to break the cycle of poverty by bringing the pleasure of reading to children under 11 years of age and thus through improving literacy. It offers a weekly reading and library service delivered directly to family homes on estates by trained volunteers. They work in pairs, carrying a backpack full of books and small stools to sit on, visiting each family once a week during term-time, reading stories with the children and lending them books to exchange when the volunteers return the following week. The volunteers also engage with the parents to show how important and easy it is for them to spend time reading with their children, and where appropriate they also broker connections for parents to local or national services that might support them. For the Literacy Special Initiative, Doorstep Library targeted new estates in Camden, prioritising wards with the highest proportion of children living in poverty.

Get Islington Reading was a programme created by the National Literacy Trust and the Reading Agency for the Mercers' Special Initiative. The National Literacy Trust is the UK's largest independent literacy charity which aims to improve the reading, writing, speaking and listening skills in the UK's poorest communities. The Reading Agency was established to promote reading across diverse communities to support skills and learning, health and wellbeing, and community cohesion. Get Islington Reading took an integrated approach to engaging and inspiring a love of reading in children from disadvantaged backgrounds, this was focused at the transition between primary and secondary school and brought together inspiring activities in school with those in the local community, including public libraries. It provided curated library collections, author engagement and continuing professional development for teachers. The National Literacy Trust and the Reading Agency worked across two secondary schools, ten primary schools and five public libraries and community venues with the aim of developing a model for integrated working transferable to other locations.

The Ministry of Stories (MoS) provides a range of inspirational after-school and in-school writing programmes to engage disadvantaged children and young people aged 8 to 18. For the Literacy Special Initiative MoS expanded its work in the London Borough of Tower Hamlets, enabling it to work with a consortium of 8–10 primary schools to inspire, enthuse and support their students to write for pleasure, including through continuing professional development with the teaching team. The charity worked collaboratively with each school to co-design a programme of work between the school and professional writers, poets and storytellers. MoS published books of the students' work and writing programmes in each school led to other additional finished 'products' such as podcasts or films. In this work, MoS trialled a new consortium approach to facilitate learning and sharing of innovative practice between schools operating in some of the most disadvantaged areas of London.

Literacy Pirates provides an after-school, year-long programme to improve the reading, writing and confidence of children who are falling behind at school and are also from disadvantaged backgrounds. The children are aged 9–12 and have been identified as potentially needing some extra support by teachers from local schools. The learning programme, which is held at the charity's premises, designed as a pirate ship, is devised and led by ex-teachers employed by Literacy Pirates with input from the participating children, and involves them each week receiving extra help with their reading from an adult volunteer one-to-one or in small groups. Each term the children work on a creative project such as: to write their own book, film script or website app with the work then published and celebrated. For the Literacy Special Initiative, The Literacy Pirates expanded their programme in the London Borough of Haringey, targeting young people at the point of/during transition from primary into secondary school, and began work on their online programme.

The Primary Shakespeare Company (PSC) work with children in primary schools to raise their attainment and achievement by engaging with Shakespeare. PSC's approach involves working with a cluster of schools in each borough over six months. Each school is supported by creative professionals to devise and rehearse a performance that tells the story of one act of the focus play. PSC also supports the class teachers, through training and online resources, to use the play to plan and deliver lessons across the curriculum with literacy as the focus. All schools in a borough come together on one day at a theatre venue to share their work in a festival of performance. For the Literacy Special Initiative, PSC aimed to develop children's writing for pleasure by devising and writing an opera based on a theme arising from a Shakespeare play, they worked with new schools in disadvantaged areas of Islington, Harrow and Tower Hamlets.

World Book Day (WBD) promotes and encourages reading for pleasure for children and young people up to 18 years of age. Every year, booksellers, publishers, authors, illustrators, librarians and teachers help the charity achieve its mission by celebrating books and reading for pleasure through storytelling, author and illustrator events, and a huge variety of fun and creative activities. A key feature of WBD is that it distributes £1 book tokens to schools across the UK and curates a list of bespoke £1 books by well-known, well-loved and well-respected children's authors to offer to young readers. For the Literacy Special Initiative, WBD created a new project to develop its educational resources in collaboration with teachers, in order to provide the many teaching staff visiting its website with free of charge, more sustained, richer and evidence-based reading for pleasure materials to use. This included a new quality assurance framework which was applied to the creation of new, and the evaluation of existing, WBD resources.

The Literacy Special Initiative commenced in January 2020 with all organisations planning to offer their programmes later that year. Despite the challenges of the COVID-19 pandemic, all programmes rose to the challenge, and pivoted their plans in various ways, some moved to work online and when it was feasible all developed their full face-to-face programme. Working alongside the OU team in that first year, the programmes explored the notions of reading and writing for pleasure. They were not alone in this regard, at least in relation to reading.

Considering the concepts of reading and writing for pleasure

Over the last two decades, policy makers, practitioners, researchers, literacy organisations and parents across the globe have begun to attend to reading for pleasure – to young people's volitional reading, their dispositions, interests and practices as readers. This 'reading for pleasure turn' (Cremin and Scholes, 2024, p. 2) has not been matched by global attention to writing for pleasure, but both concepts deserve consideration.

The International Literacy Association (2018) define reading for pleasure as the opportunity to read freely, voluntarily and with delight, and argue it does not include reviews, written responses or tests for the young to complete, rather they deem it to be choice-led reading, primarily for enjoyment. Furthermore, they position it as the right of every child (International Literacy Association, 2018). Across the world, different terminology is deployed to capture the motivations and dispositions of those children and young people who not only choose to read for their own purposes and in their own time, but who do so regularly. In England, where the Literacy Special Initiative was situated, reading for pleasure has been mandated since 2013, there the curriculum states 'Pupils should be taught to develop pleasure in reading' (Department for Education, 2013, p. 21). Nonetheless, teachers cannot require children to find pleasure in reading, although they can entice, invite, model and engage young people as readers. The autonomy-focused nature of reading for pleasure sits uncomfortably with 'teaching children to develop pleasure'. Its significance is also seen, as noted by Oxley and McGeown (2023), in the other UK curricula. In Scotland, under the reading 'Enjoyment and Choice' category, it is noted that learners should be able to select texts that they 'enjoy and find interesting' and to explain to others their text and author preferences (Scottish Government, 2009, p. 2). In Wales it is stated that 'Learners should be given opportunities to ... read for different purposes, e.g. for personal pleasure' (Welsh Government, 2016, p. 5), and in Northern Ireland, it is specified that 'Children should be encouraged to develop a love of books and the disposition to read' (CCEA, 2019, p. 20). In other countries also, including, for example, Australia, Finland, New Zealand, Norway, Portugal, Singapore, South Korea, Qatar and the United Arab Emirates, the phrase reading for pleasure or local cultural equivalents are present in policy and practice.

Arguably, in response to the widespread decline in young people enjoying reading or choosing to read in their own time, the phrase is emerging into global public discourse. Researchers have described such reading as 'recreational' (Ross et al., 2006), 'a purposeful volitional act' (Powell, 2014, p. 129), 'spontaneous pleasure reading – ludic reading' (Nell, 1988), 'independent', 'free voluntary reading' (Krashen, 2004), 'self-selected reading' (Krashen, 2019) and reading that serves 'the private purposes of the reader' (Mackey, 2019).

'Writing for pleasure' is far less recognised and accepted as a term by policy makers, practitioners and researchers internationally. The field of reading research is a far larger and broader one than that which examines writing in education, and within the latter, the concept of writing for pleasure has not been subject to significant research scrutiny or exploration. Writing, like reading, is a social practice which is shaped by social and historical understandings of what reading and writing are and what texts do. So, when educators teach children to write they instruct them in what is valued by their culture. In primary education, in England at least, the knowledge and skills of writing are foregrounded at the relative expense of composition and effect and developing a sense of young people as authors. Yet both are essential. Additionally, in many countries, while teachers recognise writing as a means of expression and a form of meaning making, the notion of 'being a writer' tends to be associated with 'creative writing' and perceived almost exclusively as the domain of published authors, for example playwrights, poets, novelists and journalists (Wilson, 2009). Yet arguably all writing can be approached creatively, it always involves creative and critical skills and such associations eschew the range of writing in which many children and adults engage in every day. Combined with the very high profile afforded the writing proficiency agenda, the lack of prominence given to volitional writing in research and policy contexts no doubt alters what counts as writing or being a writer in primary classrooms.

Developing children's love of writing, seeing writing as a leisure time pursuit undertaken for the joy of it does not appear to be part of common parlance in society or in educational contexts. Furthermore, no known national curricula state for example, as they do for reading, that children should be encouraged 'to develop the disposition to write' or to 'write for personal pleasure'. The process approach to writing, evident to some degree in England, the United States, Australia and New Zealand, profiled and prioritised personal writing from the outset (e.g. Calkins, 1991; Graves, 1994), but there is scant known research that explicitly focuses on children's pleasurable engagement in the experience or on the consequences of such approaches for children choosing to write in their own time. Some studies view children as emerging authors (e.g. Collier, 2010; Cremin, 2020), others stress the need to focus on them as children and avoid offering them up as imitations of professional writers based on adult values and beliefs as to what constitutes 'a good writer' (Dyson and Dewayani, 2013). In recent years in England, triggered perhaps by the profile afforded reading for pleasure, a writing for pleasure movement has begun to develop (Young and Ferguson, 2021) and considerable professional interest has been shown. Additionally, newly emerging research papers have begun to explore 'how to know/be/teach writers/writing differently' (Honeyford and Watt, 2025, p. 108). But with narrow notions of writing as proficiency persisting in many curricula, alongside narrow assessment frames, young people's lived experience of writing and opportunities to adopt the identity position of writer are likely to remain somewhat constrained.

The concept of reading for pleasure is frequently associated with reader engagement, or seen as a proxy for it and can, by extension, be linked to writer engagement. Engaged readers and writers are those who want to read and write, who regularly make time for it, and who find satisfaction in and through the process of thinking about and making meaning through texts, sometimes with others. This summary aligns with the Organization for Economic Co-operation and Development's (OECD) (2016) broadened conception of reading, which acknowledges that reading encompasses motivational and behavioural characteristics, as well as cognitive ones. This OECD conceptualisation of reading was first used in the 2019 Programme for International Student Assessment (PISA) survey and is complemented by the definition of reader engagement deployed within that assessment framework. They observe that education must 'cultivate not only proficiency but also engagement with reading'.

> Engagement in this context implies the motivation to read and comprises a cluster of affective and behavioural characteristics that include an interest in and enjoyment of reading, a sense of control over what one reads, involvement in the social dimension of reading and diverse and frequent reading practices.
>
> *(OECD, 2019, p. 29)*

Through the motivated process of making meaning and thinking about it, engaged readers, and arguably, engaged writers, develop their understanding and capacity to reflect upon and evaluate what they have read or written. As the OECD states, literacy engagement implies motivation, and encompasses interest, enjoyment, a sense of control and social involvement. Yet a systematic review of the field of reader engagement (Lee et al., 2021) reveals that researchers have paid more attention to young people's behavioural engagement than their cognitive, affective and social engagement. Perhaps because reading is commonly viewed as a solitary act of engagement, few studies have considered children's social engagement. Nonetheless, reading is an inherently social practice, which cannot easily be separated from young people's engagement with others and their motivation is always situated in a social context.

Potentially, these four intertwined dimensions of engagement exist for writers too, who may also be cognitively, affectively, behaviourally and socially engaged, although as Myhill et al. (2023) observe, there is no substantive parallel body of research from over the decades examining writers' motivation or engagement. Whilst Camacho et al (2023) do offer a review of writing motivation studies, this indicates that most have examined writers' self-efficacy, and the concept of writers' engagement remains unexamined.

Problematising the concepts of reading, writing and pleasure

In formal educational contexts, the concepts of reading and writing for pleasure, children choosing to read or write, can represent a challenge; indeed, by their very nature, volitional reading and writing stand in marked contrast to that which is assigned or required within the curriculum. Schooling in many countries and jurisdictions does not explicitly seek to enable learner agency and choice within the literacy curriculum. It is often constrained by professional knowledge, pedagogy and the available resources (Hempel-Jorgensen et al., 2018; Vaughn et al., 2020). Additionally, whilst teachers may plan literacy activities for English and across the curriculum that are engaging and potentially enjoyable, the goal of these may well be skill development, not the development of the desire to read, write or nurture children's positive literate identities. Furthermore, in countries in which the standards agenda is prioritised and performativity holds sway (Ball, 2000), the concept of pleasure is often sidelined or at least positioned as separate from the core business of work and learning. As a consequence, literacy activities which profile 'pleasure' (and by implication fun, enjoyment, relaxation), may not be deemed worthy of full inclusion within the curriculum. The 'push and pull' (Cremin and Moss, 2018) of the dual literacy 'skill and will' agendas create tensions and dilemmas for schools and teachers. Pleasure-focused activities may merely be offered as occasional enrichment events and positioned as 'extras', so that author visits, reading cafes or booknics (reading picnics) for instance may be seen as stand-alone activities, possible to include only when money and time allow.

Historically too reading and writing have been viewed as solitary acts, undertaken alone and assessed individually. Yet, seminal literacy research (Barton and Hamilton, 1998; Brice-Heath, 1983) and focal studies based in classrooms attest to the significance of the social aspects of reading and writing (e.g. Boyask et al., 2022; Ivey and Johnston, 2023; Myhill et al., 2023), and the influence of the wider environment and culture (see Chapters 4, 6 and 7). Nonetheless, in cultures of high accountability, notions of the sociality involved and the influence of peers on young people's literate identities and development sit uncomfortably alongside the predominant focus on individual proficiency and progress.

Additionally, whilst notions of reading and being a reader are frequently aligned to the reading of fiction (often long-form printed fiction), children and young people may choose to read many kinds of texts, including magazines, newspapers, comics, poetry and non-fiction, and in electronic and printed forms. Debates about what counts as reading and indeed writing remain matters for constant consideration, and researchers from different disciplinary and theoretical perspectives continue to advance these fields. Nonetheless, those focused on motivating children's engagement as readers and writers consistently state that choice and agency are critical (e.g. Brandt et al., 2021; Zumbrunn et al., 2019). As the 'affective turn' (Clough, 2007) has entered education, reading for pleasure has begun to be seen as far more than an individual's emotional response to a text (e.g. Boyask et al., 2022; Burnett and Merchant, 2018), although this might well be present. Burnett and Merchant for instance, draw attention to the pleasures that are often generated as children and adults read and engage, often fleetingly, with digital media, and argue for 'seeing reading for pleasure as an affect generated in the relations between readers, texts and things' (Burnett and Merchant, 2018, p. 63). Furthermore, they posit that everyday engagement with digital media has the potential to create a mood of playful enchantment for readers, and that this propels interaction and further engagement. This is also seen in a study of adults' socio-material and affective engagement in writing outdoors (Honeyford and Watt, 2025). Taking a more psycho-social conceptualisation of enjoyment, Boyask et al. (2022, p. 170) emphasise 'the fundamental sociality of emotion', thus foregrounding the social and emotional strands of the pleasure involved.

Another related conceptual challenge is that the word 'pleasure' is often associated with positive emotions, such as delight, joy and happiness, and limited readings of the term tend to suggest reading and writing will produce these pleasing states. Yet children and adults read, respond and write texts drawing on a wide range of emotions and may for instance feel aggrieved at a character's actions, saddened by the turn of event or driven to write to explore a sense of loss or to voice their views about a disturbing world issue. Such experiential textual engagement can be deeply satisfying. Both reading and writing offer opportunities for young people (and adults) to think through ideas, connect with others, consider and handle their emotions, and shape and share their knowledge and understanding. Arguably therefore, pleasure *in* reading and writing refers to pleasure *in* the experience, the deep involvement felt for example as a narrative unfolds, the satisfaction of curiosity and the aesthetic engagement in sculpting a text. Engagement may also arise from memories triggered by a text – written or read. However, there are nuanced differences between pleasure *in* the experience and reading or writing *for* pleasure. Whilst children may find the experience of hearing a book read aloud, or composing their own poem enjoyable, it does not follow that the pleasure engendered in such contexts will lead to increased reading or writing of choice in their own time.

Furthermore, both reading and writing can be cognitively as well as emotionally demanding. Shaping thoughts into words is complicated and whatever the genre, writing is always an intellectually demanding process, involving the writer in combining cognitive, socio-cultural and linguistic understanding (Myhill et al., 2020). Indeed, in contrast to many other activities which become easier with time and practice, writing remains an effortful and mentally demanding activity even for skilled writers. So young writers may not readily associate writing with enjoyment due to the need to generate and shape ideas, and to attend to grammar, spelling and punctuation. Nonetheless, as Young and Ferguson (2021) assert, writers can experience pleasure *in* the process of making meaning and crafting their texts and, through expressing their views and finding their voices, can experience a high degree of satisfaction which may motivate further engagement.

Writing or reading *for* pleasure is somewhat more volitional in nature and concerned with choosing to read or write in one's own time. With all the competing commitments and opportunities available to young people, those who choose to spend free-choice time or their breaktime in school engaged in these literacy practices, or who make time beyond the school day to read or write, are demonstrating a deep desire to do so. By regularly seeking out these aesthetically engaging experiences and participating in them on their own terms, they are exerting their agency. Some may take part in online communities of readers or writers, others may participate alone, perhaps prior to sharing their thoughts about their self-chosen texts- written or read with others. As the extensive evidence detailed in Chapter 1 indicates, those young people who develop the childhood habit of reading and writing will benefit academically, socially and emotionally (e.g. Clark et al., 2023; Graham et al., 2017; Sun et al., 2024; Torppa et al., 2020).

So, whilst pleasure *in* reading and writing matters, the long-term goal for educationalists must surely be to nurture children's reading and writing *for* pleasure, such that they volitionally choose to make time to read and write in their own ways and for their own purposes, some of which may also be social and relational. Hearing why some children and young people choose to engage as readers and writers in their own time is therefore invaluable.

Attending to young people's views

The reasons which young people give for engaging as readers and writers in their own time offer an insight into their literacy experiences. However, as noted earlier, the notion of writing for pleasure has not been extensively examined, the phrase is infrequently used in research, policy or practice domains and is almost completely absent in educational discourse internationally. With a few notable exceptions, writing researchers have paid relatively little attention to children's experience of writing and reasons for writing.

Studies demonstrate that affective engagement is the dominant driver for some young readers, they value the feelings and emotions triggered by reading and the opportunity to become immersed in texts (e.g. McGeown et al., 2020). The role of affect as an underlying dimension and motivator of reading for pleasure is often linked to the immersive experience of reading literature which can enable a state of 'flow' (Csikszentmihalyi, 2014), a positive emotional state. This is likely to encompass visualising scenes and events and vicariously experiencing characters' challenges, and has salience for supporting children to access texts that enable them to make life to text and text to life connections, which are in themselves valuable affective motivators. Exploring the inner experience of becoming relocated in a story world, or 'lost in a book' among 9–12-year-old readers (n:28), Kuzmičová et al. (2022) noted the children's diverse, but often affectively engaged responses. For example, several appeared to become suspended in the text through their emotional attachment with characters, and others, in order to reach a stage of emotional absorption, persevered with the skills needed.

Investigating the role of pleasure reading in the lives of 12–15-year-old Canadian adolescents (n:68), Howard (2011) found that they valued this for academic, social and personal reasons. Academically, these young people recognised that volitional reading would likely lead to greater success in school by developing their literacy skills and that the act of reading itself had prompted them to consider their own vocational goals. This focus on aspiration and success in reading was also discerned in data drawn from the 2009 PISA (Cheung et al., 2016). The young people in Howard's study perceived that their pleasure in reading empowered them to develop their beliefs about the world, their social conscience and empathy, and many found reading a valuable form of entertainment, escapism, relaxation, reassurance and a space to imagine. Interviews with Scottish 15–16-year-olds (n:39) indicate that they too valued book reading for intrinsic reasons (Wilkinson et al., 2020). Common factors that younger Scottish youngsters, aged 13–15 (n:46), reported would entice them to read more included: access to quality books aligned with their interests and the skills to choose these, increased autonomy, reading practices that were sociable and enjoyable, and quality time and space to read (Webber et al., 2025). These teenagers also noted that reading promotions attuned to their own ways of communicating would support them.

In exploring 10–11-year-olds' (n:114) experience of writing, Zumbrunn et al. (2017) invited children from eight schools to draw 'a recent experience they had with writing and how that made them feel' (p. 668). The children described their drawings, and these were inductively analysed. The findings indicate that over half reported valuing the experience as a relaxing and calming one which helped them feel 'at peace', and many were motivated by choice and agency. However, a proportion of this writing was school-led writing, not volitional writing undertaken in their own time. In another writing study which specifically attended to children's beliefs about leisure writing, Birnbaum et al. (2020) drew on data from 8–9-year-olds (n:963) in 23 schools across Germany. These researchers defined leisure writing as being 'an inherently valuable cultural activity' (p. 857) and found that the intrinsic value of it played a pivotal role that correlated with the frequency of the children's writing. The themes identified in the children's beliefs about leisure writing included:

- *intrinsic value comprising fun, fantasy, and autonomy* (e.g. 'I write because I can decide by myself what I want to write')
- *beliefs concerning congruent consequences* (e.g. 'I write letters because I can keep in contact with others')
- *beliefs concerning incongruent consequences* (e.g. 'I'd rather play outside than write something')

- *normative beliefs operationalised by children's perceptions of others' expectations* (e.g. 'My parents approve of me writing').
- *person-related control beliefs* (e.g. 'Writing is easy for me')
- *environmental-related control beliefs* (e.g. 'I can write in peace during my leisure time').

(adapted from Birnbaum et al., 2020, p. 681)

Both these studies of young people's writing experience underscore the influence of young writers' volition and agency, and connect to Young and Ferguson's (2021, p. 21) view of writing for pleasure as 'a volitional act undertaken for enjoyment and satisfaction'. Although the nature of that satisfaction and enjoyment will vary for different writers in different contexts, having a strong sense of ownership or control over the process appears to be integral to being motivated to write (e.g., Dyson, 1997; Marinak et al., 2012; Myhill et al., 2023).

An American study of avid adolescent readers' perceptions of free reading offers another range of reasons and pleasures (Wilhelm, 2016). In the eyes of these teenagers (n:29), free reading, including the reading of genres typically marginalised in their school (e.g. romance, fantasy, vampire, dystopia and horror), offered them distinct kinds of pleasure. Wilhelm categorised these, noting that the first, the immersive pleasure of play, was seen to be an essential prerequisite for the other 'pleasures'.

- *The immersive pleasure of play*: e.g. through getting lost in a book and living through the text.
- *Intellectual pleasure*: e.g. finding out about issues of interest in the world and solving problems in narratives.
- *Social pleasure*: e.g. belonging to a community of readers and connecting to others through reading as well as identifying as a reader.
- *The pleasure of functional work*: e.g. using reading to learn, think and act in different ways, and using reading to shape one's writing.
- *The pleasure of inner work*: e.g. using reading to learn about oneself, to imagine oneself in different situations and consider options.

(adapted from Wilhelm, 2016)

However, this study of young people's perceptions, undertaken through four in-depth interviews across three years, indicates that only their intellectual pleasure was directly fostered in school. Other studies also suggest that immersive, affective, social forms of pleasure in reading or writing are not always nurtured or recognised by young people in school (e.g. Hempel-Jorgensen et al., 2018; Fletcher and Nicholas, 2016; Maybin, 2013; Sellers, 2019; Zumbrunn et al., 2017). In these, some children viewed reading as 'a commodity to be acquired rather than a skill to allow them to read for pleasure' (Fletcher and Nicholas, 2016, p. 491), as a matter of 'proficiency' (Hempel-Jorgensen et al., 2018) or as simply 'uncool and anti-social' (Sellers, 2019) and in the case of writing both 'isolating' and a 'horrible experience' (Zumbrunn et al., 2017, p. 671). Where this is the case, then the young may come to adopt indifferent attitudes to reading and writing, may position themselves as resistant or disengaged, and seek to prioritise other social pursuits that can connect them to their peers. Indeed, as Chapter 1 details, attitudes to reading and writing are declining among the young, alongside the frequency with which they choose to read or write for pleasure in their own time (e.g. Clark et al., 2024; Mullis et al., 2023).

It is invaluable for educators to attend to young people's reasons for reading and writing in their own time, and to explore how to prioritise the development of competent and committed readers and writers, who engage deeply with the meanings and possibilities offered by texts. Nonetheless, it is not only educators who shape and influence young people's volitional reading and writing – families, friends, peers and the young people themselves, as well as the available texts and contexts – influence their literate identities and shape their engagement in reading.

Moving forwards

In the Literacy Special Initiative (2020–2023), the OU team worked with six London-based literacy programmes to explore the concepts of 'reading and writing for pleasure', the terms used by the Mercers' Company in their framing of the study. Staff from the programmes were encouraged to examine the ways in which pleasurable engagement in literacy was evident within their work, as well as the extent to which they sought to nurture children's recreational involvement in reading or writing in their own time. Slightly adapting a definition by Cremin and Scholes (2024, p. 2), the team came to view reading and writing for pleasure as:

> Volitional reading and writing, driven by the child's own goals and interests – which may include social and relational ones – in anticipation of some form of satisfaction.

Throughout this book, although many of the terms used globally are also deployed, this definition of reading and writing for pleasure is foregrounded. It is recognised that these agentic acts of meaning making are both individual *and* social literacy practices.

The book is divided into four sections each exploring a component of the research study. The first explores the wider context by examining international research evidence in this area and the relative strength of this. The first chapter details the evidenced and multifaceted benefits of children reading for pleasure, encompassing cognitive development, academic impact and more nuanced social and emotional influences, and the less well researched area of young people choosing to write. It also considers the decline in young people's attitudes to reading and writing and their changing literacy habits and behaviours The many complex and intersectional influences on children's engagement as readers and writers, including parents and home circumstances, gender and more are examined in Chapter 2. This chapter also reflects on the relationship between reading and writing. With this context underpinning the book, Chapter 3 moves to explain the project's methodology, and process of data collection and analysis, in order to explore the set question 'What approaches and methodologies seem to be effective in inspiring and encouraging children and young people to read and to write for pleasure?'.

In Part II, synergies in approaches to reading and writing for pleasure derived from the reviews of the extant research literature are examined. Four themes are identified as significant, and the imbalance between research into reading and writing for pleasure is acknowledged throughout. In each chapter, where possible, commonalities and differences are shared, alongside counter views, contradictions and foci for new inquiries. Initially in Chapter 4, the research literature which examines readers and writers identities and their motivation to engage in these literacy practices is considered. Chapter 5 discusses the impact of texts, text access and choice, and research around the time and space needed to nurture reader and writer engagement. Building on the earlier discussion of motivation, the role of social interaction between adults and children, and between peers, and the link between sociality and motivation are explored in Chapter 6. The salience of reading and writing role models and ways in which different networks enable children to participate as members of literacy communities is examined in Chapter 7.

Part III focuses on sharing findings from the qualitative data collected from the six London literacy programmes involved in the Literacy Special Initiative. This section draws out themes from the analysis which illustrate the research team's understanding of the programmes' practices and common features. It begins in Chapter 8 by examining the aims or expectations of the different programmes and how these shaped their support for children as readers and writers. The programmes' different ways of working with stakeholders, participants and the delivery teams are examined in Chapter 9, which also considers the diversity and expertise involved in the programmes and the influence of their shared values in relation to children's engagement reading and writing. Chapter 10 explores in more detail how the different roles and responsibilities in the programmes supported the children, whether leading, volunteering, or delivering, and the essential role of these adults. The nature of activities and interactions which nurture reader and writer engagement are examined in Chapter 11, which highlights findings related to the ways in which programmes used and created resources to support their work and the impact of these on children's engagement as readers and writers.

Finally, Part IV draws together the learning from the research study as whole, combining the findings from the data collection and the synthesis of international literature to explore the Reading and Writing for Pleasure Framework for Practice. The Framework is introduced fully in Chapter 12 and the inter-related elements are explained, as evidenced in the literature and work with the programmes. This chapter also explores the organisational characteristics of the programmes and considers how these may be realised in schools and other contexts. Recommendations are also offered for practitioners, to enable them to consider ways forward with using the Framework to enhance their practice. Chapter 13 shares examples of practice in two schools and two charitable literacy programmes to illustrate the Framework elements in action. These are offered as a potential stimulus for practitioners to reflect on their own contexts and consider how the inter-related elements of the Framework might influence their own practice and approaches to nurturing children's reading and writing for pleasure.

In response to the three-year study and collective understanding from over 20 years of research considering children's volitional reading and writing, the Conclusion, whilst recognising the challenges and limitations of the work, urges policy makers, researchers and educators to pay more attention to young people's engagement as readers and writers. It highlights gaps in the extant research, makes recommendations, and considers the dilemmas and possibilities involved in seeking to 'measure' and document children's pleasure in reading and writing. The Conclusion also foregrounds the significance of the social and relational connections that appear to motivate children to engage as readers and writers, linking this to the structured informality and rapport seen in studies of relational pedagogy. Finally, ways forward are explored, including the development of multi-agency approaches that have the potential to strengthen professional practice and help create a new generation of motivated readers and writers.

In drawing together what is a complex and nuanced field, this book highlights consensus, challenges and gaps in the reading and writing for pleasure research base as well as ways forward for applying what is known in the field, in the form of the Reading and Writing for Pleasure Framework for Practice. Whilst there is still much to be learned, a convincing body of international evidence and practical examples in a wide variety of contexts provide potential routes ahead. Ultimately, it is the intention that the book will empower all concerned with a deeper understanding of why reading and writing for pleasure matter, and how individuals and organisations can enable children and young people to experience the deep satisfaction of engaging as readers and writers, with texts, with adults and with each other.

References

Ball, S.J. (2000) 'Performativities and fabrications in the education economy: Towards the performative society?', *The Australian Educational Researcher*, 27(2), pp. 1–23.

Barton, D. and Hamilton, M. (1998) *Local Literacies: Reading and Writing in One Community*, London: Routledge.

Birnbaum, L., Schüller, E.M. and Kröner, S. (2020) 'Who likes to engage in writing? The role of children's beliefs and intrinsic value regarding leisure writing', *Educational Psychology*, 40(7), pp. 856–874.

Boyask, R., Harrington, C., Milne, J. and Smith, B.H.B. (2022) '"Reading enjoyment" is ready for school: Foregrounding affect and sociality in children's reading for pleasure', *New Zealand Journal of Educational Studies*, 58, pp. 169–182.

Brandt, L., Sharp, A.C. and Gardner, D.S. (2021) 'Examination of teacher practices on student motivation for reading', *Reading Teacher*, 74(6), pp. 723–731.

Brice-Heath, S. (1983) *Ways with Words: Language, Life and Work in Communities and Classrooms*, Cambridge: Cambridge University Press.

Burnett, C. and Merchant, G. (2018) 'Affective encounters: Enchantment and the possibility of reading for pleasure', *Literacy*, 52(2), pp. 62–69.

Calkins, L.M. (1991) *Living Between the Lines*, Portsmouth, NH: Heinemann.

Camacho, A., De Smedt, F., Maoi, R., Cadmia, J., Van Keer, H. and Alves, R.A. (2023) 'Writing motivation profiles and their association with writing performance: A person-centered approach', *Topics in Language Disorders*, 43(2), pp. 169–186.

CCEA (2019) *The Northern Ireland Curriculum Primary*, Belfast: Council for the Curriculum Examinations and Assessment.

Cheung, K., Mak, S.-K., Sit, P.-S. and Soh, K.-C. (2016) 'A typology of student reading engagement: Preparing for response to intervention in the school curriculum', *Studies in Educational Evaluation*, 48, pp. 32–42.

Clark, C., Picton, I. and Galway, M. (2023) *Children and Young People's Reading in 2023*, London: National Literacy Trust.

Clark, C., Picton, C., Cole, A. and Bonafede, F. (2024) *Children and Young People's Writing in 2024*, London: National Literacy Trust.

Clough, P.T. (2007) 'Introduction', in Clough, P.T. and Halley, J (eds), *The Affective Turn: Theorizing the Social*, Durham, NC: Duke University Press, pp. 1–33.
Collier, D.R. (2010) 'Journey to becoming a writer: Review of research about children's identities as writers', *Language and Literacy*, 12(1), pp. 147–164.
Cremin, T. (2020) 'Apprenticing authors: Nurturing children's identities as writers', in Chen, H., Myhill, D. and Lewis, H. (eds), *Developing Writers Across Primary and Secondary Years*, London and Sydney: Routledge, pp. 113–130.
Cremin, T. and Moss, G. (2018) 'Reading for pleasure: Supporting reader engagement', *Literacy*, 52(2), pp. 59–61.
Cremin, T. and Scholes, L. (2024) 'Reading for pleasure: Scrutinising the evidence base – benefits, tensions and recommendations', *Language and Education*, 38(4), pp. 537–559.
Csikszentmihalyi, M. (2014) *Applications of Flow in Human Development and Education: The Collected Works of Mihaly Csikszentmihalyi*, Cham: Springer Science + Business Media.
Department for Education (2013) *The National Curriculum in England: Key Stages 1 and 2 Framework Document*, London: Department for Education.
Dyson, A.H. (1997) *Writing Superheroes: Contemporary Childhood, Popular Culture, and Classroom Literacy*, New York: Teachers College Press.
Dyson, A.H. and Dewayani, S. (2013) 'Writing in childhood cultures', in Hall, K., Cremin, T., Comber, B. and Moll, L.C. (eds), *International Handbook of Research on Children's Literacy, Learning, and Culture*, Malden, MA: Wiley, pp. 258–274.
Fletcher, J. and Nicholas, K. (2016) 'What can we learn from young adolescents' perceptions about the teaching of reading?', *Educational Review*, 68(4), pp. 481–496.
Graham, S., Kiuhara, S.A., Harris, K.R. and Fishman, E.J. (2017) 'The relationship among strategic writing behaviour, writing motivation, and writing performance with young, developing writers', *Elementary School Journal*, 118(1), pp. 82–104.
Graves, D. (1994) *A Fresh Look at Writing*, Portsmouth, NH: Heineman.
Hempel-Jorgensen, A., Cremin, T., Harris, D. and Chamberlain, L. (2018) 'Pedagogy for reading for pleasure in low socio-economic primary schools: Beyond "pedagogy of poverty"?', *Literacy*, 52(2), pp. 86–94.
Honeyford, M. and Watt, J. (2025) 'Opening the door to writing relationalities: Moving writing and the teaching of writing', *Literacy*, 59(1), pp. 108–117.
Howard, V. (2011) 'The importance of pleasure reading in the lives of young teens: Self-identification, self-construction and self-awareness', *Journal of Librarianship and Information Science*, 43(1), pp. 46–55.
International Literacy Association (2018) *The Case for Children's Rights to Read*. Newark, DE:Author.
Ivey, G. and Johnston, P. (2023) *Teens Choosing to Read: Fostering Social, Emotional, and Intellectual Growth Through Books*, New York: Teachers College Press.
Krashen, S. (2004) 'False claims about literacy development', *Educational Leadership*, 61(6), pp. 18–21.
Krashen, S. (2019) 'Self-selected voluntary reading: The missing link', *Language and Language Teaching*, 8(1), pp. 58–62.
Kuzmičová, A., Supa, M., Segi Lukavská, J. and Novák, F. (2022) 'Exploring children's embodied story experiences: A toolkit for research and practice', *Literacy*, 56, pp. 288–298.
Lee, Y., Gee Jang, B. and Conradi Smith, K. (2021) 'A systematic review of reading engagement research: What do we mean, what do we know and where do we need to go?', *Reading Psychology*, 42(5), pp. 540–576.
Mackey, M. (2019) 'Literacy constants in a context of contemporary change', *English in Education*, 53(2), pp. 116–128.
Marinak, B.A., Gambrell, A.B. and Mazzoni, S.A. (2012) *The Teacher, the Text and the Context as Factors in Motivating Students to Write: The Motivation to Write Scale in Maximizing Motivation for Literacy Learning*, New York: Guilford Publications.

Maybin, J. (2013) 'What counts as reading? PIRLS, EastEnders and The Man on the Flying Trapeze', *Literacy*, 47(2), pp. 59–66.
McGeown, S., Bonsall, J., Andries, V., Howarth, D., Wilkinson, K. and Sabeti, S. (2020) 'Growing up a reader: Exploring children's and adolescents' perceptions of "a reader"', *Educational Research*, 62(2), pp. 216–228.
Mullis, I.V.S., von Davier, M., Foy, P., Fishbein, B., Reynolds, K.A. and Wry, E. (2023) *PIRLS 2021 International Results in Reading*, Boston: Boston College, TIMSS and PIRLS International Study Center.
Myhill, D., Cremin, T. and Oliver, L. (2023) 'The impact of changed writing environment on students' motivation to write', *Frontiers in Psychology*, 14.
Myhill, D., Lines, H. and Jones, S. (2020) 'Writing like a reader: Developing metalinguistic understanding to support reading-writing connections', in Alves, R.A., Limpo, T. and Joshi, R.M. (eds), *Reading-Writing Connections: Towards Integrative Literacy Science*, Cham: Springer, pp. 107–122.
Nell, V. (1988) 'The psychology of reading for pleasure: Needs and gratifications', *Reading Research Quarterly*, 23(1), pp. 6–50.
OECD (2016) *Innovating Education and Educating for Innovation: The Power of Digital Technologies and Skills*, Paris: OECD Publishing.
OECD (2019) *PISA 2018 Assessment and Analytical Framework*, Paris: OECD Publishing.
Oxley, E. and McGeown, S. (2023) 'Reading for pleasure practices in school: Children's perspectives and experiences', *Educational Research*, 65(3), pp. 375–391.
Powell, S. (2014) 'Influencing children's attitudes, motivation and achievements as readers', in Cremin, T., Mottram, M., Collins, F. and Powell, S. (eds) *Building Communities of Engaged Readers*, London: Routledge, pp. 128–146.
Ross, C.S., McKechnie, L. and Rothbauer, P.M. (2006) *Reading Matters: What Research Reveals about Reading, Libraries and Community*, Westport: Libraries Unlimited.
Scottish Government (2009) *Curriculum for Excellence: Literacy and English Experiences and Outcomes*, Author.
Sellers, C. (2019) '"Fitting in" and "standing out": the peer group and young people's development of reader identity', *British Journal of Sociology of Education*, 40(7), pp. 938–952.
Sun, Y.-J., Sahakian, B.J., Langley, C., Yang, A., Jiang, Y., Jujiao K., Zhao, X., Li, C., Cheng, W. and Fen, J. (2024) 'Early initiated childhood reading for pleasure: Associations with better cognitive performance, mental well-being and brain structure in young adolescence', *Psychological Medicine*, 54(2), pp. 359–373.
Torppa, M., Niemi, P., Vasalampi, K., Lerkkanen, M.-K., Tolvanen, A. and Poikkeus, A.-M. (2020) 'Leisure reading (but not any kind) and reading comprehension support each other: A longitudinal study across grades 1 and 9', *Child Development*, 91(3), pp. 876–900.
Vaughn, M., Jang, B.G., Sotirovska, V. and Cooper-Novack, G. (2020) 'Student agency in literacy: A systematic review of the literature', *Reading Psychology*, 41(7), pp. 712–734.
Webber, C., Wilkinson, K., Duncan, L.G. and McGeown, S. (2025) 'Motivating book reading during adolescence: Qualitative insights from adolescents', *Educational Research*, 67(1), pp. 79–97.
Welsh Government (2016) *Curriculum for Wales: Programme of Study for English: Key Stages 2–4*, Cardiff: Department for Education and Skills, Welsh Government.
Wilhelm, J. (2016) 'Recognising the power of pleasure: What engaged adolescent readers get from their free-choice reading, and how teachers can leverage this for all', *Australian Journal of Language and Literacy*, 39(1), pp. 30–41.
Wilkinson, K., Andries, V., Howarth, D., Bonsall, J., Sabeti, S. and McGeown, S. (2020) 'Reading during adolescence: Why adolescents choose (or do not choose) books', *Journal of Adolescent and Adult Literacy*, 64(2), pp. 157–166.
Wilson, A.C. (2009) 'Creativity and constraint: Developing as a writer of poetry culture', in Beard, R., Myhill, D., Riley, J. and Nystrand, M. (eds), *The SAGE Handbook of Writing Development*, London: SAGE, pp. 387–401.

Young, R. and Ferguson, F. (2021) *Writing for Pleasure: Theory, Research and Practice*, London: Taylor & Francis.

Zumbrunn, S., Ekholm, E., Stringer, J.K., McKnight, K. and DeBusk-Lane, M. (2017) 'Student experiences with writing: Taking the temperature of the classroom', *The Reading Teacher*, 70 (6), pp. 667–677.

Zumbrunn, S., Marrs, S., Broda, M., Ekholm, E., DeBusk-Lane, M. and Jackson, L. (2019) 'Toward a more complete understanding of writing enjoyment: A mixed methods study of elementary students', *AERA Open*, 5(2), pp. 1–16.

PART I

Setting the Context

1

THE EVIDENCED BENEFITS AND YOUNG PEOPLE'S ATTITUDES

Introduction

Children and young people who read or write for pleasure, volitionally making meaning from texts in their own time, are recognised as keen readers and writers. As the Introduction explored, these young people have the habit of reading and/or writing and participate regularly in these literacy practices. Intrinsically motivated, they find the experience enjoyable and are likely to have a strong sense of their own self-efficacy and identities as readers and/or writers. In this chapter the multiple evidenced benefits that are associated with volitional reading and writing are examined, and the need to consider these in detail is acknowledged. The flow on from volitional reading into comprehension, for example, is not straightforward and as research reveals is influenced by multiple factors. The nature of the studies in this area, most of which are large-scale and qualitative in nature, are also considered. In addition, the chapter examines young people's attitudes to reading and writing and reflects upon their decline in desire to read and write (e.g. Clark et al., 2023; Mullis et al., 2023; OECD, 2021) and the changes reported in their reading and writing behaviours. These large surveys tend to indicate that more girls than boys, and more young people from higher rather than lower socio-economic backgrounds, voice positive attitudes to reading and writing. This remains a matter of concern and provides a strong rationale for the focus of the Literacy Special Initiative funded by the Mercers' Company in which six literacy programmes worked with children and young people from disadvantaged contexts.

It should be acknowledged that reading itself, and reading for pleasure in particular, has been subject to far closer scrutiny by researchers than writing and writing for pleasure. Scholars persistently argue that how children learn to write and become engaged and successful writers remains a significantly under-researched area (Kress, 1994; Kucirkova et al., 2019; Myhill et al., 2023). Furthermore, the term 'writing for pleasure', that is, pleasure in the experience and engagement in the volitional practice of writing in one's own time, is rarely the focus of research studies. The term is not in

DOI: 10.4324/9781003532606-3

common use in educational contexts, nationally or internationally. In contrast, volitional reading is recognised as an aim within many national curricula and plays a part within wider public discourse. As a consequence, this chapter is skewed towards the available evidence on the consequences of being a keen reader. Where known and related data exists for writing it has been drawn upon. The final sections encompass attention to young people's attitudes and behaviours towards both reading and writing, although once again there is a narrower body of research documenting the dispositions and motivations of young writers.

Reading for pleasure and reading achievement

Towards the end of the 1980s, studies began to show an association between the amount of reading children do outside of school and their reading achievement in school (e.g. Anderson et al., 1988) and evidence of a reciprocal relationship between reading engagement and reading achievement was established (Campbell et al., 1997). Additionally, research revealed that disaffected readers fail to benefit from reading teaching (Guthrie and Wigfield, 2000). Unsurprisingly, therefore, attention turned to the importance of intrinsic motivation and the desire to read. Young people who are proficient and confident readers tend to spend more time reading volitionally and, in the process, they further their development as readers and support their desire to read (Guthrie et al., 1999), thus nurturing the will to read and the skill.

The introduction of the Programme of International Student Assessment (PISA) in 2000 and the Progress in International Reading Literacy Study (PIRLS) a year later, enabled this relationship between the will and the skill to be examined further. These Organization for Economic Co-operation and Development (OECD) surveys not only report reading attainment scores but also provide insights into young people's engagement in reading. This currently encompasses the motivation to read, and young people's interest, enjoyment, sense of control, frequency and nature of their reading practices, alongside their 'involvement in the social dimensions' (OECD, 2019b, p. 29). Over the ensuing decades, analysis of this large-scale dataset has consistently demonstrated a bi-directional relationship between reader engagement and reading attainment (e.g. Brozo et al., 2007, Cheema, 2018; Kirsch et al., 2002; Lindorff et al., 2023; McGrane et al., 2017; Mullis et al., 2023). Nationally, this has also been noted in many countries, for example in England (Lindorff et al., 2023; McGrane et al., 2017), in Ireland (Gilleece and Eivers, 2018), in Germany (Schiefele et al., 2012), in the Netherlands (Rogiers et al., 2020), in Turkey (Tavsancil et al., 2019) and the United States (Troyer et al., 2019). Other studies of leisure reading, drawing on their own data sets and often examining slightly different issues, have also affirmed the presence of this reciprocity, including, for instance, Mol and Bus's (2011) meta-analysis of studies examining print exposure from infancy to early adulthood and Malanchini and colleagues' study (2017), which examined longitudinal data from Wales and England. This found evidence of a reciprocal association between motivation and achievement in the domain of reading, with the researchers observing what many others have also found, that:

> Compared to their peers, children with more confidence and interests in reading are more likely to become more competent readers over time, and more skilled readers are also more likely to become more confident in their ability to read and interested in reading.
>
> *(Malanchini et al., 2017, p. 708)*

The research team note that this association was also seen when 'reading enjoyment and reading self-perceived ability were considered separately' (Malanchini et al., 2017, p. 709). The not inconsiderable body of international evidence noted thus far demonstrates that reading for pleasure is very closely associated with reading attainment. This not a matter for debate, it is now widely accepted. However, understanding the nuances within this research is vital as multiple mediating factors influence this significant relationship.

Mediating factors

Studies have found that age, socio-economic and cultural factors as well as reading frequency/amount and the nature of the texts themselves can make a difference to the association between reading motivation, print exposure and reading achievement. For example, Van Bergen et al. (2021) conclude that although the will and skill reciprocally influence each other throughout development, it is the amount of time that children spend independently reading at age 9–10 years that particularly predicts growth in the skills of fluency and comprehension. Age is also recognised as salient in another Finnish study: in this, Torppa et al. (2020) argue that the strength of the reciprocal association between leisure reading and reading comprehension is much stronger in the later years, specifically in 12–15-year-olds. These researchers assert that in the earlier years, whilst reading fluency and comprehension predict leisure reading, leisure reading does not predict reading competence (Torppa et al., 2020).

In addition, two studies have documented a more uni-directional relationship; both observe the influence of literacy skills on enjoyment not vice versa (Erbeli et al., 2020; van Bergen et al., 2023). The former notes that for the adolescents in their research, choosing to read was influenced by their proficiency in reading comprehension which led to increased print exposure (Erbeli et al., 2020). The latter study, drawing on teacher and child report data from a longitudinal Finnish twin cohort study, highlights the critical influences on early skill development which lead to enjoyment, although it should be acknowledged that this research focused broadly on literacy development (van Bergen et al., 2023). Nonetheless, these studies act as a salient reminder that individual children's early decoding ability and speed as readers can constrain their volitional reading for pleasure and thus their attainment over time. This has been coined as the 'Matthew effect' (Stanovich, 1986) whereby 'the rich get rich and the poor get poorer'. According to this, able young readers who are motivated to read, read more, are more persistent in coping with difficulties, and so become better readers. Low achievement, contrarily, reduces children's desire to read, which further lowers their achievements and self-efficacy, creating a cycle of disadvantage.

The mediating influence of socio-economic factors was observed by Schugar and Dreher (2017) when analysing their survey of 165,000 children aged 9–10 years old.

Whilst this analysis of data from the US National Assessment of Educational Progress study documented positive associations between children's reading engagement beyond school and their information text comprehension in school, it also found that the out-of-school reading engagement of children from low-income households was not as positively associated as that of their peers from higher-income households. The team postulate that the less economically advantaged group had reduced access to reading resources in their homes and communities, and that their beyond school reading experiences may have been 'less well matched' to the demands of school information text reading (Schugar and Dreher, 2017). Additionally, Rogiers et al. (2020) found that boys, second language learners and those children on vocational learning tracks reported enjoying reading far less than girls and their peers on academic track programmes, with negative consequences for their reading attainment.

The degree to which enjoyment of reading is a strong predictor of reading achievement has also been found to vary considerably between countries; it is seen to predict as much of 18 per cent of variation in countries' reading achievement (Cheema, 2018). This analysis of 65 countries' PISA results also indicates that positive associations are most evident in high and average academic performance countries (Cheema, 2018). Not dissimilarly, an Israeli study of secondary school students has shown that the beneficial effects of volitional reading on assessed reading outcomes were most evident for those adolescents working at or above their grade level (Vaknin-Nusbaum et al., 2018). Additionally, in a longitudinal national study of over 4,000 German students, which again revealed a positive correlation between intrinsic reading motivation and reading competence, differences were noted for immigrant students (Miyamoto et al., 2018). Whilst the effect of reading competence on intrinsic reading motivation was evident for all students over two grade years, for the immigrant students, intrinsic motivation did not impact on competence. The researchers posit that immigrant students have high levels of drive and commitment to learning overall and that this may mean intrinsic reading motivation is of less importance to them (Miyamoto et al., 2018).

In addition, reading amount is also seen to impact upon the relationships between intrinsic reading motivation and reading achievement (Miyamoto et al., 2018). Drawing on a review of research into this association, Allington and McGrill-Franzen (2021) conclude that this relationship only appears once children have acquired adequate proficiency in independent reading. In contrast however, Troyer et al. (2019) found no significant effect of reading volume on reading comprehension. Instead, these researchers suggest that the association between intrinsic reading motivation, reading amount and reading comprehension, is not only mediated by motivation, but by the text and its quality, alongside the opportunities offered to young people to talk about their self-chosen texts and to develop their sense of self-efficacy as readers. As they observe:

> Simply increasing the amount that students read is unlikely to increase their comprehension. Instead, attention must be paid both to the quality of materials that students read, and to increasing students' intrinsic motivation to read by building their self- efficacy, curiosity and involvement with texts.
>
> *(Troyer et al., 2019, p. 1216)*

The influence of reading materials on the connections between reading for pleasure and achievement has been noted in other studies (e.g. Jerrim et al., 2020; Jerrim and Moss, 2019; Pfost et al., 2013; Schaffner et al., 2016; Spear-Swerling et al., 2010). For instance, the reading of 'classic literature' has been seen to correlate negatively with adolescents' reading motivation (Locher et al., 2019), and two Finnish studies indicate that teenagers' leisure reading of books (in contrast to comics, magazines, newspapers and digital reading) is more closely associated with reading comprehension than other texts (Leino et al., 2017; Torppa et al., 2020).

However, another team of researchers who evidence the positive relationship between book reading and attainment posit that it is often only the able or 'academic track' readers in Germany who have access to richly layered texts, and that this disadvantages less assured readers (Schaffner et al., 2016). Significantly, the presence of a clear 'fiction effect' has been revealed by Jerrim and Moss (2019). Through a process of sustained regression analyses applied to PISA 2009 data from 35 OECD countries (250,000+ students), Jerrim and Moss (2019) assert that the association between reading and young people's academic attainment is confined to fiction. They found this relationship did not hold for other types of text, such as non-fiction, newspapers or magazines. This may be because reading fiction requires time and commitment, a willingness to concentrate and high cognitive demands, and it is also likely to encompass new vocabulary and syntactic structures that require, and may well enhance, the reader's capacity to handle the experience. Additionally, reading fiction seems to have an important effect on young people's success in the subject mother tongue (e.g. Harjunen and Rautopuro, 2015; Sulkunen and Nissinen, 2014).

Volition is key to reading for pleasure, and young people's interests and preferences need to be respected, and not all of them prefer to read fiction; studies show their reading motivation varies across different text types (McGeown et al., 2020) and that some value non-fiction equally (Ives et al., 2020). Nonetheless, the potency of fiction arguably deserves enhanced educational attention, in particular in order to help address systemic inequalities (Simpson and Cremin, 2022). In the UK, classroom-based research has highlighted the positive impact of fiction through a study of the skills and attitudes of less experienced 'poorer' readers (Westbrook et al., 2019). The teachers involved read challenging, complex novels aloud and at a fast pace, to 12–13-year-old classes. The opportunity for sustained engagement with high-quality novels was seen not only to influence the 'poorer' readers' attitudes, motivation and engagement, but it also enhanced their reading attainment, on average they made 16 months progress over a 12-week period. Such practice may be particularly relevant for less experienced readers, who may come from low-income households, where the available resource to access books is reduced (Neuman and Celano, 2001). Less experienced readers are also more likely to be placed in 'low-ability' sets, offered simplified reading books and opportunities to practice discrete decoding skills or comprehension, and potentially reduced opportunities to develop their agency and interest in reading for pleasure (Dunne and Gazeley, 2008; Hempel-Jorgensen et al., 2018). Therefore, those who struggle to read are less likely to read for pleasure. This underlines both the challenge and the importance of educators focusing on children who find reading difficult and offering both 'skill and will' focused support. Balanced reading provision (with skill instruction and ongoing support for developing the will and desire to read) is essential if children are to accrue the range of benefits associated with developing the habit of reading.

In sum, whilst recognising the diverse foci examined, the studies thus far reviewed, taken together, indicate strong evidence of a reciprocal relationship between volitional reading and reading competence as measured in reading comprehension tests. Children who are motivated to read and who regularly read recreationally, enhance their attainment and their pleasure in reading.

Writing for pleasure and writing achievement

Compared to the number of studies which examine the relationship between the will and the skill of reading, there are far fewer that have explicitly considered the academic benefits that may be derived from writing for pleasure. As noted earlier, children's volitional writing has not been subject to scrutiny by research, policy or practice, and the media also, in contrast to the attention they offer reading for pleasure, pay scant attention to children or adults' desire to write, the purposes for which they might choose to do so and the benefits therein. Writers are commonly perceived to be published authors, albeit working within diverse fields and whilst examining the research practices of these professional writers does represent a research focus, the insights established have rarely been mediated and explored in primary and early secondary phase education. The field is also hampered by the absence of any large-scale data sets, such as exist in the form of PISA and PIRLS for reading, which researchers could mine to discern the presence of correlations between writing enjoyment and writing attainment.

Nonetheless, based on the available evidence, it is argued that young people who are more positive about writing and have a stronger sense of self-assurance as writers are more likely to engage willingly, to persevere during times of challenge and potentially to find the teaching of writing an enjoyable experience (e.g. Graham et al., 2007; Pajares, 2003). One US study by Graham et al. (2017) has shown that motivation and self-efficacy in turn predict writing performance. This correlational study, which used self-report instruments and assessed the children's narrative writing quality, did not seek to show causality. However, it did demonstrate that children who are confident about their writing competence are likely to develop a positive attitude towards writing and, fuelled by their sense of self efficacy as writers, are also likely to achieve highly. This work is largely consistent with other research that indicates relationships between various motivational constructs and writing outcomes (e.g. Camacho et al., 2021), and the value of motivating child writers and supporting their strategic behaviours (De Smedt et al., 2018; Guay et al., 2003). The systematic review of writing motivation in schools undertaken by Camacho et al. (2021) found a moderate association between student motivation and performance measures. De Smedt et al. (2018) also indicate that young people's motivation to write is associated with their sense of self-efficacy as writers and linked to their writing outcomes and Guay et al. (2003) argue a reciprocal relationship exists between motivation and success. The implications of this work is that once a child has composed something of which they are proud, this has the potential to change their sense of self-efficacy, enabling them to see themselves as a successful writer, and that, over time, more success will follow. None of these studies however explicitly examine whether this sense of self-efficacy or success affords pleasure to the young people or leads to them to write in their own time (see Chapter 4 for a more detailed consideration of writing motivation and self-efficacy and its potential relationship to volitional writing). Another group of research studies have found a positive relationship between children's attitudes and writing outcomes (e.g. Graham et al., 2007, 2017; Lee, 2013), and a UK survey has shown that 8–18-year-olds who enjoy writing 'very much' were far more likely to write above the level expected for their age compared with those who did not enjoy writing at all (50.3 per cent versus 7.2 per cent) (Clark, 2016). Nonetheless, in reviewing this field, Ekholm et al. (2018) observe that it is not a substantial one.

Additional benefits associated with reading and writing for pleasure

Studies also indicate there are other benefits associated with children choosing to engage in reading and writing in their own time. These benefits go well beyond reading performance.

Overcoming social and educational inequalities

Positive correlations between early volitional reading and cognitive growth during the years of adolescence are not only seen in richer comprehension scores in PISA and PIRLS as noted earlier (e.g. Cheema, 2018; Lindorff et al., 2023; Mullis et al., 2023), but in cognitive growth and wider academic attainment beyond English (e.g. Sullivan and Brown, 2015; Sun et al., 2024; Whitten et al., 2016). Drawing on evidence from a 1970s British cohort study, which encompassed a nationally representative sample of 3,583 16-year-olds, Sullivan and Brown (2015) show that being a frequent reader of choice in childhood is associated with substantial intellectual progress. As the scholars note:

> Once we controlled for the child's test scores at age five and ten, the influence of the child's own reading remained highly significant, suggesting that the positive link between leisure reading and cognitive outcomes is not purely due to more able children being more likely to read a lot, but that reading is actually linked to more cognitive progress over time.
>
> *(Sullivan and Brown, 2015, p. 37)*

Indeed, this research reveals that volitional reading is more strongly linked than parental education to cognitive progress in adolescence. The large-scale longitudinal work of Froiland and Oros (2014) also found that 10–11-year-olds' intrinsic motivation and desire to read predicted their later reading outcomes aged 13–14, and this was regardless of their socio-economic status, gender and ethnicity. As discussed in the Introduction, OECD findings consistently indicate that engagement in reading by choice 'is correlated with reading performance and is a mediator of gender and socio-economic status' (OECD, 2021, p. 28). As a result, the OECD asserts that being a keen engaged reader can help leverage social change. Later OECD summaries also indicate that low-income students with high reading engagement attain higher reading performance scores than high-income students with low reading engagement (Schleicher, 2023). So, supporting volitional reading is a matter of social justice.

Wider knowledge

Reading for pleasure is positively associated with higher numeracy scores in adolescence (Sullivan and Brown, 2015), which is affirmed by Whitten et al. (2016), who also found that high school students who reported reading for pleasure not only showed higher grade averages in mathematics but in science subjects, in addition to English. Furthermore, Sikora et al. (2019) evidence that growing up as an adolescent in a 'book-orientated environment' enhances adults' literacy, numeracy and technology skills. As a consequence of choosing to read regularly, researchers also assert children will be developing a wider general knowledge and understanding of the world (e.g. Clark and Rumbold, 2006; Cunningham and Stanovich, 1998; Mol and Bus, 2011) and will be developing 'information capital' essential for successful learning in different subjects (Neuman and Celano, 2012). Enhanced prior knowledge derived through wide reading supports young people's comprehension and learning right across the curriculum; arguably it offers them a distinct cognitive advantage compared to their peers who do not choose to read in their own time (Schugar and Dreyer, 2017).

Whilst there is no known research which documents the development of young people's general knowledge through their engagement in writing for pleasure, Graham and Hebert's (2011) meta-analysis of previous studies of writing instruction indicates that writing about a topic can improve children's comprehension of it. As Graham (2020) has also noted, in order to help their readers understand, writers work to make their meanings clear and, in the process, may clarify their own knowledge and understanding. It is logical therefore to suggest that through choosing to write about a self-selected topic, in which the child is likely to be invested and have some familiarity, they may well develop their understanding of the topic.

Enriched vocabulary

Several studies attest to the association between reading for pleasure and vocabulary. Summarising the findings of analyses of book language studies, Nation et al. (2022) highlight that books expose young children to a far greater range of expressions than they would encounter in normal conversations, and that their experience of book language supports the development of oral language as well as literacy skills. Drawing on a very different, and longitudinal, data set, Sullivan and Brown (2015) also show that being a frequent reader of choice in childhood is associated with marked vocabulary growth between the ages of 10 and 16. Furthermore, the development of oral language skills over time is connected to reading in Mol and Bus's (2011) meta-analysis:

> In preschool and kindergarten, print exposure explained 12% of the variance in oral language skills, in primary school 13%, in middle school 19%, in high school 30%, and in college and university 34%.
>
> *(Mol and Bus, 2011, p. 267)*

In addition, in alignment with Sullivan and Brown's (2015) and Mol and Bus' (2011) findings on vocabulary, there are both experimental and correlational studies that claim leisure reading impacts on vocabulary acquisition (e.g. Sénéchal and LeFevre, 2002; Swanborn and de Glopper, 1999). In reviewing such studies, Krashen (2004) concludes that silent sustained reading, alongside additional reading opportunities (such as hearing texts read aloud), was as good as or even better than traditional reading instruction in encouraging vocabulary and enhanced reading comprehension. Other studies have also found that reading recreationally is correlated with and predictive of enriched vocabularies (e.g. Anderson et al., 1988) and have noted medium effect sizes for both vocabulary and comprehension (Jeon and Day, 2016).

Additionally, McQuillan (2019) drawing on a meta-analysis of the impact of 14 studies of 'free reading' and comparing these with studies of the impact of explicit language instruction, concludes that free reading is far more efficient in terms of time and vocabulary acquisition, both in the short term (1.7 times) and the long term (12 times), than direct instruction. He thus posits that choice-led leisure reading offers incidental vocabulary gains, and that such reading provides a bridge to more challenging academic reading and sub-technical vocabulary. As he states, this is advantageous for children's vocabulary and wider language development (McQuillan, 2019). Specifically engaging with complex and often long literary texts has also been shown to expand 10–13-year-olds' vocabularies and support the development of their linguistic repertoires (Pfost et al., 2013), and in a not wholly dissimilar manner, a study of undergraduates' reading habits indicates a predictive link between reading enjoyment, identifying as a reader and verbal language skills (Martin-Chang et al., 2021).

Reading and writing enrich each other

Studies also indicate that those young people who read for pleasure and gain extensive experience from print exposure, particularly from reading fiction, tend to be better writers than their peers who do not choose to read in their own time (e.g. Jouhar and Rupley, 2021; Sénéchal et al., 2018). Likewise, there is some evidence that when increased time and space is given to writing and writing instruction, this can lead to improved reading comprehension (Graham and Hebert, 2011). The influence of reading on writing is unsurprising given the wealth of texts, tunes, language, styles and genres that avid young readers can lean upon and texts are often been positioned as models for children's writing. Wolf and Brice Heath (1992) argue that children 'collect clues' (p. 20) about characters, patterns and narration from the texts they meet, use these elements in their early socio-dramatic play, and later transform this in their writing. As professional writers frequently attest, they draw upon their reading, both from childhood and more contemporaneously, when they write (e.g. Cremin et al., 2017).

In order to scrutinise the relationship between recreational reading and writing, Jouhar and Rupley (2021) undertook a systematic review of experimental studies (1970–2019) and in particular examined the impact of reading on the writing performance of 10–16-year-olds. On the basis of this work, they conclude that independent reading enhances the quality of narrative and descriptive writing. They speculate that volitional reading offers models of written texts on which writers can draw and that this improves their compositions, text organisation, content, spelling and grammatical accuracy. The work of Sullivan and Brown (2015) also noted the impact of childhood reading on young people's spelling and vocabulary. In addition, Sénéchal et al. (2018), analysing a cohort of 300 9–10-year-old students' narratives, established an association between volitional reading and written text cohesion. Other studies also indicate this reciprocity between reading and writing (e.g. Andersen et al., 2018; Barrs and Cork, 2001; Corden, 2000; Graham, 2020). Through choosing to spend time reading or writing, young people arguably enhance their skills in both domains (Anderson et al., 2018). In a rare study which combined attention to 9–10-year-olds' free choice reading and writing, Taylor and Clarke (2021) showed that the kinds of texts the children chose to write were shaped and influenced both by their experience as readers of their chosen genre and by their own interests and literacy identities. Parry and Taylor (2018) also assert that

> children are not only drawing on cultural texts but are very specifically learning from them about significant and essential aspects of literacy, such as narrative cohesion, the affordances of different modalities and the use of language appropriately in context.
> *(Parry and Taylor, 2018, p. 109)*

In this work, the authors draw on Oatley's (2003) concept of the act of 'writingandreading', which highlights the inextricably integrated and bound nature of reading and writing. The arguably reciprocal nature of reading and writing is examined more fully in Chapter 2.

Enhanced wellbeing

In the last decade an increasing number of studies have revealed relationships between reading for pleasure and psychological wellbeing (e.g. Batini et al., 2021; Clark and Teravainen-Goff, 2018; Kennewell et al., 2022; Vaknin-Nusbaum and Tuckwiller, 2023). Young people who read regularly report higher levels of wellbeing than their peers who read rarely and for many of them, as research indicates, reading is a form of relaxation, immersion, a place to escape everyday challenges, a source of entertainment, of agency and of opportunities to connect with others (e.g. McGeown et al., 2020; Wilhelm, 2016). Based on a systematic review of the association between reading and emotional development, Batini et al. (2021) show that time spent reading has a positive impact on young children's socio-emotional development, regardless of factors such as age, gender or the setting of the implementation.

Positive correlations between reading motivation and school related wellbeing have also been documented in an Israeli study of 7–8-year-old Hebrew speakers from low-medium socio-economic backgrounds (Vaknin-Nusbaum and Tuckwiller, 2023). Wellbeing was interpreted as 'covitality' in this project, and included gratitude, optimism, zest and persistence. The research team found that both reading motivation and covitality were positively correlated to reading skills and language abilities, such that children with lower reading motivation demonstrated lower levels of wellbeing and were less assured as readers. The work of Bozgün and Akın-Kösterelioğlu (2021) underscores this, demonstrating a relationship between volitional reading and writing, 'academic grit' and young people's social emotional development. Longitudinal work from a UK millennium cohort study also reveals that daily reading for pleasure outside school by 7-year-olds is associated both with lower levels of emotional problems and better prosocial behaviour by age 11 (Mak and Fancourt, 2020). Furthermore, another large-scale US national cohort study, of 10,000-plus teenagers, affirms that early reading for pleasure is not only longitudinally associated with better mental health, but also with advanced brain structure and higher levels of cognitive performance (Sun et al., 2024).

Literary scholars and educationalists have long argued that volitional reading and, in particular, reading literature, supports young people's personal, emotional and cultural development (e.g. Arizpe et al., 2014a, 2014b; Cliff-Hodges, 2010; Mar et al., 2011). Reading literature can trigger memories and reminiscences, and this aesthetic invitation to connect, which operates regardless of one's background (Kuzmičová and Cremin, 2022), can enhance children's depth of understanding of texts (Barber and Klauda, 2020) and their pleasurable engagement. Additionally, qualitative research indicates that the volitional reading of literature offers young people opportunities to explore their personal and social identities (Appleyard, 1990; Rothbauer, 2004), and develop new reader to reader connections, which can, in turn, help to build socially supportive communities of readers (Cremin et al., 2014; Ng, 2018). Indeed, readers of all ages, depending on text and context, may become affectively engaged in their reading, and are motivated by a legacy of past pleasurable engagements, both with texts themselves and related social interaction.

In relation to volitional writing, the annual National Literacy Trust (NLT) surveys in the UK indicate that those young people who are most engaged with, and invested in, their writing are more likely to report higher levels of mental wellbeing (Clark and Teravainen-Goff, 2018; Clark et al., 2023). During the COVID-19 lockdown, many UK children reported using writing to cope with anxiety and to connect with people (Clark et al., 2021), indicating that some writing for self and writing for and alongside others has social and emotional value. This links to findings from the field of creative writing therapy, which indicate the significance of expressive writing (e.g. Kashuba and Masterson, 2022; Niles et al., 2014). Although these studies are not based in classrooms, and represent a small sample from a large field, they reflect the value that writing can have for psychological wellbeing and mental health. In 2024, the NLT survey indicated that, whilst few children chose to engage in free-choice writing for pleasure at home, those that did reported that they:

> Wrote to be creative, to express their ideas and imagination or their thoughts and feelings, to support their mental wellbeing, to relax and, remarkably, because it made them feel happy. Responses highlight the vital role writing for pleasure plays in the lives of young writers, allowing them to express their interior lives and support their mental wellbeing through developing a personal writing practice.
>
> *(Clark et al., 2024, p. 28)*

The potential role that writing can play personally and socially for young people, to support their emotional wellbeing, deserves closer examination with and for young people. In particular this is needed in the UK, where evidence from the Children's Society (Chollet et al., 2024) indicates levels of happiness are at an all-time low for teenagers. Drawing on PISA (OECD, 2023) data, the Good Childhood report (Chollet et al., 2024) highlights that the UK's 15-year-olds have the lowest average life satisfaction in Europe. This represents a cause for concern, one which a movement to support personal and expressive writing for pleasure might be able to respond.

Social cognition

Studies additionally suggest that reading fiction provides a space for the development of empathy and can enrich children's ability to recognise and appreciate others' perspectives, which may in turn lead to social action. Claims have been made regarding book reading leading to prejudice reduction in children (Vezzali et al., 2015) and perspective taking and social action in adults (e.g. Kidd and Castano, 2019; Mar et al., 2009). But this work, which is mainly with adults, has not always been replicated with similar results, and debates abound about the relative influence of the nature of the text, the reader and the interaction on the development of empathy (see Eekhof et al., 2022, for a review). Nonetheless, it is widely accepted that narratives can nurture children's imaginations (Nikolajeva, 2009), enabling them to infer characters' thoughts and feelings (Kümmerling-Meibauer, 2014), with one study indicating that books which deal with real-world relationships may be most appropriate for prompting thinking and making connections (Kuzmičová and Cremin, 2022). A quantitative study of the relationship between lifetime book reading and empathy in adolescents (Lenhart et al., 2022) highlights that emotional engagement in reading, for instance through immersion in a narrative, exploration of personal interest and feelings of excitement or enjoyment, can influence social and emotional outcomes and nurture empathy. Furthermore, a meta-analysis of extant studies in this area concludes that fiction reading, compared to non-fiction reading and no reading, leads to an improvement in social cognition (Dodell-Feder and Tamir, 2018). Studies with young children at home also appear to indicate that narrative exposure aids the development of social-cognitive development and empathy (Mar et al., 2010). But whether this is due to the narrative per se, or the interaction accompanying the shared text, has not been extensively examined.

To summarise, in addition to the academic benefits associated with reading for pleasure, (including cognitive growth, enhanced reading comprehension, wider vocabulary and enriched narrative writing), potentially multiple social and emotional benefits accrue for those young people who choose to read recreationally in childhood and beyond. Those who choose to write in their own time also benefit, although there is comparatively less evidence in this regard.

Reflecting on the evidence base

In considering the evidence, it should be reasserted that research into the potential benefits associated with volitional writing is limited, and also acknowledged that measuring leisure reading and writing and assessing children's pleasure in and attitudes to these literacy practices is inherently problematic. It is important to avoid over-claiming or generalising findings about relationships and to pay attention to the context and consequences on children's volitional engagement in literacy.

Predominantly, the studies reviewed are quantitative in nature, they do not claim causality but are explicitly correlational in nature. Many rely on self-reported data from surveys, in the form of parental reports for pre-readers or children in the early stages of reading and the reported views of older readers taken at a particular moment in time, and although some of these studies are longitudinal, drawing on cohort data over time, such studies are relatively few. Surveys have been criticised due to their inherent bias towards social desirability (Sénéchal et al., 1996) and the underlying assumption that children and young people's motivation to read is stable, neither varying over time or across contexts (Schiefele and Löweke, 2018). Yet most reading research surveys stand alone and are not repeated over the years. Additionally, as Jang and Protacio (2020) highlight, historically many such research instruments were designed for monolingual students and may be unable to capture multilingual learners' diverse reading practices. So, in this respect also, caution in generalising must be exercised. In addition, the orthographies of languages differ, and these impact upon the ease with which children learn to read and develop reading fluency in different countries, thus shaping their sense of self as a reader and their volitional reading. Yet comparisons are often made without attention to cultural or linguistic differences. Finally, it is vital to acknowledge that whilst most commonly volitional reading is deemed to be measured by the time spent reading reported in the various studies, different aspects of reader motivation, engagement and attainment are considered. These included, for example, intrinsic and extrinsic motivation, reading fluency, volume, text genres and/or comprehension and their inter-relationships. Depending on discipline, as Lee et al. (2021) comment with regard to the concept of 'reader engagement', researchers tend to define their constructs somewhat differently. Furthermore, as Cremin and Scholes (2024) note:

> Drawing on large scale self report data from surveys can offer valuable correlational insights, yet seen through the lens of such surveys reading is framed more as a measurable result than a socially lived experience, surveys alone cannot capture young people's effective textual social and relational engagement as readers.
>
> *(Cremin and Scholes, 2024, p. 543)*

Mixed methods and qualitative studies of young readers' and writers' motivations, preferences, practices and behaviours as readers and writers recognise the influence of the social context and those within it. Often adopting an identity lens, these more ethnographically oriented studies tend to document the ways in which children's literacy engagement interacts with socio-cultural factors (see Chapters 4–7).

Declining attitudes towards reading and writing

The PIRLS (Mullis et al., 2023) and PISA (OECD, 2021) surveys attend, respectively, to 10-year-olds' and 15-year-olds' reading attitudes and behaviours across multiple countries. There are no comparable international surveys conducted in relation to writing. However, within the UK, the NLT undertakes annual in-school survey-based research about 5–18-year-olds' attitudes and behaviours towards both reading and writing (Clark et al., 2023, 2024) and since the Literacy Special Initiative was based in England, these have been included.

The PIRLS, PISA and NLT surveys consistently document a decline in the number of children and young people who express enjoyment in reading. In the 2021 PIRLS survey a global average of only 42 per cent of children reported that they 'very much like reading' (Mullis et al., 2023). Similarly, the 2018 PISA results indicate that there is limited appetite for reading for pleasure among 15-years-olds internationally, with a minority of young people stating that reading is one of their favourite hobbies (OECD, 2021). The international insights from PISA 2018 and PIRLS 2021 into reading attitudes are mirrored by the NLT's surveys (Clark et al., 2023). Indeed, these annual UK surveys have documented consistent declines in attitudes towards reading for pleasure since 2005. Although a brief increase in reading enjoyment was documented in 2020 during the early lockdowns of the COVID-19 pandemic, which as Clark and Picton (2020) note was probably due to increased free time at home. However, subsequent surveys have shown a return to the decline (Clark et al., 2023) and that reading enjoyment decreases with age. Other studies, from America and Canada, respectively, support the observation that younger children report greater reading for pleasure, with pre-adolescents and adolescents enjoying reading less (e.g. Adelson et al., 2019; Nootens et al., 2019).

Children and young people's attitudes to writing, in general, mirror their limited interest in reading. Since 2010, when the NLT began collecting data on children and young people's attitudes towards writing, a near consistent decline in choosing to write and enjoying writing has been documented (Clark et al., 2024). Moreover, resembling trends in relation to reading, the older the child, the more likely they are to dislike writing. Interestingly, despite these declining attitudes, the 2021 survey (Clark et al., 2021) documented 8–18-year-olds' opinions that writing makes them feel better, with many using writing during the early part of the pandemic to cope with anxiety and to connect with people. This links to the finding, noted earlier, that those young people who are most engaged with reading and writing are more likely to have higher levels of mental wellbeing (Clark and Teravainen-Goff, 2018; Clark et al., 2023).

Despite these benefits, other studies similarly indicate negative attitudes towards writing on the part of some children (e.g. Dunsmuir and Blatchford, 2004) providing useful insights into the multiple reasons underpinning these feelings. For instance, Gadd et al.'s (2019) survey of New Zealand children (n:449), aged 5–12, indicated that generating content can be challenging for some children. Moreover, these children experienced negative attitudes towards writing when it was presented as obligatory and when mandated writing was perceived as boring and irrelevant to the young. Zumbrunn et al.'s (2017) American-based study of 10–11-year olds' pictorial representations of writing experiences revealed similar attitudes. The analysis of the 114 children's drawings suggested writing evoked powerful emotions, such as anxiety, frustration and anger, indicating the need for adults to be sensitive to the intense emotions the writing process can evoke. However, in this same study, some young writers valued the writing experience and found writing relaxing and calming, helping them feel 'at peace'.

Countering the insights of the above studies, the US-based Pew Research Center's study (Lenhart et al., 2008) on the influence of technology on the writing attitudes and behaviours of 12–17-year-olds (n:700) found that the participating teenagers enjoyed writing, particularly writing for personal reasons. This included using electronic platforms to communicate with friends or using creative writing to write songs and multimedia content. Their personal writing practices suggest the need for an expanded view of what constitutes writing in schools. In contrast, writing in or for school was characterised as arduous, although these adolescents did report satisfaction when they received positive feedback on school assignments.

Other studies highlight that children and young people's attitudes to writing are shaped by experiences in the classroom, with children equating the image of a 'good writer' as someone who is proficient in transcriptional aspects of writing (Wray, 1995), and goes about the task of writing quietly and individually (Bearne et al., 2011). Worryingly, a survey in England demonstrated that children's writing engagement was detrimentally impacted by their teachers' adoption of a 'skills discourse' (Lambirth, 2016). This approach prioritised spelling, punctuation and grammar over the more creative elements of writing, such as compositional content, style and ideas. Lambirth argued that this approach alienated children from writing. Barrs has also documented how the consistent focus in England on assessing 'form over content' (2019, p. 18) led to children and young people focusing on vocabulary choices and grammatical conventions sequences for their attitudes. In a US-based survey, researchers found that children's attitudes to writing were linked to teacher feedback, with one third of children reporting not liking feedback (Marrs et al., 2016). Collectively, these studies point to a highly performative writing culture within various international educational contexts, leading to children and young people feeling they must write to meet technical criteria, not to express meaning (Barrs, 2019).

Nonetheless, there are smaller scale studies which show more positive attitudes towards writing (e.g. Barratt-Pugh et al., 2021; Colognesi and Niwese, 2020). For example, Colognesi and Niwese (2020) reported on one Belgian teacher's introduction of some principles of 'effective writing' for 10–12-year-olds (n:40). These reflective and social principles included goal setting, strategy instruction, peer assessment and rewriting. The researchers found that the students who experienced this style of teaching made greater progress, developed a new desire to write, voiced enjoyment in writing and viewed writing as less of a technical task and more of a 'means of communication'. In Australia, Barratt-Pugh et al. (2021) found that the majority of 5–6-year-olds (n:109) liked writing, believed it was easy and felt that they were good at it. However, a few children expressed dislike for writing, and some did not seem to see it as purposeful. Accordingly, their teachers adapted their practices to offer more authentic writing experiences. These two studies draw attention to the importance of providing children and young people with specific writing strategies and of ensuring that writing has a purpose for the child writer. Indeed, writing for pleasure and for specific purposes can, as Young and Ferguson (2021, p. 23) assert, offer children 'a feeling of empowerment' and a sense that their 'writing has enriched their lives and the lives of others'.

Despite the hope offered by these studies, the persistent decline in many children and young people's interest in reading and writing is alarming, especially when such attitudes are seen to be coupled by an understanding of their literacy behaviours.

Reading and writing behaviours

In addition to increasingly negative attitudes towards reading for pleasure and writing for pleasure, the PIRLS, PISA and NLT surveys also provide insights into young people's related habits, in terms of how often they read or write, and what and why they choose to do so. The NLT survey found that a minority of young people engaged in reading and writing on a daily basis (Clark et al., 2024). In contrast, the 2018 PISA survey indicated a slight increase internationally in the amount of time children spent reading (OECD, 2021). However, this increase in time spent reading does not denote sustained periods of immersion. Across the OECD nations, only 6 per cent of young people reported reading for more than two hours a day and 11 per cent reported reading for between one and two hours a day. The 2021 PIRLS survey of younger readers also attended to the amount of time spent reading, interpreting this behaviour as another marker of reading engagement (Mullis et al., 2023). In this, children from across North America, Europe, Asia and Australia were more likely to read for shorter than longer periods of time each day (Lindorff et al., 2023). To this end, some PIRLS 2021 countries have sought to implement reading initiatives, such as Drop Everything and Read in Ireland (Delaney et al., 2022), to increase time spent reading and, hopefully, to improve attitudes to reading. However, PISA results (OECD, 2019a) suggest that increased amounts of time spent reading are not coupled with increases in enjoyment. Instead, there were occasions when young people appeared to be enjoying reading less, even though they were reading more.

These insights raise challenging questions about the link between time spent reading and its purpose. The PIRLS survey data suggested that reading is increasingly used for information retrieval (Mullis et al., 2023). For instance, just over half of children surveyed spent 30 minutes or less per school day, using digital devices such as laptops, tablet or smartphones, to find and read information. Similarly, the PISA results indicated that young people were less likely to read for pleasure and more likely to read to fulfil practical tasks (OECD, 2021). In turn, reading to complete practical objectives was also associated with reading fewer fiction books. For instance, in Hungary, Serbia and Thailand, young people who expressed less enjoyment in reading spent more time reading but read a lower-than-average amount of fiction in comparison to the OECD average (OECD, 2019c). Given the association between fiction reading and high attainment (Jerrim and Moss, 2019) this is a concern. Overall, the data indicate a shift in reading's purpose for some young people. It may not be perceived as a pleasurable or leisurely activity in its own right. Instead, reading may be positioned by some as a functional task.

Regarding writing behaviours, while it is to be expected that children who enjoy writing may do so more frequently in their own free time, this has not been extensively examined, and as noted earlier no international data sets exists that are comparable to the PISA and PIRLS surveys. However, the UK NLT survey and the US-based Pew study provide useful nuances. Contrary to the international PISA and PIRLS data that suggested a shift towards reading for logistical/ functional purposes, the NLT survey suggests that those children who chose to write in their own time do so for personal, creative, emotional and social reasons (Clark et al., 2024). They want for instance, to exercise their imaginations, to share their ideas, engage with issues of importance to them and to connect with the world around them. The Pew study (Lenhart et al., 2008) into teenagers' writing also seemed to contrast with international reading data, showing that the majority of those involved reported choosing to write. However, this observation needs qualifying; volitional writing was not synonymous with frequent writing in this study, the 'majority' referred to teenagers who reported choosing to write over the course of a year. In fact, only a committed minority of them reported frequently choosing to write. So once again, careful scrutiny of the research evidence is essential in order to avoid misinterpretations and generalisations.

Conclusion

The international evidence is clear that reading for pleasure has considerable power and potential in supporting the academic, personal and social development of young people. Children's motivation as writers, their self-efficacy and engagement in writing, is also recognised as influential. Additionally, research from around the globe indicates a decline in children's and young people's desire to read and the frequency with which they do so. These studies, which tend to rely on large-scale surveys and self-report data, offer valuable correlational insights and reveal the complexities involved and the multiple mediating influences between variables. They benefit from being considered alongside qualitatively derived research findings of the wider volitional reading and writing landscape in order that the contextual factors which shape and influence children and young people's lived experience of reading and writing are also considered.

References

Adelson, J.L., Cash, K.M., Pittard, C.M., Sherretz, C.E., Possel, P. and Blackburn, A.D. (2019) 'Measuring reading self-perceptions and enjoyment: Development and psychometric properties of the reading and me survey', *Journal of Advanced Academics*, 30(3), pp. 355–380.

Allington, R.L. and McGill-Franzen, A.M. (2021) 'Reading volume and reading achievement: A review of recent research', *Reading Research Quarterly*, 56(S1), S231– S238.

Andersen, S.C., Christensen, M.V., Nielsen, H.S., Thomsen, M.K., Østerbye, T. and Rowe, M.L. (2018) 'How reading and writing support each other across a school year in primary school children', *Contemporary Educational Psychology*, 55, pp. 129–138.

Anderson, R., Wilson, P.T. and Fielding, L.G. (1988) 'Growth in reading and how children spend their time outside of school', *Reading Research Quarterly*, 23(3), pp. 85–303.

Appleyard, J. (1990) *Becoming a Reader: The Experience of Fiction from Childhood to Adulthood*, Cambridge: Cambridge University Press.

Arizpe, E., Colomer, T. and Martínez-Roldán, C. (2014a) *Visual Journeys Through Wordless Narratives*, London: Bloomsbury Academic.

Arizpe, E., Bagelman, C., Devlin, A.M., Farrell, M. and McAdam, J.E. (2014b) 'Visualising intercultural literacy: Engaging critically with diversity and migration in the classroom through an image-based approach', *Language and Intercultural Communication*, 14(3), pp. 304–321.

Barber, A.T. and Klauda, S.L. (2020) 'How reading motivation and engagement enable reading achievement: Policy implications', *Policy Insights from the Behavioral and Brain Sciences*, 7(1), pp. 27–34.

Barratt-Pugh, C., Ruscoe, A. and Fellowes, J. (2021) 'Motivation to write: Conversations with emergent writers', *Early Childhood Education Journal*, 49(2), pp. 223–234.

Barrs, M. (2019) 'Teaching bad writing', *English in Education*, 53(1), pp. 18–31.

Barrs, M. and Cork, V. (2001) *The Reader in the Writer: The Influence of Literature upon Writing at KS2*, London: Centre for Literacy in Primary Education.

Batini, F., Luperini, V., Cei, E., Izzo, D. and Toti, G. (2021) 'The association between reading and emotional development: A systematic review', *Journal of Education and Training Studies*, 9(1), pp. 12–48.

Bearne, E., Chamberlain, L., Cremin, T. and Mottram, M. (2011) *Teaching Writing Effectively: Reviewing Practice*, Leicester: UKLA.

Bozgün, K. and Akın-Kösterelioğlu, M. (2021) 'The roles of social-emotional development, academic grit and subjective well-being in primary school students' reading-writing motivation', *Reading Psychology*, 42(8), pp. 836–857.

Brozo, W.G., Shiel, G. and Topping, K. (2007) 'Engagement in reading: Lessons learned from three PISA countries', *Journal of Adolescent and Adult Literacy*, 51(4), pp. 304–315.

Camacho, A., Alves, R.A. and Boscolo, P. (2021) 'Writing motivation in school: A systematic review of empirical research in the early twenty-first century', *Educational Psychology Review*, 33, pp. 213–247.

Campbell, J., Voelkl, K. and Donahue, P. (1997) *NAEP 1996 Trends in Academic Progress. Achievement of US Students in Science, 1969 to 1996; Mathematics, 1973 to 1996; Reading, 1971 to 1996; Writing, 1984*, Washington, DC: US Department of Education.

Cheema, J. (2018) 'Adolescents' enjoyment of reading as a predictor of reading achievement: New evidence from a cross-country survey', *Journal of Research in Reading*, 41, S149– S162.

Chollet, D., Turner, A., Marquez, J., O'Neill, J. and Moore, L. (2024) *The Good Childhood Report 2024*, London: The Children's Society.

Clark, C. (2016) *Children and Young People's Writing in 2015: Findings from the National LIteracy Trust's Annual Literacy Survey*, London: National Literacy Trust.

Clark, C. and Picton, I. (2020) *Children and Young People's Reading in 2020 Before and During the COVID-19 Lockdown*, London: National Literacy Trust.

Clark, C. and Rumbold, K. (2006) *Reading for Pleasure: A Research Overview*, London: National Literacy Trust.

Clark, C. and Teravainen-Goff, A. (2018) *Mental Wellbeing, Reading and Writing. National Literacy Trust Report*, London: National Literacy Trust.

Clark, C., Best, E. and Picton, I. (2021) *Children and Young People's Writing in 2021 and Their Reflections on Writing During the Covid-19 Pandemic in 2020*, London: National Literacy Trust.

Clark, C., Picton, I. and Galway, M. (2023) *Children and Young People's Reading in 2023*, London: National Literacy Trust.

Clark, C., Picton, C., Cole, A. and Bonafede, F. (2024) *Children and Young People's Writing in 2024*, London: National Literacy Trust.

Cliff-Hodges, G. (2010) 'Reasons for reading: Why literature matters', *Literacy*, 44(2), pp. 60–68.

Colognesi, S. and Niwese, M. (2020) 'Do effective practices for teaching writing change students' relationship to writing: Exploratory study with students aged 10–12 years', *Educational Studies in Language and Literature*, 20(1), pp. 1–25.

Corden, R. (2000) 'Reading-writing connections: The importance of interactive discourse', *English in Education*, 34(2), pp. 35–44.

Cremin, T. and Scholes, L. (2024) 'Reading for pleasure: Scrutinizing the evidence base – benefits, tensions recommendations', *Language and Education*, 38(4), pp. 537–559.

Cremin, T., Lillis, T., Myhill, D. and Eyres, I. (2017) 'Professional writers' identities', in Cremin, T. and Locke, T. (eds), *Writer Identity and the Teaching and Learning of Writing*, London: Routledge, pp. 18–36.

Cremin, T., Mottram, M., Collins, F.M., Powell, S. and Safford, K. (2014) *Building Communities of Engaged Readers: Reading for Pleasure*, Oxon: Routledge.

Cunningham, A.E. and Stanovich, K.E. (1998) 'The impact of print exposure on word recognition', in Metsala, J.L. and Ehri, L.C. (eds), *Word Recognition in Beginning Literacy*, New York: Lawrence Erlbaum Associates Publishers, pp. 235–262.

Delaney, E., McHugh, G., McAteer, S. and O'Neill, B. (2022) 'PIRLS 2021 Encyclopedia: Ireland', in Reynolds, K.A., Wry, E., Mullis, I.V.S. and von Davier, M. (eds), *PIRLS 2021 Encyclopedia: Education Policy and Curriculum in Reading*, Boston: Boston College, TIMSS & PIRLS International Study Center.

De Smedt, F., Merchie, E., Barendse, M., Rossell, Y., De Naeghel, J. and Van Keer, H. (2018) 'Cognitive and motivational challenges in writing: Studying the relationship with writing performance across students' gender and achievement level', *Reading Research Quarterly*, 53 (2), pp. 249–272.

Dodell-Feder, D. and Tamir, D. (2018) 'Fiction reading has a small positive impact on social cognition: A meta-analysis', *Journal of Experimental Psychology*, 147(11), pp. 1713–1727.

Dunne, M. and Gazeley, L. (2008) 'Teachers, social class and underachievement', *British Journal of Sociology of Education*, 29(5), pp. 451–463.

Dunsmuir, S. and Blatchford, P. (2004) 'Predictors in writing competence in 4-to-7 year old children', *British Journal of Educational Psychology*, 74(3), pp. 461–483.

Eekhof, L.S., van Krieken, K. and Willems, R.M. (2022) 'Reading about minds: The social-cognitive potential of narratives', *Psychonomic Bulletin and Review*, 29, pp. 1703–1718.

Ekholm, E., Zumbrunn, S., and De Busk-Lane, M. (2018) 'Clarifying an elusive construct: A systematic review of writing attitudes', *Educational Psychology Review*, 30(3), pp. 827–856.

Erbeli, F., van Bergen, E. and Hart, S.A. (2020) 'Unraveling the relation between reading comprehension and print exposure', *Child Development*, 91(5), pp. 1548–1562.

Froiland, J.M. and Oros, E. (2014) 'Intrinsic motivation, perceived competence and classroom engagement as longitudinal predictors of adolescent reading achievement', *Educational Psychology*, 34(2), pp. 119–132.

Gadd, M., Parr, J., Robertson, J., Carran, L., Ali, Z., Gendall, L. and Watson, K. (2019) 'Portrait of the student as a young writer: Some student survey findings about attitudes to writing and self-efficacy as writers', *Literacy*, 53(4), pp. 226–235.

Gilleece, L. and Eivers, E. (2018) 'Characteristics associated with paper-based and online reading in Ireland: Findings from PIRLS and ePIRLS 2016', *International Journal of Educational Research*, 91, pp. 16–27.

Graham, S. (2020) 'The sciences of reading and writing must become more fully integrated', *Reading Research Quarterly*, 55(S1), S35–S44.

Graham, S. and Hebert, M. (2011) 'Writing to read: A meta-analysis of the impact of writing and writing instruction on reading', *Harvard Educational Review*, 81(4), pp. 710–744.

Graham, S., Berninger, V. and Fan, W. (2007) 'The structural relationship between writing attitude and writing achievement in first and third grade students', *Contemporary Educational Psychology*, 32(3), pp. 516–536.

Graham, S., Kiuhara, S.A., Harris, K.R. and Fishman, E.J. (2017) 'The relationship among strategic writing behaviour, writing motivation, and writing performance with young, developing writers', *Elementary School Journal*, 118(1), pp. 82–104.

Guay, F., Marsh, H. and Boivin, M. (2003) 'Academic self-concept and academic achievement: Developmental perspectives on their causal ordering', *Journal of Educational Psychology*, 95, pp. 124–136.

Guthrie, J.T. and Wigfield, A. (2000) 'Engagement and motivation in reading', in Kamil, M.L., Mosenthal, P.B., Pearson, P.D. and Barr, R. (eds), *Handbook of Reading Research*, Vol. 3, Mahwah, NJ: Lawrence Erlbaum, pp. 403–422.

Guthrie, J.T., Wigfield, A., Metsala, J.L. and Cox, K.E. (1999) 'Motivational and cognitive predictors of text comprehension and reading amount', *Scientific Studies of Reading*, 3(3), pp. 231–256.

Harjunen, E. and Rautopuro, J. (2015) *Thinking about Language Use and Language Thinking: Learning Outcomes in Mother Tongue and Literature at the End of Basic Education in 2014*, Helsinki: Finnish Education Evaluation Centre.

Hempel-Jorgensen, A., Cremin, T., Harris, D. and Chamberlain, L. (2018) 'Pedagogy for reading for pleasure in low socio-economic primary schools: Beyond "pedagogy of poverty"?', *Literacy*, 52(2), pp. 86–94.

Ives, S., Parsons, S., Ward Parsons, A., Dana A., Robertson, D., Daoud, N., Young, C. and Polk, L. (2020) 'Elementary students' motivation to read and genre preferences', *Reading Psychology*, 41(7), pp. 660–679.

Jang, B.G. and Protacio, M.S. (2020) 'Use of cognitive interviews to test the validity of a reading motivation instrument for English learners', *Reading Psychology*, 41(8), pp. 913–933.

Jeon, E.-Y. and Day, R.R. (2016) 'The effectiveness of ER on reading proficiency: A meta-analysis', *Reading in a Foreign Language*, 28(2), pp. 246–265.

Jerrim, J. and Moss, G. (2019) 'The link between fiction and teenagers' reading skills. International evidence from the OECD PISA study', *British Educational Research Journal*, 45(1), pp. 181–200.
Jerrim, J., Lopez-Agudo, L.A. and Marcenaro-Gutierrez, O.D. (2020) 'Does it matter what children read? New evidence using longitudinal census data from Spain', *Oxford Review of Education*, 46 (5), pp. 515–533.
Jouhar, M.R. and Rupley, W.H. (2021) 'The reading–writing connection based on independent reading and writing: A systematic review', *Reading and Writing Quarterly*, 37(2), pp. 136–156.
Kashuba, J. and Masterson, T.L. (2022) 'The effects of therapeutic writing on juvenile justice populations', *Journal of Correctional Education*, 73(1), pp. 19–30.
Kennewell, E., Curtis. R.G., Maher, C., Luddy, S. and Virgar, R. (2022) 'The relationships between school children's wellbeing, socio-economic disadvantage and after-school activities: a cross-sectional study', *BMC Pediatrics*, 22(1), Article 297.
Kidd, D. and Castano, E. (2019) 'Reading literary fiction and theory of mind: Three preregistered replications and extensions of Kidd and Castano (2013)', *Social Psychology and Personality Science*, 10(4), pp. 522–531.
Kirsch, I., de Jong, J., LaFontaine, D., McQueen, J., Mendelovits, J. and Monseur, C (2002) *Reading for Change: Performance and Engagement across Countries – Results from PISA 2000*, Paris: OECD.
Krashen, S. (2004) *The Power of Reading*, 2nd edn, Portsmouth, NH: Heinemann.
Kress, G.R. (1994) *Learning to Write*, London: Routledge.
Kucirkova, N., Wells Rowe, D., Oliver, L. and Piestrzynski, L.E. (2019) 'Systematic review of young children's writing on screen: What do we know and what do we need to know', *Literacy*, 53(4), pp. 216–225.
Kümmerling-Meibauer, B. (2014) 'What goes on in strangers' minds? How reading children's books affects emotional development', *Narrative Works*, 4(2), pp. 64–85.
Kuzmičová, A. and Cremin, T. (2022) 'Different fiction genres take children's memories to different places', *Cambridge Journal of Education*, 52(1), pp. 37–53.
Lambirth, A. (2016) 'Exploring children's discourses of writing', *English in Education*, 50(3), pp. 215–232.
Lee, J. (2013) 'Can writing attitudes and learning behavior overcome gender difference in writing? Evidence from NAEP', *Written Communication*, 30, pp. 164–193.
Lee, Y., Gee Jang, B., and Conradi Smith, K. (2021) 'A systematic review of reading engagement research. What do we mean, what do we know and where do we need to go?', *Reading Psychology*, 42(5), pp. 540–576.
Leino, K., Nissinen, K., Puhakka, E. and Rautopuro, J. (2017) *Lukutaito luodaan yhdessä: kansainvälinen lasten lukutaitotutkimus* [*Reading Skills are Created Together: International Survey on Reading*], Jyväskslä: Finnish Institute for Educational Research.
Lenhart, A., Arafeh, S., Smith, A. and Rankin MacGill, A. (2008) *Writing, Technology and Teens*, Washington, DC: Pew Internet.
Lenhart, J., Dangel, J. and Richter, T. (2022) 'The relationship between lifetime book reading and empathy in adolescents: Examining transportability as a moderator', *Psychology of Aesthetics, Creativity, and the Arts*, 16(4), pp. 679–693.
Lindorff, A., Stiff, J. and Kayton, H. (2023) *PIRLS 2021: National Report for England Research Report*, London: Department for Education.
Locher, F.M., Becker, S. and Pfost, M. (2019) 'The relation between students' intrinsic reading motivation and book reading in recreational and school contexts', *AERA Open*, 5(2), 233285841985204.
Mak, H.W. and Fancourt, D. (2020) 'Longitudinal associations between reading for pleasure and child maladjustment: Results from a propensity score matching analysis', *Social Science and Medicine*, 253, 112971.

Malanchini, M., Wang, Z., Voronin, I., Schenker, V.J., Plomin, R., Petrill, S. and Kovas, Y. (2017) 'Reading self-perceived ability, enjoyment and achievement: A genetically informative study of their reciprocal links over time', *Developmental Psychology*, 53(4), pp. 698–712.

Mar, R., Oatley, K. and Peterson, J. (2009) 'Exploring the link between reading fiction and empathy: Ruling out individual differences and examining outcomes', *Communications*, 34(4), pp. 407–428.

Mar, R.A., Tackett, J.L. and Moore, C. (2010) 'Exposure to media and theory-of-mind development in preschoolers', *Cognitive Development*, 25(1), 69–78.

Mar, R.A., Oatley, K., Djikic, M. and Mullin, J. (2011) 'Emotion and narrative fiction: Interactive influences before, during, and after reading', *Cognition and Emotion*, 25(5), pp. 818–833.

Marrs, S., Zumbrunn, S., McBride, C. and Stringer, J. (2016) 'Exploring elementary student perceptions of writing feedback', *Journal of Educational Psychology*, 10(1), pp. 16–28.

Martin-Chang, S., Kozak, S., Levesque, K.C., Calarco, N. and Mar, R.A. (2021) 'What's your pleasure? Exploring the predictors of leisure reading for fiction and nonfiction', *Reading and Writing: An Interdisciplinary Journal*, 34, pp. 1387–1414.

McGeown, S., Bonsall, J., Andries, V., Howarth, D. and Wilkinson, K. (2020) 'Understanding reading motivation across different text types: Qualitative insights from children', *Journal of Research in Reading*, 43(4), pp. 597–608.

McGrane, J., Stiff, J., Baird, J.-A., Lenkeit, J. and Hopfenbeck, T. (2017) *Progress in International Reading Literacy Study (PIRLS): National Report for England*, Oxford: Department for Education and University of Oxford.

McQuillan, J. (2019) 'Where do we get our academic vocabulary? Comparing the efficiency of direct instruction and free voluntary reading', *The Reading Matrix: An International Online Journal*, 19(1), pp. 129–138.

Miyamoto, A., Pfost, M. and Artelt, C. (2018) 'Reciprocal relations between intrinsic reading motivation and reading competence: A comparison between native and immigrant students in Germany', *Journal of Research in Reading*, 41(1), pp. 176–196.

Mol, S.E. and Bus, A.G. (2011) 'To read or not to read: A meta-analysis of print exposure from infancy to early adulthood', *Psychological Bulletin*, 137(2), pp. 267–296.

Mullis, I.V.S., von Davier, M., Foy, P., Fishbein, B., Reynolds, K.A. and Wry, E. (2023) *PIRLS 2021 International Results in Reading*, Boston: Boston College, TIMSS and PIRLS International Study Center.

Myhill, D., Cremin, T. and Oliver, L. (2023) 'The impact of changed writing environment on students' motivation to write', *Frontiers in Psychology*, 14.

Nation, K., Dawson, N.J. and Hsiao, Y. (2022) 'Book language and its implications for children's language, literacy, and development', *Current Directions in Psychological Science*, 31(4), pp. 375–380.

Neuman, S.B. and Celano, D. (2001) 'Access to print in low-income and middle-income communities: An ecological study of four neighborhoods', *Reading Research Quarterly*, 36(1), pp. 8–26.

Neuman, S. and Celano, D.C. (2012) *Giving Our Children a Fighting Chance: Poverty, Literacy, and the Development of Information Capital*, New York: Teachers College Press.

Ng, C. (2018) 'Using student voice to promote reading engagement for economically disadvantaged students', *Journal of Research in Reading*, 41(4), pp. 700–715.

Nikolajeva, M. (2009) *Power, Voice and Subjectivity in Literature for Young Readers*, New York: Routledge.

Niles, A.N., Haltom, K.E., Mulvenna, C.M., Lieberman, M.D. and Stanton, A.L. (2014) 'Randomized controlled trial of expressive writing for psychological and physical health: The moderating role of emotional expressivity', *Anxiety Stress Coping*, 27(1), pp. 1–17.

Nootens, P., Morin, M.F., Alamargot, D., Gonçalves, C., Venet, M. and Labrecque, A.M. (2019) 'Differences in attitudes toward reading: A survey of pupils in grades 5 to 8', *Frontiers in Psychology*, 9, 2773.

Oatley, K. (2003) 'Writingandreading: The future of cognitive poetics', in Gavins, J. and Steen, G. (eds) *Cognitive Poetics in Practice*, London: Routledge, pp. 161–174.
OECD (2019a) *PISA 2018 Insights and Interpretations*, Paris: OECD Publishing.
OECD (2019b) *PISA 2018 Assessment and Analytical Framework*, Paris: OECD Publishing.
OECD (2019c) *PISA 2018 Results (Volume II): Where All Students Can Succeed*, Paris: OECD Publishing.
OECD (2021) *21st-Century Readers: Developing Literacy Skills in a Digital World*, Paris: OECD Publishing.
OECD (2023) *PISA 2022 Results (Volume I): The State of Learning and Equity in Education*, Paris: OECD Publishing.
Pajares, F. (2003) 'Self-efficacy beliefs, motivation, and achievement in writing: A review of the literature', *Reading Writing Quarterly*, 19, pp. 139–158.
Parry, B. and Taylor, L. (2018) 'Readers in the round: Children's holistic engagements with texts', *Literacy*, 52(2), pp. 103–110.
Pfost, M., Dörfler, T. and Artelt, C. (2013) 'Students' extracurricular reading behavior and the development of vocabulary and reading comprehension', *Learning and Individual Differences*, 26, pp. 89–102.
Rogiers, A., Merchie, E. and Van Keer, H. (2020) 'What they say is what they do? Comparing task-specific self-reports, think-aloud protocols, and study traces for measuring secondary school students' text-learning strategies', *European Journal of Psychology of Education*, 35(2), pp. 315–332.
Rothbauer, P. (2004) '"People aren't afraid anymore, but it's hard to find books": Reading practices that inform the personal and social identities of self-identified lesbian and queer young women', *Canadian Journal of Information and Library Science*, 28(3), pp. 53–74.
Schaffner, E., Philipp, M. and Schiefele, U. (2016) 'Reciprocal effects between intrinsic reading motivation and reading competence? A cross-lagged panel model for academic track and nonacademic track students', *Journal of Research in Reading*, 39(1), pp. 19–36.
Schiefele, U. and Löweke, S. (2018) 'The nature, development, and effects of elementary students' reading motivation profiles', *Reading Research Quarterly*, 53(4), pp. 405–421.
Schiefele, U., Schaffner, E., Möller, J. and Wigfield, A. (2012) 'Dimensions of reading motivation and their relation to reading behavior and competence', *Reading Research Quarterly*, 47 (4), pp. 427–463.
Schleicher, A (2023) *PISA 2022: Insights and Interpretations*, Paris: OECD Publishing.
Schugar, H.R. and Dreher, J. (2017) 'U.S. fourth graders' informational text comprehension: Indicators from NAEP', *International Electronic Journal of Elementary Education*, 9(3), pp. 523–552.
Sénéchal, M. and LeFevre, J.A. (2002) 'Parental involvement in the development of children's reading skill: A five-year longitudinal study', *Child Development*, 73(2), pp. 445–460.
Sénéchal, M., Hill, S. and Malette, M. (2018) 'Individual differences in grade 4 children's written compositions: The role of online planning and revising, oral storytelling, and reading for pleasure', *Cognitive Development*, 45, pp. 92–104.
Sénéchal, M., LeFevre, J.-A., Hudson, E. and Lawson, E.P. (1996) 'Knowledge of storybooks as a predictor of young children's vocabulary', *Journal of Educational Psychology*, 88(3), pp. 520–536.
Sikora, J., Kelley, J. and Evans, M.D.R. (2019) 'Scholarly culture: How books in adolescence enhance adult literacy, numeracy, and technology skills in 31 societies', *Social Science Research*, 77, pp. 1–15.
Simpson, A. and Cremin, T. (2022) 'Responsible reading: Children's literature and social justice', *Education Sciences*, 12(4), 264.
Spear-Swerling, L., Brucker, P.O. and Alfano, M.P. (2010) 'Relationships between sixth graders' reading comprehension and two different measures of print exposure', *Reading and Writing*, 23(1), pp. 73–96.
Stanovich, K. (1986) 'Matthew effects in reading: some consequences of individual differences in the acquisition of literacy', *Reading Research Quarterly*, 21(4), pp. 360–407.

Sulkunen, S. and Nissinen, K. (2014) 'Reader profiles of Finnish youth', *Finnish Journal of Educational Sciences*, 45(1), pp. 34–48.

Sullivan, A. and Brown, M. (2015) 'Reading for pleasure and progress in vocabulary and mathematics', *British Educational Research Journal*, 41(1), pp. 971–991.

Sun, Y-J., Sahakian, B.J., Langley, C., Yang, A., Jiang, Y., Jujiao K., Zhao, X., Li, C., Cheng, W. and Fen, J. (2024) 'Early initiated childhood reading for pleasure: Associations with better cognitive performance, mental well-being and brain structure in young adolescence', *Psychological Medicine*, 54(2), pp. 1–15.

Swanborn, M.S.L. and de Glopper, K. (1999) 'Incidental word learning while reading: A meta-analysis', *Review of Educational Research*, 69(3), pp. 261–285.

Tavsancil, E., Yildirim, O. and Bilican Demir, S. (2019) 'Direct and indirect effects of learning strategies and reading enjoyment on PISA 2009 reading performance', *Eurasian Journal of Educational Research*, 82, pp. 169–190.

Taylor, L. and Clarke, P. (2021) 'We read, we write: Reconsidering reading–writing relationships in primary school children', *Literacy*, 55(1), pp. 14–24.

Torppa, M., Niemi, P., Vasalampi, K., Lerkkanen, M.-K., Tolvanen, A. and Poikkeus, A.-M. (2020) 'Leisure reading (but not any kind) and reading comprehension support each other: A longitudinal study across grades 1 and 9', *Child Development*, 91(3), pp. 876–900.

Troyer, M., Kim, S.J., Hale, E., Wantchekon, K.A. and Armstrong, C. (2019) 'Relations among intrinsic and extrinsic reading motivation, reading amount, and comprehension: A conceptual replication', *Reading and Writing*, 32(5), pp. 1197–1218.

Vaknin-Nusbaum, V. and Tuckwiller, E.D. (2023) 'Reading motivation, well-being and reading achievement in second grade students', *Journal of Research in Reading*, 46(1), pp. 64–85.

Vaknin-Nusbaum, V., Nevo, E., Brande, S. and Gambrell, L. (2018) 'Developmental aspects of reading motivation and reading achievement among second grade low achievers and typical readers', *Journal of Research in Reading*, 41(3), pp. 438–454.

van Bergen, E., Vasalampi, K. and Torppa, M. (2021) 'How are practice and performance related? Development of reading from age 5 to 15', *Reading Research Quarterly*, 56(3), pp. 415–434.

van Bergen, E., Hart, S.A., Latvala, A., Vuoksimaa, E., Tolvanen, A. and Torppa, M. (2023) 'Literacy skills seem to fuel literacy enjoyment, rather than vice versa', *Developmental Science*, 26, e13325.

Vezzali, L., Stahi, S., Giovanni, D., Capozza, D. and Trifiletti, E. (2015) 'The greatest magic of Harry Potter: Reducing prejudice', *Journal of Applied Psychology*, 45(2), pp. 105–121.

Westbrook, J., Sutherland, J., Oakhill, J. and Sullivan, S. (2019) '"Just reading": The impact of a faster pace of reading narratives on the comprehension of poorer adolescent readers in English classrooms', *Literacy*, 53(2), pp. 60–68.

Whitten, C., Labby, S. and Sullivan, S.L. (2016) 'The impact of pleasure reading on academic success', *The Journal of Multidisciplinary Graduate Research*, 2(4), pp. 48–64.

Wilhelm, J. (2016) 'Recognising the power of pleasure: What engaged adolescent readers get from their free-choice reading, and how teachers can leverage this for all', *Australian Journal of Language and Literacy*, 39(1), pp. 30–41.

Wolf, S.A. and Brice Heath, S. (1992) *The Braid of Literature: Children's Worlds of Reading*, Cambridge, MA and London: Harvard University Press.

Wray, D. (1995) 'What do children think about writing?', *Educational Review*, 45(1), pp. 67–77.

Young, R. and Ferguson, F. (2021) *Writing for Pleasure: Theory, Research and Practice*, London: Taylor & Francis.

Zumbrunn, S., Ekholm, E., Stringer, J.K., McKnight, K. and DeBusk-Lane, M. (2017) 'Student experiences with writing: Taking the temperature of the classroom', *The Reading Teacher*, 70(6), pp. 667–677.

2

THE WIDER LANDSCAPE OF INFLUENCE

Introduction

Key factors that influence and shape children's attitudes towards and behaviours around reading and writing are considered in this chapter. In particular, studies that look at the enabling or hindering influence of socio-economic status, parental involvement, the home environment, gender and technology are examined. Although few studies consider parental involvement in children's volitional literacy, an increasing number attend to the influence of gender, and provide welcomed nuances to the long-established image of boys as being less engaged literacy learners than girls (e.g. Scholes et al., 2021). Indeed, such research suggests that gendered attitudes towards reading and writing may be subtly changing in response to different texts and contexts in this new media age. Accordingly, the chapter progresses to consider how children's attitudes and behaviours may be influenced by digital, screen and online experiences. More of the research reviewed in this chapter attends to influences on reading and readers, there is less in the literature specifically on the influences on young writers' engagement, however, it is possible to contemplate impacts on writing given the mutually beneficial relationship between reading and writing. An appraisal of this relationship closes the chapter.

Socio-economic, parental and home influences

Evidence suggests that socio-economic, parental and home factors are capable of influencing experiences of reading and writing. However, the impact of these factors is nuanced and worthy of in-depth consideration. A noticeable body of international and localised data has attended to differences in reading and writing attainment along socio-economic lines (e.g. Jha and Pouezevara, 2016; McGinnity et al., 2022; OECD, 2021). Although such data is not explicitly concerned with attitudes towards or volitional engagement with reading and writing, given the relationship between attainment and enjoyment, discussed in Chapter 1, such apparent gaps in attainment

DOI: 10.4324/9781003532606-4

warrant consideration. In the Progress in International Reading Literacy Study (PIRLS) 2021 data, internationally, children from higher socio-economic backgrounds scored, on average, 86 points higher in reading achievement than those children from lower socio-economic backgrounds (Mullis et al., 2023). Within the United States, through analysing national data from a large-scale, longitudinal cohort study (n:25,000) along socio-economic grounds, Reardon et al. (2012) found that, on average, 13–14-year-olds from the lowest-income families had comparable literacy skill scores to 8–9-year-olds from the highest-income families. In Ireland, McGinnity et al. (2022) found that children from lower socio-economic status households held lower reading scores. This pattern has been observed with regards to writing, too. A Turkish study, by Dölek and Hamzadayı (2018), that analysed 13–14-year-olds' (n:120) expressive writing, indicated that those from a higher socio-economic status scored more highly in terms of text organisation, choices of vocabulary and grammatical complexity.

Turning to attitudes and behaviours towards reading and writing, the influence of socio-economic status appears to be more mixed between reading and writing. For instance, international survey responses from the Programme for International Student Assessment (PISA) 2018 (OECD, 2021) indicated that young people from more advantaged backgrounds reported more volitional reading. Plus, one study in England indicated that higher socio-economic status predicted more reading of fiction (McGeown et al., 2016). However, the 2023 National Literacy Trust (NLT) survey (Clark et al., 2023b) on writing attitudes and behaviours indicate a different picture. With regards to expressions of enjoyment in relation to writing, more children who received free school meals (FSM), a proxy for lower socio-economic status, said they enjoyed writing than those who did not receive FSM (34 per cent as compared to 26 per cent). Moreover, more recipients of FSM said they wrote daily in comparison to non-FSM recipients. The somewhat mixed picture regarding the influence of socio-economic status on volitional reading and writing suggests that socio-economic status should not be seen as homogeneous.

Some studies consider the influence of parental attitudes and activities. However, this research is predominantly focused on impacts on reading. Using PISA 2018 and PIRLS 2011 data related to Portugal, Araújo and Costa (2023) found a correlation between parents reading at home to their children and children's attainment. Significantly, evidence from England, Scotland and Wales (Flouri and Buchanan, 2004) and from Ireland (Gilleece and Eivers, 2018) suggests that parental attitudes towards reading can have more influence on children's reading experiences than social class and parents' education level:

> Parental education, the number of books in the home, parental enjoyment of reading, and early home literacy activities are all positively associated with achievement.
>
> *(Gilleece and Eivers, 2018, p. 22)*

Data from Hong Kong indicates a similar situation. Using PISA data, Ho and Lau (2018) found that although socio-economic background is a significant predictor of reading performance, it does not have a strong effect on reading engagement. Instead, their study suggests that parents' own engagement in and enjoyment of reading can lead to higher levels of enjoyment among children. Moreover, when parents emphasise enjoyment and entertainment in relation to reading activities, rather than the acquisition of skills, children appear to develop more positive views of reading (Baker and Scher, 2002; Sonnenschein et al., 2000).

Several studies document the beneficial impact of parental involvement in reading activities (Scholes, 2019b, 2021; Villiger et al., 2012). For instance, in Switzerland, Villiger et al. (2012) designed a homework intervention where the emphasis was on parents supporting, not controlling, a child's reading. Parents did this by 'providing material such as dictionaries, remaining available for questions, and giving the child hints as to strategy use rather than complete solutions' (Villiger et al., 2012, p. 81). In so doing, Villiger et al. observed children's independence was strengthened and connections with parents were developed. Moreover, these homework tasks were in preparation for the following day of school, helping the children to feel ready for and confident as readers and learners. Scholes' (2019b, 2021) research has also shown how parents can influence young people's positive attitudes towards reading, including those who might been characterised as having 'anti-reading' identities. Specifically, Scholes drew attention to parents recommending and sharing texts that might not normally be available in schools, such as teen magazines or cook-books. Scholes (2019b) noted in particular that boys benefited from sharing in their dad's reading of more stereotypically 'masculine' topics. Although this particular study by Scholes points to how gender stereotypes can be used to positively influence engagement with reading, there is a body of research that suggests parental involvement can be influenced by gendered assumptions. For instance, parents may prioritise early literacy activities for girls, more so than boys (Gustaffson et al., 2013; Hencke et al., 2023). Moreover, research shows that parents can make gendered assumptions about reading competencies, in favour of girls, which are detrimental to boys, thereby reinforcing gender differences (Muntoni and Retelsdorf, 2019).

Connected to the role of parents is the home environment, through which young people can engage with a wide range of reading and writing practices. Studies indicate both reading skills and a love of reading can be supported through the home environment (European Commission, Directorate-General for Education, Youth, Sport and Culture, 2012). In turn, the home environment, like parental involvement, can counter the link between socio-economic status and reading engagement. For instance, in monolingual and multilingual families from different socio-economic status backgrounds, a wealth of reading materials has been noted which are much more diverse than the children's book focused 'school reading' diets (Cremin et al., 2015; Gregory and Williams, 2000). Specifically, in a detailed ethnographic study of multi-ethnic communities in London, Gregory and Williams (2000) found a rich range of reading related activities and literacy practices in their day-to-day lives, even though these communities were often viewed through a deficit lens by others, being seen as disadvantaged and therefore 'deprived' of literacy. In these families there were many opportunities and reasons to engage in reading in the home. This insight is in common with a more recent study of multilingual families' literacies, with Little (2021) observing how children provide

> a complex network of emotional and linguistic reasons, woven into narratives of heritage language learning journeys, migratory experiences, and family cohesion.
> *(Little, 2021, p. 11)*

However, with regard to multilingual home environments, it is possible that some parents may be unsure about the value of reading in their home language. Using case study data from Chinese-Australian families Hu et al. (2021) suggest that parents may prioritise reading in the language of instruction based on a desire to support their child. Yet, this may limit their child's multi-literate identities and opportunities to enjoy reading in their home language. Therefore, even parents who want to read at home with their children may need help with how best to engage them in reading for pleasure and what sort of interactions and discussions can support this.

Ensuring young children have access to a range of writing activities at home is also seen to be beneficial to writing attainment and writing enjoyment. In one study, the frequency of early writing activities was shown to explain variance in later transcription skills at school (Adams et al., 2021). Plus, studies indicate that child autonomy during home writing tasks and independent writing practices is significant in relation to their later confidence and competence as writers (e.g. Aram and Levin, 2001; Guo et al., 2020). For example, when preschoolers write at home independently or with parents, Puranik et al. (2018) found that they experience more positive writing outcomes when they begin school (e.g. in letter writing, spelling and composing). Other research also indicates that opportunities for writing at home continues to impact the quality of children's writing through the first years of school (Dunsmuir and Blatchford, 2004).

Given the diversity of home reading and writing experiences, it is clear that there are opportunities for schools to recognise and build on such experiences. However, in the case of reading, research indicates that, in the relationship between home and school, school expectations are dominant. Schools tend to send materials to homes rather than facilitating more equal partnerships and sharing knowledge and practices (Marsh, 2003; Thomson, 2002). When teachers build new relationships with families and engage in shared dialogue about reading practices, this can help children and parents recognise and validate their reading practices and widen understanding of reading (Cremin et al., 2015). Such collaborative interactions may help to nurture practices in the home capable of supporting reading and writing for pleasure.

The role of gender

International research has long highlighted gender gaps in young people's experiences of both reading and writing in relation to attainment, attitudes and behaviours. Yet, studies also point to how gender gaps can be unhelpfully maintained by stereotypical assumptions about competencies and interests. Increasingly however, researchers have drawn attention to nuances within perceived gender gaps, suggesting adults working with children remain alert to individuals' needs and interests to support their literacy engagement.

Both PIRLS and PISA data highlight an ongoing gender gap in reading attainment. In the 2018 PISA girls consistently outperformed boys, with the mean average scores for reading performance for girls being 502 and for boys being 472 (e.g. OECD, 2019a, 2019c). Similarly, in the 2021 PIRLS, girls were observed to perform better than boys in measured reading competencies. The international average reading performance scores for girls was 509 and for boys it was 493 (Mullis et al., 2023). These observations from both PISA and PIRLS were also replicated in data specific to England, albeit less pronounced, with girls out-scoring boys (Lindorff et al., 2023; OECD, 2019c). There is not a comparable international data set that considers writing, attainment and gender. However, interesting insights can be gained from smaller-scale studies.

In this regard, the writing picture is nuanced. In a city-level study, in England, González-Díaz et al. (2022) analysed features of children's writing and found some differences between boys and girls against a number of measures, however, not all. For instance, girls wrote 10 per cent more than boys, used a greater range of different words, employed different grammatical constructs more frequently and had more accurate spelling. However, regarding factors such as readability, length of words, use of 'difficult words' and range of grammatical constructs, there were not significant differences between boys' and girls' writing. These findings are similar to those established by Adams and Simmons (2019). Through analysing young children's (n:116) writing from across six UK schools, they found that boys wrote shorter compositions with less spelling accuracy. This writing was judged to be of a lower quality than writing produced by girls, suggesting an emphasis on transcriptional elements. Indeed, returning to González-Díaz et al.'s (2022) study, these researchers asserted that boys' writing is often appraised by teachers using quantitative measures, e.g. length or frequency of output, not qualitative measures.

Attitudes towards reading and writing are also subject to a gender divide, with girls reporting enjoyment of both activities more than boys. In 2018, in all PISA-participating countries, girls reported much higher levels of reading enjoyment than boys (OECD, 2021). The 2021 PIRLS indicated the same attitudinal gap (Mullis et al., 2023), even though PIRLS surveys younger aged children who generally have more positive attitudes to reading (Clark et al., 2023a). In the UK, the 'gender gap' in reading for pleasure has been visible over many years through the NLT survey (Clark et al., 2024). With regards to writing, survey data from various countries consistently indicate that more girls than boys voice a positive attitude to writing, especially in the later primary and secondary years. For instance, in a Finnish study (Merisuo-Storm, 2006) of 10–11-year-olds (n:145), boys were significantly more reluctant writers than girls. Likewise, in a New Zealand study, 65 per cent of girls reported liking writing compared with 49 per cent of boys (Gadd et al., 2019). Finally, an American study (Graham et al., 2007) involving 6–7-year-olds (n:128) and 8–9-year-olds (n:113) indicated girls had more positive attitudes towards writing than boys, even though there was no statistical difference in their writing achievement.

Beyond attitudes, a similar gender divide has been detected in relation to reading and writing behaviours. In the 2018 PISA results, girls were more likely to report higher levels of reading frequency and to read for longer periods of time. In total, the data show that girls spent close to two hours a week more reading for enjoyment than boys, reading on average for 4.8 hours a week in comparison to 2.6 hours (OECD, 2019c). In the UK, the NLT detected a similar trend, with girls being more likely to state that they read daily in comparison to boys (Clark et al., 2023a). The NLT's annual survey also provides useful insights into differences in writing behaviours, with more girls choosing to write daily in comparison to boys (Clark et al., 2024). Interestingly, though, more girls (47 per cent) than boys (41 per cent) reported experiencing more difficulty deciding what to write. González-Díaz et al. (2022) found that girls and boys had differing perspectives regarding the challenges associated with writing. Boys tended to be concerned about handwriting and punctuation. In contrast, girls were concerned about spelling. Beyond transcriptional concerns, girls were more concerned about compositional aspects of writing such as ideas generation, vocabulary choice and emulating genres. Developing nuanced understandings of gender divides and differences is important, since research reveals that gender divides can be unhelpfully reinforced through stereotypes and assumptions on the part of peers, parents and teachers (Hempel-Jorgensen et al., 2018; Scholes, 2019a, 2021). For example, influential community members may view reading as 'feminine', not 'masculine' (Jha and Pouezevara, 2016).

Moreover, within school settings, boys can be prone to viewing reading as 'nerdy' and associate anti-reading sentiments with popularity (Scholes, 2019a). However, this view of reading as uncool has also been discerned in girls (Scholes, 2021). In addition to these peer perceptions of reading, research suggests that barriers to positive reading engagement may stem from teachers' gendered expectations of pupils (Hempel-Jorgensen, 2015; Hempel-Jorgensen et al., 2018). In one study of English schools, teachers viewed girls as having better reading skills and behaviours (Hempel-Jorgensen et al., 2018). In contrast, teachers viewed boys' reading behaviours and the actions of boys' parents less favourably or through a deficit framing:

> Boys were not seen to conform to the kinds of reading behaviour teachers saw as commensurate with being a good reader.
>
> *(Hempel-Jorgensen et al., 2018, p. 3)*

This research suggests that assumptions can be bound up with intersectional identity components, including parental influence and socio-economic status. Such views, coupled with pedagogic choices in the schools, appeared to have a detrimental impact on boys' engagement in reading for pleasure.

In contrast to such stereotypes, the long-established divide between boys and girls, with the former being seen as less engaged readers and writers, may be subtly changing in response to different texts and contexts (e.g. Scholes et al., 2021). Accordingly, a nuancing of perceived gender gaps in relation to reading and writing is necessary. For instance, some earlier research indicates that boys may not dislike all reading, but, instead, like particular text types, preferring non-fiction and comics over fiction and magazines (McGeown et al., 2016; OECD, 2010). Moss (2007), drawing on empirical work, suggested that boys who struggle with reading may select non-fiction as they perceive it to be easier to read in small sections, while boys who are more confident readers may choose fiction. However, Australian research further complicates this picture, demonstrating that boys may favour specific fiction authors and novel series (Scholes et al., 2021). Thus, perceived differences in engagement between girls and boys may result from a difference between text preferences and access, leading the researchers to argue that: 'We may well have underestimated the range of boys' preferences for reading and the changing nature of those preferences as they develop as readers' (Scholes et al., 2021, p. 176).

In addition to text types, studies suggest that boys and girls may express different preferences in reading formats, with non-print-based formats seemingly offering new opportunities for positive engagement. However, the picture emerging from data is far from simple. For instance, some studies suggest that girls are more likely to engage positively with reading on digital devices (Jang and Ryoo, 2019; OECD, 2021). Yet, boys have also been documented as having positive attitudes towards digital reading opportunities (McKenna et al., 2012) and as enjoying audio books more than girls (Clark and Picton, 2020). This indicates the complex picture surrounding young people's reading and writing habits and how they are shifting with changes in communication, text formats and technology.

The influence of technology

There is increasing interest in the possible role technology may play in young people's volitional reading and writing, with some studies suggesting that it may help to redress the decline in attitudes to these literacy practices (e.g. Clark and Picton, 2019; Cole et al., 2022; Mullis et al., 2023). However, these assertions are made against the backdrop of conflicting research on the impact of digital literacy experiences on literacy skills and a wider public discourse surrounding the benefits and detriments of screentime (Kucirkova and Flewitt, 2022). This last point indicates the importance of attending to the views of influential individuals who regularly interact with young readers and writers, such as parents and teachers. Research indicates that technological changes and resulting alterations in reading and writing opportunities may help to shift the aforementioned divides along socio-economic and gender lines in relation to attitudes and behaviours. However, the research suggests that such possibilities are dependent on developing expanded views of what reading and writing can or should look like.

Studies attending to the influence of technology have frequently focused on the role of digital reading practices on literacy skills, not engagement. This area of research reveals contested terrain, with some studies suggesting digital reading can enhance literacy skills (e.g. López-Escribano et al., 2021), while others caution against using digital reading for school-related activities (Vargas et al., 2024). Adding to this, Altamura et al. (2025) drew upon a meta-analysis to suggest that the influence of technology changes over time as literacy needs and experiences alter over the lifespan. They suggest that digital reading could be detrimental to young children's comprehension but beneficial for young people and young adults. This contrasting picture is accompanied by conflicting societal views regarding the possible value of digital reading and writing opportunities. For instance, in a study of Swedish primary school teachers (n:289), Fälth and Selenius (2024) indicated that teachers who viewed technology as capable of facilitating early reading and writing reported using digital support more frequently. In contrast, Kucirkova and Flewitt (2022) outlined parental concerns about the value of digital reading. Using interview data with parents, following the use of digital books during shared reading, parents reported concerns about whether they could trust specific digital texts, particularly brands which are less well-known to them. They also raised questions about children's ability to independently use digital texts and were aware of a disconcerting difference in their own young reading experiences and those of their child. Indicating a convergence of influences, these parental perspectives, the researchers noted, had the ability to impact on young children's experiences of reading.

The hesitancy in adults' views towards digital reading and writing is replicated in the attitudes of young people. The previous chapter noted that the US Pew Research Center's study on the influence of technology on 12–17-year-olds (n:700) reported that in contrast to international data, young people do choose to write, or at least did in 2008 (Lenhart et al., 2008). Those teenagers who reported choosing to write included their writing on 'electronic' texts, suggesting an expansive view of writing. Yet the young people themselves were unsure as to whether these activities should be or could be counted as writing. The hesitancy of this cohort indicates the need to scrutinise how technological changes can contribute to a re-classification of what constitutes 'writing'. Researchers such as Marsh et al. (2009) and Pahl and Rowsell (2012) have contributed to this agenda within academia. Arguably though, more work needs to be done by policy makers and practitioners to ensure the contemporary digitally enabled reading and writing practices of children are affirmed.

Reflecting the insights of the Pew study, PISA survey results show that young people are engaging with more digital reading activities, such as using digital devices and accessing online content (Sizmur et al., 2019; OECD, 2021). Indeed, across the Organization for Economic Co-operation and Development (OECD) countries, young people read online material more frequently than printed materials, chatting online being a major source of online reading activities (Sizmur et al., 2019). Similarly, the NLT surveys show that a large percentage of 8–18-year-olds engage in reading and writing experiences that are only available in a screen-based format, such as direct messages, in-game communications and social media content (Clark et al., 2023a, 2023b). Of particular note is how, in an earlier NLT survey, children reported being inspired by being able to find more relevant and relatable reading materials online (Cole et al., 2022). Drawing attention to the intersection of influences, the NLT surveys show that boys and children in receipt of FSM are more likely to read a range of materials on screen (Clark and Picton, 2019).

Beyond survey-based data, several recent studies have indicated the potential for technology to become part of young people's established reading habits, leading to engagement and enjoyment of reading. Using a case study approach of two adolescent boys' mobile phone reading habits, Lim et al. (2024) found that while one boy only occasionally chose to engage with reading on his phone, the other regularly used his to read informative text to stay up to date with world issues. In contrast to engaging in volitional digital reading, Loh et al. (2024) pointed to how teenage girls (n:11) read online Korean Manhwa, a form of digital comic, for entertainment and escapism. Similarly, using a mobile ethnography approach, Loh (2024) showed that some adolescents' (n:12) digital reading experiences are interest-driven and allow for immersion in imagined worlds. It is possible to suggest that this immersion helps to support sustained engagement in volitional reading.

Although the above studies indicate there is an increased interest in digital reading and writing, paper-based reading and writing activities remain important. For instance, the NLT's surveys show that children continue to engage with paper-based reading more than screen-based reading, plus, these young people are more likely to write their own fiction on paper than on a screen (Clark et al., 2023b). Moreover, the results of the 2018 PISA survey indicate that reading print-based materials is associated with enjoyment as those who chose to read printed texts also spent more time reading for pleasure (OECD, 2019d). Although, those young people who reported reading an equal combination of texts in paper-based formats and on digital devices also reported reading for enjoyment. Finally, regarding changing reading habits, although digital reading for information purposes has become more prominent, fiction texts remain the most popular text for young people surveyed across the PISA OECD countries (OECD, 2019b). These surveys indicate the complex picture surrounding young people's reading and writing habits and how they are shifting with changes in communication and text formats.

The relationship between reading and writing

Research into the relationship between writing and reading has often adopted a skills-focused approach, indicating how reading practices may improve writing (Graham et al., 2018), how the teaching of writing can improve reading attainment (e.g. Graham and Hebert, 2011; Graham et al., 2021; Salvador and Martins, 2018; Williams and Larkin, 2013) and how 'balanced' approaches can strengthen both reading and writing competencies (Graham et al., 2018). Moving beyond skills, Wyse and Hacking (2024) have argued for recognising the myriad connections between reading and writing and that young children's experiences in school should be rooted in recognising that reading and writing are meaningful and purposeful.

Attending to the impact of reading on writing, studies suggest that more experiences with reading tend to support writing competencies. Specifically, as noted in Chapter 1, research has highlighted how frequent reading enriches children's vocabularies that can subsequently be utilised in writing (e.g. McQuillan, 2019; Pfost et al., 2013; Sullivan and Brown, 2015). Other studies have illustrated how wide and reflective reading can support later composition, whereby children can 'read like a writer, in order to learn how to write like a writer' (Smith, 1983, p. 562) (e.g. Barrs and Cork, 2001; Broekkamp et al., 2009; Corden, 2001; Fitzgerald and Shanahan, 2000; Graham, 2020). In the UK-based Teaching Reading and Writing Links project, Corden (2001) showed that when children read widely and have their attention drawn to literacy devices in the texts they are reading, they can transfer this knowledge about authorship to their own writing. Likewise, Barrs and Cork (2001) and Parry and Taylor (2018) have highlighted that the texts children read influence their writing, with children drawing upon literary styles and utilising fictional contexts. Moreover, one study (Taylor and Clarke, 2021) of free reading and writing in England showed that children (n:170) with broader reading repertoires also had a broader range of approaches to writing. These children wanted to write the kinds of texts they had enjoyed reading and felt competent and able to work in that style. In their free writing, the young people skilfully replicated stylistic and linguistic features of these text types. Consequently, the researchers argued that teachers should allow children to write freely and try to understand more about the texts children encounter outside of school, positioning them as 'reader–writers'.

These forms of 'literacy borrowing' (Lancia, 1997) point to the interactions between reading and writing in the complex '*braid*' of literature and literacy (Wolf and Brice Heath, 1992). In sum, such studies draw attention to the value of reading in relation to writing, suggesting that competent, wide and reflective readers develop useful 'meta-knowledge' about both practices:

> knowing about the functions and purposes of reading and writing; knowing that readers and writers interact; monitoring one's own meaning-making (metacomprehension) and monitoring word identification or production strategies; and monitoring one's own knowledge.
>
> *(Fitzgerald and Shannon, 2000, p. 40)*

Of particular relevance is the suggestion that such 'metaknowledge' can be motivating (Fitzgerald and Shannon, 2000, p. 40). It includes 'expectation of success', with young people knowing what components are involved in accomplished reading and writing. Yet, for some, reading like a writer can be challenging and may not necessarily transfer into their writing. In such instances, more explicit instructional support via meaningful contexts can be valuable. In particular, 'mentor' texts are often used to model quality writing (Graham and Perin, 2007). Drawing on interview data with young people, Lines (2020) suggested that quality 'mentor texts' can offer rich exemplars, making explicit to young people the choices writers make and, thereby, benefiting the 'students' agency as writers' (p. 243). However, concerns have been expressed about mentor texts being tightly used, resulting in children spending disproportionate amounts of time spotting discrete literary features instead of developing rich understandings of texts in their entirety (Myhill et al., 2018).

Writing is also understood to support reading, with a meta-analysis study indicating that explicit instruction and increased time spent on writing improved reading outcomes (Graham and Hebert, 2011). Interestingly, this observed beneficial impact is understood to be particularly salient when writing activities draw upon texts that have already been read:

> Writing about material read improves student's comprehension of it; that teaching students how to write improves their reading comprehension, reading influence and word reading; and that increasing how much students write enhances their reading comprehension.
>
> *(Graham and Hebert, 2011, p. 710)*

The importance of familiar texts indicates that there is a bi-directional relationship between writing and reading. Arguing in favour of this reciprocal relationship, Graham (2020) outlined how, when writing texts for others, children learn to make their ideas clear and explicit to imagined readers. He proposed that this led to them being better equipped to consider how the authors of other texts they are reading do the same. In turn, reading exposes young people to different text types, new vocabulary and information, which young writers can adopt and adapt in their own writing. Andersen et al.'s (2018) Danish study with 6–9-year-olds (n:1,160) supports Graham's assertion. Mobilising the suggestion that 'skills build upon skills', Andersen et al. (2018) found that children's skills at word level in both reading and writing, i.e. decoding and spelling, respectively, predicted competencies with higher-level skills, such as at sentence (reading/composing) and text (comprehension/narrative) levels. Interestingly, though, the team found that skills at word level predicted competencies in the opposite domain. In short, reading skills impacted upon writing and writing skills impacted upon reading.

Despite the value of these studies in articulating the relationship between reading and writing competencies, it is noted that the above studies do not explicitly attend to time spent writing recreationally or the consequences for children's desire to write. There are only a few studies that draw attention to the impact of volitional reading on writing and vice versa (e.g. Jouhar and Rupley, 2021; Sénéchal et al., 2018). For instance, Jouhar and Rupley (2021) used a systematic review of experimental studies to examine the relationship between 'independent', meaning volitional, reading and writing. They found that time spent independently reading enhances narrative and descriptive writing. In turn, independent writing was seen to improve literal reading comprehension for beginning, low-performing and at-risk students, and significantly improves both literal and inferential reading comprehension for 'average' students. In a separate study that analysed 9–10-year olds' (n:300) writing, Sénéchal et al. (2018)

demonstrated an association between children's reading for pleasure and text cohesion in written narratives. These findings are bolstered by another study in which professional writers (including scientists, scriptwriters, children's authors and journalists) reflected upon their early reading experiences and the influence of these on their later writing (Cremin et al., 2017). In this, the 12 adult writers made frequent references to their childhood pleasure in reading, and the potency associated with listening to the tunes and rhythms of language at home, school and in the community. They also noted that in these early years they had frequently mapped out and made up stories at home and school and now perceived this had influenced their later professions, pleasures and practices as writers. Thus, the data from previous studies indicate a relationship between enjoying reading activities and being enthused to create narratives and to write from a young age.

Conclusion

Through considering a range of international studies, it is clear that myriad factors influence children's reading and writing for pleasure. The chapter has brought into sharp relief the challenges that impact upon the realisation of the benefits associated with being a keen childhood reader or writer, these include socio-economic context, parental attitudes and the home environment, gender, technology and the relationship between reading and writing. Whilst the research evidence is complex and at times contradictory, it does suggest that when more expansive and less restrictive views of reading and writing are nurtured, whether related to text types, format or reader and writer identities, children and young people can become more motivated and engaged. Moreover, when they are encouraged to reflect upon their experiences of reading and writing they begin to recognise themselves as readers and writers. These glimmers of hope point to the kinds of approaches that appear to support reading and writing for pleasure which are explored in Part III.

References

Adams, A.M. and Simmons, F.R. (2019) 'Exploring individual and gender differences in early writing performance', *Reading and Writing*, 32, pp. 235–263.

Adams, A.M., Soto-Calvo, E., Francis, H.N., Patel, H., Hartley, C., Giofre, D. and Simmons, F.R. (2021) 'Characteristics of the preschool home literacy environment which predict writing skills at school', *Reading and Writing*, 34, pp. 2203–2225.

Altamura, L., Vargas, C. and Salmerón, L. (2025) 'Do new forms of reading pay off? A meta-analysis on the relationship between leisure digital reading habits and text comprehension', *Review of Educational Research*, 95(1), 53–88.

Andersen, S.C., Christensen, M.V., Nielsen, H.S., Thomsen, M.K., Østerbye, T. and Rowe, M.L. (2018) 'How reading and writing support each other across a school year in primary school children', *Contemporary Educational Psychology*, 55, pp. 129–138.

Aram, D. and Levin, I. (2001) 'Mother-child joint writing in low ES: Sociocultural factors, maternal mediation and emergent literacy', *Cognitive Development*, 16(3), pp. 831–852.

Araújo, L. and Costa, P. (2023) 'Reading to young children: Higher home frequency associated with higher educational achievement in PIRLS and PISA', *Education Sciences*, 13(12), 1240.

Baker, L. and Scher, D. (2002) 'Beginning readers' motivation for reading in relation to parental beliefs and home reading experiences', *Reading Psychology*, 23(4), pp. 239–269.

Barrs, M. and Cork, V. (2001) *The Reader in the Writer: The Influence of Literature upon Writing at KS2*, London: Centre for Literacy in Primary Education.

Broekkamp, H., Janssen, T. and Van Den Bergh, H. (2009) 'Is there a relationship between literature reading and creative writing?', *Journal of Creative Behaviour*, 43(4), pp. 281–297.

Clark, C. and Picton, I. (2019) *Children, Young People and Digital Reading*, London: National Literacy Trust.

Clark, C. and Picton, I. (2020) *Children and Young People's Reading in 2020 Before and During the COVID-19 Lockdown*, London: National Literacy Trust.

Clark, C., Picton, I. and Galway, M. (2023a) *Children and Young People's Reading in 2023*, London: National Literacy Trust.

Clark, C., Bonafede, F., Picton, I. and Cole, A. (2023b) *Children and Young People's Writing in 2023*, London: National Literacy Trust.

Clark, C., Picton, C., Cole, A. and Bonafede, F. (2024) *Children and Young People's Writing in 2024*, London: National Literacy Trust.

Cole, A., Brown, A., Clark, C. and Picton, I. (2022) *Children and Young People's Reading Engagement in 2022: Continuing Insight into the Impact of the Covid-19 Pandemic on Reading*, London: National Literacy Trust.

Corden, R. (2001) 'Teaching reading–writing links (TRAWL Project)', *Literacy*, 35(1), pp. 37–40.

Cremin, T., Lillis, T., Myhill, D. and Eyres, I. (2017) 'Professional writers' identities', in Cremin, T. and Locke, T. (eds), *Writer Identity and the Teaching and Learning of Writing*, London: Routledge, pp. 18–36.

Cremin, T., Mottram, M., Collins, F.M., Powell, S. and Drury, R. (2015) *Researching Literacy Lives: Building Communities Between Home and School*, London: Routledge.

Dölek, O. and Hamzadayı, E. (2018) 'Comparison of writing skills of students of different socioeconomic status', *International Journal of Progressive Education*, 14(6), pp. 117–131.

Dunsmuir, S. and Blatchford, P. (2004) 'Predictors in writing competence in 4-to-7-year-old children', *British Journal of Educational Psychology*, 74(3), pp. 461–483.

European Commission, Directorate-General for Education, Youth, Sport and Culture (2012) *EU High Level Group of Experts on Literacy: Final Report*, Luxembourg: EU Publications Office.

Fälth, L. and Selenius, H. (2024) 'Primary school teachers' use and perception of digital technology in early reading and writing education in inclusive settings', *Disability and Rehabilitation: Assistive Technology*, 19(3), pp. 790–799.

Fitzgerald, J. and Shanahan, T. (2000) 'Reading and writing relations and their development', *Educational Psychologist*, 35(1), pp. 39–50.

Flouri, E. and Buchanan, A. (2004) 'Early father's and mother's involvement and child's later educational outcomes', *British Journal of Educational Psychology*, 74(2), pp. 141–153.

Gadd, M., Parr, J., Robertson, J., Carran, L., Ali, Z., Gendall, L. and Watson, K. (2019) 'Portrait of the student as a young writer: Some student survey findings about attitudes to writing and self-efficacy as writers', *Literacy*, 53(4), pp. 226–235.

Gilleece, L. and Eivers, E. (2018) 'Characteristics associated with paper-based and online reading in Ireland: Findings from PIRLS and ePIRLS 2016', *International Journal of Educational Research*, 91, pp. 16–27.

González-Díaz, V., Parr, E. and Mandya, A. (2022) *Gap-Minding, Gap-Closing, Gapworrying: Addressing the Gender Gap in Primary Children's Writing*, Liverpool: Heseltine Institute for Public Policy, Practice and Place.

Graham, S. (2020) 'The sciences of reading and writing must become more fully integrated', *Reading Research Quarterly*, 55(S1), S35–S44.

Graham, S. and Hebert, M. (2011) 'Writing to read: A meta-analysis of the impact of writing and writing instruction on reading', *Harvard Educational Review*, 81(4), pp.710–744.

Graham, S. and Perin, D. (2007). *Writing Next: Effective Strategies to Improve Writing of Adolescents in Middle and High School*, New York: Carnegie Corporation of New York.

Graham, S., Berninger, V. and Fan, W. (2007) 'The structural relationship between writing attitude and writing achievement in first and third grade students', *Contemporary Educational Psychology*, 32(3), pp. 516–536.

Graham, S., Liu, K., Aitken, A., Ng, C., Bartlett, B., Harris, K.R. and Holzapel, J. (2018) 'Effectiveness of literacy programs: Balancing reading and writing instruction: A meta-analysis', *Reading Research Quarterly*, 53(3), pp. 279–304.

Graham, S., Aitken, A.A., Hebert, M., Camping, A., Santangelo, T., Harris, K.R., Eustice, K., Sweet, J.D. and Ng, C. (2021) 'Do children with reading difficulties experience writing difficulties? A meta-analysis', *Journal of Educational Psychology*, 113(8), pp. 1481–1506.

Gregory, E. and Williams, A. (2000) *City Literacies: Learning to Read Across Generations and Cultures*, London: Routledge.

Guo, Y., Puranik, C., Kelcey, B., Sun, J., Dinnesen, M.S. and Breit-Smith, A. (2020) 'The role of home literacy practices in kindergarten children's early writing development: A one-year longitudinal study', *Early Education and Development*, 32(2), pp. 209–227.

Gustaffson, J.E., Hansen, K.Y. and Rosen, K. (2013) 'Effects of home background on achievement in reading, mathematics and science at the fourth grade', in Martin, M.O. and Mullis, I. V.S. (eds), *TIMSS and PIRLS 2011: Relationships Among Reading, Mathematics, and Science Achievement at the Fourth Grade – Implications for Early Learning*, Boston: TIMSS and PIRLS International Study Centre, pp. 181–287.

Hempel-Jorgensen, A. (2015) 'Working class girls and child-centred pedagogy: What are the implications for social justice?', *International Studies in Sociology of Education*, 23(4), pp. 531–554.

Hempel-Jorgensen, A., Cremin, T., Harris, D. and Chamberlain, L. (2018) 'Pedagogy for reading for pleasure in low socio-economic primary schools: Beyond "pedagogy of poverty"?', *Literacy*, 52(2), pp. 86–94.

Hencke, J., Eck, M., Sass, J., Hastedt, D., Meinck, S., Kennedy, A. and Liu, T. (2023) 'Early learning activities matter for girls' and boys' mathematics and science achievement', *IEA Compass: Briefs in Education No. 21*, Amsterdam: IEA.

Ho, E.S.C. and Lau, K. (2018) 'Reading engagement and reading literacy performance: Effective policy and practices at home and in school', *Journal of Research in Reading*, 41(4), pp. 657–679.

Hu, J., Hao, Y. and Yang, N. (2021) 'Chinese Australian children's shared reading experiences at home and in preschools: A case study on parents and educators' attitudes and practices', *SAGE Open*, 11(2), pp. 1–12.

Jang, B.G. and Ryoo, J.H. (2019) 'Multiple dimensions of adolescents' reading attitudes and their relationship with reading comprehension', *Reading and Writing*, 32(7), pp. 1769–1793.

Jha, J. and Pouezevara, S. (2016) *Boys' Underachievement in Education: A Review of the Literature with a Focus on Reading in the Early Years*, Durham, NC:RTI International and United States Agency for International Development.

Jouhar, M.R. and Rupley, W.H. (2021) 'The reading–writing connection based on independent reading and writing: A systematic review', *Reading and Writing Quarterly*, 37(2), pp.136–156.

Kucirkova, N., and Flewitt, R. (2022) 'Understanding parents' conflicting beliefs about children's digital book reading', *Journal of Early Childhood Literacy*, 22(2), pp. 157–181.

Lancia, P. (1997) 'Literary borrowing: The effects of literature on children's writing', *The Reading Teacher*, 50(6), pp. 470–475.

Lenhart, A., Arafeh, S., Smith, A. and Rankin MacGill, A. (2008) *Writing, Technology and Teens*, Washington, DC: Pew Internet.

Lim, F.V., Loh, C.E. and Teravainen, T. (2024) 'Adolescents' use of digital media during the pandemic: Implications for literacy', *Journal of Adolescent & Adult Literacy*, 68, pp. 234–243.

Lindorff, A., Stiff, J. and Kayton, H. (2023) *PIRLS 2021: National Report for England Research Report*, London: Department for Education.

Lines, H. (2020) 'Articulating authorial intentions: making meaningful connections between reading and writing in the secondary classroom', in Chen, H., Myhill, D. and Lewis, H. (eds), *Developing Writers Across Primary and Secondary Years*, London and Sydney: Routledge, pp. 237–255.

Little, S. (2021) 'Rivers of multilingual reading: exploring biliteracy experiences among 8–13-year-old heritage language readers', *Journal of Multilingual and Multicultural Development*, 45(2), pp. 1–14.

Loh, C.E. (2024) 'What makes adolescents want to read? Examining adolescents' contemporary print and new media (fiction) leisure reading through mobile ethnography', *Language and Education*, 38(4), pp. 596–616.

Loh, C.E., Rosli, N.F.S.B. and Krishnan, M.Z. (2024) 'Not just reading the romance online: Adolescent girls' reading Korean Manhwa', *Changing English*, 31(2), pp. 117–129.

López-Escribano, C., Valverde-Montesino, S. and García-Ortega, V. (2021) 'The impact of e-book reading on young children's emergent literacy skills: An analytical review', *International Journal of Environmental Research and Public Health*, 18, 6510.

Marsh, J. (2003) 'One-way traffic? Connections between literacy practices at home and in the nursery', *British Educational Research Journal*, 29(3), pp. 369–382.

Marsh, J., Robinson, M. and Willett, R. (2009) *Play, Creativity and Digital Cultures*, London and New York: Routledge.

McGeown, S., Osborne, C., Warhurst, A., Norgate, R. and Duncan, L. (2016) 'Understanding children's reading activities: Reading motivation, skill and child characteristics as predictors', *Journal of Research in Reading*, 39(1), pp. 109–125.

McGinnity, F., McMullin, P., Murray, A., Russell, H. and Smyth, E (2022) 'Understanding differences in children's reading ability by social origin and gender: The role of parental reading and pre- and primary school exposure in Ireland', *Research in Social Stratification and Mobility*, 81, 100729.

McKenna, M.C., Conradi, K., Lawrence, C., Jang, B.G. and Meyer, J.P. (2012) 'Reading attitudes of middle school students: Results of a U.S. Survey', *Reading Research Quarterly*, 47 (3), pp. 283–306.

McQuillan, J. (2019) 'Where do we get our academic vocabulary? Comparing the efficiency of direct instruction and free voluntary reading', *The Reading Matrix: An International Online Journal*, 19(1), pp. 129–138.

Merisuo-Storm, T. (2006) 'Girls and boys like to read and write different texts', *Scandinavian Journal of Educational Research*, 50(2), pp. 111–125.

Moss, G. (2007) *Literacy and Gender: Researching Texts, Contexts and Readers*, London: Routledge.

Mullis, I.V.S., von Davier, M., Foy, P., Fishbein, B., Reynolds, K.A. and Wry, E. (2023) *PIRLS 2021 International Results in Reading*, Boston:Boston College, TIMSS and PIRLS International Study Center.

Muntoni, F. and Retelsdorf, J (2019) 'At their children's expense: How parents' gender stereotypes affect their children's reading outcomes', *Learning and Instruction*, 60, 95–103.

Myhill, D., Lines, H. and Jones, S. (2018) 'Texts that teach: Examining the efficacy of using texts as models', *L1-Educational Studies in Language and Literature*, 18(2), pp. 1–24.

OECD (2010) *PISA 2009 Results: Learning to Learn: Student Engagement, Strategies and Practices*, Vol. 3, Paris: OECD Publishing.

OECD (2019a) *PISA 2018 Insights and Interpretations*, Paris: OECD Publishing.

OECD (2019b) *PISA 2018 Assessment and Analytical Framework*, Paris: OECD Publishing.

OECD (2019c) *PISA 2018 Results (Volume II): Where All Students Can Succeed*, Paris: OECD Publishing.

OECD (2019d) *PISA 2018 Results (Volume I): What Students Know and Can Do*, Paris: OECD Publishing.

OECD (2021) *21st-Century Readers: Developing Literacy Skills in a Digital World*, Paris: OECD Publishing.

Pahl, K. and Rowsell, J. (2012) *Literacy and Education: Understanding the New Literacy Studies in the Classroom* (2nd edn), London: SAGE.

Parry, B. and Taylor, L. (2018) 'Readers in the round: Children's holistic engagements with texts', *Literacy*, 52(2) pp. 103–110.

Pfost, M., Dörfler, T. and Artelt, C. (2013) 'Students' extracurricular reading behavior and the development of vocabulary and reading comprehension', *Learning and Individual Differences*, 26, pp. 89–102.

Puranik, C.S., Phillips, B.M., Longian, C.J. and Gibson, E. (2018) 'Home literacy practices and preschool children's emergent writing skills: An initial investigation', *Early Childhood Research Quarterly*, 42(1), pp. 228–238.

Reardon, S.F., Valentino, R.A. and Shores, K.A. (2012) 'Patterns of literacy among U.S. students', *The Future of Children*, 22(2), 17–37.

Salvador, L. and Martins, M.A. (2018) 'The impact of a writing programme on reading acquisition of at risk first grade children', *Bellaterra Journal of Teaching and Learning Language and Literature*, 11(2), pp. 74–90.

Scholes, L. (2019a) 'Differences in attitudes towards reading and other school-related activities among boys and girls', *Journal of Research in Reading*, 42(3–4), pp. 485–503.

Scholes, L. (2019b) 'Working-class boys' relationships with reading: Contextual systems that support working-class boys' engagement with, and enjoyment of, reading', *Gender and Education*, 31(3), pp. 344–361.

Scholes, L. (2021) 'Popular girls aren't into reading: reading as a site for working-class girls' gender and class identity work', *Critical Studies in Education*, 62(2), pp. 179–194.

Scholes, L., Spina, N. and Comber, B. (2021) 'Disrupting the "boys don't read" discourse: Primary school boys who love reading fiction', *British Educational Research Journal*, 47(1), pp. 163–180.

Sénéchal, M., Hill, S. and Malette, M. (2018) 'Individual differences in grade 4 children's written compositions: The role of online planning and revising, oral storytelling, and reading for pleasure', *Cognitive Development*, 45, pp. 92–104.

Sizmur, J., Ager, R., Bradshaw, J., Classick, R., Galvis, M., Packer, J., Thomas, D. and Wheater, R. (National Foundation for Educational Research) (2019) *Achievement of 15-year-olds in England: PISA 2018 Results*, London:Department for Education.

Smith, F. (1983) 'Reading like a writer', *Language Arts*, 60(5), pp. 558–567.

Sonnenschein, S., Serpell, L. and Schmidt, D. (2000) 'Shared book reading at home and preschoolers' socio-emotional competence', in Roskos, K. and Christie, I. (eds), *Play and Literacy in Early Childhood: Research from Multiple Perspectives*, New York: Lawrence Erlbaum, pp. 125–137.

Sullivan, A. and Brown, M. (2015) 'Reading for pleasure and progress in vocabulary and mathematics', *British Educational Research Journal*, 41(1), pp. 971–991.

Taylor, L. and Clarke, P. (2021) 'We read, we write: Reconsidering reading–writing relationships in primary school children', *Literacy*, 55(1), pp. 14–24.

Thomson, P. (2002) *Schooling the Rustbelt Kids: Making the Difference in Changing Times*, Stoke on Trent: Trentham Books.

Vargas, C., Altamura, L., Blanco-Gandía, M.C., Gil, L., Mañá, A., Montagud, S. and Salmerón, L. (2024) 'Print and digital reading habits and comprehension in children with and without special education needs', *Research in Development Disabilities*, 146, 104675.

Villiger, C., Niggli A., Wandeler, C. and Kutzelmann, S. (2012) 'Does family make a difference? Mid-term effects of a school/home-based intervention program to enhance reading motivation', *Learning and Instruction*, 22(2), pp. 79–91.

Williams, G.J. and Larkin, R.F. (2013) 'Narrative writing, reading and cognitive processes in middle childhood: What are the links?', *Learning and Individual Differences*, 28, pp. 142–150.

Wolf, S.A. and Brice Heath, S. (1992) *The Braid of Literature: Children's Worlds of Reading*, Cambridge, MA and London: Harvard University Press.

Wyse, D. and Hacking, C. (2024) 'Decoding, reading and writing: The double helix theory of teaching', *Literacy*, 58(3), pp. 256–266.

3

THE RESEARCH STUDY

Introduction

This chapter shares the provenance of the research findings that led to the Reading and Writing for Pleasure Framework for Practice. It explains the study's methodology, the narrative literature review deployed and its inclusion and exclusion criteria, and the way in which third generation Cultural Historical Activity Theory (Daniels, 2004; Engeström, 2001, 2008, 2014) was used as a lens to better understand the programmes' implementation of reading and writing for pleasure practices. It also details the processes involved in data collection and analysis and the ways in which the team identified synergies between the research literature and the empirical data.

Research methodology

This Literacy Special Initiative (2020–2023), as previously shared, was commissioned by the Mercers' Company and supported by an Open University (OU) team as the research partner. The team were tasked to respond to the question: 'What methodologies and approaches seem to be effective in inspiring and encouraging children and young people to read and/or write for pleasure?'

The planned outcome of this study was the development of a Reading and Writing for Pleasure Framework, the creation of which involved drawing together insights from the existing research literature and the analysis of the data collected from the six London-based literacy programmes (see Figure 3.1). In order to achieve this, the OU research team planned the following strands of work:

Strand 1: Review and synthesise existing research literature in the field of reading and writing for pleasure.
Strand 2: Collect and analyse research data from the six participating London-based literacy programmes.

DOI: 10.4324/9781003532606-5

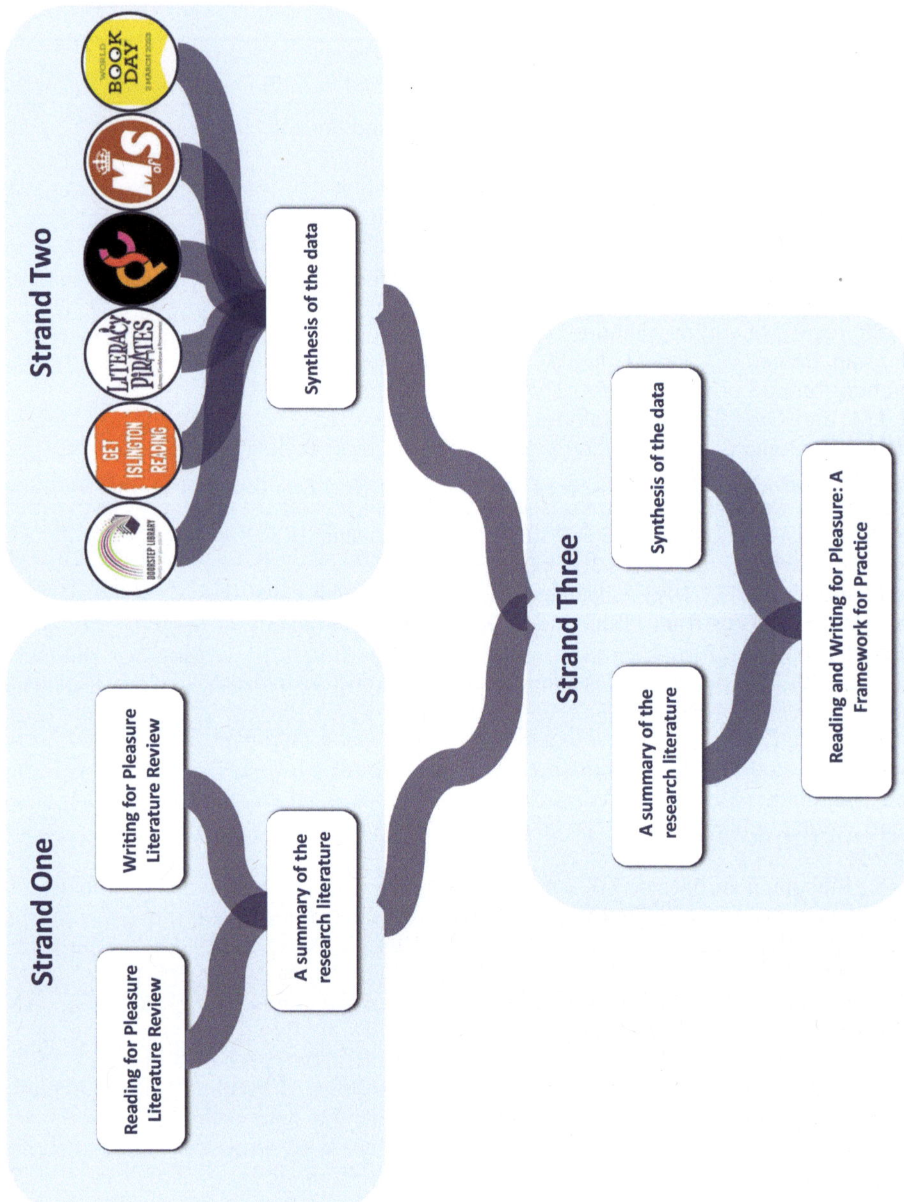

FIGURE 3.1 Overview of the research approach and process used for the Literacy Special Initiative

Strand 3: Examine if and in what ways the synergies between the research literature and the empirical data from the programmes might be connected.

The first two strands of work provided a solid foundation to inform the construction of the Framework through a process of cross-referencing between the summary of the two combined literature reviews and the synthesis of the data empirically derived from the programmes. The ongoing and iterative process of thinking and reflection continued throughout Strand 3, until the final version of the research-informed Framework was agreed.

Supporting programme learning

As the Literacy Special Initiative focused on identifying the common features of effective practice in nurturing reading and writing for pleasure, the research team sought to develop relationships with programme members. To support this, the process of data collection utilised a research partner approach – programmes were assigned a 'linked researcher' – a member of the OU team to work with across the three years. In addition, the lead researcher met regularly with programme leads in the role of a critical friend, these sessions were designed to offer guidance and support and build capacity. They were not recorded or transcribed and represented an opportunity for programme leads to raise issues and explore concerns in a safe space, which also involved challenge and debate. This collegiate approach to data collection, informed by the perspective of a critical friend, enabled the research team to collect data 'in action'. As relationships developed, so did the understanding of the everyday practices of the programmes, and the OU team were able to document the changes made by programmes as the Literacy Special Initiative evolved.

Another way in which the team sought to support programmes and build their capacity across the life of the project was through the cross-programme meetings, later entitled Cohort Learning Days. In these, programmes learned about each other's work and were enabled to reflect on their own. Whilst this activity did not contribute specifically to the Strand 2 data collection, it facilitated the sharing of principles and practices between the programmes, built their networks and sought to widen programme members understanding of key issues, including reading and writing for pleasure, disadvantage, evaluation and more. Two members from each programme, and representatives from the Mercers' Company and the OU team attended these days. Six were held across the three years, although initially due to the COVID-19 pandemic, those in Year 1 were shortened and held online. In the later meetings, in Year 2 and Year 3, updates of the research to date were shared, and particular research-related focus points were examined, enabling everyone to share and develop their experiences and understandings. These meetings also enabled the research team to learn more about the programmes and reflect upon their understanding of the literature and data to date.

Cultural Historical Activity Theory

Several theoretical approaches were considered, including Bronfenbrenner's ecosystems theory (Bronfenbrenner, 1986), but Activity Theory, specifically, third generation

'Cultural Historical Activity Theory' (Daniels, 2004; Engeström, 2001, 2008, 2014), was chosen as an appropriate conceptual frame to underpin the research design. In Engeström's (2014) model of Activity Theory, organisations can be conceptualised as 'activity systems', where individuals ('subjects') engage in activities motivated by individual and shared purposes or 'objects'. Positioning the programmes in this way enabled discussion across and within the scope of their various offers, whilst also enabling the team to look across programmes to understand the common features, approaches and elements directed towards the overarching goal of their activity, i.e. supporting children to read and/or write for pleasure. The outcome of the interaction between subject and object is mediated by different activity system elements. Conventionally, these elements are referred to as 'community', 'division of labour', 'rules' and 'artefacts' (Daniels et al., 2010; Engeström, 2014). For the Literacy Special Initiative, the team decided to re-label the last three of these elements to better reflect the nature of the programmes. Accordingly, the outcome of the interaction between subject and object as mediated by the community comprised other individuals and their corresponding *roles* (formerly 'divisions of labour') and *expectations* (formerly 'rules'), as well as by the availability and suitability of *resources* (formerly 'artefacts').

Applying an Activity Theory informed perspective, the team viewed each programme as an 'activity-system' which enabled them to analyse how the elements of each programme interacted to shape children and young people's engagement. Across all the programmes the children and young people were the subject, and the intended object or goal of all the programmes was defined as the provision of motivating literacy activities and their impact on children's reading and writing for pleasure according to each organisation's aims (see Figure 3.2). In summary the elements comprised:

- *Subject*: the 'target' participants.
- *Object*: aims and objectives.
- *Outcome*: specific outcomes.
- *Resources*: the objects, documentation, language and environment.
- *Expectations*: codes of conduct, rules and routines.
- *Community*: stakeholders and their engagement and relationships.
- *Roles*: responsibilities before, during, after the programme for those involved.

The programmes evaluated the objects or 'outcomes' of their work in terms of the children's attitudes, behaviour and engagement with reading and/or writing. However, these were not part of focused data collection as the impact of the programmes was not within the remit of the Literacy Special Initiative. Nonetheless, through analysis of the elements the children's engagement was discernible and in particular the focus groups with children enabled the team to discern qualitative insights into the perceived impact of the programmes on the young people's identities as readers and writers. They reflected on their sense of confidence, competence, value and belonging within the various programmes' reading and writing provision.

The benefit of using activity system elements for the conceptual model was that these elements offered a systematic and rigorous route to identifying effective approaches and methodologies at both the individual programme level *and* across the programmes. Accordingly, the team investigated commonalities across the programmes, for example:

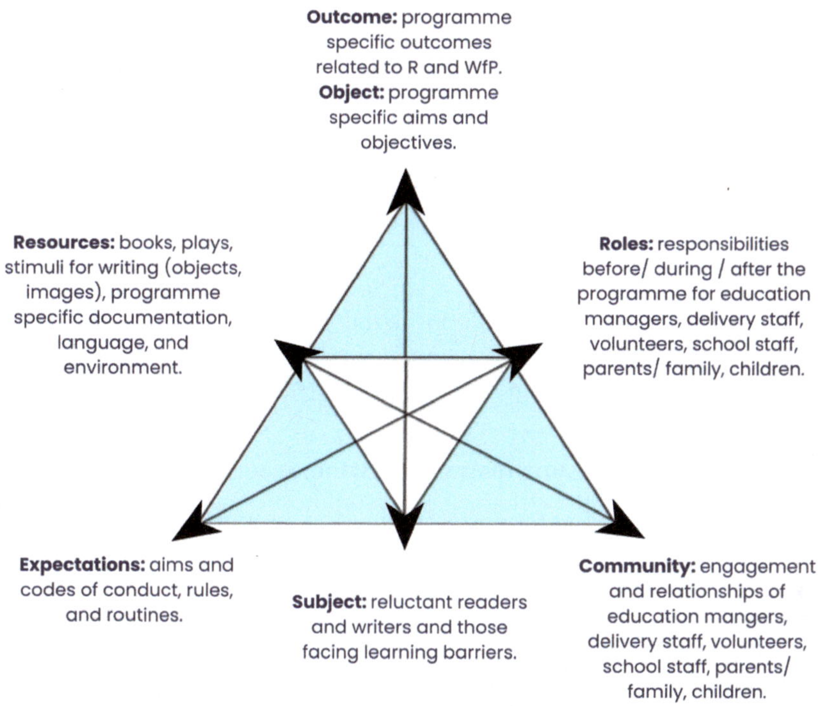

FIGURE 3.2 Activity system elements used within the Literacy Special Initiative

the ways that texts are used, what artefacts support writing and how they motivate readers and writers (resources); routines that encourage children's choice and independence in reading and writing (expectations); the relationships that delivery staff develop with children that nurture reading and writing for pleasure (community); how the educational managers develop a shared vision with their team (roles). Through these common elements, we were able to explore both a single programme in depth and all elements across the six programmes. Thus, using activity system elements offered insights without needing to compare or evaluate the programmes. This approach was valuable given that the six programmes were exceptionally diverse in form, nature and scale (see the Introduction for a summary).

Ethical considerations

The Literacy Special Initiative took place over three years and involved a broad range of individuals, including programme staff, creative practitioners, authors, volunteers, school staff, public librarians, children and their families. Given the evolving range of participants over the course of the Special Initiative, a phased approach to ethical review was adopted. This involved seeking an initial ethical review for the overall Literacy Special Initiative study and then subsequent reviews for specific aspects of the study (Human Resources Ethics Committee HREC reference number: 672/Cremin). Conducting multiple, staggered reviews for specific aspects of the initiative enabled the team to develop the precise focus of the data collection tools (e.g. interview questions) based on emerging insights and drawing on the ongoing programme interactions and iterative analysis. This proved particularly useful during the onset of the COVID-19 pandemic (2020–2022), which necessitated switching from in-person data collection methods to online approaches.

The interactional restrictions created by the pandemic not only had an impact on the nature of data collection activities, but also had an impact on the manner in which participants' consent was sought. Part of this involved working with the programmes to tailor the presentation of information to ensure it was accessible to all their participants. The families involved had varying levels of confidence with reading and accessing documents in English. This consideration, when combined with the remote methods of communication necessitated by the pandemic, meant the team had to ensure information about the programmes was as clear and unambiguous as possible.

Strand 1: Reviewing and synthesising existing research literature

In order to produce two comprehensive reviews of research relating respectively to reading and writing for pleasure, the team undertook databases searches, comparing insights gleaned from this process with known, key studies from peer-reviewed research across the last 30 years. This additionally included a focus on the consequences of young people's positive engagement as readers and writers and factors of influence beyond the classroom (see Chapters 1 and 2). Following the completion of the core reviews, which attended to the research evidence relating to approaches that were capable of supporting reading and writing for pleasure, the team identified themes within, and synergies across these core reviews. A combined review was then created of this research literature (see Chapters 4–8).

Search parameters

The database searches were conducted using several different research indexes, including for example: the British Education Index, Scopus, the Education Resources Information Centre and Web of Science. Searches were conducted using a range of terms, including: *'reading for pleasure', 'reading for enjoyment', 'volitional reading', 'voluntary reading', 'leisure reading', 'engaged reading', 'independent reading'* and *'recreational reading'*. In writing, the terms used included: *'writing for pleasure', 'writing for enjoyment', 'volitional writing', 'voluntary writing', 'independent writing', 'writer engagement', 'recreational writing'* and *'free-choice writing'*. In addition, searches were conducted using terms linked to the characteristics of reading for pleasure as an act of volitional engagement, including, for example, *'choice', 'agency'* and *'autonomy'*, these were also co-located with the word *'writing'*.

Whilst acknowledging the term writing for pleasure is rarely used in policy, practice or research, the OU team framed it as 'volitional writing', which, in line with notions of reading for pleasure, is seen to be driven by an individual's own goals and interests, often including social ones in anticipation of some kind of satisfaction. The papers selected for review mainly included peer-reviewed empirical work, articles concerned with children of primary and early secondary school age (aged 5–13 years old) and articles written in English. Additionally, reference list searches of particularly relevant meta-analyses were conducted (e.g. Mol and Bus, 2011; de Bondt et al., 2020). Some additional texts were also gathered through manual search in reference lists from retrieved articles, and significant research studies published in books and chapters across the last 30 years were included in order to deepen understanding of particular associated benefits or approaches to nurturing volitional reading and writing. Research focused on later reading, such as post-16 education and adult reading, reading in second languages or English as a foreign language, was not included, nor studies which exclusively examined digital literacy. However, where a given theme had been examined with adult participants and had more recently been examined in research with younger readers, the adult studies are referenced for context (e.g. Kidd and Castano, 2019, in relation to the development of empathy).

Appraising existing sources

The studies reported and synthesised in the review were drawn mainly from cognitive psychology, education, literary studies and linguistics. All the empirical and conceptual studies on reading that were included attended directly or indirectly to the motivational approaches used. This body of research demonstrates that there are multiple perspectives of the reading experience and that these draw on different ways of thinking about reading and reading for pleasure. Not dissimilarly, studies of writing draw on different disciplinary perspectives and models, both cognitive and educational models of writing, and pay attention to the opportunities the young are offered to compose, in educational settings, at home and online, and how particular spaces and the approaches deployed in these contribute to shaping their identities as writers.

Both reviews encompassed qualitative, quantitative and mixed methods studies. Whilst children's reading for pleasure is tracked in large-scale quantitative studies (e.g. the Progress in International Reading Literacy Study [Mullis et al., 2023] and the Programme for International Student Assessment [OECD, 2021]), there is no parallel global data set for young people's volitional engagement or performance in writing. A national data set for writing is however offered in the UK by the National Literacy Trust (2010–onwards). This annual survey includes attention to the writing behaviours and attitudes of young people and uses self-reports to discern their engagement in writing across genres, in both school and out-of-school contexts. These are invaluable, although it is recognised that surveys have limitations (see Chapter 1 for a discussion of these).

The available qualitative studies of children's volitional reading and writing are often ethnographically styled and observational in nature, tracking attitudes and seeking to understanding practices in homes, classrooms or projects. Some pay attention to the socio-cultural context in which children's choice-led reading and writing occurs, and some offer detailed accounts of the lived experience of writing and being a writer (e.g. Chamberlain, 2019; Moses and Kelly, 2018; Taylor and Clarke, 2021). These studies frequently draw upon small numbers, often through case studies of young people over short periods of time, and document the socially constructed nature of reading and writing. Relatively few however take into account the views and experiences of the young people involved, although there is an emerging tradition of more participatory research in this area (e.g. McGeown et al., 2020). Studies which have deployed mixed methods in order to understand reader motivation and the nature of self-directed reading are also encompassed (e.g. Nolen, 2007), although these are not common.

The evidence-based approach

The two reviews prioritised international peer-reviewed research over 'grey' literature (e.g. 'in house evaluations', graduate dissertations, magazine articles and government reports that have not been subject to scrutiny by academic peer-review systems) and polemical, scholarly texts, instructional articles and editorials were also excluded. In response to the remit from the Literacy Special Initiative and in order to ensure the findings were derived from evidence-based practices, peer-reviewed literature was foregrounded. This also enabled gaps in empirical knowledge to be identified. The reading for pleasure review drew upon several pre-existing reviews. Three previously commissioned and conducted OU narrative reviews on reading for pleasure (Coles, 2019), on reading aloud and shared reading in homes and schools (Mukherjee, 2020), and on intersectionality and reading for pleasure (Harris, 2017), and two earlier narrative reviews of reading for pleasure research (Clark and Rumbold, 2006; Department for Education, 2012). Additionally, a review of reading interventions and their impact on adolescent reading motivation (Webber et al., 2021), and the review undertaken for the research study and book 'Teachers as Readers: Building Communities of Readers' (Cremin et al., 2014) were included. The new review, in order to widen and enrich the breadth of work examined, revisited the insights from these previous reviews, but was far more expansive and in particular focused on 2020–2024. Small, targeted reviews in response to the work of the six programmes were also undertaken, for example in relation to extracurricular literacy provision.

Synthesising the findings from the two reviews

As papers were found, their appropriacy was assessed with reference to the inclusion and exclusion criteria, and when included, summaries were entered into a review template which recorded key information about the sample, location, duration, data sources, methods and main findings of each study alongside the country of origin. The papers were filed according to their core focus and then all papers related to a particular focus (e.g. book talk or children's agency as writers) were re-read and summarised. Members of the research team read across these focal reviews and in the process identified corresponding themes and insights, alongside a few additional themes which were then subject to closer examination.

After scrutinising the finally agreed themes arising from each of the separate research reviews related to reading and writing for pleasure, five synergies were identified. It was noted that the existing research literature that focuses exclusively on developing choice-led writing is relatively small compared to the number of studies that examine practices that connect to recreational reading. It should be noted that due to the complexity and multiple foci within the research literature, the five synergies inevitably overlap and intersect in complex dynamic ways. The first related to the construction of young people's literate identities and focused on children developing a sense of themselves as readers and writers through their social interactions with others, whether at home, at school or with peers. The second synergy illustrated the connection between motivation, time spent reading or writing, and self-efficacy. This highlighted the importance of enabling young readers and writers to feel a sense of agency, competence and social connection through reading and writing. Chapter 4 further explores these first two synergistic connections.

Text access, time and space represented the third synergistic set of connections identified from the research literature and drew attention to the importance of being able to access and produce a range of personally relevant and affectively engaging texts as part of reading and writing for pleasure (see Chapter 5). The fourth connection underscored the importance, as identified within the research literature, of social interaction. This synergy revealed the role that sharing and talking about texts plays, whether written or read, in non-assessed relaxed contexts. Studies indicate that such social interaction nurtures enjoyment and builds relational connections between readers and/or writers (see Chapter 6). The final synergy identified was entitled role models and connected communities and recognised the importance of significant others, sharing their literate identities. In addition, this synergy outlined the importance of positioning reading and writing for pleasure as a communal, collective and relational practice. By so doing, the research literature suggests that connected communities of engaged readers and writers can be cultivated (see Chapter 7).

Strand 2: Collecting and analysing research data from the participating literacy programmes

To understand the approaches used by the programmes involved in the Literacy Special Initiative, a range of data collection methods were used, including programme-specific documentation; interviews with programme staff, practitioners, teachers and volunteers; focus groups with teachers and volunteers; visits to programme activities; and focus groups with children. See Table 3.1 for an overview.

TABLE 3.1 Overview of data corpus

Data type	*Participants*	*Participant numbers*	*Documentation*	*Phase of the project*
Programme-specific documentation	(not applicable)	(not applicable)	24 documents	Year 1
Interviews	Programme staff	12	20 transcribed interviews	Year 1 and 2
Focus groups	Children	40	10 transcribed discussions	Year 2
	Teachers, practitioners, volunteers	9	5 transcribed discussions	Year 2 and 3
Observations	Children, parents teachers, practitioners, volunteers, librarians, programme staff	(various)	12 observation schedules	Year 2 and 3
Post-observation interviews	Teachers, practitioners, volunteers	9	10 transcribed group interviews	Year 2 and 3

The initial focus in Year 1 was on understanding the six programmes and their approaches and methodologies. Programme-specific information was collected, and interviews were held with the programme leads and/or education managers. Learning cohort days and critical friend meetings were held, but neither were used for data collection. In Years 2 and 3, the team enriched their understanding of the programmes' work by involving a more diverse group of stakeholders. This involved observations, interviews and focus groups with volunteers and teachers aligned to the six programmes, as well as young people. In addition to focus groups with volunteers and teachers, the research team carried out visits over these years. These included interviews with the individuals involved, which not only encompassed reflecting on the sessions, but also focused on their roles and how the programmes supported them in these roles.

Data collection

Programme-specific documentation

The programmes shared varying documentation particular to their work, for example, training handbooks, theories of change, job descriptions, workshop plans, online resources and so forth. This documentation was read by the linked researcher, but for consistency in the starting initial analysis, four pieces of documentation common to all programmes were identified. These were: the programme's application to the Mercers' Company; an evaluation report; a business/strategic plan; and a volunteer handbook (where available, or another document which offered structural/organisational information regarding staff roles). These documents were selected to give a common and rounded view of the programmes from different perspectives.

Interviews

These online interviews with the programme lead and/or the education manager were undertaken across the period of the Literacy Special Initiative and, aligned with Activity Theory, had a particular focus on the subject, object, outcomes and roles at play within the programmes. Questions probed an understanding of the programme's aims, the children involved, the object and outcomes regarding reading or writing for pleasure, and so forth. Additionally, group interviews were undertaken in order to widen the perspectives being listened to, these involved a more diverse group of stakeholders, and focused on individuals' experiences of the expectations, communities, roles and resources associated with the programmes.

Focus groups

Two cross-programme focus groups were undertaken, one with programme volunteers and one with teachers. Again, these were framed to relate to activity system elements and information was sought about volunteer and teacher perspectives on their own roles and the roles of programmes, and the resources they used within and around this work. A sequence of focus groups with children and young people who participated in the programmes were also undertaken. In total, 40 children across nine focus groups representing five programmes were involved in this work. A children's focus group was not included for World Book Day as their work for the Literacy Special Initiative did not directly involve children. For consistency, a consultant with experience in researching children's engagement with literacy practices and resources ran all the focus groups, reducing any bias or insider knowledge from the linked researchers. These conversations were arranged where possible to coincide with children's attendance at regular programme sessions, which reduced the logistical demands placed on children or their families. The semi-structured interview schedule, again influenced by the overarching interest in activity system elements, attended to the children's understanding of the roles of individuals involved in programmes, their interactions with associated resources and how these elements impacted on their feelings towards reading and writing, as an outcome. However, the schedule was designed to be flexible to the interests and perspectives of the participating young people. Accordingly, questions at the outset invited the children to share their experiences of the programme; for example, 'Can you tell me a little bit about what you do during a visit/session?'

Observations and visits

The team carried out observational visits to all programmes, some involved observing the programme's online offer (as a result of the pandemic), but all programmes were visited in action twice. Team members also attended final events, shows, and other occasions when children shared their work with their families and others. Observations of World Book Day leading sessions with teachers were undertaken and the five most downloaded resources they developed with teachers in 2022 were analysed. Researchers kept chronological narrative notes of the sessions observed, which included verbatim quotes, timing, the activities, interactions and children's engagement. Following the session, these were linked to the activity system elements at play. The visits also included in-person follow-up interviews with the individuals involved.

Data analysis

In the first year of the Literacy Special Initiative, the OU team set the foundations for data analysis by deciding on: a computer assisted qualitative data analysis software (CAQDAS), a structured analytic plan, and the agreed operationalisation of the activity system elements. Dedoose, a qualitative and mixed methods CAQDAS, was chosen as it is a web-based application that enables simultaneous use and has a secure log-in process, with an additional, optional layer of security, which was employed. Using Dedoose supported the team's approach to the gradual and collaborative creation of common sub-codes across the programmes related to the elements of Community, Expectations, Roles and Resources. This deliberate approach enabled rigour in the coding as the team were working with agreed definitions of these activity system elements. The development of a structured analytic plan offered a systematic and rigorous approach to the analysis of programmes' data. The three-stage plan was a phased approach to each activity system element in each of the data sets over time.

Stage 1 involved working with the programme's documentation, the research team coded for all the activity system elements – subject, object, outcome, community, roles, resources and expectations – with a focus on creating common understandings and definitions of the elements. Stage 2 involved a more in-depth analysis making use of new sets of data and creating sub-codes for the four activity system elements: expectations, community, roles and resources. The construction of these sub-codes involved extensive discussions, scrutinising data examples and considering the appropriateness or uniqueness of the sub-codes across the programmes. Natural overlaps and commonalities between as well as within elements emerged in both the coding and the interpretive analysis which can be seen in the patterns in the codes applied. See Figure 3.3 for the final coding table.

Stage 3 of the data analysis involved applying the codes and sub-codes developed in Stage 2 across the rest of the data corpus as it was collected. Through discussion, and for consistency of presentation, each team member was assigned one of the four elements to focus on and a written analysis with data extracts was created for each element. This third stage, continued to be iterative and rigorous with regular meetings between members of the team as parts of the data corpus were coded, enabling continued reflection and cross moderation. Common features of practice were identified across the six programmes, albeit some were evidenced unevenly. Whilst each activity system element is explored separately in Part III (see Chapters 8–11), in practice they are interlinked as part of a dynamic system and, in the final strand of the analysis, the learning arising from scrutinising data within each element was viewed holistically in conjunction with the synthesis from the literature reviews.

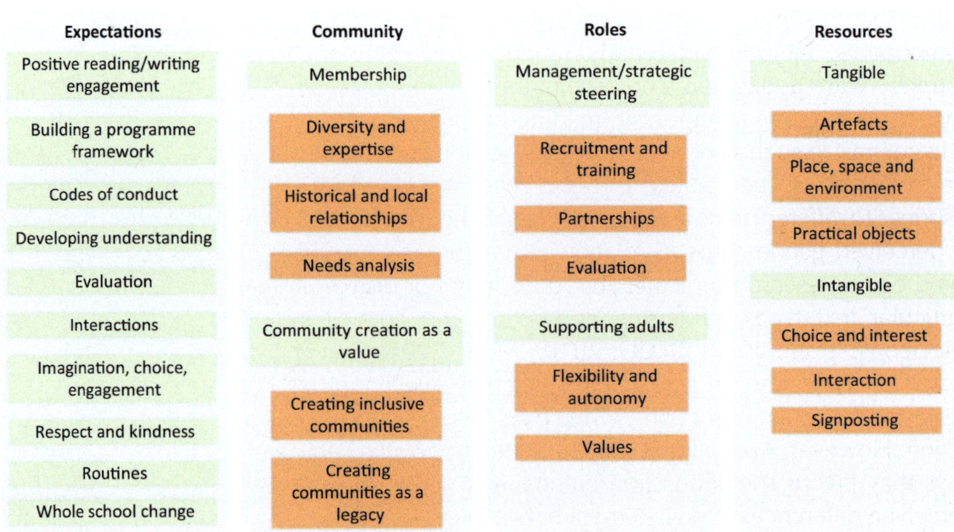

FIGURE 3.3 Elements, codes and sub-codes

Strand 3: Exploring synergies between the research literature and the empirical data

This third strand of the study involved considering the insights from both sets of literature, which had been combined into one synthesised review (Strand 1) in conjunction with the insights from the data collection from the programmes (Strand 2). Commonalities in approaches, identified in both the research literature and the programme data, led to the creation of the research-informed Reading and Writing for Pleasure Framework (see Chapter 12). This involved an extended process of identifying connections across the two strands of work and conceptualising potential ways to combine and present these. Whilst there were many possible ways of representing the Strand 3 synergies, the team sought to identify a way that was not only firmly grounded in the evidence from the first two strands, but which was also potentially accessible, in order that the insights could be shared with policy makers, the education profession and third sector organisations involved in supporting young people's literacy.

Three limitations need to be recognised however, namely that the research literature reviewed is somewhat skewed towards reading for pleasure, that the work did not include evaluation of the impact of the programmes, and finally that the context of the research reviewed differed from that of several of the programmes. The remit of the Literacy Special Initiative did not encompass attention to the impact of the programmes on the children's reading and writing for pleasure, and each of the programmes used different tools to understand their efficacy in nurturing reading and writing for pleasure, nonetheless, the data analysis indicates that all programmes impacted positively on children as readers and/or writers. The range of data collection tools, including observations and focus groups with children, enabled the team to appreciate their engagement, involvement, and positive dispositions and sense of themselves as readers and writers. This is particularly noteworthy since many of the programmes targeted their work at less engaged, reluctant readers and writers.

With regard to the research literature, this predominantly drew on research undertaken in classrooms, whereas the Strand 2 data were drawn from programmes, not all of whom worked in mainstream education contexts. The Primary Shakespeare Company and Ministry of Stories both worked in schools, their programmes were integrated into the timetable. Literacy Pirates worked with children referred from schools but in their own extracurricular space. Get Islington Reading primarily provided intracurricular opportunities alongside an extracurricular initiative with the public library service. Doorstep Library worked solely in homes and World Book Day, for this initiative, focused on resource development with teachers. The work of all the programmes was however aligned to the national curriculum which mandated reading for pleasure in 2013 (Department for Education, 2013).

Despite these differences and challenges, common approaches between the research literature and the data from the programmes were discerned and summarised in the Reading and Writing for Pleasure Framework for Practice. In addition, and perhaps significantly, in the course of the data collection and analysis, common organisational characteristics across the different programmes were identified, these appeared to underpin the programmes' approaches to supporting children's reading and writing for pleasure and they also have value for schools and other organisations seeking to nurture children's reading and writing for pleasure (see Chapter 12 for an account of these).

Conclusion

The research study (2020–2023) undertaken as part of the Literacy Special Initiative into reading and writing for pleasure was systematically organised, professionally conducted and undertaken in collaboration with the six programmes funded by the Mercers' Company. It encompassed three strands of work: reviewing and synthesising existing research literature in the fields of reading and writing for pleasure; collecting and analysing research data from the six participating London-based literacy programmes; and examining if and in what ways the synergies between the research literature and the empirical data from the programmes might be connected.

Two comprehensive narrative reviews were undertaken, respectively of reading and writing for pleasure, drawing on previous reviews. These sought to consolidate and summarise the existing research literature mainly from peer-reviewed studies with 5–13-year-olds. These were synthesised to create a combined review. A qualitative approach was taken to data collection with the six programmes, utilising Activity Theory as a lens to understand their implementation of reading and writing for pleasure practices and each programme was viewed as an activity system. The methods of data collection included interviews, focus groups, observations of the programmes in action, as well as programme documentation. The core activity system elements of expectations, communities, roles and resources were examined. Data analysis involved collaborative scrutiny of the data corpus, and through rigorous analysis, codes were generated, negotiated and agreed for each element. Commonalities in approaches, identified in both the research literature and the programme data led to the creation of the Reading and Writing for Pleasure Framework for Practice.

References

Bronfenbrenner, U. (1986) 'Ecology of the family as a context for human development: Research perspectives', *Developmental Psychology*, 22(6), pp. 723–742.

Chamberlain, L. (2019) 'Places, spaces and local customs: Honouring the private worlds of out-of-school text creation', *Literacy*, 53(1), pp. 39–45.

Clark, C. and Rumbold, K. (2006) *Reading for Pleasure: A Research Overview*, London: National Literacy Trust.

Coles, B. (2019) *A Narrative Review of Reading for Pleasure Research 2014–2019*, Milton Keynes: The Open University.

Cremin, T., Mottram, M., Collins, F.M., Powell, S. and Safford, K. (2014) *Building Communities of Engaged Readers: Reading for Pleasure*, Oxon: Routledge.

Daniels, H. (2004) 'Activity theory, discourse and Bernstein', *Educational Review*, 56(2), pp. 121–132.

Daniels, H., Edwards, A, Engeström, Y., Gallagher, T. and Ludvigsen, S.R. (2010) *Activity Theory in Practice: Promoting Learning across Boundaries and Agencies*, Oxford: Routledge.

de Bondt, M., Willenberg, I.A. and Bus, A.G. (2020) 'Do book giveaway programs promote the home literacy environment and children's literacy-related behaviour and skills?', *Review of Educational Research*, 90(3), pp. 349–375.

Department for Education (2012) *Research Evidence on Reading for Pleasure*, London: Department for Education.

Department for Education (2013) *The National Curriculum in England: Key Stages 1 and 2 Framework Document*, London: Department for Education.

Engeström, Y. (2001) 'Expansive learning at work: Toward an activity theoretical reconceptualization', *Journal of Education and Work*, 14(1), pp. 133–156.

Engeström, Y. (2008) *From Teams to Knots: Activity-Theoretical Studies of Collaboration and Learning at Work*, Cambridge: Cambridge University Press.

Engeström, Y. (2014) *Learning by Expanding: An Activity-Theoretical Approach to Developmental Research* (2nd edn), Cambridge: Cambridge University Press.

Harris, D. (2017) *Understanding 'Disadvantaged', 'Struggling' Boy Readers' (Dis)Engagement with Reading for Pleasure*, Milton Keynes: The Open University.

Kidd, D. and Castano, E. (2019) 'Reading literary fiction and theory of mind: Three preregistered replications and extensions of Kidd and Castano (2013)', *Social Psychology and Personality Science*, 10(4), pp. 522–531.

McGeown, S., Bonsall, J., Andries, V., Howarth, D., Wilkinson, K. and Sabeti, S. (2020) 'Growing up a reader: Exploring children's and adolescents' perceptions of "a reader"', *Educational Research*, 62(2), pp. 216–228.

Mol, S.E. and Bus, A.G. (2011) 'To read or not to read: A meta-analysis of print exposure from infancy to early adulthood', *Psychological Bulletin*, 137(2), pp. 267–296.

Moses, L. and Kelly, L.B. (2018) '"We're a little loud. That's because we like to read!": Developing positive views of reading in a diverse, urban first grade', *Journal of Early Childhood Literacy*, 18 (3), 307–337.

Mukherjee, S.J. (2020) *A Literature Review of Read Aloud*, Milton Keynes: The Open University.

Mullis, I.V.S., von Davier, M., Foy, P., Fishbein, B., Reynolds, K.A. and Wry, E. (2023) *PIRLS 2021 International Results in Reading*, Boston:Boston College, TIMSS and PIRLS International Study Center.

Nolen, S.B. (2007) 'Young children's motivation to read and write: Development in social contexts', *Cognition and Instruction*, 25(2–3), pp. 219–270.

OECD (2021) *21st-Century Readers: Developing Literacy Skills in a Digital World*, Paris: OECD Publishing.

Taylor, L. and Clarke, P. (2021) 'We read, we write: Reconsidering reading–writing relationships in primary school children', *Literacy*, 55(1), pp. 14–24.

Webber, C., Wilkinson, K., Duncan, L.G. and McGeown, S.P. (2021) *Reading and Literacy Interventions for Improving Reading and Motivation in Adolescence: A Narrative Review*, OSF Preprints.

PART II

Examining Synergies in Approaches to Reading and Writing for Pleasure

4

YOUNG PEOPLE'S LITERATE IDENTITIES AND MOTIVATION

Introduction

Children and young people's sense of themselves as readers and writers is constructed and re-constructed by the literacy activities in which they participate, both those required by schools and those in which they choose to engage in school at home or in other community contexts, online or off. For instance, they may engage at home (e.g. writing text messages, homework), at school (e.g. reading at break, written comprehension) and in wider 'community' contexts (e.g. fan fiction writing online, visiting the library). Their literate identities are thus always in flux. They are influenced by the environment, the current text (they are reading or composing), their past and present experiences of literacy, and by the identity positions as readers and writers that are made available to them by parents, peers, teachers and others, and those that they choose to adopt in any given context. In this sense, each young person is always in the process of becoming a reader/writer or learning how to be a reader/writer in different situations, actively shaping and reshaping their identities and being positioned as particular kinds of readers or writers by others, as well as adopting particular identity positions in the moment.

Existing studies indicate that young people's literate identities play a significant role in their wider sense of self, as well as their motivation and desire to read and write. Those young people with a positive sense of self as a reader and/or writer are likely to engage in volitional literacy activities more frequently than their peers who are less assured and do not perceive themselves to be readers or writers. Research indicates that children with a more negative sense of their literate self are less inclined to read or write in their own time and may only do so at the behest of others.

So in this chapter, in addition to exploring children's identities, research into reading and writing motivation is examined. Literacy motivation is widely recognised as a multidimensional construct comprising several factors, including young people's sense of self-efficacy as readers and writers, their attitudes and the extent to which they enjoy and value the experiences of reading and writing, as well as their personal

DOI: 10.4324/9781003532606-7

purposes and goals. Research into children's motivation is predominantly skewed towards reading; far fewer studies have documented what motivates children to want to write and the chapter thus reflects this, nonetheless, there are studies which consider children's identities as writers.

Young people's literate identities

Research examining children's perceptions of what it means to be a reader and writer reveals the marked impact of lived experience. Even before they start school, their family's attitudes to literacy, and the literacy practices and interactions that they participate in, position young people as particular kinds of readers and writers. Research indicates diversity amongst parents' attitudes to reading and reading practices in the home, which position young people differently (Levy et al., 2018). Social interactions with grandparents and siblings are also seen to support the habit of recreational reading and a positive sense of self as a reader (Gregory, 2001; Knoester and Plikuhn, 2018; Cliff-Hodges, 2018: Levy and Harrison, 2025). Studies that encompass attention to writing interactions in the home are rare (Brady, 2017; Chamberlain, 2019) and there are no known studies that take an identity lens or explicitly consider the social interactions or positioning of young writers in this context. However, when parents or educators talk to children about their out-of-school writing, show interest and affirm their communicative intent, they are in effect recognising and naming them as writers (Rowe et al., 2022), and supporting their self-efficacy as writers. Children build their identities as readers and writers as they establish their personal positions within literacy practices at home, in the classroom and the wider world. So as Collier (2010) notes:

> Identity may be viewed as a narrative or story that one tells about oneself, but identity is also constrained by practices, by time and space, in interaction with others.
>
> *(Collier, 2010, p. 149)*

Young people's literate identities are commonly associated with their perceived and received sense of competence and self-efficacy, and as research indicates, this predicts reading and writing attitudes and the frequency with which the young engage in these activities volitionally (e.g. Guthrie and Davis, 2003; McCarthy et al., 1985; Pajares and Johnson, 1994; Pajares and Valiante, 1999; Schüller et al., 2017; Weber, 2018). Indeed, as Compton-Lily (2025) argues, volitional reading and writing are 'tightly welded with identity'.

Teachers influence young people's literate identities

Who defines what a good reader or writer is and what counts as good reading/writing is dependent on context and is constructed and negotiated through interaction in different social environments. Children's literacy histories, others' perceptions of them as readers/writers and teachers', parents' and peers' interactions around reading and writing also influence their attitudes to and understanding of what it might mean to be a reader (Clark et al., 2008; Hall, 2012a, 2016; Hempel-Jorgensen et al., 2018; McGeown et al., 2020a; Scholes, 2019a), or a writer (Bourne, 2002; Brady, 2017; Nolen, 2007) in particular contexts.

For example, in a class of 9–11-year-olds from a school in Scotland, it was commonly agreed that a reader is someone who reads frequently for enjoyment, not because they feel obliged (McGeown et al., 2020a), and this aligned with their teachers' views. Some of the children also perceived that readers know their own reading interests, how to make the 'right choices' and are 'imaginative thinkers'. Self-identifying as a reader in this particular class at the time of the study suggests recognising oneself as an agentic thinker and meaning maker. This contrasts markedly with studies of other classes of primary aged learners who viewed reading and being a reader as merely a matter of proficiency – a set of skills (Hall, 2012a, 2016; Hempel-Jorgensen et al., 2018). In these classrooms, teachers understood reading as 'proficiency' in line with the US and UK accountability cultures in which they worked. The children in the UK research viewed 'good readers' as those who read fluently, accurately, at speed and who demonstrate high levels of attainment in reading (Hempel-Jorgensen et al., 2018). This had negative consequences for those who were deemed to be 'struggling'; they were seen to lack the skills to produce a 'technically correct performance', were required to practice for this and were not supported to develop a love of reading. In Hall's (2012a) US study, those children who perceived they were 'bad' or 'poor' readers interacted in particular ways in order to avoid their peers identifying them as struggling. For example, they held back from participating in discussions or reading aloud, and kept their heads down, despite not understanding the texts. In effect these children engaged in reading behaviours that they knew would prevent them from improving as readers. As a result they retained a low sense of self-efficacy and remained disengaged.

The adolescent readers in Frankel's (2017) study held very different understandings of what it means to be a reader from their teachers. These US teenagers tended to focus on the outcomes of being a good reader – having agency and being educated – whereas their teachers viewed 'good readers' as those who read frequently and who used the particular reading strategies that had been taught. As one of the boys did not engage in the kinds of behaviour expected by his teacher, he remained positioned as a 'struggler' in his teacher's eyes, which held him back. Being positioned as a struggling or able reader (or positioning oneself in this way) will dictate the types of interactions offered or participated in, thus constraining or expanding children's skills and sense of self-efficacy as readers. In a later study, Frankel and Fields (2019) showed how through thoughtful reflection and engagement with theory, teachers can come to re-view students' resistance or deviation from official expectations and can learn to see these as signs of their 'active, strategic meaning-making and self-authoring' (p. 158). Indeed, the researchers argued that one boy's deviations from his teacher's storyline were in fact:

> Acts of agency that were mediated by his identity as a reader, writer, and person, all of which were informed by his history-in-person and enacted self-understandings of himself as a reader and writer within and beyond the tutorial context, as well as by the positions available to him in that context.
>
> *(Frankel and Fields, 2019, p. 159)*

Nonetheless, this research context was one-to-one tutoring and in many of the whole class studies, the teachers involved did not appear to question the reader identity models they held or their often-narrow ways of describing readers. The influence of the performative systems in which many teachers work permeates practice, arguably constraining the reader identity positions made available to some children. For instance, in an ethnographic study of remedial reading classes, Masterson (2022) found that even though the students possessed the skills to decode and interpret texts, they did not see themselves as readers as attending this class framed them as less competent. Moreover, the students found these classes to be repetitive and boring, leading to them to viewing reading in the same light – consequently, they disengaged from it. One of the teachers in Hempel-Jorgensen et al. (2018) made visible the 9–10-year-olds' identities as readers through ability grouping, with the different groups experiencing significantly different reading opportunities. The less assured, mainly boys, were offered a more impoverished reading diet and reduced opportunities for interactions around texts of their own choice. Other studies, as discussed in Chapter 2, also indicate the marked influence of gender, and its interaction with social class and ethnicity, texts and time for social interaction around reading, and teachers' and parents' gendered expectations of children's identities as readers (Jang and Ryoo, 2019; Scholes, 2019a, 2019b, 2021).

In relation to writing, studies indicate that teachers tend to conceive of writing practices hierarchically and frequently associate writing with 'creative writing', perceiving this to be literary in nature and related to published works (e.g. McKinney and Giorgis, 2009; Wilson, 2009). Pre-service teachers too voice such views, and some consider that children's ability as 'creative writers' is innate or 'fixed' and cannot therefore be shaped by opportunities, instruction or feedback (Norman and Spencer, 2005). Such exclusive conceptions of writing limit opportunities for the young to develop as writers and find satisfaction in the experience. Teachers' views of writing in the classroom are additionally framed by institutional and assessment discourses and prescribed curricula, which in contexts of high stakes accountability tend to profile spelling, grammar and punctuation, and sideline writing as communication and meaning making (Clarkson, 2024; Cremin and Myhill, 2012; Guo et al., 2021; Lambirth, 2016; Locke, 2017; Ryan and Barton, 2014).

As with reading, adults' perceptions of writing and what it means to be a writer shape the kinds of writer identities on offer to young people in schools. For example, teachers' perceptions of writing impact on the nature of the feedback given to individuals and such feedback can have significant consequences for children's sense of self as writers and the perceived quality of their writing (Bourne, 2002). Young people's own conceptions of writing as a mechanical activity have also been seen to influence their self-esteem and identities as writers negatively (Auguste, 2018). A US classroom-based study showed that ability grouping, which represents a public formalisation of how teachers view pupils as writers, affects young people's performance and attitudes to writing (McCarthey, 2001). Frequent writers in the 'higher' groups had a stronger sense of personal self-efficacy and more positive writer identities. In contrast, those in 'lower' groups saw themselves as slow performers, tended to avoid writing and voiced their dislike of it (McCarthey, 2001). Another study which tracked the opportunities offered to two Australian 6-year-olds, from lower and higher writing groups, discerned that despite initially positive attitudes at the start of the year, the children's differently assigned writing goals influenced their peers' perceptions of them as writers (Kervin et al., 2020). This in turn impacted on their self-efficacy, with challenging consequences for the less experienced writer, in effect the children were obliged to accept the writer identity of their assigned group (Kervin et al., 2020). Whilst some research shows that children and young people are agentic and may adopt or reject the identity positions offered to them (e.g. Collier, 2010; Dyson, 2019; Rowe and Neitzel, 2010), ability grouping, and narrow definitions of writers and writer identities can have damaging consequences. This may, in part, explain why so many children express indifference to or report disliking writing and rarely write in their own time (Clark et al., 2023).

However, some studies show the possibilities which exist when teachers co-construct the nature and place of writing alongside their pupils, pay attention to the young learners' emerging identities, make use of conferences, dialogue and build in space for talk and choice among young writers (Collier, 2010; Dobson and Stephenson, 2017; Dutro et al., 2006; McCarthey and Woodard, 2017; McKinney, 2017; Nolen, 2006). Critically, these studies highlight a shift in traditional classroom hierarchies and the importance of the practitioner's awareness of their own writer identity positioning. As two of these researchers conclude:

> The success of the community as a whole depends on the teacher's sensitivity to individual children's identity enactments and their ability to reposition their own identity accordingly.
>
> *(Dobson and Stephenson, 2017, p. 167)*

It is clear teachers play a key role in forming and re-forming children's reader and writer identities and that this can inhibit as well as expand their volitional engagement.

Peers influence on young people's literate identities

Children and young people's social networks also have a strong influence on individuals' identities, and can shape their relationship with reading (e.g. McFarland and Pals, 2005; Protacio, 2019). This has rarely been documented specifically in relation to writing. Young people often choose particular literacy practices as a means of identity formation and cultural participation in their peer groups (Brady, 2017; Cremin and Swann, 2017; Ivey and Johnston, 2023), so understanding the ways in which they position themselves as readers and writers can help to illuminate why some do not choose to volitionally read or write. In one case study of teenage English language learners, the students found themselves either being positioned or positioning themselves as 'outsiders', the 'same' or 'disengaged' readers in their peer group. This had consequences for their reading opportunities and the extent of their reading engagement with their peers (Protacio, 2019). Such work highlights that the construction of social connections with peers serves to impact upon the creation and flux of young people's identities as readers. Through researching the perspectives of 13–14-year-olds, Sellers (2019) identified four categories of readers, each of which significantly influenced the adolescents' reading habits in their various social groups, as follows:

- *Resistant* readers were affected by the dominant view of reading as something that is individual. This involved reading books in isolation. Consequently, they viewed reading as anti-social and resisted reading for fear of being socially excluded and seen as 'uncool'.
- *Indifferent* readers viewed reading as non-social and while they did not see that as a problem, felt they didn't have time for it and more social activities took priority.
- *Outsider* readers used reading to actively position themselves in opposition to norms.

- *Social* readers experienced reading as social activity integral to their social participation as their peer group were reading and talking about books.

Viewed in terms of identity formation, the reading practices of these adolescents indicate the potential for positive social influence on their reader identities. But more research is needed to explore the instantiation of this in schools and classrooms where strong cultures of reading prevail and to discern the shaping influence of peers on young people's identities and practices as readers and writers. Dyson's (e.g. 2001, 2009, 2013, 2020) body of work has shown that many young writers value working alongside each other, co-authoring, appropriating and recontextualising the practices endorsed by their teachers, although her work does not explicitly take an identity lens. Compton-Lily's (2025) longitudinal work tracing the literacy identity shifts of one boy over 15 years reveals the significant fluidity involved, and, depending on the conceptual identity lens used, the different ways James' identity can be viewed. More longitudinal ethnographic research focused on students' identities as writers, and the influence of others in homes and classrooms, is needed. Young people's writer identities have a significant role to play in their volitional engagement in writing.

Motivating reading and writing for pleasure

Whilst there is a long history of research into the relationship between reading motivation and achievement, this has mainly been undertaken from a psychological perspective with attention to reading as a cognitive process. There is less research around writing motivation, but increasingly in both fields, as conceptions of reading and writing have broadened, more attention has been paid to the shaping influence of social cultural practices. Young people are motivated to read and write for multiple reasons, often related to their own goals, purposes and interests and those accepted from others. Drawing on a review of studies from 2003 to 2013, Conradi Smith et al. (2013) define reading motivation as:

> The drive to read resulting from a comprehensive set of an individual's beliefs about, attitudes toward, and goals for reading.
>
> *(Conradi Smith et al., 2013, p. 154)*

Individuals may be intrinsically motivated (e.g. by a desire for involvement, self-expression and curiosity), extrinsically motivated (e.g. by the desire to compete, be recognised and receive high grades) and also socially motivated (e.g. by a desire to be connected to others and enabled to make meanings with and through social interaction). Many researchers in the field make use of Self Determination Theory (SDT) (Deci and Ryan, 1980, 2000; Ryan and Deci, 2000, 2017) to understand the development of the desire to read. This theory suggests that for optimal human functioning, people are driven by three core psychological needs: autonomy, competence and relatedness. Applying this to reading and writing, it is clear pupils need a high degree of agency, volition and choice (autonomy), a sense of self-efficacy and a positive literacy identity (competence), and that they need to feel part of a network of readers and writers with whom they can connect (relatedness). This trio of needs are inter-related, such that feelings of competence will not enhance intrinsic motivation unless accompanied by a sense of autonomy and relatedness. Linking to SDT, researchers of literacy motivation often stress the difference between autonomous or self-determined motivation and controlled motivation. The former involves choice and volition, whereas controlled motivation involves an external expectation or an internal sense of compulsion (Assor et al., 2004). The autonomous motivation to write is seen to decrease with age (De Smedt et al., 2020), which, the researchers argue, may be linked to an increase in controlled motivation, as writing instruction in schools focuses more on the production of specified outcomes. This study, like many others in the area, stresses the value of young people being offered agency and choice as literacy learners.

Reading motivation

Turning specifically to reading motivation, the research evidence indicates that the intrinsic motivation to read is more closely associated with reading frequency and skill than extrinsic motivation (e.g. Baker and Wigfield, 1999; Becker et al., 2010; Hebbecker et al., 2019; Marinak et al., 2015; McGeown et al., 2012, 2016; Miyamoto et al., 2018; Orkin et al., 2017; Wang and Guthrie, 2004). Even at the early stages of learning to read, it is argued that intrinsic motivation and reading competence are reciprocal and mutually reinforce each other (Schiefele et al., 2016) and studies of readers in later years mostly affirm this. For example, one study with 10–14-years-olds (n:8,960) revealed that readers' intrinsic motivation and perceived competence, alongside teacher-reported classroom engagement, combined to predict reading achievement at 14 years (Froiland and Oros, 2014). Another study longitudinally showed that a high decline in students' intrinsic reading motivation is associated with a smaller growth of reading proficiency between primary and early secondary schooling (Miyamoto et al., 2020). Drawing on their research, Hebbecker et al. (2019) recommend that teachers should be supported to understand the relevance and potential of:

> Positive reading experiences and performance feedback to strengthen positive effects on students' intrinsic reading motivation … [They also note] Performance feedback should support autonomy to promote intrinsic motivation to learn, to encourage rich engagement with reading, and to give students the feeling of competence.
>
> *(Hebbecker et al., 2019, p. 431)*

Whilst some studies have found that extrinsic reading motivation may be advantageous if coupled with high levels of intrinsic motivation (McGeown et al., 2012; Park, 2011; Wang and Guthrie, 2004), others have found it can detrimentally affect reading comprehension (Schaffner et al., 2013) and is negatively associated with reading skills (McGeown et al., 2016). However, findings depend on the measures of motivation deployed in each study. Exploring the impact of a summer remedial reading intervention, designed to motivate disengaged readers (aged 7–10-years), the research team, drawing on SDT, undertook a randomised control trial (Orkin et al., 2017). In the intervention group, the children's intrinsic need for autonomy, competence, meaning and belonging was well supported, whereas for those children in the control group it was not. This made a marked difference not only to the frequency of the children in the intervention group's reading engagement behaviours, but also to their comprehension in the post-test. In contrast, the control group's reading avoidance behaviours remained largely the same, even when they were offered extrinsic motivational strategies, such as gold stars, stickers and other material rewards for reading (Orkin et al., 2017).

The relative impacts of different dimensions of intrinsic motivation have been examined and highlight that for younger primary age children 'involvement' is closely related to recreational reading (Schiefele and Löweke, 2018; Stutz et al., 2017). Another study, using an adapted version of the Motivation to Read Questionnaire (MRQ) (Wigfield and Guthrie, 1997), found that the intrinsic dimensions of 'involvement' (the desire to experience positive feeling states such as getting lost in a story or experience imaginative actions) and 'challenge' (the desire to master complex texts) predicted the reading of fiction books (McGeown et al., 2016). In contrast, 'curiosity' (the desire to learn more about topics of one's interest) and 'challenge' predicted the reading of factual texts. However, in a meta-analysis of school-based reading interventions, McBreen and Savage (2023) found that none of the interventions reported in the studies they examined made a significant difference to children's intrinsic motivation to read. They hypothesise that this may have been due to the obligatory nature of school-based interventions, making it harder to discern children's volitional engagement. Nonetheless, the interventions did impact positively on the perceived value of reading in the children's eyes. This highlights the challenge for educators who seek to nurture children's autonomy and pleasure in reading in regulated environments where reading is required.

Looking across the body of predominantly quantitative research studies focused on reading motivation, substantial evidence is offered about some of the factors involved in choosing to read. Whilst these studies tend to lack the openness, nuance and contextual details afforded by qualitative studies, the findings around the importance of intrinsic motivation and 'involvement' align well with those of qualitative and mixed-methods research exploring readers' motivation. In addition, new questionnaires measuring motivation have been developed, offering alternatives to the MRQ (Wigfield and Guthrie, 1997) which was used for many years. For example, Schüller et al. (2017), basing their questionnaire on 'the theory of planned behaviour' (Ajzen, 1985, 1991), emphasise the importance of environmental motivators, such as access to a setting amenable to reading, the absence of competing alternative activities that one would miss out on by reading and, as others have found, the importance of reading to relieve boredom (e.g. Nippold et al., 2005; Schiefele et al., 2016). Another study also highlights that environmental factors impact on adolescents' levels of reading motivation (Neugebauer and Gilmour, 2020) and further underscores the value of deploying practices based on SDT (Deci and Ryan, 1980; Ryan and Deci, 2000, 2017). In this mixed methods work, multi-level modelling, combined with observations in context, captured dynamic understandings of students' reading motivation. The researchers assert that irrespective of the content area or the characteristics of students, the way in which the classroom is organised socially, the nature of the texts and readers' interpersonal preferences influence students' daily motivation to read (Neugebauer and Gilmour, 2020).

The social dimensions of reading motivation have begun to receive increased attention in recent years, often linked to the concept of relatedness in Ryan and Deci's work (2000) and to wider understandings of literacy as social practice (e.g. Brice-Heath, 1983; Street,

1998). Historically, whilst this aspect was recognised in the MRQ (Wigfield and Guthrie, 1997), it was not always evident in later studies, and in Schiefele et al.'s (2012) review of papers in the field, the sociality which exists around reading was absent. Nonetheless, reading for pleasure is a social as well as a solitary practice, and several newer studies recognise that children may be socially motivated to read, driven and encouraged by their relationships or desire for connections with others – whether peers or adults (e.g. Barber and Klauda, 2020; Cantrell et al., 2017; Cremin et al., 2024; Ivey and Johnston, 2013, 2023; Klauda and Wigfield, 2012; Merga, 2017; Neugebauer and Gilmour, 2020; Wilhelm, 2016). As the seminal definition of reader engagement notes, engaged readers are

> Motivated to read, strategic in their approaches to comprehending what they read, knowledgeable in their construction of meaning from text, and socially interactive while reading.
>
> *(Guthrie et al., 2012, p. 602)*

For instance, in a study of the reading motivation of over 1,100 young people, Merga (2017) found that 64 per cent agreed that someone had exerted a significant positive influence on their attitudes towards reading and some typologies of reading for pleasure make detailed reference to the social activation of children's identities and activities (Alexander and Jarman, 2018; Wilhelm et al., 2013; Wilhelm, 2016). Other research has drawn attention to the importance of reading experiences that are shared, relevant and enjoyable and support the reader's identity so as to lead to engagement and potential enjoyment of reading (Barber and Klauda, 2020; Cantrell et al., 2017; Cremin et al., 2009).

To summarise, this body of literature produces well-evidenced claims that the experience of involvement, curiosity and autonomy are essential dimensions of reading motivation and that social and environmental contexts also influence whether children choose to read in their own time.

Writing motivation

Writing motivation has been defined as '[t]he variety of reasons a child may choose to engage in a writing task or decide to take steps to avoid that task' (Wright et al., 2020, p. 153). The interaction between motivation and writing is acknowledged to be complex; it is connected to writing skills, attitudes to writing, a sense of self-efficacy, interest levels, apprehension levels, as well as behaviours relating to both interest and apprehension. It also encompasses the values, goals and dispositions that students bring to any given act of writing, whether self-chosen or set by others (Boscolo and Gelati, 2019). These will be shaped over time as students engage in writing in different contexts. In a review of empirical studies, Graham (2006) underscored this point, that the data on the relationships between writing skills, positive attitudes towards writing and self-efficacy are highly nuanced. Research in this area shows a mixed situation, with self-efficacy seen to decrease with age in some studies, but remain consistent in others. Indeed, in more recent research into attitudes towards writing, Graham (2020) found that the attitudes of younger writers (6–7-year-olds) did not predict their writing performance, whereas for slightly older writers (8–9-year-olds) their attitudes towards writing did impact on their writing performance. Nonetheless, overall, the data appears to show that there are differences in motivation between more and less skilled writers, with more skilled writers unsurprisingly experiencing both a stronger desire to write and more self-efficacy.

The complex interplay between motivational and cognitive challenges related to children's writing performance is also seen in a large-scale Belgian study of 10–12-year-olds (n:1,500) (De Smedt et al., 2018). These researchers found that autonomous writing motivation made a positive contribution to students' writing performance. Such motivation is a combination of intrinsic and internalised motivation, demonstrated by a young writer being personally invested in their writing and not simply undertaking it because of external pressure or expectation. Additionally, De Smedt et al. (2020) show that students who were more self-efficacious concerning the regulation of their own writing processes, applied more thinking, planning, revision and control strategies, and that this supported their writing development. In a Portuguese study which focused on different motivational profiles and writing performance of students aged 11–12 (n:212), Camacho et al. (2023) found that some students reported a 'growth mindset' (the ability to adapt, often positively associated with self-efficacy and mastery goals) and that these children were less concerned with performance in writing. Others, however, held a more 'fixed mindset' and were more orientated towards performance-related goals. The former group wrote better quality opinion texts and achieved higher grades than those young people with a fixed mindset. The researchers also compared the students' actual writing performance, self-reported and teacher-reported writing performance, with each strand reflecting higher scores for those with a growth mindset. Their argument and the findings from De Smedt et al. (2018) support the notion of offering choice and agency in writing, and the importance of encouraging teachers to develop autonomy-oriented practices to nurture volitional writing and positive writer identities. The environment too makes a significant difference, as Slavin et al. (2019) state:

> Perhaps more than any other subject writing demands a supportive environment, in which students want to become better writers because they love the opportunity to express themselves, and to interact in writing with valued peers and teachers.
>
> *(Slavin et al., 2019)*

In sum, looking across the research into children's literacy motivation, it can be argued that those young people who are intrinsically motivated to read and/or write are more likely to hold positive attitudes to these literacy practices, be volitionally driven by their own purposes and interests, and have positive self-efficacy as readers and/or writers. They are also likely to identify as readers and/or writers and position themselves and be positioned in this way by others, in other words they are more likely to hold positive literacy identities. They show competence, autonomy and relatedness (Ryan and Deci, 2000, 2017). Linking also to the reader engagement studies of Lee et al. (2021) and McGeown and Conradi Smith (2024), it is argued that these intrinsically motivated young people are frequently capable, reflexive readers and/or writers who use strategies to support them (cognitive engagement), they are keen to read and/or write in their own time (behavioural engagement), and are emotionally invested in and connected to their reading and/or writing (affective engagement). They are also likely to share their views and experiences as readers and writers with others (socially engagement). Young people who are intrinsically motivated to read and write find pleasure in the experience through their active engagement as readers and writers (see Figure 4.1).

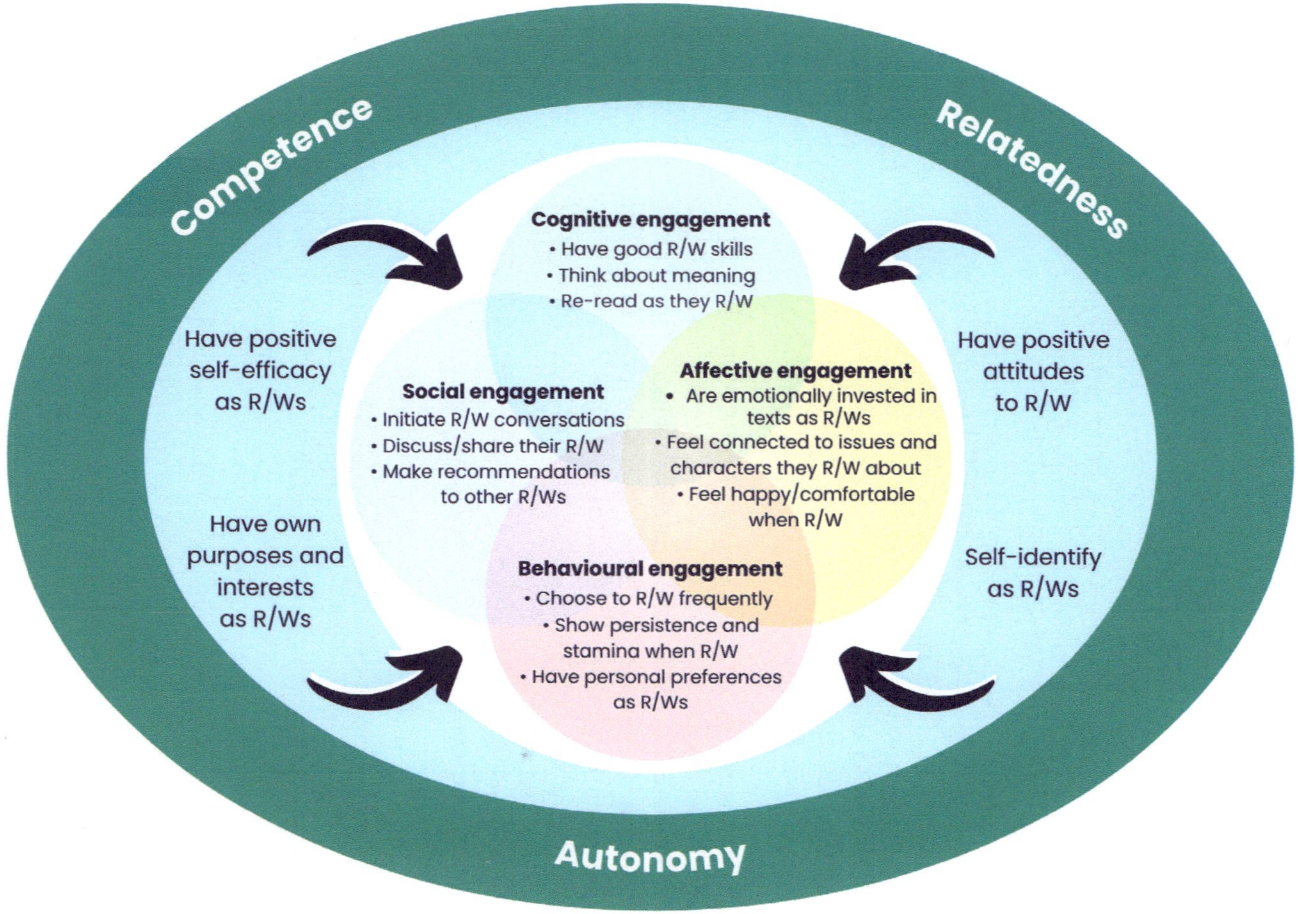

FIGURE 4.1 Intrinsically motivated and engaged readers and writers

Studies in this area, of both reading and writing, highlight that motivation is not fixed; it represents 'a fluctuating function of classroom practice' (Neugebauer, 2016) and, like readers' and writers' identities, is always influenced by the text and the wider social context in which their engagement occurs. Studies also highlight the significance of young people's intrinsic motivation and their need for autonomy, competence and relatedness.

Young people's autonomy, competence and relatedness

As noted earlier, to understand what motivates children to read, researchers often use SDT (Deci and Ryan, 1980, 2000; Ryan and Deci, 2000, 2017). Although other theoretical frameworks are deployed in examining reader motivation, including, for instance, the reading engagement model (Guthrie and Wigfield, 2000), SDT is more commonly used. Applied to motivating readers, SDT highlights the significance of readers' agency and the autonomy to exercise it, the need for a sense of self-efficacy and success as a reader, and to feel connected socially to others through reading. The value of pedagogy which explicitly addresses these needs has been shown to motivate reading in primary aged children (e.g. De Naeghel et al., 2012; Orkin et al., 2017) and in adolescents (e.g. De Naeghel et al., 2014; Neugebauer and Gilmour, 2020). It has also been used in professional development contexts (Kennedy and Shiel, 2010). Furthermore, a study of university students' memories of reading underscores the significance of these psychological needs (Zare et al., 2023). The students' memories of classroom practices that combined all three strands of SDT 'were vividly recalled as positive. In contrast, participants expressed feelings of frustration when these psychological needs were not met' (Zare et al., 2023, p. 271).

In seeking to understand the literacy practices of 9–11-year-olds (n:69) beyond the school gate, Cummings et al. (2018) employed a mixed methods approach linked to SDT (Ryan and Deci, 2000) and revealed a range of motivations and factors influenced the children's engagement with literacy. These included: communication, family practices, social relatedness, participation, identity and a desire for autonomy and competence. As they summarise:

> Engaging with traditional print, new technologies and social networks create feelings of flow and meet children's needs for autonomy, competence and relatedness. These positive experiences support children's motivation and engagement in literacy-related activities in their leisure time.
>
> *(Cummings et al., 2018, p. 113)*

Focusing specifically on the trio of autonomy, competence and relatedness, De Naeghel et al. (2014) argue that attending to each creates 'an optimally motivating classroom climate' for reading (p. 1549). Later, the research team tested this out through a teacher workshop which concentrated on the development of an autonomy-supportive stance, alongside structured teacher behaviours (De Naeghel et al., 2016). The practitioners were encouraged to make more reading activities explicitly autonomy-supportive (e.g. offering support for text choices, setting time aside for reading independently, highlighting the relevance of reading in daily life), while also offering structure (e.g. making reading expectations clear, offering reading challenges for optimal and positive feedback). This approach appeared to successfully promote 10–11-year-old boys' recreational reading motivation (De Naeghel et al., 2016).

Drawing on different conceptual lenses and terms, other qualitative studies similarly identify agency, assurance and reader relationships as critical to the development of recreational readers (e.g. Cremin et al., 2014; Cummings et al., 2018; Ivey and Johnston, 2013; Kennedy, 2018; Moses and Kelly, 2018, 2019). These investigations all affirm the impact of offering increased agency, supporting the development of readers' assurance, and making connections through a socially oriented ethos and environment. So, research examining these three concepts and the ways in which they motivate readers and writers is now examined.

Autonomy

When control in the classroom is shared by teachers and students, this has been seen to lead to increased intrinsic motivation, participation and enthusiasm for learning (Zhou et al., 2009). This also applies within the domain of recreational reading. Researchers have documented the ways in which young people's views about reading are sought, and the positive consequences when they are enabled to shape and own their experience of reading (e.g. Ivey and Johnston, 2013; Kennedy, 2018; McGeown et al., 2020b; Ng, 2018; Nolen, 2007; Reedy and De Carvalho, 2021; Webber et al., 2022). For example, in one UK class of 9–10-year-olds, the children made it clear that they valued the freedom they had at home to choose what they wished to read for their own purposes, and that they preferred quiet, comfortable reading environments with few distractions (Reedy and De Carvalho, 2021). When their teacher made responsive changes, the class had more autonomy as readers and were far more motivated to read.

Researching teenagers' recreational reading, Ivey and Johnston (2013) also found that over the course of a year, as teachers stepped back from delivering more traditional English lessons with a set class reader, this enhanced students' autonomy. The young people could choose personally meaningful texts, read at their own pace, discuss books with whom they wished and, as a result, became far more motivated and engaged as readers. These scholars argue that over time the adolescents showed increased assurance in talking about texts and a 'newfound confidence' in voicing their views in other contexts too (p. 263). Young readers' autonomy is bolstered by the opportunities offered to them or created by them, to exert a sense of ownership over their reading and to engage agentically in ways that they find valuable. This agency and autonomy as readers is closely related to their beliefs in their own ability – their self-efficacy, sense of mastery and reader identities (Adelson et al., 2019). The significance of this is underscored by classroom-based studies which Ivey and Friddle (2025) summarise when stating that: 'Positive reading identities appear to develop, fueled by student agency, in classroom contexts that prioritize meaningfulness for students, even for those with long histories of reading difficulty' (Ivey and Friddle, 2025).

Such studies indicate that when teachers develop detailed knowledge of children's literate identities, become more attuned to their difficulties and dispositions, and prioritise a more learner-led, autonomy-focused offer, this motivates children's engagement (Cremin et al., 2014, 2024; Cummings et al., 2018; Ivey and Johnston, 2023; Reedy and De Carvalho, 2021). As Cummings et al. (2018) found, teachers' autonomy-focused support and personal interest is highly significant in motivating children to read. Furthermore, teachers who invest in getting to know their young readers often enable children to exert their rights as readers and foster a sense of autonomy in and through their provision, which in some cases results in 'pedagogies of re-connection' (Comber and Kamler, 2004). Such pedagogies draw on young people's literate identities and practices beyond school, enabling them to develop relational reading connections with their teacher and motivating them to engage in the social acts of reading and writing. This is seen to impact upon their competence and self-efficacy.

In relation to writing, greater autonomy and more choice in writing are frequently noted within empirical studies and reviews of approaches to writing that fuel self-efficacy (Graham et al., 2017). Autonomy is also often linked to the teaching of self-regulation (Pajares and Valiante, 2006; Wright et al., 2019). Helping young people to reflect on and understand their challenges as they negotiate the writing process, and to strategically cope with their problems, shifts control from the teacher to the student, thus increasing their autonomy and authorial agency. Nonetheless challenges exist, since as Wright et al. (2019, p. 64) argue, young people's agency and autonomy as writers reduces when the curriculum becomes more subject oriented, and they are 'required to produce discipline-specific texts'.

In one study, following their teachers' engagement in a writing retreat, young people, aged 9–13 years, experienced increased opportunities for choice and control as writers (Cremin et al., 2020; Myhill et al., 2023). This was enabled through a range of writing approaches, including for example free writing and content selection – the expectation to conform to a given topic and genre was removed. The young people commented that they valued this way of working which encouraged them to feel more free and more creative when approaching writing, and several commented on 'owning' their own writing. The opportunities offered to them to exercise their agency and ownership as authors and share their writing in the supportive social environments appeared to reshape their experience of writing, triggering more positive attitudes and a stronger desire to write.

The impact of increased autonomy on children's attitudes to writing is also evidenced in the ethnographic longitudinal work of Nolen (2007), who tracked the views of 6–9-year-olds (n:67) and their teachers from two primary schools over three years. Nolen (2007) drew on interviews and observations and showed that the constraints and affordances of each teacher's methods shaped the young people's motivation to write. Some approaches were predominantly teacher-directed, teacher-owned and with structured writing tasks, whereas other teachers developed more collaborative student-centred workshop style approaches. The latter involved children making their own choices in topic and style and extensive sharing of their writing with each other and their parents. This approach, which foregrounded their agency as authors, promoted children's intrinsic motivation and engagement in writing and raised awareness of writing as a key element of the social life of the classroom (Nolen, 2007). In addition to increasing the children's creative choice and control of their writing, Nolen (2007) noted the importance of developing a classroom community and sense of identity and purpose in and through writing. This is connected to other research in which authentic real-world writing which was autonomously chosen was seen to enhance student motivation (Bruning and Horn, 2000; Hidi and Boscolo, 2006).

Competence and self-efficacy

Reading competence is closely related to reading self-efficacy, which is recognised by some researchers as a dimension of motivation (e.g. Guthrie et al., 1999), and develops in response to the lived experience of reading. Children's competence and self-efficacy represents a critical element of young people's sense of self as readers. Those whose teachers rate them more highly as readers and thus have higher sense of received self-efficacy and positive reader identities report that they enjoy reading more than their less confident peers (Adelson et al., 2019). In a study of 7–8-year-olds, Vaknin-Nusbaum et al. (2018) found that those who began the school year with low levels of reading achievement became less motivated over time; their self-concepts as readers declined, this was despite retaining an awareness of the value of reading. Conversely, when students experience success, receive positive affirmation about their views about a text for instance, and are positioned and recognised as readers by adults and their peers, this supports the development of enhanced self-efficacy, self-competence and confidence (De Naeghel et al., 2012; Kennedy, 2018). In turn, this not only increases their willingness and ability to discuss texts (Hall, 2012b; Ho and Lau, 2018; Moses and Kelly, 2018), but also supports their wider learning.

Research indicates that enabling students to participate in literature discussion groups (Venegas, 2018), scaffolding children's book choices (Weber, 2018) and offering pre-reading support when the chosen book is beyond a child's reading level (Kennedy, 2018) can all increase the self-efficacy of less engaged or assured readers, as well as offering positive messages, guidance and feedback about their effectiveness (De Naeghel et al., 2012, 2014). Reading with therapy dogs has also been seen to support the development of children's confidence, reading skills and self-efficacy (Noble and Holt, 2018), and, in this small-scale study, contributed to improvements in their willingness to read. Studies in this area tend to focus on individual routes to develop a stronger sense of personal self-efficacy, but given the shaping influence of the social context, more research which explicitly examines the social construction of individual readers' self-efficacy would be valuable.

As noted earlier, the motivation to write, shaped by children's attitudes to writing and sense of self-efficacy as a writer, predicts writing performance (Graham et al., 2017), so paying attention to their writer identities is essential. Indeed, as Zumbrunn et al. (2017) states:

> The beliefs students have about themselves as writers matter, as do their beliefs about the writing process.
>
> *(Zumbrunn et al., 2017, p. 667)*

Drawing on reviews of studies of writer identity, both Collier (2010) and Pajares and Valiante (2006), argue that some writing practices appear to nurture competent writer identities for more students; these practices, the reviews assert, are more inclusive and supportive of developing strong writing self-efficacy beliefs and positive attitudes to writing, thus potentially influencing children's volitional engagement. Collier (2010) asserts these practices include valuing students' choices for content, genre and preferences, and offering time for teacher–student dialogues and peer support. Pajares and Valiante (2006) conclude that autonomy, choice and collaboration matter and note the value of self-regulation development, less competitive writing environments, effective modelling and engagement in meaningful writing activities. The work of Graham and Harris (2016), drawing on meta reviews, additionally suggests that the degree to which young people's strengths are made visible to them through feedback and praise also shapes their self-efficacy and writing motivation. This has also been noted in classroom case studies (Cremin and Baker, 2010).

Furthermore, the relationship between children's motives for writing, self-efficacy and time spent on writing has also been explored (Ng et al., 2021). Using questionnaire responses from 9–10-year-olds (n:619) in Shanghai and Hong Kong, Ng et al. constructed four pathways to illustrate how varying motives for writing interacted with each other before interacting with and impacting on self-efficacy and time spent choosing to write. These pathways prioritised four key motives for writing: social recognition, curiosity, competition and grades. Overall, the pathway that prioritised grades was seen to align best with the responses of the children against a writing motivation questionnaire. However, reflecting the complex relationship between writing motivation, self-efficacy and writing behaviours, Ng et al. (2021) noted further complexity in the data. Specifically, they observed that individual's different motivation levels led to different motives for writing being prioritised. Highly motivated writers, for instance, held multiple motives for writing. In contrast, averagely motivated writers cared about curiosity and weakly motivated writers were focused on grades.

Relatedness

Supporting young people's need for relatedness, connection to and acceptance by others has also been seen to motivate recreational reading. This has been studied with peers (Sellers, 2019), parents (Merga and Ledger, 2018), librarians (Cremin and Swann, 2017; Merga and Ferguson, 2021), and teachers (Cockroft and Atkinson, 2017; Cremin et al., 2014; De Naeghel et al., 2014; Ivey and Johnston, 2013, 2023; Merga, 2020a; Neugebauer and Gilmour, 2020). The motivating power of para-belonging, which can develop though readers' engagement with series book characters, offers another dimension to relatedness in reading (Gabriel and Young, 2011). Collectively these studies indicate the motivational value of young readers connecting socially and imaginatively to others, interacting about texts, about reading and being a reader, and thus building relational connections.

In particular, research in this area highlights the significance of teacher involvement, and the extent to which adults invest in their relationships with young people as readers, offering acceptance, showing interest and making connections with them. In De Naeghel et al.'s (2014) study, through multi-level modelling based on a survey of 4,269 Flemish 15-year-olds, these researchers found that perceived teacher involvement in reading was more strongly associated with students' intrinsic reading motivation than autonomy or competence, although all these factors were significant. In commenting on the impact of personal relationships around reading, the research team note:

> Teachers investing personal resources, expressing affection, and enjoying time with students are interpersonally involved and thus support students' need for relatedness with teachers and peers.
>
> *(De Naeghel et al., 2014, p. 1549)*

Additionally, in an intervention study that aimed to help disengaged adolescent readers, Cockroft and Atkinson (2017) found that when their teachers got to know them as readers and enabled the young people to explore and challenge their own ambivalence towards reading, this impacted positively on the time they spent reading. The students perceived that in the process their self-efficacy and confidence as readers improved. The predictive power of teacher relatedness on children's reader self-concept and motivation has also been tracked in studies with kindergarten children through structural equation modelling (Guay et al., 2019) and with older primary aged learners (Neugebauer and Gilmour, 2020). In the latter case, the researchers show that focused interpersonal connections and reading relationships with teachers nurtured the children's desire to read (Neugebauer and Gilmour, 2020). Their work indicates that higher levels of reading motivation are associated with contexts in which teachers and adolescent readers interact in one-to-one or in small groups, not in whole-class contexts, and they note that these 'more intimate and tailored interactions with teachers supported students' motivation with text' (Neugebauer and Gilmour, 2020, p. 357). Some researchers also observe that teacher involvement is evidenced through professionals' positioning themselves as adult readers alongside the young, allowing interactive and reciprocal reader-to-reader relationships to develop that are less hierarchical than more traditional conceived teacher–pupil relationships (e.g. Cremin et al., 2014; Merga, 2020b). See Chapter 7 for a fuller discussion.

Turning to writing, the research evidence indicates that the social context and the degree of agency offered to children are key to their motivation to write. In turn these connections can help create a sense of belonging and community. In studies in which writing was observed to be an important part of the conversational ethos of classrooms (e.g. Collier, 2017; Myhill et al., 2023), children were observed to express a degree of interest and enjoyment in each other's writing, and writing became something to do with friends. In the latter study, the young people valued the opportunities to work with writing buddies and with talk partners. Their teachers, positioned alongside them as writers, enabled the development of more relaxed writing cultures that facilitated connections between everyone in the collaborative writing communities which developed. In a study of teenagers who choose to participate in creative writing opportunities, within and beyond school, Magnifico (2013) found the young people she studied were driven by the desire to explore ideas together. Whilst they drew on life, others' stories and texts, each wrote to express their emotions and personal experiences and to reflect upon their identities. In different ways, each subverted the norms of the context to explore their lives through writing and through conversations with their peers.

These studies indicate that when children can select subjects that are personally purposeful and offer a high degree of autonomy or agency as authors *and* they are enabled to connect to their friends, peers and teachers through the social experience of writing, they are more motivated to write. As Slavin et al.'s (2019) review of writing intervention studies also indicates:

> If students love to write, because their peers as well as their teachers are eager to see what they have to say, then they will write with energy and pleasure. Perhaps more than any other subject, writing demands a supportive environment, in which students want to become better writers because they love the opportunity to express themselves, and to interact in writing with valued peers and teachers.
>
> *(Slavin et al., 2019, p. 26)*

In his 'writer(s)-within-community' model of writing, Graham (2018) recognises both the salience of the writers, their collaborators and what they bring to the act of writing, as well as the wider community, that is the social and cultural context in which the writing occurs. This aligns to Myhill et al.'s argument that more research is needed that recognises 'motivation is not simply an internal characteristic of an individual but is situated within the context of a community of writers' (2023, p. 14).

In sum, the research literature linked to SDT indicates the importance of developing young people's autonomy and assurance as literate individuals, nurturing their self-efficacy through positive feedback and close attention to each unique reader's and writer's interests and identity. It also suggests that fostering young people's relational connections to their peers as readers and writers will support their desire to read and write. Additionally, the evidence base indicates that when teachers step back organisationally and reduce their control over literacy, are open to learning about the young people as readers and writers and act responsively, they tend to create autonomy supportive contexts which foster volitional engagement in literacy.

Conclusion

To summarise, young people's literate identities are seen to play a key role in their desire to read and write in their own time, influencing their volitional engagement. Studies of children's motivation to read and write indicate reinforcing and positive relationships between intrinsic motivation, self-efficacy and literacy attainment. Those young people who perceive themselves to be – at least to some degree – autonomous, competent and connected to other readers and writers appear to be motivated to sustain their engagement in these practices in their own time. Increased attention arguably needs to be paid to children's literate identities within and beyond the classroom, and support offered to nurture their autonomy, competence and relatedness as readers and writers.

References

Adelson, J.L., Cash, K.M., Pittard, C.M., Sherretz, C.E., Possel, P. and Blackburn, A.D. (2019) 'Measuring reading self-perceptions and enjoyment: Development and psychometric properties of the reading and me survey', *Journal of Advanced Academics*, 30(3), pp. 355–380.

Ajzen, I. (1985) 'From intentions to actions: A theory of planned behaviour', in Kuhl, J. and Beckmann, J. (eds), *Action Control: From Cognition to Behaviour*, Berlin: Springer, pp. 11–39.

Ajzen, I. (1991) 'The theory of planned behaviour', *Organisational Behaviour and Human Decision Processes*, 50(2), pp. 179–211.

Alexander, J. and Jarman, R. (2018) 'The pleasures of reading non-fiction', *Literacy*, 52(2), pp. 78–85.

Assor, A., Roth, G. and Deci, E.L. (2004) 'The emotional costs of parents' conditional regard: A self-determination theory analysis', *Journal of Personality*, 72(1), pp. 47–88.

Auguste, E. (2018) 'The balancing act of kindergarten writing instruction', *Educational Leadership*, 75(7), pp.61–64.

Baker, L. and Wigfield, A. (1999) 'Dimensions of children's motivation for reading and their relations to reading activity and reading achievement', *Reading Research Quarterly*, 34(4), pp. 452–477.

Barber, A.T. and Klauda, S.L. (2020) 'How reading motivation and engagement enable reading achievement: Policy implications', *Policy Insights from the Behavioral and Brain Sciences*, 7(1), pp. 27–34.

Becker, M., McElvany, N. and Kortenbruck, M. (2010) 'Intrinsic and extrinsic reading motivation as predictors of reading literacy: A longitudinal study', *Journal of Educational Psychology*, 102(4), pp. 773–785.

Boscolo, P. and Gelati, C. (2019) 'Motivating writers', in Graham, S., MacArthur, C.A. and Hebert, M.A. (eds), *Best Practices in Writing Instruction*, New York: Guilford Press, pp. 51–78.

Bourne, J. (2002) '"Oh, what will Miss say!": Constructing texts and identities in the discursive processes of classroom writing', *Language and Education*, 16(4), pp. 241–259.

Brady, J. (2017) 'Being in the world: Students writing identities beyond school', in Cremin, T. and Locke, T. (eds), *Writer Identity and the Teaching and Learning of Writing*, London and New York: Routledge, pp. 151–168.

Brice-Heath, S. (1983) *Ways with Words: Language, Life and Work in Communities and Classrooms*, Cambridge: Cambridge University Press.

Bruning, R. and Horn, C. (2000) 'Developing motivation to write', *Educational Psychologist*, 35 (1), pp. 25–37.

Camacho, A., De Smedt, F., Maoi, R., Cadmia, J., Van Keer, H. and Alves, R.A. (2023) 'Writing motivation profiles and their association with writing performance: A person-centered approach', *Topics in Language Disorders*, 43(2), pp. 169–186.

Cantrell, S.C., Pennington, J., Rintamaa, M., Osborne, M., Parker, C. and Rudd, M. (2017) 'Supplemental literacy instruction in high school: What students say matters for reading engagement', *Reading and Writing Quarterly*, 33(1), pp. 54–70.

Chamberlain, L. (2019) 'Places, spaces and local customs: Honouring the private worlds of out-of-school text creation', *Literacy*, 53(1), pp. 39–45.

Clark, C., Osborne, S. and Akerman, R. (2008) *Young People's Self-Perceptions as Readers: An Investigation Including Family, Peer and School Influences*, London: National Literacy Trust.

Clark, C., Bonafede, F., Picton, I. and Cole, A. (2023) *Children and Young People's Writing in 2023*, London: National Literacy Trust.

Clarkson, R. (2024) '"It's missing the heart of what writing is about": Teachers' interpretations of writing assessment criteria', *British Educational Research Journal*, 50(1), pp. 134–161.

Cliff-Hodges, G. (2018) 'Rivers of reading: A research method to explore young adults' personal reading histories', in Arizpe, E. and Cliff-Hodges, G. (eds), *Young People Reading: Empirical Research across International Contexts*, London: Routledge, pp. 55–70.

Cockroft, C. and Atkinson, C. (2017) '"I just find it boring": Findings from an affective adolescent reading intervention', *Support for Learning*, 32(1), pp. 41–59.

Collier, D.R. (2010) 'Journey to becoming a writer: Review of research about children's identities as writers', *Language and Literacy*, 12(1), pp. 147–164.

Collier, D. (2017) 'Glancing sideways at young writers becoming', in Cremin, T. and Locke, T. (eds), *Writer Identity and the Teaching and Learning of Writing*, London: Routledge, pp. 169–183.

Comber, B. and Kamler, B. (2004) 'Getting out of deficit: Pedagogies of reconnection', *Teaching Education*, 15(3), pp. 293–310.

Compton-Lily, C. (2025) 'Reading identities and recreational reading', in Cremin, T. and McGeown, S. (eds) *Reading for Pleasure: International Perspectives*, London and New York: Routledge.

Conradi Smith, K., Jang, B.G., Bryant, C., Craft, A. and McKenna, M.C. (2013) 'Measuring adolescents' attitudes toward reading', *Journal of Adolescent and Adult Literacy*, 56(7), pp. 565–576.

Cremin, T. and Baker, S. (2010) 'Exploring teacher-writer identities in the classroom: Conceptualising the struggle', *English Teaching: Practice and Critique*, 9(3), pp. 8–25.

Cremin, T. and Myhill, D. (2012) *Writing Voices: Creating Communities of Writers*, London: Routledge

Cremin, T. and Swann, J. (2017) 'School librarians as leaders of extracurricular reading groups', in Pihl, J., van der Kooij, K. and Carlsten, T. (eds), *Teacher and Librarian Partnerships in Literacy Education in the 21st Century*, Rotterdam: Sense Publishers, pp. 119–137.
Cremin, T., Bearne, E., Mottram, M. and Goodwin, P. (2009) 'Teachers as readers in the 21st century', in Styles, M. and Arizpe, E. (eds), *Acts of Reading: Teachers, Text and Childhood*, Staffordshire: Trentham Books, pp. 201–218.
Cremin, T., Hendry, H., Rodriguez Leon, L. and Hulston, S.J. (2024) 'Informal book talk: Digging beneath the surface', *English 3–13*, 52(7), pp. 930–945.
Cremin, T., Mottram, M., Collins, F.M., Powell, S. and Safford, K. (2014) *Building Communities of Engaged Readers: Reading for Pleasure*, Oxon: Routledge.
Cremin, T., Myhill, D., Eyres, I., Wilson, A., Oliver, L. and Nash, T. (2020) 'Teachers as writers: Learning together', *Literacy*, 53(2), pp. 49–59.
Cummings, S., McLaughlin, T. and Finch, B. (2018) 'Examining preadolescent children's engagement in out-of-school literacy and exploring opportunities for supporting literacy development', *Australian Journal of Language and Literacy*, 41, pp. 103–116.
Deci, E.L. and Ryan, R.M. (1980) 'Self-determination theory: When mind mediates behavior', *The Journal of Mind and Behavior*, 1(1), pp. 33–43.
Deci, E.L. and Ryan, R.M. (2000) 'Psychological inquiry: The "what" and "why" of goal pursuits: Human needs and the self-determination of behavior', *Psychological Inquiry*, 11(4), pp. 227–268.
De Naeghel, J., Van Keer, H., Vansteenkiste, M. and Rosseel, Y. (2012) 'The relation between elementary students' recreational and academic reading motivation, reading frequency, engagement, and comprehension: A self-determination theory perspective', *Journal of Educational Psychology*, 104(4), pp. 1006–1021.
De Naeghel, J., Van Keer, H., Vansteenkiste, M., Haerens, L. and Aelterman, N. (2016) 'Promoting elementary school students' autonomous reading motivation: Effects of a teacher professional development workshop', *The Journal of Educational Research*, 109(3), pp. 232–252.
De Naeghel, J., Valcke, M., De Meyer, L., Warlop, N., Van Braak, J. and Van Keer, H. (2014) 'The role of teacher behavior in adolescents' intrinsic reading motivation', *Reading and Writing*, 27, pp. 1547–1565.
De Smedt, F., Rogiers, A., Heirweg, S., Merchie, E. and Van Keer, H. (2020) 'Assessing and mapping reading and writing motivation in third to eight graders: A self-determination theory perspective', *Frontiers in Psychology*, 11, 1678.
De Smedt, F., Merchie, E., Barendse, M., Rossell, Y., De Naeghel, J. and Van Keer, H. (2018) 'Cognitive and motivational challenges in writing: Studying the relationship with writing performance across students' gender and achievement level', *Reading Research Quarterly*, 53(2), pp. 249–272.
Dobson, T. and Stephenson, L. (2017) 'Primary pupils' creative writing: Enacting identities in a community of writers', *Literacy*, 51(3), pp. 162–168.
Dutro, E., Kazemi, E. and Balf, R. (2006) 'Making sense of "The Boy Who Died": Tales of a struggling successful writer', *Reading and Writing Quarterly*, 22(4), pp. 325–356.
Dyson, A.H. (2001) 'Where are the childhoods in childhood literacy? An exploration in outer (school) space', *Journal of Early Childhood Literacy*, 1(1), pp. 9–39.
Dyson, A.H. (2009) 'Writing in childhood worlds', in Beard, R., Myhill, D., Riley, J. and Nystrand, M. (eds), *The SAGE Handbook of Writing Development*, London: SAGE, pp. 232–245.
Dyson, A.H. (2013) 'The place of childhoods in school writing programmes: A matter of ethics', in Marsh, J. and Larson, J. (eds), *The SAGE Handbook of Early Childhood Literacy*, London: SAGE, pp. 485–500.
Dyson, A.H. (2019) 'Ethnography upside down', in Kucirkova, N., Rowsell, J. and Falloon, G. (eds), *The Routledge International Handbook of Learning with Technology in Early Childhood*, London: Routledge, pp. 74–90.

Dyson, A.H. (2020) '"This isn't my real writing": The fate of children's agency in too-tight curricula', *Theory Into Practice*, 59(2), pp. 119–127.

Frankel, K.K. (2017) 'What does it mean to be a reader? Identity and positioning in two high school literacy intervention classes', *Reading & Writing Quarterly*, 33(6), pp. 501–518.

Frankel, K.K. and Fields, S.S. (2019) 'Disrupting storylines: A case study of one adolescent's identity, agency, and positioning during literacy tutoring', *Literacy Research and Instruction*, 58(3), pp. 142–163.

Froiland, J.M. and Oros, E. (2014) 'Intrinsic motivation, perceived competence and classroom engagement as longitudinal predictors of adolescent reading achievement', *Educational Psychology*, 34(2), pp. 119–132.

Gabriel, S. and Young, A. (2011) 'Becoming a vampire without being bitten: The narrative collective-assimilation hypothesis', *Psychological Science*, 22(8), pp. 990–994.

Graham, S. (2006) 'Writing', in Alexander, P. and Winne, P. (eds), *Handbook of Educational Psychology* (2nd ed.), Mahwah, NJ: Erlbaum, pp. 457–478.

Graham, S. (2018) 'Conceptualizing writing: Implications for development and future research', *Educational Psychologist*, 53(4), pp. 217–219.

Graham, S. (2020) 'The sciences of reading and writing must become more fully integrated', *Reading Research Quarterly*, 55(S1), S35–S44.

Graham, S. and Harris, K.R. (2016) 'A path to better writing: Evidence-based practices in the classroom', *The Reading Teacher*, 69(4), pp. 359–365.

Graham, S., Kiuhara, S.A., Harris, K.R. and Fishman, E.J. (2017) 'The relationship among strategic writing behaviour, writing motivation, and writing performance with young, developing writers', *Elementary School Journal*, 118(1), pp. 82–104.

Gregory, E. (2001) 'Sisters and brothers as language and literacy teachers: Synergy between siblings playing and working together', *Journal of Early Childhood Literacy*, 1(3), pp. 301–322.

Guay, F., Stupnisky, R., Boivin, M., Japel, C. and Dionne, G. (2019) 'Teacher's relatedness with students as a predictor of student's intrinsic motivation, self-concept, and reading achievement', *Early Childhood Research Quarterly*, 48(3), pp. 215–225.

Guo, Y., Puranik, C., Kelcey, B., Sun, J., Schneider, M. and Breit-Smith, A. (2021) 'The role of home literacy practices in kindergarten children's early writing development: A one-year longitudinal study', *Early Education and Development*, 32(2), pp. 209–227.

Guthrie, J.T. and Davis, M.H. (2003) 'Motivating struggling readers in middle school through an engagement model of classroom practice', *Reading and Writing Quarterly*, 19(1), pp. 59–85.

Guthrie, J.T. and Wigfield, A. (2000) 'Engagement and motivation in reading', in Kamil, M.L., Mosenthal, P.B., Pearson, P.D. and Barr, R. (eds), *Handbook of Reading Research*, Vol. 3, Mahwah, NJ: Lawrence Erlbaum, pp. 403–422.

Guthrie, J.T., Wigfield, A. and You, W. (2012) 'Instructional contexts for engagement and achievement in reading', in Christenson, S.L., Reschly, A.I. and Wylie, C. (eds), *Handbook of Research on Student Engagement*, New York and London: Springer, pp. 601–634.

Guthrie, J.T., Wigfield, A., Metsala, J.L. and Cox, K.E. (1999) 'Motivational and cognitive predictors of text comprehension and reading amount', *Scientific Studies of Reading*, 3(3), pp. 231–256.

Hall, L.A. (2012a) 'Rewriting identities: Creating spaces for students and teachers to challenge the norms of what it means to be a reader in school', *Journal of Adolescent and Adult Literacy*, 55(5), pp. 368–373.

Hall, L.A. (2012b) 'The role of reading identities and reading abilities in students' discussions about texts and comprehension strategies', *Journal of Literacy Research*, 44(3), pp. 239–272.

Hall, L.A. (2016) 'The role of identity in reading comprehension development', *Reading and Writing Quarterly*, 32(1), pp. 56–80.

Hebbecker, K., Förster, N. and Souvignier, E. (2019) 'Reciprocal effects between reading Achievement and intrinsic and extrinsic reading motivation', *Scientific Studies of Reading*, 23(5), pp. 419–436.

Hempel-Jorgensen, A., Cremin, T., Harris, D. and Chamberlain, L. (2018) 'Pedagogy for reading for pleasure in low socio-economic primary schools: Beyond "pedagogy of poverty"?', *Literacy*, 52(2), pp. 86–94.

Hidi, S. and Boscolo, P. (2006) 'Motivation and writing', in MacArthur, C.A., Graham, S. and Fitzgerald, J. (eds), *Handbook of Writing Research*, New York: The Guilford Press, pp. 144–157.

Ho, E.S.C. and Lau, K. (2018) 'Reading engagement and reading literacy performance: Effective policy and practices at home and in school', *Journal of Research in Reading*, 41(4), pp. 657–679.

Ivey, G. and Friddle, R. (2025) 'Agency within pleasure reading', in Cremin, T. and McGeown, S. (eds), *Reading for Pleasure: International Perspectives*, London and New York: Routledge, pp. 95–110.

Ivey, G. and Johnston, P. (2013) 'Engagement with young adult literature outcomes and processes', *Reading Research Quarterly*, 48(3), pp. 1–21.

Ivey, G. and Johnston, P. (2023) *Teens Choosing to Read: Fostering Social, Emotional and Intellectual Growth Through Books*, New York: Teachers College Press.

Jang, B.G. and Ryoo, J.H. (2019) 'Multiple dimensions of adolescents' reading attitudes and their relationship with reading comprehension', *Reading and Writing*, 32(7), pp. 1769–1793.

Kennedy, E. (2018) 'Engaging children as readers and writers in high-poverty contexts', *Journal of Research in Reading*, 41(4), pp. 716–731.

Kennedy, E. and Shiel, G. (2010) 'Raising literacy levels with collaborative on-site professional development in an urban disadvantaged school', *The Reading Teacher*, 63(5), pp. 372–383.

Kervin, L., Comber, B. and Woods, A. (2020) 'Children learning to write in early primary classrooms', in Chen, H., Myhill, D. and Lewis, H. (eds), *Developing Writers across the Primary and Secondary Years: Growing into Writing*, Oxon: Routledge, pp. 19–39.

Klauda, S.L. and Wigfield, A. (2012) 'Relations of perceived parent and friend support for recreational reading with children's reading motivations', *Journal of Literacy Research*, 44(1), pp. 3–44.

Knoester, M. and Plikuhn, M. (2018) 'Influence of siblings on out-of-school reading practices', *Journal of Research in Reading*, 39(4), pp. 469–485.

Lambirth, A. (2016) 'Exploring children's discourses of writing', *English in Education*, 50(3), pp. 215–232.

Lee, Y., Gee Jang, B. and Conradi Smith, K. (2021) 'A systematic review of reading engagement research: What do we mean, what do we know and where do we need to go?', *Reading Psychology*, 42(5), pp. 540–576.

Levy, R. and Harrison, A. (2025) 'Home, parents and siblings', in Cremin, T. and McGeown, S. (eds), *Reading for Pleasure: International Perspectives*, London and New York: Routledge, pp. 141–154.

Levy, R., Hall, M. and Preece, J. (2018) 'Examining the links between parents' relationships with reading and shared reading with their pre-school children', *International Journal of Educational Psychology*, 7(2), pp. 123–150.

Locke, T. (2017) 'Developing a whole school culture of writing', in Cremin, T. and Locke, T. (eds), *Writer Identity and the Teaching and Learning of Writing*, London and New York: Routledge, pp. 132–148.

Magnifico, A.M. (2013) '"Well, I have to write that": A cross-case qualitative analysis of young writers' motivations to write'. *International Journal of Educational Psychology*, 2(1), pp. 19–55.

Marinak, B.A., Malloy, J.B., Gambrell, L.B. and Mazzoni, S.A. (2015) 'Me and my reading profile: A tool for assessing early reading motivation', *The Reading Teacher*, 69(1), pp. 51–62.

Masterson, J.E. (2022) 'Reading in "purgatory": Tactical literacies in a remedial reading class', *Reading Research Quarterly*, 57(1), pp. 91–109.

McBreen, M. and Savage, R. (2023) 'The effectiveness of a cognitive-plus-motivational reading intervention: A multiple-baseline study with four pupils at-risk for reading difficulties', *Educational and Child Psychology*, 40(1), pp. 96–115.

McCarthey, S.J. (2001) 'Identity construction in elementary readers and writers', *Reading Research Quarterly*, 36(2), pp. 122–151.

McCarthey, S.J. and Woodard, R. (2017) 'Faithfully following, adapting, or rejecting mandated curriculum: Teachers' curricular enactments in elementary writing instruction', *Pedagogies: An International Journal*, 13(1), pp. 56–80.

McCarthy, P., Meier, S. and Rinderer, R. (1985) 'Self-efficacy and writing: A different view of self-evaluation', *College Composition and Communication*, 36(4), pp. 465–471.

McFarland, D. and Pals, H. (2005) 'Motives and contexts of identity change: A case for network effects', *Social Psychology Quarterly*, 68(4), pp. 289–315.

McGeown, S. and Conradi Smith, K. (2024) 'Reading engagement matters! A new scale to measure and support children's engagement with books', *The Reading Teacher*, 77(4), pp. 462–472.

McGeown, S., Goodwin, H., Henderson, N. and Wright, P. (2012) 'Gender differences in reading motivation: Does sex or gender identity provide a better account?', *Journal of Research in Reading*, 35(3), pp. 328–336.

McGeown, S., Bonsall, J., Andries, V., Howarth, D. and Wilkinson, K. (2020b) 'Understanding reading motivation across different text types: Qualitative insights from children', *Journal of Research in Reading*, 43(4), pp. 597–608.

McGeown, S., Osborne, C., Warhurst, A., Norgate, R. and Duncan, L. (2016) 'Understanding children's reading activities: Reading motivation, skill and child characteristics as predictors', *Journal of Research in Reading*, 39(1), pp. 109–125.

McGeown, S., Bonsall, J., Andries, V., Howarth, D., Wilkinson, K. and Sabeti, S. (2020a) 'Growing up a reader: Exploring children's and adolescents' perceptions of "a reader"', *Educational Research*, 62(2), pp. 216–228.

McKinney, M. (2017) 'Being a writer and teaching writing on the rackety bridge', in Cremin, T. and Locke, T. (eds), *Writer Identity and the Teaching and Learning of Writing*, London: Routledge, pp. 83–97.

McKinney, M. and Giorgis, C. (2009) 'Narrating and performing identity', *Journal of Literacy Research*, 41(1), pp.104–149.

Merga, M.K. (2017) 'Becoming a reader: Significant social influences on avid book readers', *School Library Research*, 20, pp. 1–21.

Merga, M.K. (2020a) '"We talk books": Teacher librarians promoting book discussion to foster reading engagement', *English in Australia*, 55(1), pp. 22–33.

Merga, M.K. (2020b) 'School librarians as literacy educators within a complex role', *Journal of Library Administration*, 60(8), pp. 889–908.

Merga, M.K. and Ferguson, C. (2021) 'School librarians supporting students' reading for pleasure: A job description analysis', *Australian Journal of Education*, 65(2), pp. 153–171.

Merga, M.K. and Ledger, S. (2018) 'Parents' views on reading aloud to their children: Beyond the early years', *Article in Australian Journal of Language and Literacy*, 41(3), pp. 177–189.

Miyamoto, A., Murayama, K. and Lechner, C.M. (2020) 'The developmental trajectory of intrinsic reading motivation: Measurement invariance, group variations, and implications for reading proficiency', *Contemporary Educational Psychology*, 63, 101921.

Miyamoto, A., Pfost, M. and Artelt, C. (2018) 'Reciprocal relations between intrinsic reading motivation and reading competence: A comparison between native and immigrant students in Germany', *Journal of Research in Reading*, 41(1), pp. 176–196.

Moses, L. and Kelly, L.B. (2018) '"We're a little loud. That's because we like to read!": Developing positive views of reading in a diverse, urban first grade', *Journal of Early Childhood Literacy*, 18(3), pp. 307–337.

Moses, L. and Kelly, L.B. (2019) 'Are they really reading? A descriptive study of first graders during independent reading', *Reading and Writing Quarterly*, 35(4), pp. 322–338.

Myhill, D., Cremin, T. and Oliver, L. (2023) 'Writing as a craft: Re-considering teacher subject content knowledge for teaching writing', *Research Papers in Education*, 38(3), pp. 403–425.

Neugebauer, S. (2016) 'Stable or situated understandings of adolescent reading engagement across readers and raters', *The Journal of Educational Research*, 109(4), pp. 391–404.

Neugebauer, S.R. and Gilmour, A.F. (2020) 'The ups and downs of reading across content areas: The association between instruction and fluctuations in reading motivation', *Journal of Educational Psychology*, 112(2), pp.344–363.

Ng, C. (2018) 'Using student voice to promote reading engagement for economically disadvantaged students', *Journal of Research in Reading*, 41(4), pp. 700–715.

Ng, C., Graham, S., Lau, K.-L., Liu, X. and Tang, K.-Y. (2021) 'Writing motives and writing self-efficacy of Chinese students in Shanghai and Hong Kong: Measurement invariance and multigroup structural equation analyses', *International Journal of Educational Research*, 107, 101751.

Nippold, M.A., Duthie, J.K. and Larsen, J. (2005) 'Literacy as a leisure activity: Free-time preferences of older children and young adolescents', *Language, Speech, and Hearing Services in Schools*, 36(2), pp. 93–102.

Noble, O. and Holt, N. (2018) 'A study into the impact of the Reading Education Assistance Dogs scheme on reading engagement and motivation to read among Early Years Foundation Stage children', *Education 3–13*, 46(3), pp. 277–290.

Nolen, S.B. (2006) 'The role of social context in the development of motivation to write', in Hidi, A. and Boscolo, P. (eds), *Motivation to Write*, Dordrecht: Kluwer, pp. 241–255.

Nolen, S.B. (2007) 'Young children's motivation to read and write: Development in social contexts', *Cognition and Instruction*, 25(2–3), pp. 219–270.

Norman, K.A. and Spencer, B.H. (2005) 'Our lives as writers: Examining preservice teachers' experiences and beliefs about the nature of writing and writing instruction', *Teacher Education Quarterly*, 32(1), pp. 25–40.

Orkin, M., Pott, M., Wolf, W., May, S. and Brand, E. (2017) 'Beyond gold stars: Improving the skills and engagement of struggling readers through intrinsic motivation', *Reading and Writing Quarterly*, 34(3), pp. 203–217.

Pajares, F. and Johnson, M. (1994) 'Confidence and competence in writing: The role of self-efficacy, outcome expectancy, and apprehension', *Research in the Teaching of English*, 28(3), pp. 313–331.

Pajares, F. and Valiante, G. (1999) 'Grade level and gender differences in the writing self-beliefs of middle school students', *Contemporary Educational Psychology*, 24(4), pp. 390–405.

Pajares, F. and Valiante, G. (2006) 'Self-efficacy beliefs and motivation in writing development', in MacArthur, C.A.Graham, S. and Fitzgerald, J. (eds), *Handbook of Writing Research*, New York: Guilford Press, pp. 158–170.

Park, Y. (2011) 'How motivational constructs interact to predict elementary students' reading performance: Examples from attitudes and self-concept in reading', *Learning and Individual Differences*, 21(4), pp. 347–358.

Protacio, M.S. (2019) 'How positioning affects English learners' social interactions around reading', *Theory into Practice*, 58(3), pp. 217–225.

Reedy, A. and De Carvalho, D. (2021) 'Children's perspectives on reading, agency and their environment: What can we learn about reading for pleasure from an East London primary school?', *Education 3–13*, 49(2), pp. 134–147.

Rowe, D.W. and Neitzel, C. (2010) 'Interest and agency in 2–3-year-olds' participation in emergent writing', *Reading Research Quarterly*, 45(2), pp. 169–195.

Rowe, D.W., Shimizu, A.Y. and Davis, Z.G. (2022) 'Essential practices for engaging young children as writers: Lessons from expert early writing teachers', *The Reading Teacher*, 75(4), pp. 485–494.

Ryan, M. and Barton, G. (2014) 'The spatialized practices of teaching writing in elementary schools: Diverse students shaping discoursal selves', *Research in the Teaching of English*, 48(3), pp. 303–328.

Ryan, R.M. and Deci, E.L. (2000) 'Self-determination theory and the facilitation of intrinsic motivation, social development, and well-being', *The American Psychologist*, 55(1), pp. 68–78.

Ryan, R.M. and Deci, E.L. (2017) *Self-Determination Theory: Basic Psychological Needs in Motivation, Development, and Wellness*, New York: The Guilford Press.

Schaffner, E., Schiefele, U. and Ulferts, H. (2013) 'Reading amount as a mediator of the effects of intrinsic and extrinsic reading motivation on reading comprehension', *Reading Research Quarterly*, 48(4), pp. 369–385.

Schiefele, U. and Löweke, S. (2018) 'The nature, development, and effects of elementary students' reading motivation profiles', *Reading Research Quarterly*, 53(4), pp. 405–421.

Schiefele, U., Stutz, F. and Schaffner, E. (2016) 'Longitudinal relations between reading motivation and reading comprehension in the early elementary grades', *Learning and Individual Differences*, 51, pp. 49–58.

Schiefele, U., Schaffner, E., Möller, J. and Wigfield, A. (2012) 'Dimensions of reading motivation and their relation to reading behavior and competence', *Reading Research Quarterly*, 47 (4), pp. 427–463.

Scholes, L. (2019a) 'Differences in attitudes towards reading and other school-related activities among boys and girls', *Journal of Research in Reading*, 42(3–4), pp. 485–503.

Scholes, L. (2019b) 'Working-class boys' relationships with reading: Contextual systems that support working-class boys' engagement with, and enjoyment of, reading', *Gender and Education*, 31(3), pp. 344–361.

Scholes, L., Spina, N. and Comber, B. (2021) 'Disrupting the "boys don't read" discourse: Primary school boys who *love* reading fiction', *British Educational Research Journal*, 47(1), pp. 163–180.

Schüller, E.M., Birnbaum, L. and Kroner, S. (2017) 'What makes elementary school students read in their leisure time? Development of a comprehensive questionnaire', *Reading Research Quarterly*, 52(2), pp. 161–175.

Sellers, C. (2019) '"Fitting in" and "standing out": the peer group and young people's development of reader identity', *British Journal of Sociology of Education*, 40(7), pp. 938–952.

Slavin, E.R., Lake, C., Inns, A., Baye, A., Dachet, D. and Haslam, J. (2019) *A Quantitative Synthesis of Research on Writing Approaches in Years 3 to 13*, London: Education Endowment Foundation.

Street, B. (1998) 'New literacies in theory and practice: What are the implications for language in education?', *Linguistics and Education*, 10(1), pp. 1–24.

Stutz, F., Schaffner, E. and Schiefele, U. (2017) 'Measurement invariance and validity of a brief questionnaire on reading motivation in elementary students', *Journal of Research in Reading*, 40(4), pp. 439–461.

Vaknin-Nusbaum, V., Nevo, E., Brande, S. and Gambrell, L. (2018) 'Developmental aspects of reading motivation and reading achievement among second grade low achievers and typical readers', *Journal of Research in Reading*, 41(3), pp. 438–454.

Venegas E.M. (2018) 'Strengthening the reader self-efficacies of reluctant and struggling readers through literature circles', *Reading and Writing Quarterly*, 34(5), pp. 419–435.

Wang, J.H.Y. and Guthrie, J.T. (2004) 'Modeling the effects of intrinsic motivation, extrinsic motivation, amount of reading, and past reading achievement on text comprehension between U.S. and Chinese students', *Reading Research Quarterly*, 39(2), pp. 162–186.

Webber, C., Wilkinson, K., Andries, V. and McGeown, S. (2022) 'A reflective account of using child-led interviews as a means to promote discussions about reading', *Literacy*, 56 (2), pp. 120–129.

Weber, S. (2018) 'How teachers can guide library book selection to maximize the value of independent reading time', *The Language and Literacy Spectrum*, 28(1), Article 4.

Wigfield, A. and Guthrie, J.T. (1997) 'Relations of children's motivation for reading to the amount and breadth of their reading', *Journal of Educational Psychology*, 89(3), pp. 420–432.

Wilhelm, J. (2016) 'Recognising the power of pleasure: What engaged adolescent readers get from their free-choice reading, and how teachers can leverage this for all', *Australian Journal of Language and Literacy*, 39(1), pp. 30–41.

Wilhelm, J.D., Smith, M.W. and Fransen, S. (2013) *Reading Unbound: Why Kids Need to Read What They Want – and Why We should Let Them*, New York: Scholastic.

Wilson, A.C. (2009) 'Creativity and constraint: Developing as a writer of poetry culture', in Beard, R., Myhill, D., Riley, J. and Nystrand, M. (eds), *The SAGE Handbook of Writing Development*, London: SAGE, pp. 387–401.

Wright, K.L., Hodges, T.S. and McTigue, E.M. (2019) 'A validation program for the self-beliefs, writing-beliefs, and attitude survey: A measure of adolescents' motivation toward writing', *Assessing Writing*, 39, pp. 64–78.

Wright, K.L., Hodges, T.S., Dismuke, S. and Boedeker, P. (2020) 'Writing motivation and middle school: An examination of changes in students' motivation for writing', *Literacy Research and Instruction*, 59(2), pp. 148–168.

Zare, M., Kozak, S., Rodrigues, M.L. and Martin-Chang, S. (2023) 'The roots of reading for pleasure: Recollections of reading and current habits', *Literacy*, 57(3), pp. 262–274.

Zhou, M., Ma, W.J. and Deci, E.L. (2009) 'The importance of autonomy for rural Chinese children's motivation for learning', *Learning and Individual Differences*, 19, pp. 492–498.

Zumbrunn, S., Ekholm, E., Stringer, J.K., McKnight, K. and DeBusk-Lane, M. (2017) 'Student experiences with writing: Taking the temperature of the classroom', *The Reading Teacher*, 70 (6), pp. 667–677.

5

TEXT ACCESS, CHOICE AND TIME

Introduction

The research literature points to the importance of access to texts, making choices about texts as well as having time and space to engage with texts in supporting volitional reading and writing. Informed by varying agendas, such as literary and cultural heritage and cultural diversity, curricula frequently stress the need for adults to expose young people to key classical or contemporary texts and significant genres (e.g. ACARA, 2022; DfE, 2014). However, the studies examined frequently highlight that experiences of reading and writing need to be of interest and relevance to young people, while also providing ample opportunities for them to engage with texts in their own time and on their own terms. The evidence suggests that the development and support of positive literate identities and children's reading and writing for pleasure cannot be restricted, rushed or cut short, it takes time and sustained support as Chapters 6 and 7 also indicate.

This chapter highlights the insights from studies in this area and indicates that access to texts in several locations can support children's desire to read. However, access to texts is far from equitable, so practices that seek to enable equitable access to texts for the young are identified as important. Connected to the concept of access, research also draws attention to the role of choice, arguing that children need to be able to make choices about what types of reading and writing they engage with. Studies highlight that adults can play a crucial role in both supporting access and in helping children to make informed and suitable choices about their reading and writing activities. In so doing, the young are enabled to exercise their rights and develop their unique identities as readers and writers. The chapter concludes by highlighting that once choices have been made, young people need time and space to engage deeply with their self-chosen texts.

Access to texts

Providing children and young people with 'access' to a number of texts is key to enabling positive reading experiences. Multiple studies attest to the significance of

DOI: 10.4324/9781003532606-8

book ownership and book borrowing as distinct and valuable forms of text access (e.g. Kennedy, 2018; Nielen and Bus, 2015). However, the issue of text access encapsulates more than the number of texts available. Indeed, studies show that in particular access to high-quality, engaging, interesting and relevant texts is crucial to developing and maintaining volitional reading (Gambrell, 2011; Guthrie et al., 2007). Moreover, given the reading–writing nexus discussed in Chapter 2, it is possible that access to quality texts can also support volitional writing.

A link between the number of books children have access to and their reading attainment and engagement has been established, alongside beneficial reading experiences (e. g. Allington et al., 2010; Evans et al., 2010; Lindsay, 2010). Specifically, these studies draw attention to the importance of book access at home. In a meta-analysis of 108 studies, Lindsay (2010) indicated that a beneficial relationship exists between book ownership and reading attainment. This research also pointed to how access to print materials encourages children to read more and to read for longer periods of time, behaviours conventionally associated with reading for pleasure (Kozak and Martin-Chang, 2019). In an international and longitudinal piece of research, involving 27 countries and 70,000 cases, Evans et al. (2010) found that the presence of a home library had considerable influence on children's attainment. The researchers posited that the presence of multiple books at home may help not only to model a preference for and pleasure in reading but also to develop reading skills that make schooling 'congenial or enjoyable' (Evans et al., 2010, p. 17). In brief, being habituated with reading through access to texts may help to make school feel more familiar. Interestingly, this study suggests that the benefits associated with book ownership are felt most in households with less books, whereby each additional book 'yields more "bang for your book" among the book-poor than among the book-rich' (Evans et al., 2010, p. 17):

> Where books are rare, each additional book matters most, not among the literate elite.
>
> *(Evans et al., 2010, p. 17)*

Of concern though is that text inequalities exist. Specifically, text access has been shown to be connected to socio-economic status, with young people living in deprived areas having reduced access (Neuman and Celano, 2012; Neuman and Moland, 2016; Pribesh et al., 2011). Moreover, these inequalities are entrenched across various locations typically associated with providing access to texts, such as schools, shops and libraries. In these US studies, children from lower income families were seen to live in locations where fewer books were available in book shops and community libraries (Neuman and Celano, 2012; Neuman and Moland, 2016). These areas are referred to as 'book deserts' (Neuman and Moland, 2016) or areas of 'book hunger' (Shaver, 2020), which Shaver notes 'is particularly resistant to market solutions because of the extreme diversity of products readers need' (p. 7). This challenge is evident in schools, many of which also appear to mirror the imbalance; schools with higher concentrations of students from lower-income families had more limited school library resources (Pribesh et al., 2011).

In attempts to redress such inequities and enhance text access, a variety of book distribution programmes exist worldwide. In a meta-analysis of studies in this area, de Bondt et al. (2020) indicate some of these programmes make an impact in the following areas: positive parental perceptions of such programmes; increased likelihood of daily shared reading and talk about texts; and enhanced early literacy skills. Building on these findings, more recently Galea et al. (2024) found that parents involved in the Dolly Parton Imagination Library (DPIL) in a region of Australia specifically benefited from the tips provided by the programme for carrying out shared reading which enhanced their confidence and frequency of reading with their child. Of those parents (n:89) who remained involved for three years in the DPIL scheme, 75 per cent reported that their children were interested in reading. Interestingly, studies also suggest that book gifting schemes can result in variations in library visiting habits. Funge et al. (2017) found that book gifting increased library visits, suggesting an increased interest in reading. However, O'Hare and Connolly (2014) found that such schemes were associated with decreased library visits. However, It is possible that this latter study indicates not a reduced interest in reading, but a reduced dependency on libraries for text access. Several factors mediate the findings about book gifting programmes. Specifically, the quality and quantity of interactions offered by caregivers (de Bondt et al., 2020) and the duration of involvement in such book gifting programmes (Tura et al., 2021). However, short-running book gifting schemes can still have an impact, if they are well-timed, and coincide with school summer holidays when children have increased free time to engage with texts (Allington et al., 2010; Allington and McGill-Franzen, 2021; Bell et al., 2020).

Despite the links between children's reading experience and engagement with writing (see Chapter 2), there appear to be fewer studies examining the connection between access to texts and volitional writing. In particular, studies note that wide reading can support composition, as young people appear to learn the craft of writing somewhat vicariously (e.g. Barrs and Cork, 2001; Corden, 2001). If these reading experiences are independent or volitional in nature, research indicates that they can support writing competencies (e.g. Jouhar and Rupley, 2021; Sénéchal et al., 2018). Indeed, one study pointed to professional writers' reflections upon their enjoyment of reading in childhood (Cremin et al., 2017), potentially indicating a sustained connection between text access, engagement and later volitional writing.

However, research suggests that access to texts may not be enough. Instead, access to a range of text types and formats appears to be significant for supporting volitional reading. For instance, printed books, in contrast to other text formats, are particularly capable of nurturing sustained reading engagement and enjoyment (Torppa et al., 2020) and fiction is seen as especially valuable for volitional reading (Jerrim and Moss, 2019; Leino et al., 2017). Studies suggest that fiction narratives are affectively engaging, prompting emotions and memories that help readers to connect with texts, which can drive further reading (Kuzmičová and Cremin, 2022). Yet not all young people will favour print-based books or fiction (Ives et al., 2020), many derive pleasure from reading non-fiction and the opportunities to learn and share facts (e.g. Alexander and Jarman, 2018; Edmunds and Bauserman, 2006; Kuzmičová and Supa, 2024). Additionally, Loh (2024) identified that a wider choice of different text types, such as e-books, online fan fiction, anime and print-based manga can motivate young people. Through a mobile ethnography with adolescents aged 14–15 (n:12), Loh found that such 'cross-media' forms of reading appeared to offer them 'immersive entertainment'. These studies indicate the value of being able to access a wide range of text types and formats for volitional reading, affirming the EU Literacy Commission's advice:

> There should not be a hierarchical ranking of reading material. Books, comic books, newspapers, magazines and online reading materials are equally valid and important entry points to reading for children and adults alike.
>
> *(European Commission, Directorate-General for Education Youth, Sport and Culture, 2012, p. 42)*

The texts themselves are significant, with studies highlighting that the range and relevance of available texts influence whether children choose to read (Gambrell, 2011; Guthrie et al., 2007). Research also frequently shows that young people believe they would be more interested in reading for pleasure if texts had more relevance to them and were representative of their lives and interests (Cantrell et al., 2017; Clark and Teravainen-Goff, 2020; Scholes et al., 2021; Vehabovic, 2021). Such texts show that reading can provide a 'window' or a way to look upon other worlds, as Sims Bishop notes (1990):

> These windows are also sliding glass doors, and readers have only to walk through in imagination to become part of whatever world has been created or recreated by the author. When lighting conditions are just right, however, a window can also be a mirror.
>
> *(Sims Bishop, 1990, p. 1)*

Texts that reflect individuals' interests and experiences also build on and connect to young people's 'funds of knowledge' (Moll et al., 1992). Studies have also shown that reading and sharing culturally relevant and representative texts enables teachers to learn more about their students' socio-cultural and linguistic assets (e.g. Clark and Fleming, 2019; Milne et al., 2022). Yet, being able to access and share quality texts that are relevant and representative can be challenging.

Children's reading repertoires can be under-recognised and under-appreciated in schools (Cremin et al., 2015; McKnight, 2018). For instance, studies suggest a marked distinction between the reading matter that is enjoyed at home and that which is sanctioned in school (e.g. Gregory and Williams, 2000; Scholes, 2019). This has led researchers to suggest children are often obliged to leave their 'virtual school bags' (Thomson, 2002), packed with life knowledge and personal interests, at home. Doing so potentially limits their interactions with texts that motivate, inspire and engage them. However, it is important to acknowledge that there is, as yet, limited evidence to suggest that children read more avidly when they encounter books that reflect their knowledge, interests and worlds. Children self-report that they would read more if they encountered reflecting and representative texts. Thus, there is arguably a need for research that tracks shifts in reading behaviours and attitudes when text access shifts from being limited to becoming rich and diverse.

In recent years, studies and reports from UK-based academia, charities and publishers (CLPE, 2024; Elliott et al., 2021; Ramdarshan Bold, 2022) have highlighted the remarkably low number of fiction texts available that enable children to see themselves in books. Specifically, such studies have focused on diverse ethnic representations. Focusing on the UK context, the annual Centre for Literacy in Primary Education's 'Reflecting Realities' report highlighted that only 17 per cent of published books from 2023 included a racially minoritised character (CLPE, 2024). This is an increase on the low baseline of 4 per cent from 2017 when the report series started, but a drop from the higher figure of 30 per cent from published books in 2022 (CLPE, 2023, 2024). Moreover, it is important to note that racially minoritised characters are rarely positioned as main characters, only 7 per cent of UK books published in 2023 had a main character from a racially minoritised background (CLPE, 2024). Of additional concern is whether representations, whether in relation to ethnicity, gender, disability or other protected characteristics, are authentic and nuanced or whether they reinforce stereotypes. For instance, an Australian study indicated that many books shared by educators included highly traditional and stereotypical views of gender and gender roles (Adam and Harper, 2023). To avoid creating and sustaining stereotypes, children need to be able to choose from stories that include authentic and positive representations of characters from diverse cultural backgrounds and a range of gender representation. Young people need stories, as Tatum (2008) found, that resonate personally, socially, emotionally or politically, as these can enhance their desire to read.

Adults play a crucial role in enabling access to a range of relevant and engaging texts. Yet research suggests that, within school settings, adults experience challenges to enacting this role. For instance, in an Australian study, educators had limited understandings of the role of literature in enabling children to experience and value diversity and lacked in using such texts (Adam et al., 2019). Plus, several studies highlight trainee teachers and practising teachers' repertoires of diverse texts are slight (Cremin et al., 2024) and lack cultural nuance (Adam, 2021). Instead, teachers tend to draw on a limited range of dated texts, based on their own childhood reading and well-known celebrity authors (Akins et al., 2018; Clark and Teravainen, 2015; CLPE, 2021; Conradi Smith et al., 2022; Cremin et al., 2008a, 2008b, 2014, 2024; Farrar, 2021). This body of work around teachers' reading repertoires suggests the existence of a 'popular childhood canon' (Cremin et al., 2024) which fails to reflect the diverse realities of young people's lives and interests and is very likely both to constrain children's repertoires and their pleasure in reading (Simpson and Cremin, 2022). Moving beyond teachers' awareness of contemporary and diverse texts, Watson et al. (2022) identified that teachers' text decision making was influenced by several factors. Based on interviews with nine teachers from Wales and England, Watson et al. found that they selected texts through reflecting on their childhood reading experiences, current reading habits and an awareness of their students' interests. Their thoughtful approach, however, was complicated by a desire to ensure students had access to classic texts, texts that included 'life lessons' as well as texts that matched assessment criteria, and they also had to navigate practicalities around the availability of texts due to resource restrictions. Whilst a principled approach to text selection and purchasing is needed (Hartsfield and Kimmel, 2020), in practice this appears to be demanding to operationalise.

Making choices about texts

Research consistently reveals that both volitional reading and volitional writing can be supported by allowing and enabling children to make their own choice (e.g. Allred and Cena, 2020; Kissel and Miller, 2015). For reading, choice relates to being able to choose to read formats and text types that are of interest to individuals (e.g. Brandt et al., 2021; Cockroft and Atkinson, 2017; De Naeghel et al., 2016; Fisher and Frey, 2018; Guthrie et al., 2007; Ives et al., 2020; Kim et al., 2017; McGeown et al., 2020b; Pihl, 2012; Scholes, 2019). However, young readers benefit from being supported to make informed text choices to ensure what they pick matches their interests and adults have a role to play in supporting reading choices (Cockroft and Atkinson, 2017; Ives et al., 2020). For writing, choice may relate to content, purpose, form and audience (e.g. Barratt-Pugh et al., 2021; Collier, 2017; Dyson, 2010; Kissel and Miller, 2015). However, making choices about what to write can be challenging, and is also enabled through sensitive and judicious adult support (Gadd et al., 2019). Thus, although choice is strongly linked to the concept of individual agency, it also hinges on the role of knowledgeable and responsive adults.

Choosing texts to read

Being able to choose what to read is seen to motivate young people. Some report enjoying being able to make their own text choices and are competent at doing so (Oxley and McGeown, 2023; Tegmark et al., 2022; Wilhelm, 2016). In one study, the children's choices seemed to be shaped by their previous literary experiences, seeing their interests reflected in texts, seeing themselves represented in texts, perceptions of genre, interest in images, engagement with blurbs, and their view of their own reading skills (Reedy and Reedy, 2024). The first three of these influences were the most prominent, indicating the importance of their identities as readers:

> The multitude of strands that influenced the choices the children made were intertwined with their own identity as a reader at that moment.
>
> *(Reedy and Reedy, 2024, p. 10)*

Reader identities are continuously shaped by what children read. Accordingly, there is value in adults taking time to get to know individual readers, their preferences, dispositions and habits. As a consequence, they are well placed to make appropriate and personalised text recommendations capable of supporting emerging reader identities and interests (e.g. Cremin et al., 2014; Francois, 2013). Strategies deployed in school-based and other research projects to find out about young readers' interests are diverse, including, for example, small group conversations and interviews (e.g. Ng, 2018; Nolen, 2007; Reedy and Reedy, 2024), surveys and questionnaires (e.g. De Naeghel et al., 2012; Mohr, 2006; Reedy and De Carvalho, 2021), home visits (Cremin et al., 2015) and the use of creative methods, such as drawing practices (Cliff-Hodges, 2010; Cremin et al., 2014). Beyond activities focused on eliciting children's opinions and interests, Allen-Lyall and Davis' (2020) research indicates the value of attending to behaviours. They advocate for teachers building reading profiles of individual children through attending to the responses and behaviours of children during shared reading – demonstrating their choices in action.

The practices noted are predominantly orchestrated or led by an adult, with the intention of improving their understanding of young readers' interests. However, these inquiry methods can also make children's interest more transparent, helping children to reflect on their own reading. Moreover, researchers have shown the value of positioning pupils as researchers of other children's reading practices (McGeown et al., 2020a; Webber et al., 2022). Doing so can help to amplify overlooked voices and perspectives (Webber et al., 2024). In turn, including broader perspectives can prompt both a re-acknowledgement and re-valuing of practices that might not immediately be recognised as reading, such as engaging with digital formats and texts, particularly when children tend to adopt a school-based lens on reading. Webber et al. (2022) suggested, for instance, that child-led interviews enable the development of natural discussions between peers that offer valuable insights about reading. Nevertheless, they acknowledged that, as the interviews in their study were undertaken in school, the children's insight may have been curtailed by a schooled conception of reading.

For children in the process of understanding their own interests as readers, choice can be challenging (Guthrie et al., 2007). Moreover, when children are left to make their own choices, they may inadvertently encounter texts that are overly difficult and therefore disengaging. Characteristics such as text difficulty levels and length can affect readers' involvement and some texts need considerable stamina to sustain attention (Hiebert et al., 2014). As Locher et al.'s (2019) longitudinal work has shown, however, present pleasure in a book – what they describe as 'intrinsic situational motivation' – influences the likelihood of the child's future engagement. They note this 'positively predicted individual differences in the development of that student's intrinsic habitual reading motivation' (p. 11). The significance therefore of children developing a legacy of past satisfactions cannot be underestimated, and to achieve this, support from knowledgeable adults is necessary. This can lead to children building confidence in their abilities to make appropriate, independent text selections. Through interviews with children (n:9) aged 9–10, Edmunds and Bauserman (2006) found that children enjoy receiving supportive recommendations from their teachers and are motivated to read them. Conversations between readers, whether adults or peers, can also support wise choices as many studies attest (e.g. Cremin et al., 2014; Fisher and Frey, 2018; Kennedy, 2018; Merga, 2020a; Moses and Kelly, 2019; Ng, 2018; Ross, 2018; Ross et al., 2018).

However, research also indicates that teachers' pedagogical approaches can hinder text choice and, thereby, enjoyment of reading. Moss and McDonald (2004) showed that one teacher who wanted to ensure breadth and quality monitored and constrained children's choices, whereas in another class children were free to choose what interested them. In the former, the children appeared to read because they were required to do so, not because they chose to do so. So, a balance between giving free choice and adults and peers being able to offer judicious support is needed.

> [S]ome students expressed that they like both making their own book choices, as well as having close, trusted others choose books for them. This suggests that perhaps students can be motivated by both personal choice and choices made by close others.
>
> *(Guthrie et al., 2007, p. 306)*

Choice is also influenced by the number and range of texts available at home, school or the wider community. For instance, in case studies of four classes of 9–10-year-olds, Hempel-Jorgensen et al. (2018) noted the number of texts available to children ranged from 147 to 802, with some classes having no poetry, news items or screen-based reading opportunities. The availability of similar books (by the same author or in the same series) is seen as a way to support text choice and retain interest (Daniels, 1996) as well as involving children in co-constructing text collections with library staff (Rudkin and Wood, 2019).

Choice within writing

As writers compose, they are obliged to make choices, related to audience, purpose, style and content. These choices are also shaped by individuals' identities as writers which in themselves are fluid and negotiated in and through interactions. In school, many of these choices are set by teachers, and influenced by schemes of work and assessment expectations. Consequently, skill-focused aspects of writing tend to be foregrounded (Guo et al., 2021; Kervin et al., 2020) at the relative expense of creating, composing and crafting texts. Research suggests that one consequence of foregrounding skills over self-expression is that children's authorial choices are often short-changed (Cremin and Myhill, 2012; Fisher, 2006; Jesson and Cockle, 2016; Myhill, 2005; Parr and McNaughton, 2013). Moreover, consistent emphasis on writing skills can have an impact on children's perceptions of what constitutes good writing. For example, online questionnaire responses from 9–11-year-olds in England suggested they associated presentational skills (handwriting) and language choices (vocabulary) with being a good writer (González-Díaz et al., 2024). Although the children did also value the status of 'being an author', recognising the role of 'creative flair' in writing. These and other studies indicate that freedom alongside form is necessary, if children are to find writing engaging.

Enabling young people to make choices about their writing can fuel motivation and engagement (Barratt-Pugh et al., 2021; Barrs and Horrocks, 2014; Fletcher, 2016; Gadd et al., 2019; Zumbrunn et al., 2019). Decisions impacting on topic and genre appear to be key to motivating young writers (Barrs and Horrocks, 2014; Fletcher, 2016; Zumbrunn et al., 2019). Choice in writing can extend to including additional modes, such as visuals in composition (Laman et al., 2025). Similarly, children can be motivated to write when they are allowed to pursue their own interests (Dyson, 1999; Kress, 1997; Laman et al., 2025). In a US survey (n:263), Zumbrunn et al. (2019) found that the children voiced clear preferences for writing about self-chosen topics and genres. Kissel and Miller (2015) affirmed this and found that where and with whom to write was also influential. When teachers offered and supported this range of choices children developed their identities as writers with valuable ideas to communicate. In another study (Healey, 2019), in Australia, children (n:8) expressed enjoyment when they felt free to create during writing, not to focus on the specifics of school writing 'tasks':

> For instance, some participants spoke about feeling as though restraints were removed, finally having the voice to express themselves. As such, many participants saw creative writing as purposeful, even if they created the purpose themselves.
>
> *(Healey, 2019, p. 190)*

Studies have also highlighted the benefits of providing young people with personal writing journals or 'just writing' books. These resources can allow young writers to pursue their own passions and concerns in writing (Cremin et al., 2020; Graham and Johnson, 2012). The interests pursued in choice-led writing are understood to emerge from children's social and cultural experiences and their home and community (Dyson, 2001; Rowe, 2008; Rowe and Neitzel, 2010). Drawing across a range of her extensive ethnographic studies undertaken in classrooms, Dyson (2020) argued that children use writing to explore their own lives and emotions, and to connect to and develop interests with their friends. Similarly, Barrs and Horrocks (2014) show that writing that has personal and emotional relevance for individual writers prompts fuller engagement, enabling students to develop a sense of pride and ownership in their work.

There is also evidence to suggest the value of children participating in authentic writing, with real purposes and audiences (e.g., Boscolo et al., 2012; Gadd et al., 2019; Gadd and Parr, 2016; Nolen, 2007; Zumbrunn et al., 2019). Such research indicates that when young people's personal purposes for writing are recognised and honoured, this can impact on their levels of engagement as well as success. For example, in New Zealand it was found that teachers who devised tasks that the children saw as purposeful and challenging, and who involved children in selecting and constructing these tasks, enabled them to make the most progress as writers (Gadd and Parr, 2016). Although the concept of audience is rarely directly examined, studies indicate its relevance. In one Australian study, Chen and Rutherford Vale (2020) examined the ways in which two primary teachers supported children's audience awareness. They displayed the children's work, modelled writing for specific audiences and offered writing circles where students could develop an understanding of the presence of an 'audience as reader' (Chen and Rutherford Vale, 2020, p. 147). In another study of primary classes in English inner-city schools, Barrs and Horrocks (2014) found that, through blogging, the pupils (n:12) were able to access and build audiences for their writing. These audiences included their families and readers from across the world which they found highly engaging. There were benefits for the teachers too, as they were able to learn more about the children's personal interests. Significantly, the children had control over their blogs, could use them for their own purposes, and were able to post from home whenever they wanted.

To exercise choice as writers, children need to be able to generate ideas, and draw on the texts they have read, heard and watched as well as their life experiences to do so (see Chapter 2). Yet, two school-based studies, both Jesson and Cockle (2016) in New Zealand and Woodard (2013) in the United States, found that the teaching of writing did not explicitly draw on the young people's engagement in reading or life experiences. In the former, children were offered no choice of genre or topic and appeared to see the features of the genre under instruction as 'a list of ingredients' they must include. In the latter, teachers restricted their modelling to align with limited curricula and thus neglected topics or genres that were personally meaningful to the children, linked to literature or life. Neither study showed evidence of the children's positive engagement in writing, rather it seems appropriate to interpret their involvement as 'doing schooled writing' with a degree of distanced engagement.

However, when young people are given freedom to draw upon their prior experiences, both lived and literary, they can re-sculpt these to support their writing practice. For instance, Parry and Taylor (2018) describe how children adapt resources from their cultural experiences when invited to freely create texts. Additionally, scholars argue, if children are offered the chance to lean on literature, this can make a contribution to their writing (e.g. Corden, 2000; Schatt and Ryan, 2021) which may enhance their writing, their self-efficacy as writers and their desire to write. Also, in a study of free reading and writing those children with broad reading repertoires also had a broad range of approaches to writing (Taylor and Clarke, 2021). They wanted to write the kinds of texts they had enjoyed reading and were skilful in so doing. In brief, when young people are given choice over what they write and how they write, they appear to experience greater engagement in being writers. Despite these reassuring insights into approaches capable of supporting engagement in and enjoyment of writing in the moment, there remains a gap in the extant literature that attends to how these choice-led writing practices may extend out and impact upon volitional writing in different settings and at different times.

Time for reading and writing

Having time to engage with reading and writing is seen to be beneficial. Research suggests that when time for reading is set aside children can practice skills, enhance stamina, build an awareness of their interests and sense of self as a reader (Hiebert and Reutzel, 2010; Reutzel et al., 2008). Time to read can be of value for young readers at the beginning stages, those struggling, those reading in their second language and those who are more assured (Hudson and Williams, 2015). The same can be said of writing, although there is less research that looks explicitly at the relationship between time and writing. Nevertheless, when time is made available for reading and writing, research indicates that this can involve more silent and private practices (e.g. Collins et al., 2022) as well as more chatty and interactive practices (e.g. Moses and Kelly, 2019), both having value in motivating and engaging young readers and writers.

Some studies draw attention to the value of giving young people enough time for independent reading. Yet, Bus et al. (2024) acknowledge, there is debate regarding effectiveness of independent reading practice, not least because studies have focused on the different effects of independent reading. For example, some studies have focused on the impact of quiet reading time on the development of reading skills and competencies (e.g. Smith and Joyner, 1990; Taylor et al., 1990), with Reutzel et al. (2008) concluding that 20–25 minutes of daily, scaffolded silent reading supported the fluency and comprehension of 8–9-year-olds in areas of high levels of deprivation. Others have identified that when children read silently, on their own, their comprehension improves (Hiebert and Reutzel, 2010). Regular, independent reading is also associated with increasing reading stamina, which can help children to engage with and comprehend more complex texts (Hiebert and Pearson, 2014). Connected to this proposal is Cuevas et al.'s (2014) research into independent, silent reading. In a study of 15–17-year-olds these researchers found that not only did young people's comprehension increase, but so too did their confidence levels. This research suggests that having quiet time to develop reading skills provides a useful foundation upon which children can become absorbed in a story, developing their engagement with and enjoyment of reading. Returning to the work of Bus et al. (2024), who conducted a meta-analysis of studies (1970–2020) concerned with in-school independent reading, they found that whilst independent reading appeared to affect both word recognition and children's reading attitudes, the link to volitional reading remains elusive.

Some studies in line with Bus et al.'s (2024) review show the positive impact on enjoyment and attitudes. For instance, drawing upon data from group interviews with 8–11-year-olds (n:59), Oxley and McGeown (2023) found that the children valued having time set aside to read their self-chosen books. Similarly, using teachers' (n:105) feedback from a reading for pleasure intervention, Collins et al. (2022) found that when text choice was embedded into a programme of regular quiet reading time, reading enjoyment was discerned among even those children who were characterised as resistant to reading. In these studies, choice and time combine, demonstrating how key aspects of volitional reading operate in tandem.

Historically, however, educators and researchers have expressed concerns about the value of reading silently, and 'fake reading', whereby individuals might pretend to read, looking superficially at texts without attempting to engage (e.g. Bryan et al., 2003; Hiebert and Reutzel, 2010; Kelley and Clausen-Grace, 2006; Reutzel et al., 2008). Indeed, in 2000, Shriver argued there was insufficient quality research to substantiate causal claims between reading time and skill-based benefits. A more recent review of studies in this area affirms the absence of this causal relationship (Erbeli and Rice, 2022), although it does recognise that the ways silent reading times are organised and facilitated are significant. If children are offered scant support and limited or irrelevant text choices for mandated reading time, they are unlikely to be motivated or engaged as readers.

When reading time is intentional and well-planned, coupled with scaffolding by adults and opportunities for conversation with peers, multiple studies indicate it can make a contribution to developing volitional reading and positive reader identities (e.g. Cremin et al., 2014; Cuevas et al., 2014; Francois, 2013; Kennedy, 2018; Manresa, 2018; Merga, 2017; Merga and Mason, 2019; Moses and Kelly, 2018). In particular, studies demonstrate that offering time to talk about texts before, during or after independent reading is of real value, alongside periods of quiet (e.g. Cremin et al., 2014; Kennedy, 2018; Moses and Kelly, 2019; Ng, 2018). These indicate the value of fluid and flexible practices, whereby quiet, independent reading can morph into relaxed and even chatty interactions. In one study (Moses and Kelly, 2019), which focused on 6–7-year-olds, the benefits of teachers being willing to take a chance on independent reading time, even if at times it might be susceptible to 'fake reading', was made evident, so long as it was situated within a broader reading for pleasure pedagogy:

> When offered a supportive early literacy environment in which the teacher provided interesting, appropriate texts and instruction in independent reading strategies and behaviours, students demonstrated many more literacy-related behaviours than off-task behaviours.
>
> *(Moses and Kelly, 2019, p. 333)*

In this study, the researchers observed that over the course of a year, the teacher engaged in one-to-one and small group coaching during this time and allowed quiet interactions between children, for example, they shared their excitement or asked for help. By the end of the school year, this class of young children primarily used independent reading time to read (Moses and Kelly, 2019), plus, most of them regularly chose to take books home to read for pleasure. In a related study (Ng, 2018), a class teacher shifted the focus during independent reading time from 'silence to reading' (Ng, 2018, p. 713). This involved teacher-initiated discussions that gave the young people time to talk, their ideas were valued, and they were invited to bring in books to read from home. These combined practices were seen to be motivating, suggesting that time to read needs to be supported in diverse ways (see Chapter 6 for a more detailed discussion of the role of social interaction in motivating readers).

Nonetheless, challenges can persist, since as Mackey (2022) suggests, giving children time to read must include trusting them to make choices not to read. Building on the work of Pennac (2006), she argues that adults need to reflect upon the behaviours they are expecting to see during this time, and the extent to which the presence or absence of these behaviours qualifies 'a person to be described as a reader' (Mackey, 2022, p. 103). Moreover, linked to the discussion of agency and autonomy in Chapter 4, it needs to be recognised that resistance and refusals are also choices, and their presence could provide valuable insights into the environment created and its consequences.

With regard to writing, debates exist regarding the amount of time needed for teaching writing and allowing children to experience being writers (e.g. Coker et al., 2018; Rietdijk et al., 2018), with Graham et al. (2015) arguing that adding a quarter of an hour of writing each day can impact significantly on writing outcomes. Nonetheless, these studies focus on writing outputs not the nurturing of writers' identities. Time is also examined in a Chinese study, which found that children spent just eight minutes a day writing (Hsiang et al., 2020). It stands to reason that if such restricted time is offered, children's pleasurable engagement and investment in writing is bound to be limited. Instead, studies recognise that if children are to become both competent and engaged writers, dedicated time is essential. Composing is a considered practice and needs direct teaching and scaffolding as well as space and time for independent exploration and innovation (De Smedt et al., 2018; Gallagher and Kittle, 2018; Graham et al., 2015). In general, research points to the value of offering time to choose to write, to engage volitionally through less structured writing activities, such as open-ended writing zones in the Early Years or the use of writing journals in older year groups (e.g. Cremin, 2020; Dyson, 2010; Nicolopoulou et al., 2006; Rowe and Neitzel, 2010; Rowe et al., 2022; Rumney et al., 2016).

The role of space

The creation of spaces for reading and writing that are welcoming and safe is recognised as valuable for supporting children's literacy engagement (e.g. Cremin and Swann, 2017; Kennedy, 2018; Loh, 2023). School libraries are often interpreted as quintessential spaces for reading and young people's views are often sought. For example, in Stewart's (2018) study, they felt libraries should: provide comfortable relaxed reading spaces with minimal noise, act as a forum to meet with peers, participate in clubs, use technologies and offer a contemplative oasis. Other studies affirm these perspectives, indicating that young people value library spaces that offer informal social opportunities to read, relax and access texts that are not otherwise accessible (Loh, 2016). The creation of such socially and emotionally supportive spaces for reading appeared to enable students in extracurricular reading groups to voice their views and debate texts in depth, even in the absence of adults (Cremin and Swann, 2017). Research also demonstrates the value of focusing on children's needs and desires in order to create and constantly iterate the design and use of school libraries (Loh, 2023). However, school leaders' understanding of the role of librarians is seen to be limited to literacy learning and study skills which constrains their potential impact on volitional reading (Hochman, 2016; Loh et al., 2021; Merga, 2020b).

There is scant research that directly addresses the configuration of school or wider community reading spaces and how such spaces might enable either quiet reading, livelier book-related interactions or both. However, one ethnographic study of a secondary school identified how staff identified and curated a range of spaces to support a reading for pleasure agenda (Francois, 2013). Students were encouraged and allowed to read in these shared reading spaces and reading was successfully positioned as a public and shared activity, with book recommendations being documented across classrooms, corridors and libraries. The rich book-related interactions discerned in myriad school spaces in Francois' study suggests the value of and possibilities enabled by extended and rich ethnographically influenced qualitative research, indicating possible next steps in the research agenda.

There appear to be fewer studies that look explicitly at the role of physical spaces in relation to writing for pleasure. However, some hint at the value of private space when engaging in volitional writing (Brady, 2017; Chamberlain, 2019). For instance, a case study of three 9- and 10-year-olds illustrated that they chose to engage with non-school, volitional writing at home in private spaces, such as their bedrooms (Chamberlain, 2019). This location allowed them to keep their personal writing activities 'secret'. Another study revealed how girls aged 7–13 years old (n:15) viewed their volitional writing at home as involving greater levels of freedom, variety, creativity, time and commitment in comparison to mandated writing at school (Brady, 2017). Given these characteristics, volitional writing can be characterised as more personal, precious and private. For instance, as Brady noted, the girls' writings of a 'more personal nature' were not 'intended for public consumption' (Brady, 2017, p. 162). In such instances, privacy was enacted through the girls, as authors, ascribing pseudonyms to their writing. This study draws attention to more abstract, or psychological conceptualisations, of space (Brady, 2017).

Other research has also indicated the need for head space for writing, one study noted that professional writers often referred to 'the privacy of writing and the need to find a mental space for writing' (Cremin and Myhill, 2012, p. 197). Similarly, Zumbrunn et al. (2019) found that young people voiced clear preferences for writing environments that were quiet and controlled. In contrast to these insights, Honeyford and Watt (2025) have drawn attention to the writing opportunities enabled through sharing writing experiences outside with others. Although their research orientated around the combination of adults walking, writing and noticing, Honeyford and Watt (2025) posit that such practices can help to enthuse teachers and identify what matters in their own writing. It is inferred that this may beneficially impact upon writing practices with children if adults seek to create physical and abstract spaces capable of supporting volitional writing.

Conclusion

To summarise, the reviewed literature repeatedly highlights that young people benefit from accessing and choosing their own experiences as readers and writers. However, these experiences are not evenly distributed, with socio-economic, curricula and pedagogical stances having an impact on children's text access and text choices. So, informed and motivated adults need to help children make judicious selections about resources and activities so as to ensure they can find texts that motivate, engage and prompt them to seek out new texts which offer further satisfaction. This foundation can be reinforced through ensuring children are given extended periods of time and varying spaces in which they can become absorbed as readers and writers. The studies considered illustrate that time needs to be carefully planned such that quiet reflexive spaces, as well as interactive and energetic ones, are offered that suit the diverse dispositions and shifting identities of young readers and writers.

References

ACARA (Australian Curriculum, Assessment and Reporting Authority) (2022) 'English F-10: Version 9.0: About the learning area'. Available from: https://australiancurriculum.edu.au/f-10-curriculum/english/structure/.

Adam, H. (2021) 'When authenticity goes missing: How monocultural children's literature is silencing the voices and contributing to invisibility of children from minority backgrounds', *Education Science*, 11, 32.

Adam, H. and Harper, L.J. (2023) 'Gender equity in early childhood picture books: A cross-cultural study of frequently read picture books in early childhood classrooms in Australia and the United States', *The Australian Educational Researcher*, 50, pp. 453–479.

Adam, H., Barratt-Pugh, C. and Haig, Y. (2019) '"Portray cultures other than ours": How children's literature is being used to support the diversity goals of the Australian Early Years Learning Framework', *The Australian Educational Researcher*, 46, pp. 549–563.

Alexander, J. and Jarman, R. (2018) 'The pleasures of reading non-fiction', *Literacy*, 52(2), pp. 78–85.

Akins, M., Tichenor, M., Heins, E. and Piechura, K. (2018) 'Teachers' knowledge of children's literature: What genres do teachers read?', *Reading Improvement*, 55(2), pp. 63–68.

Allen-Lyall, B. and Davis, V. (2020) 'Empowering students to make their own reading choices: A teaching framework', *Reading Improvement*, 1, pp. 1–10.

Allington, R.L. and McGill-Franzen, A.M. (2021) 'Reading volume and reading achievement: A review of recent research', *Reading Research Quarterly*, 56(S1), S231– S238.

Allington, R.L., McGill-Franzen, A., Camilli, G., Williams, L., Graff, J., Zeig, J., Zmach, C. and Nowak, R. (2010) 'Addressing summer reading setback among economically disadvantaged elementary students', *Reading Psychology*, 31(5), pp. 411–427.

Allred, J.B. and Cena, M.E. (2020) 'Reading motivation in high school: Instructional shifts in student choice and class time', *Journal of Adolescent and Adult Literacy*, 64(1), pp. 27–35.

Barratt-Pugh, C., Ruscoe, A. and Fellowes, J. (2021) 'Motivation to write: Conversations with emergent writers', *Early Childhood Education Journal*, 49(2), pp. 223–234.

Barrs, M. and Cork, V. (2001) *The Reader in the Writer: The Influence of Literature upon Writing at KS2*, London: Centre for Literacy in Primary Education.

Barrs, M. and Horrocks, S. (2014) *Educational Blogs and Their Effects on Pupils' Writing*, Reading: CfBT Education Trust.

Bell, S.M., Park, Y., Martin, M., Smith, J., McCallum, R.S., Smyth, K. and Mingo, M. (2020) 'Preventing summer reading loss for students in poverty: A comparison of tutoring and access to books', *Educational Studies*, 46(4), pp. 440–457.

Boscolo, P., Gelati, C. and Galvan, N. (2012) 'Teaching elementary school students to play with meanings and genre', *Reading and Writing Quarterly*, 28(1), pp. 29–50.

Brady, J. (2017) 'Being in the world: Students writing identities beyond school', in Cremin, T. and Locke, T. (eds), *Writer Identity and the Teaching and Learning of Writing*, London and New York: Routledge, pp. 151–168.

Brandt, L., Sharp, A.C. and Gardner, D.S. (2021) 'Examination of teacher practices on student motivation for reading', *The Reading Teacher*, 74(6), pp. 723–731.

Bryan, G., Fawson, P.C. and Reutzel, D.R. (2003) 'Sustained silent reading: Exploring the value of literature discussion with three non-engaged readers', *Reading Research and Instruction*, 43(1), pp. 47–73.

Bus, A.G., Shang, Y. and Roskos, K. (2024) 'Building a stronger case for independent reading at school', *AERA Open*, 10.

Cantrell, S.C., Pennington, J., Rintamaa, M., Osborne, M., Parker, C. and Rudd, M. (2017) 'Supplemental literacy instruction in high school: What students say matters for reading engagement', *Reading and Writing Quarterly*, 33(1), pp. 54–70.

Chamberlain, L. (2019) 'Places, spaces and local customs: Honouring the private worlds of out-of-school text creation', *Literacy*, 53(1), pp. 39–45.

Chen, H. and Rutherford Vale, E. (2020) 'Developing confident writers: fostering audience awareness in primary school writing classrooms', in Chen, H., Myhill, D. and Lewis, H. (eds), *Developing Writers Across Primary and Secondary Years*, London and Sydney: Routledge, pp. 131–153.

Clark, A. and Fleming, J. (2019) '"They almost become the teacher": Pre-K to third grade teachers' experiences reading and discussing culturally relevant texts with their students', *Reading Horizons: A Journal of Literacy and Language Arts*, 58(3), pp. 23–51.

Clark, C. and Teravainen, A. (2015) *Teachers and Literacy: Their Perceptions, Understanding, Confidence and Awareness*, London: National Literacy Trust.

Clark, C. and Teravainen-Goff, A. (2020) *Children and Young People's Reading in 2019: Findings From Our Annual Literacy Survey*, London: National Literacy Trust.

Cliff-Hodges, G. (2010) 'Reasons for reading: Why literature matters', *Literacy*, 44(2), pp. 60–68.

CLPE (2021) *Reading for Pleasure in 2020: Learning about Literacy Teaching during the Pandemic Reading for Pleasure*, London: CLPE.

CLPE (2023) *Reflecting Realities: Survey of Ethnic Representation within UK Children's Literature 2022*, London: CLPE.

CLPE (2024) *Reflecting Realities: Survey of Ethnic Representation within UK Children's Literature 2024*, London: CLPE.

Cockroft, C. and Atkinson, C. (2017) '"I just find it boring": Findings from an affective adolescent reading intervention', *Support for Learning*, 32(1), pp. 41–59.

Coker, D.L., Jennings, A.S., Farley-Ripple, E. and MacArthur, C.A. (2018) 'The type of writing instruction and practice matters: The direct and indirect effects of writing instruction and student practice on reading achievement', *Journal of Educational Psychology*, 110(4), pp. 502–517.

Collier, D. (2017) 'Glancing sideways at young writers becoming', in Cremin, T. and Locke, T. (eds), *Writer Identity and the Teaching and Learning of Writing*, London: Routledge, pp. 169–183.

Collins, V.J., Dargan, I.W., Walsh, R.L. and Merga, M. (2022) 'Teachers' perceptions of the benefits and challenges of a whole-school reading for pleasure program', *Issues in Educational Research*, 32(1), pp. 89–104.

Conradi Smith, K., Young, C.A. and Yatzeck, J.C. (2022) 'What are teachers reading and why? An analysis of elementary read aloud titles and the rationales underlying teachers' selections', *Literacy Research and Instruction*, 61(4), pp. 383–401.

Corden, R. (2000) 'Reading-writing connections: The importance of interactive discourse'. *English in Education*, 34(2), pp. 35–44.

Corden, R. (2001) 'Teaching reading–writing links (TRAWL) project in reading, literacy and language, *Literacy*, 35(1), pp. 37–40.

Cremin, T. (2020) 'Apprenticing authors: Nurturing children's identities as writers', in Chen, H., Myhill, D. and Lewis, H. (eds), *Developing Writers Across Primary and Secondary Years*, London and Sydney: Routledge, pp. 113–130.

Cremin, T. and Myhill, D. (2012) *Writing Voices: Creating Communities of Writers*, London: Routledge.

Cremin, T. and Swann, J. (2017) 'School librarians as leaders of extracurricular reading groups', in Pihl, J., van der Kooij, K. and Carlsten, T. (eds), *Teacher and Librarian Partnerships in Literacy Education in the 21st Century*, Rotterdam: Sense Publishers, pp. 119–137.

Cremin, T., Bearne, E., Mottram, M. and Goodwin, P. (2008a) 'Primary teachers as readers', *English in Education*, 42(1), pp. 8–23.

Cremin, T., Mottram, M., Bearne, E. and Goodwin, P. (2008b) 'Exploring teachers' knowledge of children's literature', *Cambridge Journal of Education*, 38(4), pp. 449–464.

Cremin, T., Lillis, T., Myhill, D. and Eyres, I. (2017) 'Professional writers' identities', in Cremin, T. and Locke, T. (eds), *Writer Identity and the Teaching and Learning of Writing*, London: Routledge, pp. 18–36.

Cremin, T., Mottram, M., Collins, F.M., Powell, S. and Safford, K. (2014) *Building Communities of Engaged Readers: Reading for Pleasure*, Oxon: Routledge.

Cremin, T., Mottram, M., Collins, F.M., Powell, S. and Drury, R. (2015) *Researching Literacy Lives Building Communities between Home and School*, London: Routledge.

Cremin, T., Myhill, D., Eyres, I., Wilson, A., Oliver, L. and Nash, T. (2020) 'Teachers as writers: Learning together', *Literacy*, 53(2), pp. 49–59.

Cremin, T., Mukherjee, S., Aerila, J.A., Kauppinen, M., Lateela, J. and Sipola, M. (2024) 'Widening teachers' reading repertoires: Moving beyond a popular childhood canon', *The Reading Teacher*, 77(6), pp. 833–841.

Cuevas, J.A., Irving, M.A. and Russell, L.R. (2014) 'Applied cognition: Testing the effects of independent silent reading on secondary students' achievement and attribution', *Reading Psychology*, 35(2), pp. 127–159.

Daniels, J. (1996) 'Is a series reader a serious reader?', in Styles, M., Bearne, E. and Watson, V. (eds), *Voices Off: Texts, Contexts and Readers*, London: Cassell, pp. 44–55.

de Bondt, M., Willenberg, I.A. and Bus, A.G. (2020) 'Do book giveaway programs promote the home literacy environment and children's literacy-related behaviour and skills?', *Review of Educational Research*, 90(3), pp. 349–375.

De Naeghel, J., Van Keer, H., Vansteenkiste, M. and Rosseel, Y. (2012) 'The relation between elementary students' recreational and academic reading motivation, reading frequency, engagement, and comprehension: A self-determination theory perspective', *Journal of Educational Psychology*, 104(4), pp. 1006–1021.

De Naeghel, J., Van Keer, H., Vansteenkiste, M., Haerens, L. and Aelterman, N. (2016) 'Promoting elementary school students' autonomous reading motivation: Effects of a teacher professional development workshop', *The Journal of Educational Research*, 109(3), pp. 232–252.

De Smedt, F., Merchie, E., Barendse, M., Rossell, Y., De Naeghel, J. and Van Keer, H. (2018) 'Cognitive and motivational challenges in writing: Studying the relationship with writing performance across students' gender and achievement level', *Reading Research Quarterly*, 53(2), pp. 249–272.

DfE (2014) *The National Curriculum in England*, London: Department for Education. Available from: https://www.gov.uk/government/uploads/system/uploads/attachment_data/file/381344/Master_final_national_curriculum_28_Nov.pdf.

Dyson, A.H. (1999) 'Transforming transfer: Unruly children, contrary texts, and the persistence of the pedagogical order', *Review of Research in Education*, 24(1), pp. 141–171.

Dyson, A.H. (2001) 'Where are the childhoods in childhood literacy? An exploration in outer (school) space', *Journal of Early Childhood Literacy*, 1(1), pp. 9–39.

Dyson, A.H. (2010) 'Writing childhoods under construction: Re-visioning "copying" in early childhood', *Journal of Early Childhood Literacy*, 10(1), pp. 7–31.

Dyson, A.H. (2020) '"This isn't my real writing": The fate of children's agency in too-tight curricula', *Theory Into Practice*, 59(2), pp. 119–127.

Edmunds, K.M. and Bauserman, K.L. (2006) 'What teachers can learn about reading motivation through conversations with children', *The Reading Teacher*, 59(5), pp. 414–424.

Elliott, V., Nelson-Addy, L., Chantiluke, R. and Courtney, M. (2021) *Lit in Colour: Diversity in Literature in English Schools*, London: Runnymede and Penguin.

Erbeli, F. and Rice, M. (2022) 'Examining the effects of silent independent reading on reading outcomes: A narrative synthesis review from 2000 to 2020', *Reading and Writing Quarterly*, 38(3), pp. 253–271.

European Commission, Directorate-General for Education, Youth, Sport and Culture (2012) *EU High Level Group of Experts on Literacy: Final Report*, Luxembourg: EU Publications Office.

Evans, M.D.R., Kelly, J., Sikora, J. and Treiman, D.J. (2010) 'Family scholarly culture and educational success: Books and schooling in 27 nations', *Research in Social Stratification and Mobility*, 28(2), pp. 1–27.

Farrar, J. (2021) '"I don't really have a reason to read children's literature": Enquiring into primary student teachers' knowledge of children's literature', *Journal of Literary Education*, 4, pp. 217–236.

Fisher, R. (2006) 'Whose writing is it anyway?', *Cambridge Journal of Education*, 36(2), pp. 193–206.

Fisher, D. and Frey, N. (2018) 'Raise reading volume through access, choice, discussion, and book talks', *Reading Teacher*, 72(1), pp. 89–97.

Fletcher, A. (2016) 'Exceeding expectations: Scaffolding agentic engagement through assessment as learning', *Educational Research*, 58(4), pp. 400–419.

Francois, C. (2013) 'Reading in the crawl space: A study of an urban school's literacy-focused community of practice', *Teachers College Record*, 115(5), pp. 1–35.

Funge, S.P., Sullivan, D.J. and Tarter, K. (2017) 'Promoting positive family interactions: Evaluating a free early childhood book distribution program', *Early Childhood Education Journal*, 45(5), pp. 603–611.

Gadd, M. and Parr, J.M. (2016) 'It's all about Baxter: Task orientation in the effective teaching of writing', *Literacy*, 50(2), pp. 93–99.

Gadd, M., Parr, J., Robertson, J., Carran, L., Ali, Z., Gendall, L. and Watson, K. (2019) 'Portrait of the student as a young writer: Some student survey findings about attitudes to writing and self-efficacy as writers', *Literacy*, 53(4), pp. 226–235.

Galea, C., Robidoux, S., Salins, A., Noble, C. and McArthur, G. (2024) 'The impact of shared book reading on children and families: A study of Dolly Parton's Imagination Library in Tamworth, Australia', *Journal of Research in Childhood Education*, pp. 1–30.

Gallagher, K. and Kittle, P. (2018) 'Giving students the right kind of writing practice', *Educational Leadership*, 75(7), pp. 14–20.

Gambrell, L.B. (2011) 'Seven rules of engagement: What's most important to know about motivation to read', *The Reading Teacher*, 65(3), pp. 172–178.

González-Díaz, V., Parr, E. and Nourie, K. (2024) 'Conceptualisations of "good" writing in the English primary school context', *Language and Education*, 39(3), pp. 656–679.

Graham, L. and Johnson, A. (2012) *Children's Writing Journals*, Leicester: United Kingdom Literacy Association.

Graham, S., Harris, K. and Santangelo, T. (2015) 'Research-based writing practices and the Common Core', *Elementary School Journal*, 115(4), pp. 498–523.

Gregory, E. and Williams, A. (2000) *City Literacies: Learning to Read Across Generations and Cultures*, London: Routledge.

Guo, Y., Puranik, C., Kelcey, B., Sun, J., Schneider, M. and Breit-Smith, A. (2021) 'The role of home literacy practices in Kindergarten children's early writing development: A one-year longitudinal study', *Early Education and Development*, 32(2), pp. 209–227.

Guthrie, J.T., Hoa, A.L.W., Wigfield, A., Tonks, S., Humenick, N.M. and Littles, E. (2007) 'Reading motivation and reading comprehension growth in the later elementary years', *Contemporary Educational Psychology*, 32(3), pp. 282–313.

Hartsfield, D.E. and Kimmel, S.C. (2020) 'Supporting the right to read: Principles for selecting children's books', *The Reading Teacher*, 74(4), pp. 419–427.

Healey, B. (2019) 'How children experience creative writing in the classroom', *Australian Journal of Language and Literacy*, 42, pp. 184–194.

Hempel-Jorgensen, A., Cremin, T., Harris, D. and Chamberlain, L. (2018) 'Pedagogy for reading for pleasure in low socio-economic primary schools: Beyond "pedagogy of poverty"?', *Literacy*, 52(2), pp. 86–94.

Hiebert, E.H. and Pearson, P. (2014) 'Understanding text complexity', *The Elementary School Journal*, 115(2), pp. 153–160.

Hiebert, E.H. and Reutzel, D.R. (2010) *Revisiting Silent Reading: New Directions for Teachers and Researchers*, Newark, DE: International Reading Association.

Hiebert, E., Wilson, K. and Trainin, G. (2014) 'Are students really reading in independent reading contexts? An examination of comprehension-based silent reading rate', in Hiebert, E. and Reutzel, D.R. (eds), *Revisiting Silent Reading: New Directions for Teachers and Researchers*, Newark, DE: International Reading Association, pp. 151–167.

Hochman, J. (2016) 'School library nostalgias', *Curriculum Inquiry*, 46(2), pp. 132–147.

Honeyford, M. and Watt, J. (2025) 'Opening the door to writing relationalities: Moving writing and the teaching of writing', *Literacy*, 59(1), pp. 108–117.

Hsiang, T.P., Graham, S. and Yang, Y.M. (2020) 'Teachers' practices and beliefs about teaching writing: A comprehensive survey of grades 1 to 3 teachers', *Reading and Writing: An Interdisciplinary Journal*, 33, pp. 2511–2548.

Hudson, A.K. and Williams, J.A. (2015) 'Reading every single day: A journey to authentic reading', *The Reading Teacher*, 68(7), pp. 530–538.

Ives, S., Parsons, S., Ward Parsons, A., Dana A., Robertson, D., Daoud, N., Young, C. and Polk, L. (2020) 'Elementary students' motivation to read and genre preferences', *Reading Psychology*, 41(7), pp. 660–679.

Jerrim, J. and Moss, G. (2019) 'The link between fiction and teenagers' reading skills: International evidence from the OECD PISA study', *British Educational Research Journal*, 45(1), pp. 181–200.

Jesson, R.N. and Cockle, V. (2016) 'The opportunities to build on existing expertise in writing classrooms: A study of writing lessons in New Zealand primary schools', *Education 3–13*, 44(6), pp. 604–616.

Jouhar, M.R. and Rupley, W.H. (2021) 'The reading–writing connection based on independent reading and writing: A systematic review', *Reading and Writing Quarterly*, 37(2), pp. 136–156.

Kelley, M. and Clausen-Grace, N. (2006) 'R5: The sustained silent reading makeover that transformed readers', *The Reading Teacher*, 60(2), pp. 148–156.

Kennedy, E. (2018) 'Engaging children as readers and writers in high-poverty contexts', *Journal of Research in Reading*, 41(4), pp. 716–731.

Kervin, L., Comber, B. and Woods, A. (2020) 'Children learning to write in early primary classrooms', in Chen, H., Myhill, D. and Lewis, H. (eds), *Developing Writers across the Primary and Secondary Years: Growing into Writing*, Oxon: Routledge, pp. 19–39.

Kim, J.S., Hemphill, L., Troyer, M., Thomson, J.M., Jones, S.M., LaRusso, M.D. and Donaovan, S. (2017) 'Engaging struggling adolescent readers to improve reading skills', *Reading Research Quarterly*, 52(3), pp. 357–384.

Kissel, B.T. and Miller, E.T. (2015) 'Reclaiming power in the writers' workshop: Defending curricula, countering narratives, and changing identities in prekindergarten classrooms', *The Reading Teacher*, 69(1), pp. 77–86.

Kozak, S. and Martin-Chang, S. (2019) 'Preservice teacher knowledge, print exposure, and planning for instruction', *Reading Research Quarterly*, 54(3), pp. 323–338.

Kress, G.R. (1997) *Before Writing: Rethinking the Paths to Literacy*, London: Routledge.

Kuzmičová, A. and Cremin, T. (2022) 'Different fiction genres take children's memories to different places', *Cambridge Journal of Education*, 52(1), pp. 37–53.

Kuzmičová, A. and Supa, M. (2024) 'Interesting facts: Holistic interviews on children's nonfiction engagement', *Language and Education*, 38(4), pp. 560–577.

Laman, T.T., Flint, A.S., Rossi, R. and Jaggers, W. (2025) '"I love my class family": Writing realities and relational pedagogies', *Literacy*, *59*(1), pp. 118–131.

Leino, K., Nissinen, K., Puhakka, E. and Rautopuro, J. (2017) *Lukutaito luodaan yhdessä: kansainvälinen lasten lukutaitotutkimus* [*Reading Skills are Created Together: International Survey on Reading*], Jyväskslä: Finnish Institute for Educational Research.

Lindsay, J.J. (2010) *Children's Access to Print Material and Education-Related Outcomes: Findings from a Meta-Analytic Review*, Naperville, IL: Learning Point Associates.

Locher, F.M., Becker, S. and Pfost, M. (2019) 'The relation between students' intrinsic reading motivation and book reading in recreational and school contexts', *AERA Open*, 5(2), pp. 1–14.

Loh, C.E. (2016) 'Levelling the reading gap: A socio-spatial study of school libraries and reading in Singapore', *Literacy*, 50(1), pp. 3–13.

Loh, C.E. (2023) 'Designing future-ready school libraries: Empowering stakeholders for evidence-based change', *Journal of the Australian Library and Information Association*, 72(3), pp. 294–305.

Loh, C.E. (2024) 'What makes adolescents want to read? Examining adolescents' contemporary print and new media (fiction) leisure reading through mobile ethnography', *Language and Education*, 38(4), pp. 596–616.

Loh, C.E., Sundaray, S., Merga, M. and Gao, J. (2021) 'Principals and teachers' perspectives of their school libraries and implications for school library policy', *Journal of library Administration*, 61(5), pp. 550–571.

Mackey, M. (2022) 'Social justice for young readers: Advocating for access, choice and time to read', *Literacy*, 56(2), pp. 97–105.

Manresa, M. (2018) 'Adolescent reading habits: The effect of school activities on reading practices', in Arizpe, E. and Cliff Hodges, G. (eds), *Young People Reading: Empirical Research Across International Contexts*, New York: Routledge, pp. 123–136.

McGeown, S., Bonsall, J., Andries, V., Howarth, D., Wilkinson, K. and Sabeti, S. (2020a) 'Growing up a reader: Exploring children's and adolescents' perceptions of "a reader"', *Educational Research*, 62(2), pp. 216–228.

McGeown, S., Bonsall, J., Andries, V., Howarth, D. and Wilkinson, K. (2020b) 'Understanding reading motivation across different text types: Qualitative insights from children', *Journal of Research in Reading*, 43(4), pp. 597–608.

McKnight, L. (2018) 'Sponsors of pleasure: Wide reading re-imagined through social curation', *Changing English*, 25(3), pp. 300–311.

Merga, M.K. (2017) 'What would make children read for pleasure more frequently?', *English in Education*, 51(2), pp. 207–223.

Merga, M.K. (2020a) '"We talk books": Teacher librarians promoting book discussion to foster reading engagement', *English in Australia*, 55(1), pp. 22–33.

Merga, M.K. (2020b) 'School librarians as literacy educators within a complex role', *Journal of Library Administration*, 60(8), pp. 889–908.

Merga, M.K. and Mason, S. (2019) 'Building a school reading culture: Teacher librarians' perceptions of enabling and constraining factors', *Australian Journal of Education*, 63(2), pp. 173–189.

Milne, J., Harrington, C. and Boyask, R. (2022) '"We read together": Collaboration, community and stories supporting children's reading for pleasure', *Literacy Forum NZ*, 37(1), pp. 44–55.

Mohr, K.A.J. (2006) 'Children's choices for recreational reading: A three-part investigation of selection preferences, rationales, and processes', *Journal of Literacy Research*, 38(1), pp. 81–104.

Moll, L., Amanti, C., Neff, D. and Gonzalez, N. (1992) 'Funds of knowledge for teaching: Using a qualitative approach to connect homes and classrooms', *Theory into Practice*, 31, pp. 132–141.

Moses, L. and Kelly, L.B. (2018) '"We're a little loud. That's because we like to read!": Developing positive views of reading in a diverse, urban first grade', *Journal of Early Childhood Literacy*, 18(3), pp. 307–337.

Moses, L. and Kelly, L.B. (2019) 'Are they really reading? A descriptive study of first graders during independent reading', *Reading and Writing Quarterly*, 35(4), pp. 322–338.

Moss, G. and McDonald, J. (2004) 'The borrowers: Library records as unobtrusive measures of children's reading preferences', *Journal of Research in Reading*, 27(4), pp. 401–412.

Myhill, D. (2005) 'Writing creatively', in Wilson, A. (ed), *Creativity in Primary Education*, Exeter: Learning Matters, pp. 58–69.

Neuman, S. and Celano, D.C. (2012) *Giving Our Children a Fighting Chance: Poverty, Literacy, and the Development of Information Capital*, New York: Teachers College Press.

Neuman, S. and Moland, N. (2016) 'Book deserts: The consequences of income segregation on children's access to print', *Urban Education*, 54(1), pp. 126–147.

Ng, C. (2018) 'Using student voice to promote reading engagement for economically disadvantaged students', *Journal of Research in Reading*, 41(4), pp. 700–715.

Nicolopoulou, A., McDowell, J. and Brockmeyer, C. (2006) 'Narrative play and emergent literacy: Storytelling and story-acting meet journal writing', in Singer, D.G., Golinkoff, R.M. and Hirsh-Pasek, K. (eds), *Play = Learning: How Play Motivates and Enhances Children's Cognitive and Social-Emotional Growth*, New York: Oxford University Press, pp. 122–144.

Nielen, T.M.J. and Bus, A.G. (2015) 'Enriched school libraries: A boost to academic achievement', *AERA Open*, 1(4).

Nolen, S.B. (2007) 'Young children's motivation to read and write: Development in social contexts', *Cognition and Instruction*, 25(2–3), pp. 219–270.

O'Hare, L. and Connolly, P. (2014) 'A cluster randomised controlled trial of "Bookstart +": A book gifting programme', *Journal of Children's Services*, 9(1), pp. 18–30.

Oxley, E. and McGeown, S. (2023) 'Reading for pleasure practices in school: Children's perspectives and experiences', *Educational Research*, 65(3), pp. 375–391.

Parr, J. and McNaughton, S. (2013) 'The unfulfilled pedagogical promise of the dialogic in writing: intertextual writing instruction for diverse settings', in Hall, K., Cremin, T., Comber, B. and Moll, L. (eds), *The Wiley Blackwell International Research Handbook of Children's Literacy, Learning and Culture*, Oxford: Wiley Blackwell, pp. 215–227.

Parry, B. and Taylor, L. (2018) 'Readers in the round: Children's holistic engagements with texts', *Literacy*, 52(2), pp. 103–110.

Pennac, D. (2006) *The Rights of the Reader*, London: Walker Books.

Pihl, J. (2012) 'Can library use enhance intercultural education?', *Issues in Educational Research*, 22(1), pp. 1–12.

Pribesh, S., Gavigan, K. and Dickinson, G. (2011) 'The access gap: Poverty and characteristics of school library media centers', *Library Quarterly*, 81(2), pp. 143–160.

Ramdarshan Bold, M. (2022) *Representation of People of Colour among Children's Book Creators in the UK (2020–2021)*, London: Book Trust.

Reedy, A. and De Carvalho, D. (2021) 'Children's perspectives on reading, agency and their environment: What can we learn about reading for pleasure from an East London primary school?', *Education 3–13*, 49(2), pp. 134–147.

Reedy, A. and Reedy, D. (2024) '"Because it reminds me of my culture." "Because I want to challenge myself." "Because I like all the stars and the swirls." What influences children's independent choice of text?', *Literacy*, 58(3), pp. 289–300.

Reutzel, D.R., Jones, C., Parker, C.F. and Smith, J.A. (2008) 'Scaffolded silent reading: A complement to guided repeated oral reading that works!', *The Reading Teacher*, 62(3), pp. 194–207.

Rietdijk, S., van Weijen, D., Janssen, T., van den Bergh, H. and Rijlaarsdam, G. (2018) 'Teaching writing in primary education: Classroom practice, time, teachers' beliefs and skills', *Journal of Educational Psychology*, 110(5), pp. 640–663.

Ross, C.S. (2018) 'Adult readers', in Ross, C.S., McKechnie, L. and Rothbauer, P. (eds), *Reading Still Matters: What the Research Reveals about Reading, Libraries, and Community*, Santa Barbara: Libraries Unlimited, pp. 137–230.

Ross, C.S., McKechnie, L.E. and Rothbauer, P.M. (2018) *Reading Still Matters: What the Research Reveals about Reading, Libraries, and Community*, Santa Barbara: Libraries Unlimited.

Rowe, D.W. (2008) 'Social contracts for writing: Negotiating shared understandings about text in the preschool years', *Reading Research Quarterly*, 43(1), pp. 66–95.
Rowe, D.W. and Neitzel, C. (2010) 'Interest and agency in 2–3-year-olds' participation in emergent writing', *Reading Research Quarterly*, 45(2), pp. 169–195.
Rowe, D.W., Shimizu, A.Y. and Davis, Z.G. (2022) 'Essential practices for engaging young children as writers: Lessons from expert early writing teachers', *The Reading Teacher*, 75(4), pp. 485–494.
Rudkin, G. and Wood, C. (2019) *Understanding the Impact and Characteristics of School Libraries and Reading Spaces*, London: Nottingham Trent University and National Literacy Trust.
Rumney, P., Kuksa, I. and Buttress, J. (2016) 'Seeing, doing, writing: The Write Here Project', *Sage Open*, 6(1).
Schatt, D. and Ryan, P. (2021) *Story Listening and Experience in Early Childhood*, Basingstoke: Palgrave Macmillan.
Scholes, L. (2019) 'Differences in attitudes towards reading and other school-related activities among boys and girls', *Journal of Research in Reading*, 42(3–4), pp. 485–503.
Scholes, L., Spina, N. and Comber, B. (2021) 'Disrupting the "boys don't read" discourse: Primary school boys who love reading fiction', *British Educational Research Journal*, 47(1), pp. 163–180.
Sénéchal, M., Hill, S. and Malette, M. (2018) 'Individual differences in grade 4 children's written compositions: The role of online planning and revising, oral storytelling, and reading for pleasure', *Cognitive Development*, 45, pp. 92–104.
Shaver, L. (2020) *Ending Book Hunger: Access to Print across Barriers of Class and Culture*, New Haven: Yale University Press.
Shriver, E.K. (2000) *Report of the National Reading Panel: Teaching Children to Read*. Available from: https://www.nichd.nih.gov/publications/pubs/nrp/smallbook.
Simpson, A. and Cremin, T. (2022) 'Responsible reading: Children's literature and social justice', *Education Sciences*, 12(4), 264.
Sims Bishop, R. (1990) 'Windows and mirrors: Children's books and parallel cultures', in *California State University San Bernardino Reading Conference. 14th Annual Conference Proceedings: Celebrating Literacy*, San Bernadino, CA: CSUSBRC, pp. 3–15.
Smith, L.L. and Joyner, C.R. (1990) 'Comparing recreational reading levels with reading levels from an informal reading inventory', *Reading Horizons: A Journal of Literacy and Language Arts*, 30(4), pp. 293–299.
Stewart, P. (2018) 'School library design, facilities and resource for sustainable cognitive and social development of students: An evaluative case study', *School Libraries Worldwide*, 24(2), pp. 30–45.
Tatum, A. (2008) 'Towards a more anatomically complete model of literacy instruction: A focus on African American male adolescents and texts', *Harvard Educational Review*, 78(1), pp. 155–180.
Taylor, B.M., Frye, B.J. and Maruyama, G.M. (1990) 'Time spent reading and reading growth', *American Educational Research Journal*, 27(2), pp. 351–362.
Taylor, L. and Clarke, P. (2021) 'We read, we write: Reconsidering reading–writing relationships in primary school children', *Literacy*, 55(1), pp. 14–24.
Tegmark, M., Alatalo, T., Vinterek, M. and Winberg, M. (2022) 'What motivates students to read at school? Student views on reading practices in middle and lower-secondary school', *Journal of Research in Reading*, 45(1), pp. 100–118.
Thomson, P. (2002) *Schooling the Rustbelt Kids: Making the Difference in Changing Times*, Stoke on Trent: Trentham Books.
Torppa, M., Niemi, P., Vasalampi, K., Lerkkanen, M.-K., Tolvanen, A. and Poikkeus, A.-M. (2020) 'Leisure reading (but not any kind) and reading comprehension support each other: A longitudinal study across grades 1 and 9', *Child Development*, 91(3), pp. 876–900.
Tura, F., Wood, C., Thompson, C. and Lushey, C. (2021) 'Evaluating the impact of book gifting on the reading behaviours of parents on young children', *Early Years*, 43(1), pp. 75–90.

Vehabovic, N. (2021) 'Picturebooks as critical literacy: Experiences and perspectives of translingual children from refugee backgrounds', *Journal of Literacy Research*, 53(3), pp. 382–405.

Watson, A., Kelly, L., Foley, J., Kneen, J., Chapman, S., Smith, L. and Thomas, H. (2022). 'Teacher agency in the selection of literary texts', *English in Education*, 56(4), pp. 340–356.

Webber, C., Wilkinson, K., Andries, V. and McGeown, S. (2022) 'A reflective account of using child-led interviews as a means to promote discussions about reading', *Literacy*, 56, pp. 120–129.

Webber, C., Wilkinson, K., Duncan, L.G. and McGeown, S. (2024) 'Adolescents' perspectives on the barriers to reading for pleasure', *Literacy*, 58(2), pp. 204–215.

Wilhelm, J. (2016) 'Recognising the power of pleasure: What engaged adolescent readers get from their free-choice reading, and how teachers can leverage this for all', *Australian Journal of Language and Literacy*, 39(1), pp. 30–41.

Woodard, R.L. (2013) 'Complicating "writing teachers must write": Tensions between teachers' literate and instructional practices', in *62nd Yearbook of the Literacy Research Association*, Altamonte Springs, FL: Literacy Research Association, pp. 377–390.

Zumbrunn, S., Marrs, S., Broda, M., Ekholm, E., DeBusk-Lane, M. and Jackson, L. (2019) 'Toward a more complete understanding of writing enjoyment: A mixed methods study of elementary students', *AERA Open*, 5(2), pp. 1–16.

6

SOCIAL INTERACTIONS

Introduction

The third theme arising from the literature review, namely the role of social interactions in reading and writing for pleasure, is explored in this chapter. Both reading and writing may be seen as independent and private activities, whereby an individual focuses on and is, ideally, absorbed by a text, either when reading or composing. In contrast, studies which attend to volitional reading and writing in varied settings show that the foregrounded literacy environments in such settings are highly social ones. Thus, instead of positioning reading and writing as individualistic cognitive endeavours, this chapter will highlight the social elements of both activities.

In this chapter, the research reviewed is presented and appraised, this suggests that the sharing of texts, at home and in school, in person and online, helps young people to develop social bonds and, in so doing, enhances their enjoyment of reading and writing. Talk in relation to reading and writing has often been positioned as supporting comprehension or meta-cognitive understandings of writing, but it affords more than this. The research indicates that informal, child-led discussions about the reading and writing of texts can enhance pleasure and engagement, not only by facilitating ideas, but also generating profound and sustainable connections with others.

Shared reading

Sharing texts through listening to others read can be enjoyable for young people (e.g. Anderson et al., 2019; Boerma et al., 2018; Vuong et al., 2021). Variously referred to as 'read alouds' (Wiseman, 2011; Worthy et al., 2012), or 'shared readings' (Batini and Toti, 2024; Levy and Hall, 2021; Zucker et al., 2021), the practice of reading texts together has the potential to both relax and inspire. In this chapter, the phrase 'shared reading' is used to emphasise the interactive qualities involved in such activities. Empirical research on shared reading has often focused on the communicative practices of adults and their impact on young children's development (e.g. Anderson et al.,

DOI: 10.4324/9781003532606-9

2012; Hindman et al., 2014). Fewer studies have sought to document the consequences of shared readings for children's affective and social engagement as readers. Nevertheless, there are some studies that do pay attention to the fundamentally social nature of shared readings both at home and in school (e.g. Batini and De Carlo, 2025; Hall et al., 2018; Levy et al., 2018; Wiseman, 2011).

Shared reading at home

Chapter 2 highlighted that children's enjoyment of reading is influenced by their caregivers' involvement in reading practices (e.g. OECD, 2010, 2021). Accordingly, it is important to attend to the practice of shared reading at home. The research evidence suggests that adults' conceptualisation of the purpose of shared reading impacts on their practice and the possible role this practice can play in fostering recreational reading. For instance, in an interview-based study in England, Levy et al. (2018) found that parents (n:29) were heavily invested in the nurturing interactions afforded through the sharing of a book with their children. Accordingly, adults were motivated to give '100%' to sharing books so that both they and their children could enjoy reading and the time together it afforded (Levy et al., 2018, p. 139). The researchers found that shared reading was viewed as a 'form of family display', supporting the expression of family roles (Levy et al., 2018, p. 363). Shared reading, in these contexts, not only gave adults and children time together but also afforded opportunities to be affectionate and tactile with one another, reinforcing family bonds and enjoyment. Involvement in such tender family moments can be interpreted as being capable of supporting enjoyment and engagement in reading:

> Parents were motivated to read to their children because their child either asked to be read to or demonstrated that they were enjoying the activity.
>
> *(Hall et al., 2018, p. 373)*

Although parents and caregivers may be highly motivated, their perceptions of 'negative' feedback from their children can result in them being hesitant to engage in subsequent readings (Preece and Levy, 2020). A key factor understood to prevent children's lack of enjoyment in shared reading at home is the inclusion of child-led or child-mediated approaches, whereby children can initiate or refuse to participate and chose texts to be shared (Hall et al., 2018). These factors appeared to support children's reading for pleasure. Indicating a connection with the later sections in this chapter, research also suggests that parents' talk during shared readings can support children's engagement. For instance, Schapira et al. (2021) observed how Israeli parents (n:50) changed the focus of their talk as they engaged in repeated readings of texts. When reading with children (aged 4–5 years old), they progressed from talk focused on depicted actions to talk about the socio-emotional aspects of the text. Significantly, the involvement of children increased during these repeated readings. This observation reinforces findings that highlight talk focused on the meanings of texts is linked to positive affective interactions (De Temple and Snow, 2003; Schapira and Aram, 2020).

The studies noted thus far indicate the importance of shared readings at home. However, home reading interactions can become dominated by 'schooled' versions of reading (Marsh, 2003; Thomson, 2002) as parents and caregivers can become worried about 'getting it right' once children start school (Levy, 2009). Moreover, studies from the UK (Picton et al., 2024) and Australia (Merga and Ledger, 2018) indicate that the use of shared reading at home is in decline, with this being particularly noticeable among children who can read independently. Thus, as Merga and Ledger (2018) observe, reading becomes an 'orphaned responsibility'. The decline in reading to and with children at home indicates the need to continue to direct attention to the likely role of shared reading in nurturing reading for pleasure. Attitudinal research in this area could increase understanding of parents' perspectives and motivations regarding reading to children as they grow older and could consider these perspectives alongside children's. Moreover, collaborative action-orientated research, involving teachers and parents, could help to generate insights into how the affectionate, affective and social mechanisms of shared reading can be mobilised for older children.

Shared reading in school

Shared reading in schools offers rich opportunities for supportive and engaging social interactions, through exploring each other's understandings, interpretations and experiences of texts (e.g. Batini et al., 2018; Leung et al., 2018; Moffatt et al., 2019; Torr, 2007). Indeed, children report that they find listening to others sharing a text to be both enjoyable (Ledger and Merga, 2018) and calming and value being introduced to a wider range of texts in this way (Oxley and McGeown, 2023). Predominantly, existing research has focused on adult-led shared readings in school, with it being positioned as part of literacy teaching and used to explicitly impart literacy skills. Additionally, some evidence suggests that adult-led shared reading can support positive reading experiences. For instance, hearing teachers confidently voice cognitively challenging texts has been seen to enable readers to experience fluency vicariously and thereby greater levels of autonomy and understanding. This benefit is seen as being particularly important for less assured or engaged teenage readers. In a study that involved 20 teachers in England reading demanding novels at pace, the 12–13-year-olds (n:343) involved were observed to make 16 months progress on standardised reading comprehension tests over three months (Westbrook et al., 2019). The researchers suggest that these adolescents may have previously been directed to spend more reading time on developing their skills. With such a focus, they may have experienced an impoverished reading diet, instead of reading widely and for enjoyment. Through the adult-led shared readings, the students gained access to engaging, contemporary texts. The researchers argue that this access 'repositioned "poorer readers" as "good" readers, giving them a more engaged uninterrupted reading experience over a sustained period' (Westbrook et al., 2019, p. 60). This study highlights the inter-relationship between shared readings and students' identities as readers.

In addition to research that highlights the value to children listening to adults read texts, evidence points to how shared readings that are adult-led and socially involving can cultivate engagement and enjoyment. Such interactive experiences provide young people with opportunities to engage in readerly behaviours, such as influencing text choices and fuelling the direction of free-flowing discussions about texts, thereby affirming their competence as readers. Interactive approaches are associated with many benefits (Batini et al., 2018; Zucker et al., 2021). In an experimental study into the use of interactive approaches to shared reading in an Italian primary school, the agency of the children (n:76) (aged 8–10) was foregrounded (Batini et al., 2018). Children were invited to influence the book choices and draw upon their personal interests and experiences, which fuelled free-flowing discussions about their own lives and about the narratives shared. This experimental study has been formalised into a 'shared reading aloud' protocol key which is the understanding that children 'have the right to speak and guide choices' (Batini and De Carlo, 2025, p. 130). This protocol has been seen to contribute not only to cognitive development, but also to expressions of creativity and empathy (Batini et al., 2018). These studies in Italy also show that regular interactive shared readings support children's wellbeing; the children connected with one another through the experiences, and a sense of belonging was also fostered.

Nurturing children's agency through interactive shared readings can be key to promoting reading for pleasure (Maloch and Beutel, 2010; Wiseman, 2011). However, research studies are also alert to the continued role teachers play in nurturing children's agency. During a nine-month ethnographic study of whole-class shared readings in an American kindergarten class (n:21), Wiseman (2011) noted that from the outset the class teacher facilitated rich discussions guided by the children's contributions and interests. Over time, this meant that the children 'led more of the conversations without prompting' (Wiseman, 2011, p. 433). This study highlights the value of teachers using shared readings to enact the behaviours of enthusiastic readers. Studies suggest that when teachers model making text choices (Brandt et al., 2021) and exemplify meaning-making practices (McClure and Fullerton, 2017), before providing time and space for children to test out these behaviours, children are supported in their engagement with reading. Crucially, the literature also acknowledges the importance of the time and space provided during interactive shared readings and these are explicitly framed as accepting of children's unique interests, queries and comments (Maloch and Beutel, 2010). The complexity of shared reading encounters is seen in a study by Rodriguez Leon and Payler (2021), which examined the different norms around teacher-initiated and child-initiated episodes of shared reading. The latter 'afforded fluid interactive, multimodal dialogue through which interpretations could emerge, develop and adapt' (p. 9) and it enabled the 3–4-year-olds to take ownership of their personal perspectives and express these. However, the opportunities for such dialogue were not always taken up due to the identity positioning of the young children. Nonetheless, interactive shared readings that foreground children's agency, involvement, self-expression and free-flowing discussions can play a key role in enabling children to derive pleasure from encountering and interpreting texts. Indeed, Leung et al. (2018) note:

> Teachers can cultivate a positive learning environment during read alouds with social interaction, in-depth dialogue, and conversations to deepen understanding and amplify the pleasure of reading
>
> *(Leung et al., 2018, p. 24).*

Part of the purpose of interactive shared reading, research reveals, is to demonstrate behaviours that children will be able to use independently when they read their own self-chosen texts. In a review of international literature, Batini and De Carlo (2025) outline how interactive shared reading has an impact not only on engagement with reading and motivation to read, but also on the development of independent reading practices. For instance, referring to their shared reading protocol used in Italy, teachers' reflective diaries indicate that their sessions were frequently followed by children imitating the readerly behaviours involved. They consistently returned to the same books, engaged in repeated re-readings, on their own, with friends and with toys (Batini, 2022). From this study, it is proposed that interactive shared reading is capable of triggering later volitional child-led shared readings.

There are few studies which explicitly focus on this proposed relationship between interactive shared reading and children's later volitional reading, whether reading on their own or sharing a reading with others. Nevertheless, two small-scale studies of single classrooms in America point to a potential connection between shared reading and later child-initiated reading (Hall and Williams, 2010; Pegg and Bartelheim, 2011). In a separate study, involving participant observations of three Canadian kindergarten classrooms, with 3–6-year-olds, researchers observed how in one classroom, in addition to adults leading shared readings, children were involved in leading shared readings (Moffatt et al., 2019). Through this, the children 'were positioned, and positioned themselves, as readers in their own right daily' (Moffatt et al., 2019, p. 159). Children would sign themselves up to read to others, seemingly with enthusiasm, and were allowed to sit in the special 'reader's chair', affording them the prestige associated with being a reader. Such research illustrates how by positioning children as agentic readers, allowing them to choose what to read, when to read and with whom to read, they develop and demonstrate a desire to read.

Although research has indicated when and how shared reading can support engagement and enjoyment, there are occasions when shared reading can be counterproductive. When it is co-opted for comprehension purposes the nature of the practice shifts, becoming increasingly adult-led with a battery of specific questions (Hempel-Jorgensen et al., 2018). In turn, research shows that when children perceive the experience as part of such school literacy, and expect that writing and assessment will follow, they voice a dislike or indifference to shared readings (Cremin et al., 2014). Furthermore, even when shared reading is not co-opted for the teaching of literacy skills, if teachers do not hold this practice in high regard, children also tend to deprioritise it (Ledger and Merga, 2018). In this Australian study of 6–12-year-olds' (n:220) attitudes to shared reading, when teachers positioned shared reading as a 'luxury', 'reward' or 'break' (Ledger and Merga, 2018, p. 134), children saw it as less important than schoolwork. Moreover, these children reported disliking shared reading due to a perceived lack of autonomy and because the time often involved teachers responding to behaviour management issues. Such insights reveal that continual efforts need to be made to appraise and raise the profile of shared reading as a valuable approach, offered in addition to reading texts aloud for instructional purposes. Shared reading is vital to support social interactions in the service of reading for pleasure.

To summarise, existing studies highlight how supportive, interactive and facilitative shared reading can be influential in nurturing positive attitudes to reading, which may lead to young people's later choice-led reading. The interactive elements of shared reading can contribute to children's development as readers in various ways. For instance, shared reading can help build connections between readers through the shared experience of being read to and the resulting conversations. Moreover, young children may choose to re-read books already explored during shared readings and their repertoires of authors and texts may be widened. Despite these insights from the available research, more empirically derived evidence is needed that tracks the movement of texts and conversations between readers and documents the shaping influence of shared reading on children's volitional reading.

Sharing writing

There are relatively few studies that explicitly investigate the social interactions involved in the sharing of writing. However, Jones (2015) has highlighted how very young children first experience the benefits of socialised sharing of writing at home, where emergent writings are shared with and appreciated by family members and friends. Beyond the early years, although there is less research, those studies that do look at sharing writing draw attention to how doing so, at home and at school, can affirm children's interests, both in terms of their lived experiences and their literary tastes (e.g. Connolly and Burn, 2019; Curwood et al., 2013; Olin-Scheller and Wikström, 2010). For instance, drawing from many of her own studies, Dyson (2020) concludes that creating designated, celebratory spaces for children to share their compositions can be supportive, allowing children's worlds, shown in their writing, to be expressed and accepted.

Sharing writing in school

Research also suggests that children are more likely to choose to share their writing when they have greater agency over what they are producing as well as when they feel that their writing has a receptive audience and may have an impact (Connolly and Burn, 2019; Jones, 2015). In a study into the writing practices of children aged 5–10 (n:14), Jones (2015) observed how children were inspired to write letters or stories when they wanted to galvanise others to action, or they had a personal experience to share. This latter emphasis on the desire to share personal experiences can also be discerned in a research project that used an online writing platform (Wyse et al., 2014). The project involved students in England, aged 11–12 (n:107), accessing the platform in their schools. Reporting on this project, Connolly and Burn (2019) describe how the platform appeared to support adolescents' creative writing. Although it was made available to students through their schools, the researchers suggested that the features of the platform were perceived to be different to schooled forms of writing and behaving, and resonated instead with the young people's cultural interests. These features involved using '[p]layful, experimental approaches to language and narrative structure, legitimising the vernacular styles of popular cultural forms and the redeployment of a wide range of cultural resources' (Connolly and Burn, 2019, p. 37). Connolly and Burn also posit that the provision of online prompts and access to mentors may have motivated the teenagers as they felt like their writing was supported and encouraged.

Sharing writing beyond school

Outside of school settings, young people appear to be motivated to share their writing when they can see that doing so connects them to others, whether in-person or online. For instance, in a study of community-based writing during the COVID-19 lockdowns in England, children were observed to volitionally create a range of texts that were shared with and developed across the local community (Chamberlain et al., 2020). Following a teacher's creation of a toy wildlife scene outside her house, local children chose to adopt and adapt this idea. They created their own stuffed animal displays and accompanied these with information posters for passers-by. They also wrote chalk pavement messages and stuck posters in their windows, using these mediums to both entertain the neighbourhood and to share sincere messages about the health service. This study indicates that agency and community are key to the sharing of writing in community spaces. The children who chose to write at home and in their communities were doing so for their own communicative purposes, but with a view to sharing with others.

Studies of online volitional writing further reinforce the argument that affirming social interactions with peers can be intensely motivating for young people (e.g. Cummings et al., 2018; Curwood et al., 2013; Olin-Scheller and Wikström, 2010). Predominantly, these studies focus on the role of fan fiction writing practices, which denotes the writing of stories using characters, settings and plots from already existing novels, films and other media. However, Cummings et al. (2018) also illustrate how digital messaging was used by 9–11-year-olds to share an interest in an activity with friends and relatives. The evidence indicates that shared interest in a pre-existing text nurtures the confidence of young writers who post their fan fiction on online sites. In the literature, these are commonly referred to as 'affinity spaces'. Through an ethnographic study of English Language Learners (ELL), one researcher proposed that these affinity spaces scaffold ELLs' writing (Black, 2005). ELLs were able to use the informal social interactions afforded by fan fiction sites to construct identities as successful writers and, thus, competent English-language users in the online community. In a Swedish study of 12–28-year-olds (n:31), Olin-Scheller and Wikström (2010) found that affinity spaces not only allowed but praised imitation of both pre-existing texts and other fan fiction writers' contributions. Indeed, the affinity spaces in this study appeared to thrive on a cycle of young writers being inspired by and inspiring others. Thus, imitative practices allowed the young people to develop their confidence and independence as writers in relation to the original texts. Furthermore, Lammers and Marsh (2015) drawing on a three-year longitudinal study of one teenager in the United States, illustrate that fan fiction sites may allow writers to take greater creative risks by enabling them to survey a range of other existing outputs.

The young people who use these spaces appear to be motivated by the prospect of connecting with like-minded individuals and having the chance to share their writing with a receptive audience. For instance, based on research from three studies, each involving between 8 and 20 participants, ranging from 11 to 23 years old, Curwood et al. (2013) proposed that sharing writing in these online spaces facilitated opportunities for sharing, feedback, reviews and competitions that pushed young people to improve their craft:

> Sheena describes writing for the [Neopian Times] and submitting to site contests to win achievements and Neopoints, but also for "friendship and feedback" from other players.
>
> *(Curwood et al., 2013, p. 681)*

Crucially, the constructive criticism offered via fan fiction sites in response to shared writing is almost invariably combined with positive and encouraging feedback. Young people make requests for more 'chappies' or ask fellow writers to 'update soon', creating safe and unintimidating spaces and supporting the development of positive writer identities (Black, 2005; Olin-Scheller and Wikström, 2010).

These studies about sharing writing online illustrate how opportunities for supportive social interactions, often via feedback, not only motivate young writers, but sustain their volitional engagement and support their growth and sense of identity as writers.

Talking about reading

There is scant research about the role of talk in relation to reading in the home, however, there is an established body of research about the role of talk in school-based reading. This emphasis on text talk has been influenced by socio-cultural approaches to learning, which highlight the impact of talk on learning (e.g. Alexander, 2011, 2018; Mercer, 1994; Mercer and Dawes, 2018; Mercer and Littleton, 2007). Building on such insights, research indicates that talk can play a crucial role in young people's experiences of and understandings of texts (e.g. Barber and Klauda, 2020; Jerasa and Boffone, 2021; Leung et al., 2018). Indeed, Oatley (2011) has eloquently expressed this sentiment: 'Works of art are surrounded by orbits of discussion. To talk about fiction is almost as important as reading it in the first place' (Oatley, 2011, p. 178). However, much of the work that looks at the connection between talk and reading attends to the impact of talk on language and literacy skills (e.g. Karrass and Braungart-Rieker, 2005), comprehension (e.g. Chambers, 1985, 2011) and creative and critical thinking capabilities (e.g. Maine, 2015; Roche, 2014, 2020). Beyond concerns about developing various competencies, research also highlights the range and significance of talk-based social interactions associated with being a reader (e.g. Ivey and Johnston, 2013; Maybin, 2013; Merga et al., 2018; Moses and Kelly, 2018). Furthermore, research illustrates how these talk-based social interactions can play a crucial role in nurturing children and young people's enjoyment of texts.

Book talk that is more informal in nature is seen to be critical to both engaging young readers and motivating them to read. Referred to as 'informal book talk' (Cremin et al., 2024), much of the research in this area focuses on school settings, recognising that talk about texts in classrooms has tended to be adult-led and orientated towards learning goals. In contrast, informal book talk is more child-led, less hierarchical and not assessed, attending instead to the interests, enthusiasms and curiosities of children. Moreover, the research shows how this type of talk can occur in multiple contexts, such as during shared reading and reading time, as well as in non-designated reading time and space, such as during break time, on the playground and in the corridor. Adding to this variety, informal book talk is understood to encompass a wide range of discourse, both fleeting and extensive, related to texts, being a reader, personal interests and life experiences. These interactions enable the sharing of views and connections and are seen to be socially motivating, supporting reading for pleasure (e.g. Coakley-Fields, 2018; Cremin et al., 2014; Ivey and Johnston, 2013, 2015; Mottram, 2014).

Children predominantly express enjoyment in being able to talk about texts. However, it is important to acknowledge that not all children are interested in talking about texts with others. Indeed, some are concerned that talking with others might prematurely reveal story plots (Oxley and McGeown, 2023), thereby impacting upon their affective engagement. In the main, though, the research indicates that children derive pleasure from informally chatting about self-chosen books (Kennedy, 2018), making text recommendations to others (Ivey and Johnston, 2013; Oxley and McGeown, 2023) and using texts to make connections, both textual and social (Alexander and Jarman, 2018; Button and Millward, 2005; Coakley-Fields, 2018; Cremin et al., 2014, 2024; Francois, 2013; Torr, 2007).

The use of informal book talk to establish social connections within class settings is increasingly receiving greater attention in the research literature. For instance, in a one-year UK study of 43 teachers in 27 schools, primary aged children were, towards the close of the year, observed to establish connections across texts they had shared with others, reciting extracts from texts they had heard and performed, and interpreting shared experiences through the lens of known texts, thereby, learning about each other's lives (Cremin et al., 2014). As the researchers noted, this 'child-initiated talk was undertaken in a mobile and fluid manner and drew on common intertextual references. It was self-perpetuating due to its motivating and engaging manner' (Cremin et al., 2014, p. 116). Similarly, in another year-long study involving 9–10-year-olds in the United States (Coakley-Fields, 2018), the children and their teacher began to seamlessly weave references to books they had read together into and across their school day. They connected texts to key parts of the class's day, such as morning registration, post-break time conflict resolution and moments of celebration, indicating 'the power of inside text talk':

> Students learned about one another's lives and experiences and honed their reading comprehension skills. This talk helped shape students' identities as valued classroom members, capable readers, and reflective problem solvers
>
> *(Coakley-Fields, 2018, p. 727).*

Younger readers too, as participating members of strong reading communities, have been seen to engage spontaneously in relaxed book-based conversations (Cremin et al., 2024; Rodriguez Leon et al., 2025). This study, undertaken in four UK classrooms with 4–7-year-olds, indicated that such talk has the potential to be an affective, positively engaging and supportive experience. In these classrooms, informal book talk was used to ask questions about well-known texts, to reminisce about texts previously shared in class and to link texts to knowledge of the wider world (Cremin et al., 2024; Rodriguez-Leon et al., 2025). In so doing, it enabled the young readers to build and sustain friendships, nurture their self-efficacy and more positive reader identities, and is thus seen as capable of supporting volitional reading.

Informal book talk is not limited to fiction texts. Talk about non-fiction can also help to position children as knowledgeable and competent readers (Alexander and Jarman, 2018; Cremin et al., 2024). In a UK-based study into non-fiction science texts and reading for pleasure, Alexander and Jarman (2018) found that such texts facilitated lively and impromptu conversations. Semi-structured interviews with children aged 8–14 (n:27) indicated that they valued being able to share facts and recommend books to their friends and family members. Moreover, the researchers reported that doing so influenced children's later reading choices. These studies indicate that informal book talk can help young people to make sense of what they are reading and the world around them through thinking and talking together. Additionally, it can reinforce friendships and nurture new ones, socially motivating children to read and thus contributing to the creation of self-sustaining communities of readers.

In addition to informal book talk taking place in classrooms, extracurricular book clubs, both in-person and online, appear to provide opportunities for older children to engage in informal book talk. The research evidence suggests that these discussions not only support comprehension but also nurture social connections and reading enjoyment. For instance, in a study of 11–13-year-olds (n:60), Whittingham and Huffman (2009) observed that the provision of an independent book club enabled discussions of the young people's self-chosen texts. In turn, these discussions supported the development of positive attitudes towards reading. More recently, in a randomised controlled trial in the Netherlands, Tijms et al. (2018) found that books clubs not only improved teenagers' attitudes to reading, but also enhanced social and emotional competencies, as well as reading comprehension. The social affordances of book clubs were also noted by Gan and Loh (2024) who discerned that 11-year-olds (n:15) participating in virtual book clubs used opportunities to talk about texts, and became more aware of how books are structured and more attuned to other attendees' perspectives. Alvermann et al.'s (1999) American study into an after-school reading club also suggests that such informal and talkative settings allow individuals to learn more about themselves. In this study, adolescents (n:20) viewed book clubs as social spaces where they could enact and test out new social positions.

Although informal book talk is characterised as being more child-led, studies illustrate that adults can play a key role in facilitating it. Teachers can facilitate informal book talk by both sensitively modelling how it is done (Fisher and Frey, 2018) and by coupling such modelling with gradual-release techniques that empower children to take control of discussions about texts (Hudson, 2016). Teacher recommendations and book promotions have likewise been seen to influence younger readers' desire to read and talk about texts (e.g. Batchelor and Cassidy, 2019; Cremin et al., 2014; Moses and Kelly, 2018). These promotions, however, rely upon professional knowledge of texts, and as many studies indicate, are enriched by knowledge of young readers. Research also indicates that teachers resisting making choices about texts can also facilitate informal book talk. For instance, in a US study of 13–14-year-olds (n:71) it was found that when teenagers were free to choose 'edgy' young adult fiction (albeit the wider list was curated by their teachers) and were free to read at their own pace and in their own way, widespread casual conversations about the texts emerged. Crucially this talk occurred not only between peers but also involved teachers and parents as the teenagers navigated often intense and affectively engaging stories and read them avidly within and beyond school.

Ivey and Johnston's study suggests that when teachers engage in practices associated with informal book talk, they need to be committed in their approach and open to the resultant student-led interactions. Moses and Kelly (2018) used the practices of one US teacher of 6–7-year-olds to exemplify this approach, also indicating the role that educators play in supporting informal book talk. The teacher in this study provided various inventive opportunities to talk about books, including author studies and discussion groups, and the children suggested they held a book exchange party. This was welcomed, and in the process, the children shared in one another's reading journeys. Plus, children broadened their knowledge of texts and began to develop a more nuanced understanding of what makes a good reader. Instead of seeing good readers as those who read quietly and accurately, these children came to associate reading with social interaction and enjoyment. Nonetheless, it can take time for children to adjust to and accept adults' use of informal book talk, especially if children are used to more formal and adult-led book talk (Cremin et al., 2014). In this UK study, for instance, the children appeared unsure of what was expected of them. However, through the teachers' widening reading repertoires and growing knowledge of children's interests, spontaneous informal book talk did develop between children and between children and adults.

Librarians are also understood to play a key role in supporting such book talk and, therefore, reading for pleasure (Merga, 2020; Schmidt, 2020). For instance, in a study in Australia, Merga (2020) noted that teacher-librarians planned numerous discussion-based opportunities, including peer-led book recommendations, author talks, book matching and guided choosing as well as both teacher and student-led book talk:

> We always encourage the students to tell everyone about a good book they've read, but just very informally. We do have discussions at the end, but the informal just 'this was a great book, I loved it because of …' and that's peer sharing of ideas and also, we do it, we model it.
>
> *(Librarian quoted in Merga, 2020, p. 28)*

Such opportunities and some studies indicate that librarians may view reading differently to many teachers (Schmidt, 2020). Studies have also identified that teachers who view reading as a matter of proficiency may see peer text talk as a waste of time (Collins et al., 2022). In contrast, librarians or teachers with library responsibilities prioritise reading for pleasure and plan book-related activities designed to support social interactions. Accordingly, library-based conversations about texts are seen to be characteristically informal and relatively non-hierarchical in nature (Cremin and Swann, 2017; Merga, 2020), creating a safe and encouraging environment for young people, which is likely to contribute to their enjoyment of reading and potentially influence their later volitional reading.

To conclude, looking across the range of studies about informal book talk, the importance of supportive, enabling and responsive social environments in developing children's enjoyment in recreational reading can be seen. In these, relaxed conversational engagement between readers is fostered. Within the classroom, these informal conversations occur when the interests and choices of children and young people are prioritised. Teachers and librarians who follow children's interests, ideas and views about texts appear to enable learner-led informal book talk. Such talk is driven by young readers' desires to explore their thoughts and to make connections and help them enhance their understandings of texts, themselves, others and the wider world around them (Barber and Klauda, 2020). However, there remains a gap in the extant research regarding whether and to what extent such talk changes reading behaviours, attitudes and identities. Thus far, research has focused on the enjoyment and other affordances of talk in the moment, with talk about texts and authors being interpreted as indicators of readerly behaviours and thus of children developing identities as readers. Research that clearly tracks the extended influence and impact of such discussions on volitional reading in the longer term would be invaluable.

Talking about writing

In this chapter, talk to generate, shape and support ideas for and interest in writing is recognised as diverse in form and content. Indeed, studies suggest that different types of talk can help young writers – before, during and after the act of writing (e.g. Davidson, 2007; Dobson and Stephenson, 2019). However, the body of research attending to talking about writing is less extensive than that which has looked at the role of talk in relation to reading. Moreover, in schools, Jones (2015) has indicated that talking about writing can be devalued when there is an emphasis on assessing individuals' skills through their siloed compositions. Yet, research with young children has consistently shown that writing is socially rooted, often involving playful and unofficial peer dialogues (Dyson, 1997, 2000, 2001, 2013). Accordingly, studies note that facilitated, supportive, relaxed and spontaneous discussions about writing, with peers or trusted adults, can help young people to generate ideas, to compose collaboratively, to rehearse texts, to reflect upon theirs and others' compositions and to develop understandings of their writing preferences (Fisher et al., 2010; Myhill and Newman, 2019). Such social interactions, when conducted sensitively, are seen to be intensely motivating (De Smedt et al., 2019). In playful, open-ended environments, children equate writing with friendship, belonging and, thus, enjoyment.

Using different forms of drama and dramatic play as a support for writing has been identified as capable of enhancing children's motivation to write and developing more positive attitudes towards it (Bearne and Grainger, 2004; Cremin et al., 2006, 2017; Dobson and Stephenson, 2018, 2019; Nicolopoulou et al., 2006; Rumney et al., 2016). Indeed, in reviewing the field, Dunn et al. (2013) highlight that engaging in drama increases children's desire to write, enriches the quality and quantity of their writing, prompts a greater range of registers to be used and enables greater empathy with characters. In particular, improvisation has been identified as a valuable tool for generating ideas for writing. In so doing, it has been shown to support writing attainment (Fleming et al., 2004), influencing the depth, detail, stance and quality of the writing produced (Cremin et al, 2006; Crumpler and Schneider, 2002; Dobson and Stephenson, 2019). Additionally, these studies suggest that by supporting the writing process, improvisation is associated with more positive attitudes to writing.

Embedded within research about the value of drama techniques is recognition of the role of the body. For instance, Dobson and Stephenson (2019) argue that the embodied elements of process drama appear to expand framings of writing that are capable of cultivating children's agency and developing their writing styles:

> Teachers should take the risk of weakening their own framing of teaching writing through the use of process drama to provide embodied experiences for the children in their classes in order to allow the act of writing to become agentic and the written text more sophisticated.
>
> *(Dobson and Stephenson, 2019, p. 77)*

Storytelling and story acting is also understood to support volitional writing (Cremin et al., 2017; Cremin, 2020; Nicolopoulou et al., 2006). Affording young children the opportunity to dictate their own story to an adult, who writes their composition down, and then to later perform this story with their classmates is understood to be stimulating. Research suggests it nurtures the young children's attention to the written word and motivates them to imitate this activity and write themselves. In Nicolopoulou et al's (2006) study, pre-schoolers appeared to become more interested in their journal writing activities, which were variously drawn and dictated and over time, the length and complexity of their dictated stories increased. Cremin et al. (2017) observed a similar impact of storytelling and story acting techniques on levels of agency and intentionality among 5–7-year-olds. These children were observed to engage unprompted in scribing their own and each other's tales for later enactments.

Such studies indicate how the prospect of enacting and performing to peers can be a significant driver for children to put theirs and others' stories to paper. Enacting with and for others is a communal social activity. In so being, it gives context, purpose and an audience for children's writing. Moreover, the above research indicates that writing with the purpose of a public enactment helps children to position themselves as accomplished authors. Taken together, the work around drama underscores the potency of interaction with peers as highly motivating, supportive of children's authorial engagement, and potentially able to prompt writing for pleasure. Talking about writing, through drama-based activities, clearly has the potential to support writing activities and to nurture young people's identities as writers. However, more empirical evidence is needed to establish a more robust understanding of how these components nurture volitional writing.

Using talk as part of collaborative writing practices is also recognised as motivating (e.g. Graham and Harris, 2016). Studies indicate that opportunities to collaborate and to co-produce writing foster children's need to connect with others which can motivate and prompt positive engagement and volitional writing (e.g. De Smedt et al., 2019). In one American study involving 8–9-year-olds (n:4), Jaeger (2021) attended to spontaneous instances of collaborative co-composition in a classroom. This research drew attention to how a small group of boys used talk in numerous ways to support their volitional collaborative composition process. They negotiated, narrated, overlapped each other's talk, reflected, took on roles and shifted perspectives as they chose to write together over an extended period of time. This talk supported the boys' social interactions and appeared to sustain their volitional engagement in writing (Jaeger, 2021).

In addition to sustaining engagement in writing, social interaction around writing is seen to be invaluable for reflecting on one's writing and identity as a writer. Research indicates that young writers benefit from a reflective language to talk about writing and themselves as writers, enabling them to voice their views, listen to others and develop new knowledge and understanding. For example, Jesson et al. argue that a dialogic space in the writing classroom 'can give voice to the silences, the tacit understandings, and the multiple discourses that surround learning to be a writer' (2016, p. 155). Moreover, such reflective conversations can help children to become more conscious of the choices they are making and the options and identity positions available to them.

Child-led conversations are seen by several studies to offer the richest support for writing for pleasure. When talk to collaborate and co-compose is learner-led it is seen to respect children's authorial agency, enabling them to sustain an interest in writing based on affirmative feedback (e.g. Graham et al., 2014; Harmey, 2021; Harmey and Rodgers, 2017; Hawkins, 2019; Jesson et al., 2016). Nonetheless, supporting adults are still playing a pivotal role in facilitating and respecting children's ideas for writing. For instance, drawing on a case study of a teacher who profiled talk as a tool to support primary phase writers, Cremin (2020) observed that the teacher modelled energetic talk and attentive listening. Alongside significant choice and agency, this approach served to develop the children's emotional engagement in writing and positive authorial dispositions. In another study, children who were supported by conversations with their teachers and enabled to take control of the compositional process were seen to make typical progress in contrast to those who were afforded less control (Harmey and Rodgers, 2017). These studies illustrate the importance of teachers affording young writers control over the writing process. When children and young people are positioned as agentic writers, they are able to take up the identity of an author, rather than a distanced observer or compliant pupil (Harmey, 2021; Hawkins, 2019). Building on the argument presented in Chapter 4, which discusses the interplay between motivation and literate identities, this positioning can be seen as capable of nurturing writing for pleasure.

Talking about texts appears to support greater levels of engagement with and motivation towards writing activities. Studies into the use of dramatic techniques, whether improvisation, enactments or storytelling, appear to provide a way forward for young writers to be apprenticed as authors. Moreover, the research literature indicates that talking about writing with others, whether teachers or peers, can help young people to generate ideas, reflect upon their choices and make the process of writing transparent. However, although it is proposed that such talk can be supportive, motivating and engaging during writing activities, it is less clear whether and how such talk leads to enhanced positive attitudes towards writing and sustained volitional writing. Opportunities for research to further consider how talk contributes to writing for pleasure remain.

Conclusion

To summarise, research suggests that being able to share the processes and experiences associated with reading and writing with others can support an interest in and enjoyment of these practices. A key insight discerned across the review relates to the value of relaxed child-led interactions and social interactions where young people can see their actions influence others. However, studies also illustrate that supportive adults still have a significant role to play in social interactions around reading and writing for pleasure. Adults who are aware of, show enthusiasm for and respond to the needs and interests of children can help these young people see themselves as accomplished readers and writers. The studies discussed here and in Chapter 4 indicate that children's identities as readers and writers influence their reading and writing for pleasure, although a larger body of research which tracks the part played by social interactions would help to underscore and enrich this evidenced argument.

References

Alexander, J. and Jarman, R. (2018) 'The pleasures of reading non-fiction', *Literacy*, 52(2), pp. 78–85.

Alexander, R. (2011) *Towards Dialogic Teaching* (4th edn), York: Dialogos.

Alexander, R. (2018) 'Developing dialogic teaching: Genesis, process, trial', *Research Papers in Education*, 33(5), pp. 561–598.

Alvermann, D.E., Young, J.P., Green, C. and Wisenbaker, J.M. (1999) 'Adolescents' perceptions and negotiations of literacy practices in after-school read and talk clubs', *American Educational Research Journal*, 36(2), pp. 221–264.

Anderson, A., Anderson, J., Lynch, J., Shapiro, J. and Eun Kim, J. (2012) 'Extra-textual talk in shared book reading: A focus on questioning', *Early Child Development and Care*, 182(9), pp. 1139–1154.

Anderson, K., Atkinson, T.S., Swaggerty, E.A. and O'Brien, K. (2019) 'Examining relationships between home-based shared book reading practices and children's language/literacy skills at kindergarten entry', *Early Child Development and Care*, 189(13), pp. 2167–2182.

Barber, A.T. and Klauda, S.L. (2020) 'How reading motivation and engagement enable reading achievement: Policy implications', *Policy Insights from the Behavioral and Brain Sciences*, 7 (1), pp. 27–34.

Batchelor, K. and Cassidy, R. (2019) 'The lost art of the book talk: What students want', *The Reading Teacher*, 73(2), pp. 230–234.

Batini, F. (2022) 'Reading aloud as a stimulus and facilitation of children's narratives', *Debates em Educação*, 14(34), pp. 113–126.

Batini, F. and De Carlo, M.E. (2025) 'Shared reading aloud as a practice to promote equity: Review, method, and evidence-based research', in Cremin, T. and McGeown, S. (eds), *Reading for Pleasure: International Perspectives from Research*, London: Routledge, pp. 125–137.

Batini, F. and Toti, G. (2024) 'Shared reading aloud to enhance language and literacy', *Education 3–13*, 52(7), pp. 946–962.

Batini, F., Bartolucci, M. and Timpone, A. (2018) 'The effects of reading aloud in the primary school', *Psychology of Education: An Interdisciplinary Journal*, 55(1 and 2), pp. 111–141.

Bearne, E. and Grainger, T. (2004) 'Raising boys achievements in writing', *Literacy*, 38(3), pp. 153–159.

Black, R. (2005) 'Access and affiliation: The literacy and composition practices of English language learners in an online fanfiction community', *Journal of Adolescent and Adult Literacy*, 49(2), pp. 118–128.

Boerma, I.E., Mol, S.E. and Jolles, J. (2018) 'Parents adjust the quality of their home literacy environment to the reading interest of their third to sixth graders', *Parenting*, 18(4), pp. 243–261.

Brandt, L., Sharp, A.C. and Gardner, D.S. (2021) 'Examination of teacher practices on student motivation for reading', *Reading Teacher*, 74(6), pp. 723–731.

Button, S. and Millward, P. (2005) 'Talking into literacy in the early years', *FORUM: For Promoting 3–19 Comprehensive Education*, 47(1), pp. 34–38.

Chamberlain, L., Lacina, J., Bintz, W.P., Jimerson, J., Payne, K. and Zingale, R. (2020) 'Literacy in lockdown: Learning and teaching in COVID-19 school closures', *The Reading Teacher*, 73 (4), pp. 243–253.

Chambers, A. (1985) *Booktalk: Occasional Writing on Children and Literature*, London: Bodley Head.

Chambers, A. (2011) *Tell Me: Children, Reading and Talk: With the Reading Environment*, Stroud: Thimble Press.

Coakley-Fields, M.R. (2018) 'Inclusive talk: Weaving fiction discussions across the school day', *The Reading Teacher*, 72(6), pp. 721–729.

Collins, V.J., Dargan, I.W., Walsh, R.L. and Merga, M. (2022) 'Teachers' perceptions of the benefits and challenges of a whole-school reading for pleasure program', *Issues in Educational Research*, 32(1), pp. 89–104.

Connolly, S. and Burn, A. (2019) 'The story engine: Offering an online platform for making "unofficial" creative writing work', *Literacy*, 53(1), pp. 30–38.

Cremin, T. (2020) 'Apprenticing authors: Nurturing children's identities as writers', in Chen, H., Myhill, D. and Lewis, H. (eds), *Developing Writers Across Primary and Secondary Years*, London and Sydney: Routledge, pp. 113–130.

Cremin, T. and Swann, J. (2017) 'School librarians as leaders of extracurricular reading groups', in Pihl, J., van der Kooij, K. and Carlsten, T. (eds), *Teacher and Librarian Partnerships in Literacy Education in the 21st Century*, Rotterdam: Sense Publishers, pp. 119–137.

Cremin, T., Hendry, H., Rodriguez Leon, L. and Hulston, S.J. (2024) 'Informal book talk: Digging beneath the surface', *English 3–13*, 52(7), pp. 930–945.

Cremin, T., Lillis, T., Myhill, D. and Eyres, I. (2017) 'Professional writers' identities', in Cremin, T. and Locke, T. (eds), *Writer Identity and the Teaching and Learning of Writing*, London: Routledge, pp. 18–36.

Cremin, T., Goouch, K., Blakemore, L., Goff, E. and Macdonald, R. (2006) 'Connecting drama and writing: Seizing the moment to write', *Research in Drama in Education*, 11(3), pp. 273–291.

Cremin, T., Mottram, M., Collins, F.M., Powell, S. and Safford, K. (2014) *Building Communities of Engaged Readers: Reading for Pleasure*, Oxon: Routledge.

Crumpler, T. and Schneider, J.J. (2002) 'Writing with their whole being: A cross-study analysis of children's writing from five classrooms using process', *Research in Drama Education: The Journal of Applied Theatre and Performance*, 7(1), pp. 61–79.

Cummings, S., McLaughlin, T. and Finch, B. (2018) 'Examining preadolescent children's engagement in out-of-school literacy and exploring opportunities for supporting literacy development', *Australian Journal of Language and Literacy*, 41, pp. 103–116.

Curwood, J., Magnifico, A. and Lammers, J. (2013) 'Writing in the wild: Writers' motivations in fan-based affinity spaces', *Journal of Adolescent and Adult Literacy*, 56(8), pp. 677–685.

Davidson, C. (2007) 'Independent writing in current approaches to writing instruction: What have we overlooked?', *English Teaching: Practice and Critique*, 6(1), pp. 11–24. Available from: http://education.waikato.ac.nz/research/files/etpc/2007v6n1art1.pdf.

De Smedt, F., Graham, S. and Van Keer, H. (2019) 'The bright and the dark side of writing motivation: Effects of explicit instruction and peer assistance', *The Journal of Educational Research*, 112(20), pp. 152–167.

De Temple, J. and Snow, C.E. (2003) 'Learning words from books', in van Kleeck, A., Stahl, S.A. and Bauer, E.A. (eds), *On Reading Books to Children: Parents and Teachers*, New York: Lawrence Erlbaum Associates, pp. 16–36.

Dobson, T. and Stephenson, L. (2018) 'Challenging boundaries to cross: Primary teachers exploring drama pedagogy for creative writing with theatre educators in the landscape of performativity', *Professional Development in Education*, 46(2), pp. 245–255.

Dobson, T. and Stephenson, L. (2019) '"I think it fits in": Using process drama to promote agentic writing with primary school children', *Literacy*, 53(2), pp. 69–76.

Dunn, J., Harden, A. and Marion, S. (2013) 'Drama and writing: overcoming the hurdle of that blank page', in Anderson, M. and Dunn, J. (eds), *How Drama Activates Learning: Contemporary Research and Practice*, London: Bloomsbury, pp. 245–259.

Dyson, A.H. (1997) *Writing Superheroes: Contemporary Childhood, Popular Culture, and Classroom Literacy*, New York: Teachers College Press.

Dyson, A.H. (2000) 'Writing and the sea of voices: Oral language in, around and about writing', in Indrisano, R. and Squire, J. (eds), *Perspectives on Writing*, Newark, DE: International Reading Association, pp. 45–65.

Dyson, A.H. (2001) 'Where are the childhoods in childhood literacy? An exploration in outer (school) space', *Journal of Early Childhood Literacy*, 1(1), pp. 9–39.

Dyson, A.H. (2013) 'The place of childhoods in school writing programmes: A matter of ethics', in Marsh, J. and Larson, J. (eds), *The SAGE Handbook of Early Childhood Literacy*, London: SAGE, pp. 485–500.

Dyson, A.H. (2020) '"This isn't my real writing": The fate of children's agency in too-tight curricula', *Theory Into Practice*, 59(2), pp. 119–127.

Fisher, D. and Frey, N. (2018) 'Raise reading volume through access, choice, discussion, and book talks', *The Reading Teacher*, 72(1), pp. 89–97.

Fisher, R., Myhill, D., Jones, S. and Larkin, S. (2010) *Using Talk to Support Writing*, London: SAGE.

Fleming, M., Merrell, C. and Tymms, P. (2004) 'The impact of drama on pupils' language, mathematics, and attitude in two primary schools', *Research in Drama Education: The Journal of Applied Theatre and Performance*, 9(2), pp. 177–197.

Francois, C. (2013) 'Reading in the crawl space: A study of an urban school's literacy-focused community of practice', *Teachers College Record*, 115(5), pp. 1–35.

Gan, S. and Loh, C.E. (2024) '"I feel like my awareness grew": Fostering dialogues to increase awareness through virtual book clubs', *Changing English*, 31(3), pp. 241–252.

Graham, S. and Harris, K.R. (2016) 'A path to better writing: Evidence-based practices in the classroom', *The Reading Teacher*, 69(4), pp. 359–365.

Graham, S., Hebert, M., Sandbank, M.P. and Harris, K.R. (2014) 'Assessing the writing achievement of young struggling writers: Application of generalizability theory', *Learning Disability Quarterly*, 39(2), pp. 72–82.

Hall, K.W. and Williams, L.M. (2010) 'First-grade teachers reading aloud Caldecott award-winning books to diverse 1st-graders in urban classrooms', *Journal of Research in Childhood Education*, 24(4), pp. 298–314.

Hall, M., Levy, R. and Preece, J. (2018) '"No-one would sleep if we didn't have books!": Understanding shared reading as family practice and family display', *Journal of Early Childhood Research*, 16(4), pp. 363–377.

Harmey, S.J. (2021) 'Co-constructing writing: Handing over the reins to young authors', *Education 3–13*, 49(4), pp. 412–421.

Harmey, S.J. and Rodgers, E.M. (2017) 'Differences in the early writing development of struggling children who beat the odds and those who did not', *Journal of Education for Students Placed at Risk*, 22(3), pp. 157–177.

Hawkins, L.K. (2019) 'Writing conference purpose and how it positions primary-grade children as authoritative agents or passive observers', *Reading Horizons: A Journal of Literacy and Language Arts*, 58(1), pp. 22–47.

Hempel-Jorgensen, A., Cremin, T., Harris, D. and Chamberlain, L. (2018) 'Pedagogy for reading for pleasure in low socio-economic primary schools: Beyond "pedagogy of poverty"?', *Literacy*, 52(2), pp. 86–94.

Hindman, A., Skibbe, L.E. and Foster, T. (2013) 'Exploring the variety of parental talk during shared book reading and contributions to preschool language and literacy: Evidence from the Early Childhood Longitudinal Study-Birth Cohort', *Reading and Writing: An Interdisciplinary Journal*, 27(2), pp. 287–313.

Hudson, A.K. (2016) 'Get them talking! Using student-led book talks in the primary grades', *The Reading Teacher*, 70(2), pp. 221–225.

Ivey, G. and Johnston, P. (2013) 'Engagement with young adult literature outcomes and processes', *Reading Research Quarterly*, 48(3), pp. 1–21.

Ivey, G. and Johnston, P. (2015) 'Engaged reading as a collaborative transformative practice', *Journal of Literacy Research*, 47(3), pp. 297–327.

Jaeger, E. (2021) 'Friends and authors: Spontaneous co-composing in a writing workshop', *Journal of Early Childhood Literacy*, 21(2), pp. 177–207.

Jerasa, S. and Boffone, T. (2021) 'BookTok 101: TikTok, digital literacies, and out-of-school reading practices', *Journal of Adolescent and Adult Literacy*, 65(3), pp. 219–226.

Jesson, R., Fontich, X. and Myhill, D. (2016) 'Creating dialogic spaces: Talk as a mediational tool in becoming a writer', *International Journal of Educational Research*, 80, pp. 155–163.

Jones, S.K. (2015) 'Authenticity and children's engagement with writing', *Language and Literacy*, 17(1), pp. 63–82.

Karrass, J. and Braungart-Rieker, J. (2005) 'Effects of shared parent-infant book reading on early language acquisition', *Journal of Applied Developmental Psychology*, 26(2), pp. 133–148.

Kennedy, E. (2018) 'Engaging children as readers and writers in high-poverty contexts', *Journal of Research in Reading*, 41(4), pp. 716–731.

Lammers, J. and Marsh, V. (2015) 'Going public: An adolescent's networked writing on fanfiction.net', *Journal of Adolescent and Adult Literacy*, 59(3), pp. 277–285.

Ledger, S. and Merga, M.K. (2018) 'Reading aloud: Children's attitudes toward being read to at home and at school', *Australian Journal of Teacher Education*, 43(3), pp. 124–139.

Leung, C., Moore, L.L., Bennett, S.V. and Gunn, A.A. (2018) 'Classroom storybook reading as a dialogic speech event', *Literacy Practice and Research*, 44(1), pp. 16–25.

Levy, R. (2009) '"You have to understand words ... but not read them": Young children becoming readers in a digital age', *Journal of Research in Reading*, 32(1), pp. 75–91.

Levy, R. and Hall, M. (2021) *Family Literacies: Reading with Young Children*, London: Routledge.

Levy, R., Hall, M. and Preece, J. (2018) 'Examining the links between parents' relationships with reading and shared reading with their pre-school children', *International Journal of Educational Psychology*, 7(2), pp. 123–150.

Maine, F. (2015) *Dialogic Readers*, Oxon: Routledge.

Maloch, B. and Beutel, D. (2010) '"Big loud voice. You have important things to say": The nature of student initiations during one teacher's interactive read-alouds', *Journal of Classroom Interaction*, 45(2), pp. 20–29.

Marsh, J. (2003) 'One-way traffic? Connections between literacy practices at home and in the nursery', *British Educational Research Journal*, 29(3), pp. 369–382.

Maybin, J. (2013) 'What counts as reading? PIRLS, EastEnders and The Man on the Flying Trapeze', *Literacy*, 47(2), pp. 59–66.

McClure, E.L. and Fullerton, S.K. (2017) 'Instructional interactions: Supporting students' reading development through interactive read-alouds of informational texts', *The Reading Teacher*, 71(1), pp. 51–59.

Mercer, N. (1994) 'The quality of talk in children's joint activity at the computer', *Journal of Computer Assisted Learning*, 10(1), pp. 24–32.

Mercers, N. and Dawes, L. (2018) *The Development of Oracy Skills in School-Aged Learners*, Cambridge: Cambridge University Press.

Mercer, N. and Littleton, K. (2007) *Dialogue and the Development of Children's Thinking: A Sociocultural Approach*, London: Routledge.

Merga, M.K. (2020) '"We talk books": Teacher librarians promoting book discussion to foster reading engagement', *English in Australia*, 55(1), pp. 22–33.

Merga, M.K. and Ledger, S. (2018) 'Parents' views on reading aloud to their children: Beyond the early years', *Australian Journal of Language and Literacy*, 41(3), pp. 177–189.

Merga, M., McRae, M. and Rutherford, L. (2018) 'Adolescents' attitudes toward talking about books: Implications for educators', *English in Education*, 52(1), pp. 36–53.

Moffatt, L., Heydon, R. and Iannacci, L. (2019) 'Helping out, signing up and sitting down: The cultural production of "read-alouds" in three kindergarten classrooms', *Journal of Early Childhood Literacy*, 19(2), pp. 147–174.

Moses, L. and Kelly, L.B. (2018) '"We're a little loud. That's because we like to read!": Developing positive views of reading in a diverse, urban first grade', *Journal of Early Childhood Literacy*, 18(3), pp. 307–337.

Mottram, M. (2014) 'Reader relationships within and beyond school', in Cremin, T., Mottram, M., Collins, F.M., Powell, S. and Safford, K. (eds), *Building Communities of Engaged Readers*, Oxon: Routledge, pp. 108–127.

Myhill, D. and Newman, R. (2019) 'Writing talk: Developing metalinguistic understanding through dialogic teaching', in Mercer, N., Wegerif, R. and Major, L. (eds), *International Handbook of Research on Dialogic Education*, London: Routledge, pp. 360–372.

Nicolopoulou, A., McDowell, J. and Brockmeyer, C. (2006) 'Narrative play and emergent literacy: Storytelling and story-acting meet journal writing', in Singer, D.G., Golinkoff, R.M. and Hirsh-Pasek, K. (eds), *Play = Learning: How Play Motivates and Enhances Children's Cognitive and Social-Emotional Growth*, New York: Oxford University Press, pp. 122–144.

Oatley, K. (2011) *Such Stuff as Dreams: The Psychology of Fiction*, London: Wiley.

OECD (2010) *PISA 2009 Results: Learning to Learn: Student Engagement, Strategies and Practices*, Vol. 3, Paris: OECD Publishing.

OECD (2021) *21st-Century Readers: Developing Literacy Skills in a Digital World*, Paris: OECD Publishing.

Olin-Scheller, C. and Wikström, P. (2010) 'Literacy prosumers: Young people's reading and writing', *Education Inquiry*, 1(1), pp. 41–56.

Oxley, E. and McGeown, S. (2023) 'Reading for pleasure practices in school: Children's perspectives and experiences', *Educational Research*, 65(3), pp. 375–391.

Pegg, L. and Bartelheim, F. (2011) 'Effects of daily read-alouds on students' sustained silent reading', *Current Issues in Education*, 14(2), pp. 1–8.

Picton, I., Moisi, I., Jackson, T. and Clark, C. (2024) *Parents' Support for Young Children's Literacy at Home in 2024*, London: National Literacy Trust.

Preece, J. and Levy, R. (2020) 'Understanding the barriers and motivations to shared reading with young children: The role of enjoyment and feedback', *Journal of Early Childhood Literacy*, 20(4), pp. 631–654.

Roche, M. (2014) *Developing Children's Critical Thinking Through Picturebooks: A Guide for Primary and Early Years Students and Teachers*, London: Routledge.

Roche, M. (2020) 'Critical thinking and book talk: Thinking ahead', in *Future Edge*, NSW Department of Education, 1, pp. 14–32.

Rodriguez Leon, L. and Payler, J. (2021) 'Surfacing complexity in shared book reading: The role of affordance, repetition and modal appropriation in children's participation', *Learning, Culture and Social Interaction*, 28, 100496.

Rodriguez Leon, L., Hulston, S.J., Hendry, H. and Cremin T. (2025) 'Informal book talk: How casual conversations support enjoyment of reading', in Cremin, T. and McGeown, S. (eds), *Reading for Pleasure: International Perspectives from Research*, London: Routledge, pp. 111–124.

Rumney, P., Kuksa, I. and Buttress, J. (2016) 'Seeing, doing, writing: The Write Here Project', *Sage Open*, 6(1).

Schapira, R. and Aram, D. (2020) 'Shared book reading at home and preschoolers' socio-emotional competence', *Early Education and Development*, 31(6), pp. 819–837.

Schapira, R., Bergman Deitcher, D. and Aram, D. (2021) 'Variability and stability in parent-child discourse during and following repeated shared book reading', *Reading and Writing: An Interdisciplinary Journal*, 34(1), pp. 273–300.

Schmidt, C. (2020) 'Librarians' book talks for children: An opportunity for widening reading practices?', *Journal of Early Childhood Literacy*, 23(3), pp. 470–492.

Thomson, P. (2002) *Schooling the Rustbelt Kids: Making the Difference in Changing Times*, Stoke on Trent: Trentham Books.

Tijms, J., Stoop, M.A. and Polleck, J.N. (2018) 'Bibliotherapeutic book club intervention to promote reading skills and social-emotional competencies in low SES community-based high schools', *Journal of Research in Reading*, 41(3), pp. 525–545.

Torr, J. (2007) 'The pleasure of recognition: Intertextuality in the talk of preschoolers during shared reading with mothers and teachers', *Early Years*, 27(1), pp. 77–91.

Vuong, Q.-H., La, V.-P., Nguyen, T.-H.T., Nguyen, M.-H., Vuong, H.-M. and Ho, M.-T. (2021) 'Impacts of parents and reading promotion on creating a reading culture: Evidence from a developing context', *Children and Youth Services Review*, 131, pp. 106–311.

Westbrook, J., Sutherland, J., Oakhill, J. and Sullivan, S. (2019) '"Just reading": The impact of a faster pace of reading narratives on the comprehension of poorer adolescent readers in English classrooms', *Literacy*, 53(2), pp. 60–68.
Whittingham, J.L. and Huffman, S. (2009) 'The effects of book clubs on the reading attitudes of middle school students', *Reading Improvement*, 46(3), pp. 130–137.
Wiseman, A.M. (2011) 'Interactive read alouds: Teachers and students constructing knowledge and literacy together', *Early Childhood Education Journal*, 38, pp. 431–438.
Worthy, J., Chamberlain, K., Peterson, K., Sharp, C. and Shih, P.-Y. (2012) 'The importance of read-aloud and dialogue in an era of narrowed curriculum: An examination of literature discussions in a second-grade classroom', *Literacy Research and Instruction*, 51(4), pp. 308–322.
Wyse, D., Bradford, H., Burn, A., Wigins, M., Bryer, T., Potter, J. and Coles, J. (2014) *Young People Writing: A Three-Year Longitudinal Research Evaluation of The Ministry of Stories (MoS): Final Report*, London: UCL, Institute of Education.
Zucker, T.A., Bowles, R., Pentimonti, J. and Tambyraja, S. (2021) 'Profiles of teacher and child talk during early childhood classroom shared book reading', *Early Childhood Research Quarterly*, 56(3), pp. 27–40.

7

ROLE MODELS AND CONNECTED COMMUNITIES

Introduction

This chapter examines the fourth theme identified in the combined literature, namely the significance of literate adult role models and building connected communities of readers and writers. It illustrates how adults, whether parents, teachers, librarians or professional writers, may act as gatekeepers, curators, mentors, monitors, assessors, fellow readers and/or writers. Scrutinising these available roles, it indicates how, when adults present themselves as engaged readers and writers, they become role models for the young. However, despite the studies which reveal that teachers' engagement as readers and writers can enable them to model the value and satisfaction they find in their own literate lives and to induct children into such pleasures, there are challenges associated with adopting this identity stance and these are examined. It is also worth noting, that in contrast to Chapters 4, 5 and 6 which examine other synergies within the evidence base linked to children's pleasure in reading and writing, the research literature on teachers as writers and role models is reasonably extensive.

The evidence overall signals that role models can positively influence children and young people's engagement in volitional reading and writing, not only through modelling relaxed and informal reading and writing practices, but also through their contribution to the creation of literate communities. In these communal and connected groups, children, young people and adults often interact reciprocally and with agency, sharing their own views and voices and contributing to a sense of belonging. A strong sense of social connectedness is evident in the literacy networks and sub-groups that nurture and sustain young people's engagement as volitional readers and writers within and beyond school. These communities appear to afford significant support for the development of young people's positive identification as readers and writers and highlight the relational nature of literacy.

DOI: 10.4324/9781003532606-10

Reading and writing role models

Role models matter, both adults and peers. In literacy environments, adults can adopt (or be assigned) multiple identity positions and, if they choose to do so, can demonstrate their authentic engagement as readers and writers. These role models can positively influence young people's engagement in volitional reading and writing (e.g. Kucirkova and Cremin, 2017; Ng, 2018; Rowe et al., 2022; Woodard, 2017; Zumbrunn et al., 2019). By reflecting on their own experience of reading and writing, studies indicate that adults may come to question 'schooled' or received perceptions of reading and writing, re-consider what counts in their context (home, school, library, community) and take a broader view. This more encompassing perspective of reading and writing for meaning, for self-expression and communication, is often positioned in contrast to reading and writing for skill development and assessment, yet both are essential. Adults who read and/or write of choice for themselves and explicitly, or implicitly, position themselves as readers or writers, in effect demonstrate what is involved and provide permission and encouragement for children to do the same (e.g. Anderson et al., 2019; Cremin et al., 2022; McDowall, 2022; Rowe et al., 2022; Vanden Dool and Simpson, 2021; Whitney, 2017; Xerri, 2017). Expanding Whitney's summary of a writer teacher to encompass reading, it can be argued that a role model is teacher writer/reader who is:

> A teacher who uses writing/reading to understand and experience their teaching. And a teacher writer/reader brings a writer's/reader's awareness, a writer's/reader's struggles and the writer's/reader's humility into the classroom.
>
> *(adapted from Whitney, 2017, p. 70)*

As reflective professionals, such pedagogues are positioned as authentic literate role models who are seen to share their enthusiasm, interests, challenges and experience as readers and writers in diverse ways, and to scaffold young people's literacy identity journeys by offering opportunities for genuine engagement and sustained support over time. Such role models are not, however, only found in school.

Role models in the home

While no known studies document parents as writing role models, research does indicate that parents who read or show reading enjoyment shape children's desire to read, in part through role modelling, discussing texts and making personal connections. International data indicates that parents who report enjoying reading the most, and who are thus likely to demonstrate such engagement at home, have teenagers with a higher index of reading enjoyment than those whose parents report not enjoying reading (OECD, 2021). Affirming this association between parents and young people's pleasure in reading, a smaller scale study with Australian adolescents also indicates that parents who find pleasure in reading themselves positively influence their young people's desire to read (Scholes, 2019). In addition, parents' engagement and pleasure in reading, as the OECD (2021) data and Ho and Lau's (2018) study reveals, influences their children's reading engagement, frequency and achievement.

Furthermore, studies with younger children show that adult engagement and modelling impacts positively on families' shared reading practices and the enjoyment of young readers (Anderson et al., 2019; Wiescholek et al., 2018). Parents appear to model their engagement in reading through singing songs and rhymes together, shared reading and reading aloud, book ownership and visiting libraries. Consequently, research highlights the importance of encouraging parents to find ways of making shared reading enjoyable for themselves as well as their children, rather than viewing it as an educational endeavour, thus a focus on pleasure is seen to be preferable (Preece and Levy, 2020). This can lead to more frequent shared reading experiences that encompass enjoyment, relational connections and a home reading culture and ethos which enriches children's enjoyment in literacy (Wiescholek et al., 2018). However, parents' gender stereotypes regarding reading can have an adverse effect on their children's engagement as readers, as one study showed that parents who viewed reading as a feminised practice impacted negatively on their boys' competence beliefs and the perceived value of reading (Muntoni and Retelsdorf, 2019).

The part played by siblings as reading role models in the home has not been extensively studied to date. Gregory (2001) observed that through book sharing in the home, older siblings were seen to scaffold the reading development of their younger siblings, however little mention is made of modelling engagement. However, in a study of the reading memories of adults, Knoester and Plikuhn (2016) did find evidence that older siblings had encouraged younger family members to find pleasure in reading and that this persisted later in life. More recently, Harrison, through observing older siblings role-modelling their reading expertise and sharing their attitudes with younger siblings at home, found that these shared reading experiences were positively supportive (see Levy and Harrison, 2025). The digital story texts shared in these contexts also appeared to offer the younger children more agency than reading print texts, triggering more spontaneous informal talk and potentially enhancing their pleasure. Whilst a plethora of studies exist into home learning environments with regard to reading (e.g. Gregory and Williams, 2000; Sénéchal and Young, 2008), there is scope for new work that overtly explores parents, caregivers, siblings and wider family members as literacy role models and the ways in which they may induct the young into reading and writing for pleasure.

Role models in school

In school contexts, headteachers, teachers, librarians and professional writers can all act as literate role models, as well as pedagogues focused on teaching reading and writing. This is not, however, without challenges, but the adoption of such a stance can, research indicates, have positive consequences for students' attitudes and engagement as readers and writers (e.g. Cremin et al., 2014; Gardner and Kuzich, 2022; Merga and Ferguson, 2021; Vanden Dool and Simpson, 2021; Yeo, 2007; Zumbrunn et al., 2019). It is argued that those who read for pleasure can implicitly and explicitly, consciously and intuitively, model the diverse range of practices and discourses that are associated with being a keen reader or writer. Children appear to be aware of their teachers' and others' attitudes to reading and writing and report that they are influenced by role models (Cole et al., 2022), although they may associate the notion with popular cultural icons rather than their class teacher. Nonetheless, studies indicate that young people recognise teachers' engagement in reading through: their personal readerly dispositions and behaviours; the time they assign to reading for pleasure within the school week; their text recommendations; and their participation in text related discussions (McDowall, 2022; Merga, 2016; Ng, 2018). Similarly, in studies where teachers write alongside students, share their own writing and assign curriculum time to free choice writing, young people perceive their teachers as fellow writers (Cremin and Baker, 2014; Cremin et al., 2020).

Teachers as reading role models

Turning specifically to reading role models, and the influence of this stance on children's attitudes to reading and desire to read, many studies indicate that by sharing their passion for reading, teachers can make a positive impact on children's engagement as readers. Studies from Australia (Merga, 2016; Ng, 2018; Simpson, 2016; Vanden Dool and Simpson, 2021), Belgium (Vansteelandt et al., 2017), Finland (Aerila et al., 2023), Spain (Granado, 2014), New Zealand (McDowall, 2021, 2022), the UK (Cremin et al., 2014, 2024a) and from the United States (Applegate et al., 2014; Commeyras et al., 2003; Daisey, 2010; Francois, 2013a; Methe and Hintze, 2003) all underscore the significance of teachers as reading role models. This has even been noted when, as in the case of an Australian educator, this was not part of the teacher's planned reader identity positioning (Vanden Dool and Simpson, 2021). Nonetheless it is not just passion that matters, positive relationships between teacher modelling and student on-task reading behaviour during reading time have also been documented (Methe and Hintze, 2003). This research highlights that when the teachers involved modelled their own focused engagement during quiet reading and offered a verbal reflection on their reading at the outset, this enhanced the number of children who also concentrated on their chosen texts. Additionally, two studies indicate that when teachers share personal connections to texts, both emotional and intellectual, and make links to their own lives in class, over time this can became reciprocal (Cremin, 2020; Cremin et al., 2014; Ng, 2018). In these studies, the teachers learnt about the children and their lives through a number of activities and through text discussions and developed new and stronger relationships with them, which supported the children's desire to read for pleasure in school and beyond.

Researchers have argued that if teachers position themselves as reading teachers – teachers who read and readers who teach – they are more likely to make a positive difference to young people's reading motivation and frequency (Commeyras et al, 2003). Coined by this US team, the concept of being a reading teacher was used initially to describe teachers who are readers in their personal lives and teachers of reading in their professional lives. More recently, it has been empirically researched and expanded to acknowledge the significant reflexivity and pedagogic consequence involved (Cremin et al., 2014, 2022, 2024a). UK classroom research suggests that such teachers are not merely teachers who read, but argues that Reading Teachers (capital R and T) are extended professionals and reading role models, who actively seek to reflect upon reading and being readers themselves, and then adjust their classroom practice to make the experience of reading more real, more relevant and more authentic (Cremin, 2010; Cremin et al., 2014). In this way it appears they both model and support children's reading for pleasure.

In one US study, teachers who ascribed the most value to reading in their own lives intentionally set more time aside in class for children to read and discuss their free-choice texts, and they also recommended books and shared reflections on their own reading far more frequently than their peers who ascribed less personal value to reading (McKool and Gespass, 2009) Again, this had positive consequences for the child readers. In another study, McDowall (2021, 2022) found advantageous shifts in students' (aged 4 to 12 years) engagement when the New Zealand teachers she was case-studying actively positioned themselves as readers, rather than teachers of reading. As she notes, the teachers considered

> being a reader themselves, to be one of the most important ways in which to support students to develop their own identities as readers.
>
> *(McDowall, 2022, p. 26)*

The dual identity position – as readers and as educators – arguably legitimates the practice of reading for pleasure, enabling students to 'witness' and participate in adults' passion for reading and to participate, formally and informally, in this shared experience and practice (Francois, 2013a, p. 22).

Few studies of librarians focus specifically on their own readerly identities, but when young people's views are sought, they consider librarians model and share their affective pleasure in reading, participate in discussions and make text recommendations (e.g. Cremin, 2010; Cremin and Swann, 2017; Merga and Ferguson, 2021). In one US secondary school study, staff created a network of library spaces across the institution, including the headteacher's library, which comprised a large collection with over 2,000 titles. The presence of this library in the headteacher's office not only provided an additional space from which students could choose books but also positioned the headteacher as a reader (Francois, 2013a). Furthermore, the staff knew the collections intimately and were thus able to recommend texts as fellow readers and role models. This contributed to the students making more regular use of the library spaces, closer relationships between staff and students, and a new sense of belonging at the school.

Primary phase research, from the United States, the UK and Finland, has shown that staff knowledge of texts is vital for Reading Teachers, although it cannot be assumed (e.g. Conradi Smith et al., 2022; Cremin et al., 2014, 2024a). Nonetheless, those teachers who work to develop rich repertoires of children's texts, and who position themselves thoughtfully as readers in the classroom, have been seen to make a more marked and a more positive impact on children's volitional reading than their peers who simply share their love of reading (Cremin, 2010; Cremin et al., 2014). Through reflection and action, these Reading Teachers became more conscious of their own identities, histories and strategies as readers, sought to learn about the children's identities as readers, and developed more engaged classroom reading communities in which they too participated. As a consequence, the research team argued:

> An enhanced personal and professional awareness of what it means to be a reader and deep pleasure in reading, can, the project suggests, serve to nurture young

> readers who, like their teachers, are likely to become engaged self-motivated and interactive readers.
>
> *(Cremin et al., 2014, p. 153)*

Later work with Reading Teachers in the UK underscores the potential of increasing teachers' consciousness of the complex personal, social and affective nature of reading in their own lives, this has been seen to result in altered classroom practices (Cremin et al., 2022) although closer documentation of the impact of these reading role models on young readers and their desire to read is still needed.

Teachers as writing role models

Turning to teachers as writers, research in this area also indicates that teachers' knowledge and conceptualisation of writing influences their teaching (Rietdijk et al., 2017; Woodard, 2017; Yeo, 2007). Also, that professional knowledge and teachers' modelling their own enjoyment and excitement in writing can support children's development as writers, potentially motivating them to engage in leisure writing (e.g. Gardner and Kuzich, 2022; Graham et al., 2015). Concluding their review of key writing practices, Graham et al. (2015) observe that amongst many other features, effective writing teachers create a safe and engaging environment for writing by modelling their own pleasure and excitement about writing, and celebrate good writing in diverse ways. A systematic review of research into teachers as writers from 1995 to 2015 signals that in pre-service and in-service community contexts, extended opportunities to write and reflect upon the processes involved can increase teachers' self-confidence as writers and their approach to developing writers (Cremin and Oliver, 2016). Teachers' assurance and investment in writing may in turn enhance their students' experiences as writers and support volitional writing within and beyond school. For instance, three-quarters of the pre-service teachers in Gardner's (2014) study perceived that the experience of writing in sessions and reflecting on being a writer would impact on their teaching, increasing their empathy for children's writing challenges, their awareness of the role of life experience and the importance of the affective dimension of writing.

Whilst the systematic review found there was limited and inconclusive evidence of the impact of teachers' writing on student writing attainment outcomes, the evidence suggests that teachers' histories and identities as writers can make a difference to children's attitudes and engagement (Cremin and Oliver, 2016). Studies indicate this is in part through teachers' personal sharing of their engagement and pleasure in writing, and in part through their openness to talk about the challenges they encounter and strategies to handle these (e.g. Dix and Cawkwell, 2011; Locke and Kato, 2012; McKinney, 2017; McKinney and Giorgis, 2009). The data suggest that even teachers who lack confidence as writers can support children's motivation to write by taking on a visible writing identity, sharing their own difficulties and relating to children as writers (Cremin and Baker, 2010; Gardner, 2014; Woodard, 2017).

Through engaging reflexively in the experience, research suggests that teachers who adopt an insider's perspective on the writing process can serve as potent writing role models (Baker and Cremin, 2017; Rowe et al., 2022). In order to offer the children living demonstrations of how, what and why they might write, early years professionals in the United States were seen to write in front of and alongside them (Rowe et al., 2022). They also invited the children to participate as writers and supported them in identifying opportunities to compose messages and texts that were regularly shared with significant others in their lives. Additionally, the pedagogues accepted and valued the children's attempts at writing, positioning these, like their own adult writing, as acts of genuine communication.

Likewise, in apprenticing story writers, teachers who make use of Paley's (1990) storytelling and story-acting approach, and scribe children's stories, offer them evidence of adult delight and expertise in capturing their narratives in writing (Cremin, 2017; Nicolopoulou et al., 2015). In the former study of this practice, children took up the mantle of the story scribe for others, in the latter this appeared to increase the children's agentic engagement with journal writing. The shaping influence of teachers' pleasure and engagement in the process of writing is also seen in Woodard's (2017) research. She tracked the journey of a teacher who did not see herself as a particularly good writer due to negative memories of school writing; she lacked confidence in sharing writing and rarely wrote for pleasure. However, after attending a US National Writing Project summer institute, this teacher took up the identity of writer with and for her students. This approach, over time, combined with legitimising children's diverse personal experiences, recognising their drawing as writing, positioning them as experts, and encouraging them to engage in fan fiction writing, for example, led to positive consequences. Through her observations, Woodard observed that this

> seemed to positively affect children's sense of themselves as writers, their motivation to write and their writing performance.
>
> *(2017, p. 130)*

Another US study has also shown that those students who perceived their teachers enjoyed teaching writing tended to have higher writing enjoyment scores (Zumbrunn et al., 2019). The authors conclude that teachers' behaviour, both implicit and explicit as writers, and their involvement in writing have the potential to make the writing process enjoyable for their students. This was borne out in an earlier UK-based case study, in which a teacher, despite lacking assurance as a writer, regularly composed in front of the class and undertook the same writing assignments as the children, in order, in his words, to 'create a writing community' (Baker and Cremin, 2017). The children viewed their teacher as a writer who was genuinely interested in them as individuals and in what they wrote. The youngsters expressed interest in their teacher's writing and voiced considerable satisfaction in the opportunities given to them to exercise their rights as writers and choose their subject matter and form. They also valued the personal and affective nature of his feedback and response. Furthermore, there was evidence to indicate that his role, and the ways he positioned the children as authors, created a more horizontal and less hierarchical classroom community 'where the status of the teacher-as-expert was eroded through the sharing of knowledges and the understanding that everyone is a learner' (Baker and Cremin, 2017, p. 107).

Whilst the range of studies reviewed indicate the potential of teachers positioning themselves as learners, readers, writers and literacy role models in the classroom, this identity stance is not without challenge.

The challenges of being a reading/writing role model

Adopting the role of Reading Teacher or becoming a fellow writer requires considerable knowledge and professional reflexivity on the part of the professional and may well involve a degree of personal sharing and risk taking. The evidence indicates that for some teachers sharing their reading and writing lives and practices with children and in particular positioning themselves as readers and writers publicly in school is difficult and may be an uncomfortable experience.

Such challenges have been more extensively documented in relation to teachers as writers than readers. Teachers, the research reveals, do not commonly view themselves as writers and tend to have negative views of their authorial capabilities when invited to write and share their writing during initial teacher education or professional development (e.g. Cremin, 2006; Gardner, 2014; Morgan, 2006; Street and Stang, 2016; Woodard, 2015; Whitney, 2008). These studies, alongside many others noted in the systematic review (Cremin and Oliver, 2016), show that considerable insecurity, anxiety and discomfort exists about writing on the part of teachers, particularly in the public forum of the classroom. These often relate to teachers' low self-confidence, negative writing histories, and the challenge of composing and enacting the dual identity positions of teacher and writer in school. As the review concludes, this is likely to shape professional practice, influencing whether teachers follow policy requirements and skills-based models of writing, or offer a more reflective, writer/author-oriented approach (Cremin and Oliver, 2016). Responding to this lack of confidence, Gardner observes:

> We need to understand the fears that children and adults alike have in regard to expressing themselves through this means [writing] and demonstrate the pleasures and benefits they are missing out on
>
> *(Gardner, 2014, p. 138).*

Less explicit discomfort has been tracked in relation to teachers as readers, although in one study some educators voiced concern about the appropriacy of sharing their own reading lives and interests with children, perceiving that this was irrelevant, too personal and not required by national policy (Cremin et al., 2009, 2014). Another challenge is that some online library systems position teachers in particular ways – often as gatekeepers of children's reading, mediating and transferring texts knowledge in the database to children in a largely hierarchical and somewhat distanced manner (Kucirkova and Cremin, 2017). Arguably these library systems, which are commonly used internationally, restrain teachers from acting as informed listeners, mentors and co-readers – as reading role models.

Furthermore teachers' conceptions of what counts as reading/writing and what being a reader/writer involves can both constrain and enable their literate identity positions in the classroom. For many teachers, the concept of a writer is tied to a published professional or expert engaged in paid work (Wilson, 2009; Woodard, 2013). Pedagogues' conceptualisations of reading and writing, as Yeo (2007) observes, often have little to do with current theories or practices in reading and composition, or with what they were taught in pre-service programmes; rather they tend to be rooted in their past experiences, historical conceptions of reading/writing and in their particular national policy codifications. Dobson and Stephenson (2017) found when they, as researcher-educators, led the creative writing and drama workshops, some teachers and teaching assistants voiced concern about the children's behaviour and progress according to their perceived and received notions of writing. Limited perceptions of school literacy proficiency and its attendant assessment can reinforce long-standing dichotomies between personal reading and writing at home and school and may well constrain classroom practice (e.g. Cremin et al., 2014; Hall, 2012; Hempel-Jorgensen et al., 2018; Yeo, 2007). Arguably therefore, widening professional understanding of literacy to encompass attention to being a reader and a writer is invaluable. Professional writers can support educators on these journeys.

Professional writers as role models

A body of work exists about authors working in schools, although relatively few peer-reviewed studies focus on the benefits of published writers working as experienced role models alongside children and whether this influences children's motivation to read or write. Considerable grey literature exists, but there is a tendency for the evaluations of partnership projects to be positively appraised and these rarely offer details of the identity positioning of the writers involved. However, the research studies that are available emphasise the significance of writers – in residence or in stand-alone visits – drawing on their professional lives, profiling children as authors and experts, and working towards the publication and performance of their work (DeFauw, 2018; Owen and Munden, 2010; Xerri, 2015). In examining the work of a long-standing Northern Ireland 'Poetry in Motion' project, Xerri (2017) indicates that the professional writers involved operate as role models, and that this is part of the project's success. They share their enthusiasm for the art form as well as their commitment and determination to write poetry, and this is seen to motivate young writers (Xerri, 2017). As Owen and Munden (2010) note in reviewing professional writer and teacher partnership work:

> The effects of working with writers can be radically different. ... This is partly due to the fact that their focus in the classroom derives directly from their professional life: their very living relies on their craft, on matters of imagery, structure and style, and this clearly makes some important connections with pupils.
>
> *(Owen and Munden, 2010, p. 56)*

Additionally, in exploring how a primary class interacted with an author over a school year, DeFauw (2018) demonstrates that the children were inspired by the author's reflections on his own experience of writing. The author not only modelled the challenges he encountered, he also performed the role of an authentic audience for the children's writing, offering feedback and considerable direct encouragement which was valued and built upon. Furthermore, researching a collaboration between a school, a writer and an art gallery, Rumney et al. (2016) found that by using play, drama and multimodal activities, the children's confidence as writers developed, irrespective of their ability. The teachers perceived that the act of writing became more meaningful for the young such that they no longer saw writing as 'work' and found increased pleasure in it.

In yet another study, the professional writers, who were positioned as learning partners, worked collaboratively with teachers, which over time helped these pedagogues to recognise, articulate and share their redeveloped expertise as writers with children (Cremin et al., 2020). In this 'Teachers as Writers' (2015–2017) project, two universities and Arvon, a creative writing foundation in the UK, sought to determine the impact of professional writers engaging with teachers. It involved a residential writing retreat for the teachers, and collaborative work in classrooms, and the team tracked changes in practice and the impact on both the teachers and students as writers. Initially anxious about sharing their writing, the teachers gradually came to write, to draw on their life experiences and share their writing in workshops during the retreat and later in school. Over time, many came to embrace the title 'writer', as they broadened their understanding of what being a writer might mean and developed a greater commitment to that identity position. For instance, one noted that she was learning '[w]hat it feels like to be a writer and how hard that can be ... and also just that it doesn't have to be perfect, you know it's the enjoyment of creating it' (Cremin et al., 2020, p. 53).

Teachers also adopted pedagogical practices demonstrated by the writers: they offered children choice and agency through personal non-assessed notebooks and positioned them as authors who regularly read their work to one another. The students voiced increased enjoyment and engagement in writing, a stronger sense of ownership and understanding of the writing process and they also perceived the project impacted positively on their motivation, confidence and skills as writers (Myhill et al., 2023). The young people attached particular significance to creative freedom, associating gains in enjoyment with less prescriptive writing tasks and more flexible drafting strategies. However, the results of this year-long randomised control trial showed that the comparison group made stronger improvement in writing outcomes than the intervention group (Cremin et al., 2020). The project raised questions about what constitutes 'good writing' nationally, institutionally and in each classroom, and highlighted the need to track the impact of young people's increased enjoyment, motivation and sense of self as writers on their writing outcomes over more sustained periods of time. This study also evidences the ways in which the teachers' engagement as adult writers shaped their pedagogy and links to many of the studies in Part III, which highlight the significance of autonomy, agency and relatedness in nurturing writing for pleasure.

As part of this study, the researchers examined the professional writers' understanding of the craft of writing; and found this knowledge encompassed five elements: the Writing Process; Being an Author; Text-level Choices; Language Choices; and the Reader–Writer Relationship (Myhill et al., 2023). Arguably, in many schools in accountability cultures, the notion of 'being an author', like being a teacher-writer, is sidelined, alongside the reader–writer relationship, whereas text and word level choices as well as simplistic notions of the writing process abound. In contrast, this work, derived from analysis of nine professional writers' perceptions and practices, represents a way for educators to think about subject knowledge for writing as being both text-oriented and writer-oriented. This conception of the craft of writing may afford more scope for developing young people's pleasure in writing, as it recognises the personal resources and intentions that writers bring alongside and as equal to, the text knowledge needed.

In sum, the research literature indicates that parents are influential reading role models, and that teachers, librarians and professional writers too can be involved as reflective readers, writers and role models in school and community contexts. Studies suggest that projects and partnerships, as well support in pre-service training and continuing professional development, can be helpful to nurture increased awareness of the potential of this identity positioning for nurturing reading and writing for pleasure. Such opportunities can enable pedagogues to teach from an insider-perspective, drawing on newly realised understandings of the complex nature of reading and writing, and an awareness of the significance of their own and young people's literacy identities. The involvement of adults in this way also serves to build a sense of community.

Communities of readers and writers

In recent years, with increased appreciation of the social nature of reading and writing, researchers have begun to pay more attention to conceptualising and understanding literacy communities classrooms and schools. Studies show that educators who intentionally offer sustained social opportunities to nurture recreational reading as a collective, create connected communities of readers (e.g. Boyask et al., 2022; Cremin et al., 2014; Lenhart et al, 2017; Ng, 2018). Writing research has also begun to focus on the nature of young people's engagement in communities of writers, both in school and online (e.g. Connolly and Burn, 2019; Zumbrunn et al., 2019). Reading in the context of a community not only enables children to develop relational connections to their peers and adults, but can serve to motivate young people to read or write in their own time. However, participation cannot be mandated and community cohesion may prove elusive with members exhibiting different levels of dis/engagement. Nonetheless, such communities, if they are built on notions of equality and the quality of human relationships – *communitas* – rather than only social systems or organisational structures (Williams, 1976), have the potential to be places of collective growth and to support pleasure and engagement in reading and writing.

Connected communities of readers

Studies that pay attention to reading collectives demonstrate the existence of a number of micro communities in different reading spaces: in schools (e.g. Boyask et al., 2022; Cremin et al., 2014; Francois, 2013a; Moss and Macdonald, 2004; Ng, 2018), in libraries (e.g. Merga, 2020a, 2020b), in homes (e.g. Fletcher, 2018), in digital reading spaces (e.g. Jerasa and Boffone, 2021) as well as in particular geographic contexts (e.g. Manresa, 2018). As Mercer (2002) acknowledges, communities can be 'distributed, multiple, and complex, and based as much on common interests as common locality' (p. 105). The adults in these communities play influential roles. Whether they are parents, grandparents, carers, teachers, librarians, volunteers, or members of reading intervention programmes for example, their conceptions of reading, reading attitudes, knowledge, practices and priorities all shape and are shaped by the community. The relationships between adults and children influence these reading networks and communities, which Kucirkova and Cremin (2020) argue, must encompass difference and diversity, as well as agreement and disagreement if volitional reading is to be fostered.

Whilst researchers have not directly examined families as connected communities of readers, studies do highlight that family reading practices are often child-led and thus relationally responsive to the young people's needs and interests (Levy et al., 2018). Also that parents appreciate the interpersonal connections that shared reading offers (Brown et al., 2017; Merga and Ledger, 2018). Additionally, neighbourhood reading interventions have been seen to increase children's recreational reading by drawing families into communal experiences, albeit often temporarily through summer reading programmes, library events and public read-alouds for instance (Compton-Lilly, 2016; Mahasneh et al., 2021). These examples highlight the potential of building relaxed reading communities locally that support the young, but more research is needed to understand the levers for optimal impact on volitional reading.

Drawing on their view of reading for pleasure as an act of sociality, based in a communal conception of being within Aotearoa New Zealand, Boyask and colleagues voice a concern that '[s]chool and school-based approaches to literacy, act as individuating technologies that underplay the pleasures of reading together and accentuate differences between readers' (Boyask et al., 2022, p. 175). Reading, they argue, is too often seen as an individual endeavor, which fails to recognise the affective and relational experience of reading as a way of being with others. In their research in a secondary school, the researchers observe that certain objects, such as the physical, virtual and temporal reading spaces, combined to 'create a landscape in which communal relations to reading' were established (Boyask et al., 2022 p. 178). They describe these relations as being connected by the young people's affective and pleasurable engagement with both objects and with people yet highlight that a community approach to developing to reading education, whilst desirable, can 'struggle with the central tension between the individual and collective' (Boyask and Derby, 2025).

Other studies which frame reading for pleasure as inevitably encompassing relating to others, highlight the myriad complex ways in which groups of young people and adults connect around texts in peer and friendship groups and as part of adult–child relationships, and stress the social and emotional value of these (e.g. Cremin et al., 2014, 2024b; De Naeghel et al., 2014; Francois, 2013a, 2013b; Ivey and Johnston, 2013, 2015, 2023; Kennedy, 2018; Milne et al., 2022). However, not all these studies describe these collectives as communities, nor do they subject the reader relationships to close scrutiny. In addition, few of them examine the affective nature of young people's social engagement in reading.

Studies that focus on classroom reading communities frequently indicate the significance of adult knowledge of the children as readers. They reveal the value of staff learning about and listening to young people's perspectives as readers. For example, in a US study, seeking out and honouring student voices clearly supported the emergence of a reading community (Ng, 2018). By developing knowledge about her students as readers, and responsively adapting her practice, the teacher in this study triggered increased interest and cultivated their agency. Over time the young people began to collaborate, share reading materials, develop reading stamina and seek out new texts of choice. The teacher also shifted from controlling and monitoring their reading time, and began to read alongside her students, discuss books with them, and model her engagement as a reader. Over the year, this shaped the development of closer relationships and connections within the classroom.

> The sharing of students' reading and related feelings at the end of the school day reinforced a culture of collaboration and continuously fortified students' interest in reading and evolving readers' community.
>
> *(Ng, 2018, p. 712)*

This sense of connection between readers and the creation of reading networks is also evidenced in the work of Ivey and Johnston (2013, 2023). The teachers in this US study sought out the adolescents' interests and preferences and carefully curated a book collection in response, with multiple copies of some texts. This enabled the teenagers to share their reading journeys and their newly formed networks were seen to support their volitional reading. In a UK study which explored the development of reading communities in 27 primary schools, teachers also sought to learn more about children's reading preferences and practices, and some pedagogues began to share their own reading lives. This wider knowledge about children and teachers as readers beyond the school gate enabled new relational connections and a basis from which to begin to build connected communities of readers (Cremin et al., 2014). As discussed in Chapter 5, in response to the children's interests and teachers' enriched repertoires of children's texts, the nature of the classroom book talk gradually shifted from being teacher-led and became more learner-led. Debate and mutuality was evidenced in the way that adults and children exchanged views and gave of themselves as readers. Connecting to other readers became part of the ethos of many of the classrooms in this study and, as in Ng's (2018) and Ivey and Johnston's (2023) research, new reader-to-reader relationships developed between children and adults as well as children and children.

Through this study, it appeared that the teachers re-viewed the concept of reading and over time came to see it not only an individual private pursuit, but also as a collaborative social experience (Cremin et al., 2009, 2014). The teachers established 'books in common', offered relaxed spaces for discussing texts, encouraged reader-to-reader recommendations, and supported informal book talk. In the process, affinity groups around particular texts, genres, interests and series iteratively developed. Characterised by reciprocity and interaction, these were underpinned by reader relationships, not by the requirement to read or the provision of reading for pleasure routines. These communities, documented within and beyond the classroom, evidenced a strong sense of social connectedness, fostered and sustained a sense of belonging and enabled the development of more positive reader identities (Cremin, 2010; Cremin et al., 2009, 2014). The case study children, initially identified as 'reluctant' and 'disinterested', became drawn into reading and their dispositions and behaviours as readers gradually changed, many showed increased pleasure in reading and began to read more frequently and participate as members of these different reading communities.

In a not dissimilar manner, Boyask's team (2021a) found that a strong focus on the encouragement of reading as a social experience and the building of inclusive reading communities can positively impact on less engaged readers. In this study of five schools, the participation of wider school communities and families was explicitly sought through multiple library and school initiatives (Boyask et al., 2021b; Harrington et al., 2021; Milne et al., 2022). This made recreational reading more visible and opened up new spaces for the young people aged 5–13 years to engage in reading voluntarily and for pleasure with others. It indicated that

> Reading for pleasure best occurs within a place of connectivity where all reading relationships are shaped by reciprocity and collective responsibility.
>
> *(Milne et al., 2022, p. 48)*

Libraries represent another space where reading relationships and networks can be created, although surprisingly few studies of library practices consider community creation, perhaps due to the temporality of visits and clubs held in them. They are noted, however, as a place of 'social connectedness' (Willis et al., 2019) and some research indicates that extracurricular reading clubs, characterised by informality and relaxed attitudes and led by librarians who modelled the pleasure to be found in reading, enabled the building of communities (Cremin and Swann, 2017). The reading spaces inhabited by these clubs, linked to the Carnegie medal shadowing scheme, were mostly non-hierarchical in nature, this was echoed in the teenagers' and adults' close reader relationships, personal connections made to texts and the communal sharing of food. Significantly, the groups effectively encouraged volitional reading. Merga and Ferguson (2021) also found the safe space of libraries fostered a sense of belonging, at least for those students who identified as readers and wanted to talk about texts.

Online spaces also offer opportunities for the creation of reading connections and networks and for learning about the key tenets of such. The recent phenomenon of BookTok as a sub-space within TikTok, created by the young for the young, once again underscores the significance of agency and autonomy in developing communities of readers, and demonstrates how young people connect through peer-led discussions of their chosen books (Jerasa and Boffone, 2021). Similarly, Asplund et al. (2024), identified how young adults (17–18-year-olds), use BookTok to find communities of readers to share their love of reading and favourite texts. Amongst the many digital literacies practiced within it, BookTok includes mini videos with young readers chatting about their current favourites and making recommendations that often involve in-jokes to which others respond, either by making videos or by creating digital discussion groups. Jerasa and Boffone (2021) suggest that such spaces alter the way young adult literature is discussed, making it more fun, memeable and socio-culturally relevant.

> It [BookTok] makes space for identities that are underrepresented in the traditional canon and allows for community with books not considered "appropriate" for academic spaces or those spaces where curriculum is created according to rigid testing "standards"
>
> *(Jerasa and Boffone, 2021, p. 222).*

Young people's local practices appear to be inspired by BookTok practices and vice versa, enabling the two communities of practice to interplay (Asplund et al., 2024). The researchers argue that if teachers acknowledge and use examples from these communities in school, this could widen professional understanding of contemporary teenagers' reader identities and support the development of school reading communities. For a fuller consideration of online social reading cultures and communities, see Reddan et al. (2024).

Connected communities of writers

Children and young people participate in different writing networks at school (e.g. Baker and Cremin, 2017; Dyson, 2001, 2003; Dyson and Dewayani, 2013; Elf, 2017), online (e.g. Black, 2005; Curwood, 2013) and at home (e.g. Brady, 2009; Chamberlain, 2019). To serve their own purposes and in response to their own interests and friendships, children may also choose to write with others in their local community, as Chamberlain et al. (2020) documented during the COVID-19 lockdown when young people in the UK, for instance, wrote messages of support for the National Health Service on the pavement. In school, if writing is framed as a personally purposeful, imaginatively engaging and socially supported experience, this can, the evidence suggests, create a felt sense of belonging and enable the development of connected communities of writers (Connolly and Burn, 2019; Cremin et al., 2020; Dobson and Stephenson, 2017, 2019; Myhill et al, 2023; Nolen, 2006, 2007; Zumbrunn et al., 2017). Such communities are not static and the characteristics, practices and individuals within them will both shape the communities and be shaped by their participation in them.

Drawing on his 'writer(s)-within-community model of writing', Graham (2018) argues that participation in writing communities will impact on young writers' development, and their cognitive, affective and behavioural engagement in writing. He posits that writing is

> Shaped and bound by the characteristics, capacity, and variability of the communities in which it takes place and by the cognitive characteristics, capacity, and individual differences of those who produce it.
>
> *(Graham, 2018, p. 258)*

The development of a classroom community of writers arguably encompasses creativity and structure, opportunities for authorial agency and explicit instruction in order that young writers are supported, and, to extend Graham's (2018) conceptualisation, are socially engaged as writers. In their study focused on creating a community of writers, Dobson and Stephenson (2017) deliberately sought to balance the freedom of creative engagement and choice (through using the open approach of process drama) with structured teaching (this involved modelling writing techniques for example). They profiled the opportunity for the 25 7–11-year-olds to 'steal' words from one another and the workshop leaders (and vice versa) and stressed this was normal practice for all writers. Adaptations and appropriations within their social groups were common, reminiscent of the borrowing within the smaller writing networks observed by Dyson (e.g. 2001) and commitment levels were high across the eight sessions. The study shows that by establishing a writing community in and through drama, in which such intertextual borrowing practices were normal, the researcher-teachers were able to facilitate the children's enjoyment and enable 'different authorial identity enactments' (Dobson and Stephenson, 2017, p. 166) that supported their engagement as writers.

When such communities emerge, as in this case, the young are supported to move with assurance between personal and social spaces for writing and often a shared communicative purpose for writing is created. Young people's writing is often published as part of community practice, for example through performances, readings, plays, debates, the production of anthologies (recorded or written), digital resources and so forth (e.g. Chen and Rutherford Vale, 2020; Connolly and Burn, 2019; Cremin et al., 2023; Young and Ferguson, 2021). Additionally, the collective support of adults and peers is evident and in two particular studies this was seen to nurture a positive sense of self as a writer (Nolen, 2007; Myhill et al., 2023). In Nolen's (2007) longitudinal study of individuals' motivation to read and write, she noted a palpable sense of community developed in some classes which impacted on the young people's drive to compose. Whilst affording more choice and authentic reasons to write were seen as essential elements, so was a socially supportive structure for writing. As Nolen notes:

> Children were observed to express pleasure and interest in each other's writing, and writing became something to do with friends as children were encouraged and given time to collaborate on joint projects. Writing was an important part of the social fabric of the classroom.
>
> *(Nolen, 2007, p. 27)*

Socially shared writing (and reading) activities were normalised within this classroom, which offered the children a communal sense of purpose and community. These findings are underscored by Myhill et al.'s (2023) work. Their analysis of pupil interviews from the 'Teachers as Writers' research highlighted the motivating power of choice and agency and the importance of a collaborative writing community. At the residential writing retreat, the 16 teachers involved developed a commitment to each other in the community created by Arvon. They wrote alone, but constantly shared their ideas and extracts from their writing with one another and their tutors in a low-key, informal manner. They also created a shared anthology to which everyone, teachers, researchers and tutors, contributed. Back in school, as noted earlier, the teachers began to position themselves as co-writers and learners, and in particular created classrooms which were more relaxed, less pressured and where collaboration was actively encouraged. The young people recognised a distinct change in the atmosphere and ethos in their classrooms as a result, they valued this and perceived it enabled the creation of a shared writing culture. As the authors observe:

> Motivation is not simply an internal characteristic of an individual but is situated within the context of a community of writers
>
> *(Myhill et al., 2023, p. 14).*

Yet as this review has shown, relatively few studies have examined the impact of the writing environment and community on young people's desire to write. In many classrooms, due in part to the pressures of the accountability agenda (Barrs, 2019), there may be limited collective engagement in writing and little sense of a community of writers.

Conclusion

To summarise, research indicates that adult involvement and authentic demonstrations of the experience, pleasures and challenges of being a reader and a writer can positively influence children's own literate identities. Yet this is not a simple matter of showcasing and role-modelling and optimally it is combined with pedagogic principles such as choice, recognition and knowledge of each unique child as a reader and writer. Additionally, through the creation and support of various connected literacy communities and kinship groups, adults invest in and involve young people, offering them agency and space to participate as readers and writers on their own terms. This can enhance children's social engagement and support the development of positive literacy dispositions. Nonetheless, more work is needed to understand the diverse needs and socio-cultural interests and identities of different groups, to consider those members who may only be peripherally engaged, and to explore wider communities of connection that stretch beyond the bounds of school and encompass families and local community members.

References

Aerila, J., Kauppinen, M., Cremin, T., Siipola, M., Mukherjee, S.J. and Lähteelä, J. (2023) 'Student teachers as readers: The reading experiences and reading pedagogy of Finnish and British student teachers', *Australian Journal of Teacher Education, 48*(9), pp. 87–99.

Anderson, K., Atkinson, T.S., Swaggerty, E.A. and O'Brien, K. (2019) 'Examining relationships between home-based shared book reading practices and children's language/literacy skills at kindergarten entry', *Early Child Development and Care*, 189(13), pp. 2167–2182.

Applegate, A., Applegate, M.D., Mercantini, M.A., McGeehan, C.M., Cobb, J.B., DeBoy, J.R., Modla, V.B. and Lewinski, K.E. (2014) 'The Peter effect revisited: Reading habits and attitudes of college students', *Literacy Research and Instruction*, 53(3), pp. 188–204.

Asplund, S.-B., Ljung Egeland, B. and Olin-Scheller, C. (2024) 'Sharing is caring: Young people's narratives about BookTok and volitional reading', *Language and Education*, 38(4), pp. 635–651.

Baker, S. and Cremin, T. (2017) 'Teachers' identities as writers: Teachers, support staff and pupil accounts of the role of emotion in the writing classroom', in Cremin, T. and Locke, T. (eds), *Writer Identity and the Teaching and Learning of Writing*, London: Routledge, pp. 98–114.

Barrs, M. (2019) 'Teaching bad writing', *English in Education*, 53(1), pp. 18–31.

Black, R. (2005) 'Access and affiliation: The literacy and composition practices of English language learners in an online fanfiction community', *Journal of Adolescent and Adult Literacy*, 49(2), pp. 118–128.

Boyask, R. and Derby, M. (2025) 'Reading communities', in Cremin, T. and McGeown, S. (eds), *Reading for Pleasure: International Perspectives*, London and New York: Routledge.

Boyask, R., Mounsey, M., Couch, D. and Smith, B. (2021a) *A Changing Story of Reading at Huntly College*, Wellington: National Library of New Zealand.

Boyask, R., Harrington, C., Milne, J. and Smith, B.H.B. (2022) '"Reading enjoyment" is ready for school: Foregrounding affect and sociality in children's reading for pleasure', *New Zealand Journal of Educational Studies*, 58, pp. 169–182.

Boyask, R., Wall, C., Harrington, C., Milne, J. and Couch, D. (2021b) *Reading for Pleasure: For the Collective Good of Aotearoa New Zealand*, Wellington: National Library of New Zealand.

Brady, J. (2009) 'Exploring teachers' perceptions of children's imaginative writing at home', *English in Education*, 43(2), pp. 129–148.

Brown, M.I., Westerveld, M. and Gillon, G. (2017) 'Early storybook reading with babies and young children: Parents' opinions and home reading practices', *Australasian Journal of Early Childhood*, 42(2), pp. 69–77.

Chamberlain, L. (2019) 'Places, spaces and local customs: Honouring the private worlds of out-of-school text creation', *Literacy*, 53(1), pp. 39–45.

Chamberlain, L., Lacina, J., Bintz, W.P., Jimerson, J., Payne, K. and Zingale, R. (2020) 'Literacy in lockdown: Learning and teaching in COVID-19 school closures', *The Reading Teacher*, 73(4), pp. 243–253.

Chen, H. and Rutherford Vale, E. (2020) 'Developing confident writers: fostering audience awareness in primary school writing classrooms', in Chen, H., Myhill, D. and Lewis, H. (eds), *Developing Writers Across Primary and Secondary Years*, London and Sydney: Routledge, pp. 131–153.

Cole, A., Brown, A., Clark, C. and Picton, I. (2022) *Role Models and Their Influence on Children and Young People's Reading*, London: National Literacy Trust.

Commeyras, M., Bisplinghoff, B. and Olson, J. (2003) *Teachers as Readers: Perspectives on the Importance of Reading in Teachers' Classrooms and Lives*, Newark, DE: International Literacy Association.

Compton-Lilly, C. (2016) *Reading Students' Lives: Literacy Learning Across Time*, New York: Routledge.

Connolly, S. and Burn, A. (2019) 'The story engine: Offering an online platform for making "unofficial" creative writing work', *Literacy*, 53(1), pp. 30–38.

Conradi Smith, K., Young, C.A. and Yatzeck, J.C. (2022) 'What are teachers reading and why? An analysis of elementary read aloud titles and the rationales underlying teachers' selections', *Literacy Research and Instruction*, 61(4), pp. 383–401.

Cremin, T. (2006) 'Creativity, uncertainty and discomfort: Teachers as writers', *Cambridge Journal of Education*, 36(3), pp. 415–433.

Cremin, T. (2010) 'Poetry teachers: Teachers who read and readers who teach poetry', in Styles, M., Joy, L. and Whitley, D. (eds), *Poetry and Childhood*, London: Trentham, pp. 219–226.

Cremin, T. (2017) 'Apprentice story writers: Exploring young children's print awareness and agency in early story authoring', in Cremin, T., Flewitt, R., Mardell, B. and Swann, J. (eds), *Storytelling in Early Childhood: Enriching Language, Literacy, and Classroom Culture*, London and New York: Routledge, pp. 67–84.

Cremin, T. (2020) 'Apprenticing authors: Nurturing children's identities as writers', in Chen, H., Myhill, D. and Lewis, H. (eds), *Developing Writers Across Primary and Secondary Years*, London and Sydney: Routledge, pp. 113–130.

Cremin, T. and Baker, S. (2010) 'Exploring teacher-writer identities in the classroom: Conceptualising the struggle', *English Teaching: Practice and Critique*, 9(3), pp. 8–25.

Cremin, T. and Baker, S. (2014) 'Exploring the discursively constructed identities of a teacher-writer teaching writing', *English Teaching: Practice and Critique*, 13(3), pp. 28–53.

Cremin, T. and Oliver, L. (2016) 'Teachers as writers: A systematic review', *Research Papers in Education*, 32(2), pp. 269–295.

Cremin, T. and Swann, J. (2017) 'School librarians as leaders of extracurricular reading groups', in Pihl, J., van der Kooij, K. and Carlsten, T. (eds), *Teacher and Librarian Partnerships in Literacy Education in the 21st Century*, Rotterdam: Sense Publishers, pp. 119–137.

Cremin, T., Hendry, H., Chamberlain, L. and Hulston, S.J. (2023) *Reading and Writing for Pleasure: Executive Summary of the Research Literature*, London: The Mercers' Company.

Cremin, T., Hendry, H., Rodriguez Leon, L. and Kucirkova, N. (eds) (2022) *Reading Teachers: Nurturing Reading for Pleasure*, London: Routledge.

Cremin, T., Hendry, H., Rodriguez Leon, L. and Hulston, S.J. (2024b) 'Informal book talk: Digging beneath the surface', *English 3–13*, 52(7), pp. 930–945.

Cremin, T., Mottram, M., Collins, F., Powell, S. and Safford, K. (2009) 'Teachers as readers: Building communities of readers', *Literacy*, 43(1), pp. 11–19.

Cremin, T., Mottram, M., Collins, F.M., Powell, S. and Safford, K. (2014) *Building Communities of Engaged Readers: Reading for Pleasure*, Oxon: Routledge.

Cremin, T., Myhill, D., Eyres, I., Wilson, A., Oliver, L. and Nash, T. (2020) 'Teachers as writers: Learning together', *Literacy*, 53(2), pp. 49–59.

Cremin, T., Mukherjee, S., Aerila, J.A., Kauppinen, M., Lateela, J. and Sipola, M. (2024a) 'Widening teachers' reading repertoires: Moving beyond a popular childhood canon', *The Reading Teacher*, 77(6), pp. 833–841.

Curwood, J. (2013) 'The Hunger Games: Literature, literacy and offline affinity spaces', *Language Arts*, 90(6), pp. 417–427.

Daisey, P. (2010) 'Secondary preservice teachers remember their favorite reading experiences', *Journal of Adolescent & Adult Literacy*, 53(8), pp. 678–687.

DeFauw, D.L. (2018) 'One school's yearlong collaboration with a children's book author', *The Reading Teacher*, 72(3), pp. 355–367.

De Naeghel, J., Valcke, M., De Meyer, L., Warlop, N., Van Braak, J. and Van Keer, H. (2014) 'The role of teacher behavior in adolescents' intrinsic reading motivation', *Reading and Writing*, 27, pp. 1547–1565.

Dix, S.M. and Cawkwell, G. (2011) 'The influence of peer group response: Building a teacher and student expertise in the writing classroom', *English Teaching-practice and Critique*, 10(4), pp. 41–57.

Dobson, T. and Stephenson, L. (2017) 'Primary pupils' creative writing: Enacting identities in a community of writers', *Literacy*, 51(3), pp. 162–168.

Dobson, T. and Stephenson, L. (2019) '"I think it fits in": Using process drama to promote agentic writing with primary school children', *Literacy*, 53(2), pp. 69–76.

Dyson, A.H. (2001) 'Where are the childhoods in childhood literacy? An exploration in outer (school) space', *Journal of Early Childhood Literacy*, 1(1), pp. 9–39.

Dyson, A.H. (2003) 'Popular literacies and the "all" children: Rethinking literacy development for contemporary childhoods', *Language Arts*, 81(2), pp. 100–109.

Dyson, A.H. and Dewayani, S. (2013) 'Writing in childhood cultures', in Hall, K., Cremin, T., Comber, B. and Moll, L.C. (eds), *International Handbook of Research on Children's Literacy, Learning, and Culture*, Malden, MA: Wiley, pp. 258–274.

Elf, N (2017) 'Taught by bitter experience: A timescales analysis of Emily's development of writer identity', in Cremin, T. and Locke, T. (eds), *Writer Identity and the Teaching and Learning of Writing*, London: Routledge, pp. 183–199.

Fletcher, J. (2018) 'Supporting and encouraging young adolescents in New Zealand to be effective readers', *Educational Review*, 70(3), pp. 300–317.

Francois, C. (2013a) 'Reading in the crawl space: A study of an urban school's literacy-focused community of practice', *Teachers College Record*, 115(5), pp. 1–35.

Francois, C. (2013b) 'Reading is about relating: Urban youths give voice to the possibilities for school literacy', *Journal of Adolescent and Adult Literacy*, 57(2), pp. 141–149.

Gardner, P. (2014) 'Becoming a teacher of writing: Primary student teachers reviewing their relationship with writing', *English Education*, 48(2), pp.128–148.

Gardner, P. and Kuzich, S. (2022) 'Ready to write? Investigating the writing experiences of pre-service teachers and their readiness to teach writing', *Issues in Educational Research*, 32(2), pp. 513–532.

Graham, S. (2018) 'A revised writer(s)-within-community model of writing', *Educational Psychologist*, 53(4), pp. 258–279.

Graham, S., Harris, K. and Santangelo, T. (2015) 'Research-based writing practices and the Common Core', *Elementary School Journal*, 115(4), pp. 498–523.

Granado, C. (2014) 'Teachers as readers: A study of the reading habits of future teachers', *Cultura y Educación*, 26(1), pp. 44–70.

Gregory, E. (2001) 'Sisters and brothers as language and literacy teachers: Synergy between siblings playing and working together', *Journal of Early Childhood Literacy*, 1(3), pp. 301–322.

Gregory, E. and Williams, A. (2000) *City Literacies: Learning to Read Across Generations and Cultures*, London: Routledge.

Hall, L.A. (2012) 'Rewriting identities: Creating spaces for students and teachers to challenge the norms of what it means to be a writer in school', *Journal of Adolescent and Adult Literacy*, 55 (5), pp. 368–373.

Harrington, C., Milne, J. and Boyask, R. (2021) *Making Reading for Pleasure Visible in Five Primary Schools from kāhui ako o tiriwā in West Auckland*, Wellington: National Library of New Zealand.

Hempel-Jorgensen, A., Cremin, T., Harris, D. and Chamberlain, L. (2018) 'Pedagogy for reading for pleasure in low socio-economic primary schools: Beyond "pedagogy of poverty"?', *Literacy*, 52(2), pp. 86–94.

Ho, E.S.C. and Lau, K. (2018) 'Reading engagement and reading literacy performance: Effective policy and practices at home and in school', *Journal of Research in Reading*, 41(4), pp. 657–679.

Ivey, G. and Johnston, P.H. (2013) 'Engagement with young adult literature outcomes and processes', *Reading Research Quarterly*, 48(3), pp. 1–21.
Ivey, G. and Johnston, P.H. (2015) 'Engaged reading as a collaborative transformative practice', *Journal of Literacy Research*, 47(3), pp. 297–327.
Ivey, G. and Johnston, P. (2023) *Teens Choosing to Read: Fostering Social, Emotional, and Intellectual Growth Through Books*, New York: Teachers College Press.
Jerasa, S. and Boffone, T. (2021) 'BookTok 101: TikTok, digital literacies, and out-of-school reading practices', *Journal of Adolescent and Adult Literature*, 65(3), pp. 219–226.
Kennedy, E. (2018) 'Engaging children as readers and writers in high-poverty contexts', *Journal of Research in Reading*, 41(4), pp. 716–731.
Knoester, M. and Plikuhn, M. (2016) 'Influence of siblings on out-of-school reading practices', *Journal of Research in Reading*, 39(4), pp. 469–485.
Kucirkova, N. and Cremin, T. (2017) 'Personalised reading for pleasure with digital libraries: Towards a pedagogy of practice and design', *Cambridge Journal of Education*, 48(5), pp. 1–19.
Kucirkova, N. and Cremin, T. (2020) *Children Reading for Pleasure in the Digital Age: Mapping Reader Engagement*, London: SAGE.
Lenhart, J., Lenhard, W., Vaahtoranta, E. and Suggate, S. (2017) 'Incidental vocabulary acquisition from listening to stories: A comparison between read-aloud and free storytelling approaches', *Educational Psychology*, 38(5), pp. 1–21.
Levy, R. and Harrison, A. (2025) 'Home, parents and siblings', in Cremin, T. and McGeown, S. (eds), *Reading for Pleasure: International Perspectives*, London and New York: Routledge, pp. 141–154.
Locke, T. and Kato, H. (2012) 'Poetry for the broken-hearted: How a marginal year 12 English class was turned on to writing', *English in Australia*, 17(1), pp. 61–79.
Mahasneh, R., Suchodoletz, A., Larsen, R. and Dajanai, R. (2021) 'Reading for pleasure among Jordanian children: A community-based reading intervention', *Journal of Research in Reading*, 44(2), pp. 360–378.
Manresa, M. (2018) 'Adolescent reading habits: The effect of school activities on reading practices', in Arizpe, E. and Cliff Hodges, G. (eds), *Young People Reading: Empirical Research Across International Contexts*, New York: Routledge, pp. 123–136.
McDowall, S. (2021) *Teachers as Readers in New Zealand Primary and Intermediate Schools*, Wellington: New Zealand Council for Educational Research.
McDowall, S. (2022) 'Teachers as readers: Listening to, reading, and talking about stories – for pleasure', *Research Information for Teachers*, 2, pp. 22–28.
McKinney, M. (2017) 'Being a writer and teaching writing on the rackety bridge', in Cremin, T. and Locke, T. (eds), *Writer Identity and the Teaching and Learning of Writing*, London: Routledge, pp. 83–97.
McKinney, M. and Giorgis, C. (2009) 'Narrating and performing identity', *Journal of Literacy Research*, 41(1), pp. 104–149.
McKool, S. and Gespass, S. (2009) 'Does Johnny's reading teacher love to read? How teachers' personal reading habits affect instructional practices', *Literacy Research and Instruction*, 48 (3), pp. 264–276.
Mercer, N. (2002) *Words and Minds: How We Use Language to Think Together*, London and New York: Routledge.
Merga, M.K. (2016) '"I don't know if she likes reading": Are teachers perceived to be keen readers, and how is this determined?', *English in Education*, 50(3), pp. 255–269.
Merga, M.K. (2020a) '"We talk books": Teacher librarians promoting book discussion to foster reading engagement', *English in Australia*, 55(1), pp. 22–33.
Merga, M.K. (2020b) 'School librarians as literacy educators within a complex role', *Journal of Library Administration*, 60(8), pp. 889–908.
Merga, M.K. and Ferguson, C. (2021) 'School librarians supporting students' reading for pleasure: A job description analysis', *Australian Journal of Education*, 65(2), pp. 153–171.

Merga, M.K. and Ledger, S. (2018) 'Parents' views on reading aloud to their children: Beyond the early years', *Australian Journal of Language and Literacy*, 41(3), pp. 177–189.

Methe, S.A. and Hintze, J.A. (2003) 'Evaluating teacher modeling as a strategy to increase student reading behavior', *School Psychology Review*, 32(4), pp. 617–623.

Milne, J., Harrington, C. and Boyask, R. (2022) '"We read together": Collaboration, community and stories supporting children's reading for pleasure', *Literacy Forum NZ*, 37(1), pp. 44–55.

Morgan, W. (2006) '"Poetry makes nothing happen": Creative writing and the English classroom', *English Teaching: Practice and Critique*, 5(2), pp. 17–33.

Moss, G. and McDonald, J. (2004) 'The borrowers: Library records as unobtrusive measures of children's reading preferences', *Journal of Research in Reading*, 27(4), pp. 401–412.

Muntoni, F. and Retelsdorf, J. (2019) 'At their children's expense: How parents' gender stereotypes affect their children's reading outcomes', *Learning and Instruction*, 60, pp. 95–103.

Myhill, D., Cremin, T. and Oliver, L. (2023) 'The impact of changed writing environment on students' motivation to write', *Frontiers in Psychology*, 14.

Ng, C. (2018) 'Using student voice to promote reading engagement for economically disadvantaged students', *Journal of Research in Reading*, 41(4), pp. 700–715.

Nicolopoulou, A., Cortina, K.S., Ilgaz, H., Cates, C.B. and de Sá, A.B. (2015) 'Using a narrative- and play-based activity to promote low-income preschoolers' oral language, emergent literacy, and social competence', *Early Childhood Research Quarterly*, 31, pp. 147–162.

Nolen, S.B. (2006) 'The role of social context in the development of motivation to write', in Hidi, A. and Boscolo, P. (eds), *Motivation to Write*, Dordrecht: Kluwer, pp. 241–255.

Nolen, S.B. (2007) 'Young children's motivation to read and write: Development in social contexts', *Cognition and Instruction*, 25(2–3), pp. 219–270.

OECD (2021) *21st-Century Readers: Developing Literacy Skills in a Digital World*, Paris: OECD Publishing.

Owen, N. and Munden, P. (2010) *Class Writing: A NAWE Research Report into the Writers-in-Schools Ecology*, York: NAWE.

Paley, V.G. (1990) *The Boy Who Would be a Helicopter*, Cambridge, MA: Harvard University Press.

Preece, J. and Levy, R. (2020) 'Understanding the barriers and motivations to shared reading with young children: The role of enjoyment and feedback', *Journal of Early Childhood Literacy*, 20(4), pp. 631–654.

Reddan, B., Rutherford, L., Schoonens, A. and Dezuanni, M. (2024) *Social Reading Cultures on BookTube, Bookstagram and BookTok*, London and New York: Routledge.

Rietdijk, S., Janssen, T., van Weijen, D., van den Bergh, H. and Rijlaarsdam, G. (2017) 'Improving writing in primary schools through a comprehensive writing program', *Journal of Writing Research*, 9(2), pp. 173–225.

Rowe, D.W., Shimizu, A.Y. and Davis, Z.G. (2022) 'Essential practices for engaging young children as writers: Lessons from expert early writing teachers', *The Reading Teacher*, 75(4), pp. 485–494.

Rumney, P., Kuksa, I. and Buttress, J. (2016) 'Seeing, doing, writing: The Write Here project', *Sage Open*, 6(1).

Scholes, L. (2019) 'Working-class boys' relationships with reading: Contextual systems that support working-class boys' engagement with, and enjoyment of, reading', *Gender and Education*, 31(3), pp. 344–361.

Sénéchal, M. and Young, L. (2008) 'The effect of family literacy interventions on children's acquisition of reading from kindergarten to grade 3: A meta-analytic review', *Review of Educational Research*, 78(4), pp. 880–907.

Simpson, A. (2016) *The Use of Children's Literature in Teaching: A Study of Politics and Professionalism within Teacher Education*, Sydney: Routledge.

Street, C. and Stang, K. (2016) 'Addressing resistance: Encouraging in-service teachers to think of themselves as writers', in Cremin, T. and Locke, T. (eds), *Writer Identity and the Teaching and Learning of Writing*, London: Routledge, pp. 53–66.

Vanden Dool, C. and Simpson, A. (2021) 'Reading for pleasure: Exploring reading culture in an Australian early years classroom', *Literacy*, 55(2), pp. 113–124.

Vansteelandt, I., Mol, S., Caelen, D., Landuyt, I. and Mommaerts, M. (2017) 'Attitude profiles explain differences in pre-service teachers' reading behavior and competence beliefs', *Learning and Individual Differences*, 54, pp. 109–115.

Whitney, A. (2008) 'Teacher trainsformation in the National Writing Project', *Research in the Teaching of English*, 43(2), pp. 144–187.

Whitney, A. (2017) 'Developing the teacher writer in professional development', in Cremin, T. and Locke, T. (eds), *Writer Identity and the Teaching and Learning of Writing*, London: Routledge, pp. 67–79.

Wiescholek, S., Hilkenmeier, J., Greiner, C. and Buhl, H.M. (2018) 'Six-year-olds' perception of home literacy environment and its influence on children's literacy enjoyment, frequency, and early literacy skills', *Reading Psychology*, 39(1), pp. 41–68.

Williams, R. (1976) *Keywords: A Vocabulary of Culture and Society*, London: Fontana.

Willis, J., Hughes, H. and Bland, D. (2019) 'Students reimagining school libraries as spaces of learning and wellbeing', in Hughes, H., Franz, J. and Willis, L. (eds), *School Spaces for Student Wellbeing and Learning: Insights from Research and Practice*, Singapore: Springer, pp. 121–137.

Wilson, A.C. (2009) 'Creativity and constraint: Developing as a writer of poetry culture', in Beard, R., Myhill, D., Riley, J. and Nystrand, M. (eds), *The SAGE Handbook of Writing Development*, London: SAGE, pp. 387–401.

Woodard, R.L. (2013) 'Complicating "writing teachers must write": Tensions between teachers' literate and instructional practices', in *62nd Yearbook of the Literacy Research Association*, Altamonte Springs, FL: Literacy Research Association, pp. 377–390.

Woodard, R.L. (2015) 'The dialogic interplay of writing and teaching writing: Teacher writers' talk and textual practices across contexts', *Research in the Teaching of English*, 50(1), pp. 35–59.

Woodard, R.L. (2017) 'Working towards "I'm a writer and a pretty good writer": An elementary teacher legitimising students' writerly identities while authenticating her own', in Cremin, T. and Locke, T. (eds), *Writer Identity and the Teaching and Learning of Writing*, London: Routledge, pp. 115–131.

Xerri, D. (2015) 'On owing one's poetic life to inspiring teachers of English', *The Use of English*, 67(1), pp. 39–44.

Xerri, D. (2017) 'Inspiring young people to be creative: Northern Ireland's poetry in motion for schools', *New Writing*, 14(1), pp. 127–137.

Yeo, M. (2007) 'New literacies, alternative texts: Teachers' conceptualisations of composition and literacy', *English Teaching: Practice and Critique*, 6(1), pp. 113–131.

Young, R. and Ferguson, F. (2021) *Writing for Pleasure: Theory, Research and Practice*, London: Taylor & Francis.

Zumbrunn, S., Ekholm, E., Stringer, J.K., McKnight, K. and DeBusk-Lane, M. (2017) 'Student experiences with writing: Taking the temperature of the classroom', *The Reading Teacher*, 70 (6), pp. 667–677.

Zumbrunn, S., Marrs, S., Broda, M., Ekholm, E., DeBusk-Lane, M. and Jackson, L. (2019) 'Toward a more complete understanding of writing enjoyment: A mixed methods study of elementary students', *AERA Open*, 5(2), pp. 1–16.

PART III

Understanding the Programmes' Practices

8

THE PROGRAMMES' EXPECTATIONS

Introduction

This chapter shares key findings from data collection with the six programmes, Doorstep Library (DL), Get Islington Reading (GIR), Literacy Pirates (LP), World Book Day (WBD), Ministry of Stories (MoS) and the Primary Shakespeare Company (PSC) that illuminate the expectations held by the different members of each programme and identifies common themes. Initially, the codes and sub-codes relating to 'expectations' for programme delivery are shared, and then each of these is explored and explained with qualitative examples from the programmes' documentation, observations of their work in action, multiple interviews with programme staff and focus groups with a range of adults (e.g. volunteers, creatives) and children gathered over the period of the Literacy Special Initiative. A wealth of expectations were articulated by programme staff in response to their own specific work, volunteers voiced their views of expected elements in the programmes and key goals and many of these were also noted by the young people.

Considering the programmes' expectations

'Expectations', a core element of any activity system, relates to the goals and anticipated actions of those involved in an activity. In this case it was interpreted to refer to the aims of each programme and the intended codes of conduct, rules and routines associated with these. By introducing these aspects at the start of Part III, which summarises the data across the six programmes, it is hoped to offer insights regarding macro-level features but also an emerging understanding of individual programmes. Ten codes were identified in relation to the expectations element (see Table 8.1). These encompassed: positive reading/writing engagement, building a programme framework, codes of conduct, developing understanding, evaluation, imagination/choice/engagement, interactions, respect/kindness, routines, and whole-school change. These were mostly common across programmes, but due to the rich diversity

DOI: 10.4324/9781003532606-12

TABLE 8.1 Definitions of codes within the 'expectations' category

Positive reading/writing engagement	Statements that indicated enjoyment in reading and writing is an expected element of programme experience, where it is observed in children and how it is facilitated by volunteers and teachers.
Building a programme framework	Evidence that building a programme framework is an intention of programme activity, mention of what kind or content of a framework is sought, or how this is done through programme activity.
Codes of conduct	Mention of what rules programmes have in place, how they are communicated and monitored, and how they are experienced by volunteers, teachers and children, to ensure consistency and desired running of programmes.
Developing understanding	Statements that evidence a desire to understand more about something, from multiple perspectives.
Evaluation	As embedded into programme activities, to know if their work is achieving their aims.
Imagination/choice/engagement	Mention of encouraging children and young people's imagination, having and exercising choice of activity/resource and willing engagement as a core element of programmes.
Interactions	Mention of the ways that exchanges are prescribed and experienced by programmes to support reading and writing for pleasure.
Respect, kindness	Statements that indicate assumptions about respectful and kind behaviours between individuals – whether children, practitioners, volunteers or teachers.
Routines	Expected or anticipated ways of doing activities that are understood and shared between those involved in the programme.
Whole-school change	How programmes support this process.

and range of the programmes' work, it was decided to include codes such as whole-school change even though not all the programmes were working towards this goal, but it was clearly salient for the four concerned. As a consequence of the range of programmes, this element generated more codes during data analysis than the other Activity Theory elements of programmes' communities, roles and resources. The expectations of each programme were pivotal to their ways of working and the children's volitional reading and writing.

Positive reading or writing engagement

Enabling positive reading and/or writing engagement was at the core of all programmes' expectations, although for some this involved reflecting on how their activities had previously been perceived and shifting expectations to bring reading or writing for pleasure more to the fore. Programme work often began by identifying barriers to children experiencing reading and writing enjoyment:

> So, a mixture of not having someone reading to them and they all talk about loving being read to. That fundamental association of skill and reading and then being bad at it and then not wanting to go anywhere near it because they're bad at it. And then not finding a book that speaks to them, so why would I bother?
>
> *(WBD Interview 2, Programme staff)*

Programme leads identified positive reading or writing engagement as an instantiation of programme aims and expectations, in ways that might be felt or expressed by children and observed by programme teams, linked to programme evaluations. Consistently staff in programmes focused on reading made mention of children's confidence as readers increasing and commented on the development of more positive attitudes towards reading (e.g. GIR, LP, DL). Children involved in the programmes also frequently expressed positive reading and writing engagement in terms of fun, enjoyment and relaxation. Moreover, they correlated this enjoyment with an increase in confidence, an enhanced sense of perceived reading and writing efficacy, and spoke of the programmes as having given them the skills and imagination needed to engage effectively in a wider than usual range of reading and writing activities which they enjoyed. The programmes also focused on the social element of literacy engagement as a sign of success, for example through children supporting this in other children:

> When you see other children encouraging children ... reading through each other's writing and suggesting editing ... where the children were not afraid to read their writing. I had so many more children happy to read their writing out and so many more children proud of what they'd done because I think they'd been able to talk through it with some people they felt comfortable with.
>
> *(Teachers' Focus Group)*

This barrier of being 'afraid', linked to the notion of 'being bad' at something, was clearly something programme staff felt determined to break through. This sometimes involved changing the frame of accessing reading and writing:

> For many children who aren't engaging with reading for pleasure, the very fact that they have to do all the decoding effort and then find an adverbial, and then write three pages afterwards in the same style, well that puts them off the whole thing in the first place.
>
> *(WBD Interview 2, Programme staff)*

At times, the children also made connections between their positive reading engagement in the programmes and their experiences of reading and writing at school. Some noted their confidence to 'level up' (PSC Children's Focus Group) with new book choices, as suggested by their teachers, while other children spoke of their ability to sound out words independently and how they could use their expanded vocabulary in school (DL Children's Focus Group).

CASE STUDY: LITERACY PIRATES – AN EXPECTATION OF READING AND WRITING ENGAGEMENT

Engagement was a key driver for LP and enjoyment too was seen as a vehicle to enable the children's positive involvement in reading and writing and in supporting school-validated achievement:

> For kids, it's about making sure that it is positive and relentlessly positive and fun to be in, but at the same time there's this rigour, because we deeply feel that children need to succeed at school and so we're not taking kids who enjoy writing and making them into creative writers.
>
> *(LP Interview 1, Programme staff)*

From the children's perspective, they reported developing trusting and genuine relationships with adults, whose positive feedback to individuals and to the group they commented upon. They expected and valued these relationships, took pride in being members of the 'pirate ship' and this appeared to facilitate their social, affective and behavioural engagement as readers and writers. In the LP focus groups, the young people were also acutely aware that they were able to access different texts and activities to those usually available in school and they appreciated this. The staff and volunteers also embedded expectations related to the break from the norm that the programme offered, in terms of giving children agency over creative activities, opportunities to make text choices, and in the ways they could engage with literacy. The children seemed to experience this as different and potentially broader than their experience in school.

> In Literacy Pirates we would do sometimes technical stuff, as in we would research for information, like since you do research, we would research things for what we're writing. As an example, we had a thing where we made a speech, we got information from the iPad, then we got the most important things, we made it into like a speech and then we're going to be telling all of it today, I think.
>
> *(LP Children's Focus Group)*

Positive reading and writing engagement therefore underpinned the design of each programme and decisions about interactions within them. The expectation of positive reading and writing engagement was foundational to frameworks developed to steer future programme development.

Building a programme framework

This code refers to data that evidenced a programme focus on building a framework for later use. Data were drawn largely from interviews with programme leads, reflecting their strategic intentions. Frameworks were not seen as end-points, but transferrable foundations to build programme strength, for example, 'such that we can use it in work within other disadvantaged communities' (GIR Interview 1, Programme staff).

Additionally, programmes recognised that frameworks took time to develop and embed, benefiting from using clearly identifiable steps (WBD Visit Observation 2). Programme staff also recognised the importance of creating clear structures for activities, while allowing for reasonable flexibility within delivery frameworks so that volunteers, practitioners and teachers could exercise some agency over activities. Their frameworks also served as springboards to communicate the underpinning principles of their work, and why their aims and expectations were important so that teacher partners for instance could seek to build on programme activity outside of scheduled programme sessions. Similarly, building a 'quality assurance framework' was referenced by some programmes, this involved recognising and critically reflecting upon their own assumptions related to reading for pleasure, so as to clearly communicate this with schools (WBD Interview 1, Programme staff). The success of such frameworks as communicative springboards seemed to be dependent on recognising the needs of teachers, partners and facilitators so that they could develop a shared understanding of the programme's intentions and operate assuredly.

Alongside these broader frameworks, programme leads also referred to a need for frameworks that supported the day to day experience for children attending sessions. Building frameworks to support and communicate programme expectations regarding children's literate and pleasurable engagement allowed programmes to spread their evidence-based work through and beyond direct involvement, to adapt in the face of challenge, and to acknowledge the importance of programme experience for the young people. Such frameworks also offered a foundation for rules, or codes of conduct.

Codes of conduct

Programme leads raised the notion of 'codes of conduct' when discussing volunteer training, this often included communicating expectations of behaviour, the core ethos of a programme, and any 'non-negotiables' of programme facilitation. Codes of conduct were often influenced by safeguarding practices. The efficacy of observing appropriate safeguarding practices was dependent on volunteers feeling that programmes would provide timely and sensitive support if challenges arose, 'She's always there. You can always ring her up' (DL Interview, Volunteer).

Some programmes referred to 'rules' such as expectations of behaviour and engagement with children attending sessions, to facilitate positive programme experiences. This was often in the school-based programmes. In contrast, home-based programmes, such as DL, reminded volunteers – as part of their code of conduct – that programme activity and engagement was at the discretion of the family and child being visited; thus, children's behaviour was not within the code of conduct, although volunteers were expected to make a note of each child and parent's engagement as part of record-keeping.

Programmes reported different mechanisms for monitoring the implementation of codes of conduct, ranging from relatively informal 'constant dialogue', through to more formal 'annual supervisions' with volunteers. Codes of conduct and the monitoring of programme expectations were implemented differently across the six programmes. However, what was important for all programmes was that relevant codes were communicated and understood amongst volunteers, children, teachers and families. Significantly, monitoring the implementation of codes of conduct was focused on developing positive and reciprocal relationships between programmes, volunteers, teachers, families and children, instead of imposing fixed outcomes and performance metrics and so linked to the programmes' aim of developing understanding.

Developing understanding

This code reflected the importance of building relationships and breaking down assumptions or negative attitudes towards reading or writing. This could be at the level of interaction between facilitators and individual children or groups, for instance: '[At a first visit to school] [children] arrived and they saw my badge saying World Book Day, they were like oh my God, are you going to make us read? And some of them were actually trembling' (WBD Interview 2, Programme staff).

Breaking down assumptions about reading, writing and what the programmes might involve helped to shape children's individual engagement, and created new relationships between children and the creatives, volunteers and programme facilitators. Recognising each child as a unique reader or writer was complemented by the need to recognise the needs of parents and carers also, with their own enthusiasms and hesitancies surrounding reading and writing. For example, staff from MoS explained some of the factors they considered as they planned their work:

> How do peers celebrate the work that young people are creating in school, or what's the relationship with the teachers in the school, or the relationship with parents when we're sharing or presenting work … we're not just working with that young person in isolation, but sitting that work in the context of the younger person's life around the interactions that they're having.
>
> *(MoS Interview 1, Programme staff)*

For programmes engaging through schools (MoS, GIR, PSC, WBD) programme leads and facilitators frequently mentioned the importance of teacher input into resource development to build understanding through their expert positioning of what might be useful for their work with children. Maintaining an open ethos in order to enrich their understanding of the children's needs underpinned all the programmes' activities and involved, for instance, reaching children through awareness of their different personal interests and working collaboratively with them. The children recognised that the programmes offered a different range of reading and writing experiences from those available at home or school and some expressed excitement in trying out new activities, or by taking part in celebrations or having special visitors. These experiences potentially afforded opportunities to develop new understandings about themselves as readers and writers, including changing children's perceptions of self-efficacy and confidence which were often measured through programme evaluations.

Evaluation

The code evaluation refers to actions embedded into programme activities, that sought to discern if their work was achieving their intended aims and expectations. In some programmes, leaders commented on pairing 'baseline' assessment of children's attitudes around enjoyment of writing or reading followed by an 'exit' assessment. Such attitudinal evaluation was often paired with observations of behavioural changes, such as children choosing their own books as indicative of reading engagement. Moreover, some programmes referenced their own evaluation tool and reading outcome toolkits to understand and evaluate any changes to children's attitudes, confidence, engagement and sense of self-efficacy as readers and writers. The programmes worked to develop multi-pronged approaches drawing on data across different stakeholder perspectives (e.g. child, parent, teacher, volunteer, creatives, facilitators), through different methods (survey, observation, interview, anecdote, work, assessment marks, 'retention rate'), at different points in time. Commonly plenary style evaluations were held after programme sessions when those involved shared their views and discussed different children's ongoing literacy journeys. Time away from routine activities was also built into some programmes to reflect on their work.

The children's evaluations of the programmes were often implied via their own self-evaluations of their reading and writing behaviours and their views were sought through programme tools as well as in the focus groups. The programme sessions were commonly appraised positively, children reported finding them enjoyable, sociable and did not appear to perceive them as 'work'. Some referred to changes in their attitudes and engagement as readers and writers, and reported choosing to read more frequently, for example, 'I think before [the MoS project] I didn't really read much books except for [xxx], but now I think I read more books and I find more books more interesting' (MoS Children's Focus Group). A few young people expressed a desire for more ways to provide feedback to share their perspectives and made suggestions. Notably, the positive changes to children's attitudes to reading and writing seem strongly influenced by the programmes' focus on child-led choice.

Imagination/choice/engagement

This code refers to data that revealed an emphasis on encouraging and making use of children's ideas and agency in sessions, encouraging their full involvement, for example:

> Children were given the opportunity to be playful, to interact with one another, to use their own ideas generated in previous weeks and to link to their story list and plans thus far... Their agency and choice was asserted as writers and ... they were encouraged to rely upon their own imaginations and resources.
>
> *(MoS Visit 1, Observation)*

The children and young people involved in the programmes frequently commented upon the pleasure they found in being agentic, making choices, sharing and developing ideas and having these valued. Often, the programmes involved them in collaborating imaginatively with their peers or the adults they were working with, and these collective reading and writing experiences were seen as enjoyable, playful and the kind of activities that they might not ordinarily associate with reading or writing:

> It boosted our imagination, when we came, we went outside and we got into groups and we just went exploring with an adult and so my group, we found this

> fox and then it was like orange, so my group, we thought of the name the Fire Fox and then Casey said it in the actual like story.
>
> *(MoS Children's Focus Group)*

The creativity and imagination fostered by these programmes spilled out beyond the boundaries of the programme into the children's play and social interactions (PSC Visit 2, Observation) and some children reported that this was sustained in self-initiated home-learning activities. Moreover, in focus groups with children, there were frequent comments connected to their creativity, autonomy and enjoyment.

> I feel that how it boosted our creativity because while I used to think that writing and reading is you have to read a book, read the pages and that's all and like about history and stuff, that's what I used to think and then when it came to writing, I just thought it would just be poetry, but they expressed the writing in fun ways, so it didn't feel like writing, it felt like you're writing a magical story.
>
> *(MoS Children's Focus Group)*

Volunteers played a key role in creating expectations around imagination, choice and engagement, many perceived their main aim was to enable children to experience enjoyment through creative play, particularly where the young people were less engaged at the outset, and many expressed the belief that stimulating the children's imaginations would feed into their choice and engagement in reading and writing. Programme staff often commented on the need to reconsider how children might be categorised or labelled in schools and how they sought to approach disengagement differently. Children across several programmes seemed delighted in being able to choose their own books, to exert their rights as writers to invent their own stories and appreciated that their opinions and preferences were heard and respected.

> I'm really lucky to have a Doorstep Library because the books they have are just amazing and you get to have all the books you would like and if you don't want this book or that book or if you have already read it, it's really nice just to tell them and tell them how you feel about this book.
>
> *(DL Children's Focus Group)*

Some children also commented on how their exposure to different texts, including Shakespeare, had sparked an interest in different genres. They perceived they were developing the confidence to choose books from a broader range and to write in a wider range of styles. Adults involved in the programmes also commented on the critical importance of enjoyment in identifying as a reader, writer and learner, and felt that curricular practices and processes tended to overlook this. They positioned the programme session in contrast to this: 'The sessions are, they are transformative, you do see children make extraordinary leaps of confidence and creativity, and I think that happening in the room, the impact of that is extraordinary and profound for the other people around it' (PSC Interview 3, Programme staff). Offering spaces to reframe, model, value and encourage children's imaginations, choice and engagement as readers and writers was therefore pivotal across all six programmes and was supported by carefully considered interactions.

Interactions

Programmes identified ways that they orchestrated interactions between children, their peers and volunteers in order to foster enjoyment of reading and writing. For children, reading and writing became associated with the warm interactions they had with programme adults. For some programmes this was intentionally achieved through using different volunteers each week to build confidence through different relationships.

> We really try to provide ... one-to-one mentoring at all the sessions, even online ones ... we pair up the volunteers and the young pirates randomly, so you never get to work with the same kid in each group, even if you come back every week.
>
> *(LP Volunteers' Focus Group)*

Other programmes orchestrated interactions to build steady relationships with the same volunteers around the child and, when part of the programmes, their families: 'We really strive hard for consistency in the relationship so that that bond can really build up between the volunteers and the families' (DL Interview 1, Programme staff). In turn, the children in this programme expressed delight that they had dependable contact with a regular adult who was interested in them as a reader.

> I really like how you get to read to them, instead of just picking the books and them leaving, you read to them so that you can finish off and we can continue reading the books and we know that we are interested in them.
>
> *(DL Children's Focus Group)*

However, at times, the willingness to interact and cultivate genuine relationships between volunteers and children was not always mirrored in interactions between parents and volunteers, some parents approached directly by programmes expressed reluctance towards visits:

> The kids want it, but the parents don't, or you struggle to find them there and available at the right time when you're going each week ... I guess maybe one of the bigger barriers is just that parental engagement and making sure that all the parents that we see ... feel confident to be able to do what we do outside of our sessions.
>
> *(DL Interview 2, Programme staff)*

Whilst interactions with parents and reluctant teachers were identified by some programmes as essential to successful implementation, close attention and individual interaction with children was identified as even more crucial, driving expectations across programmes, such that one member of staff noted: 'Our aim with volunteering is that every young person over the course of a session gets one to one attention' (MoS Interview 2, Programme staff). Despite different approaches to orchestrating programme interactions, it is clear individual attention to enable positive reading and writing engagement was focal and relied upon kind and respectful relationships between children and adults.

Respect/kindness

This code was primarily attributed to data from the children's focus groups, although there were occasional references to respectful and caring relationships in interviews with teachers and volunteers about engagement with other schools (PSC, MoS) and families (DL). In the focus group discussions, children frequently discussed the presence of considerate and kind relationships with each other, with volunteers and with practitioners: 'Usually, we have to be patient with each other to get what we're doing done, so we have to be patient and communicate with each other to do what we're supposed to do' (PSC Children's Focus Group).

When talking about the facilitators from the programmes, the children drew attention to and appreciated efforts made by them to be fair to all those involved, by making sure that everyone had an equal chance to participate and everyone was heard. Seemingly conversely, the children identified feeling special through the time, help and attention given to them by those involved. However, the offers of help were available to all based on need in the moment, meaning perceptions of unfair attention were perhaps avoided. This sense of help being available and being valued often created relationships built on trust. Sometimes this trust was fostered by broader social interactions, not just related to reading and writing, as volunteers took time to connect with the children by informally talking and playing games together (LP, DL).

Children also expressed feeling respected when their book interests or ideas were validated by adults, in the form of books of favourite authors being brought to subsequent reading sessions.

> I think I enjoy reading because normally when they come, they get prepared for my favourite books and my favourite books are Rainbow Magic books and I like Rainbow Magic books because they're like sparkly on the covers and when I read them they're very interesting and, yeah, good and there's goblins in the stories, so that's why I like the books. That's why I just like when they get prepared.
>
> *(DL Children's Focus Group)*

Overall, kind and respectful interaction and authentic relationships underpinned programme activities and routines.

Routines

Children and adults commonly commented upon programmes' material, spatial and interactional routines. For LP, these were seen to involve clear transitions, often with piracy-inspired catchphrases, between different spaces in the ship, from the more spacious reception area at the start to the more secret, hidden activity area later on (LP Visit Observation 2). For DL the predictability of regularly exchanging books seemed to be understood by all the children, alongside the adults arriving with tailored text choices in response to their interests. The in-school sessions led by MoS staff were often commented upon with regard to the children's sense of agency, they could choose their writing foci and often the facilitators checking in how they were feeling, not about their writing initially, but about their day. The children appeared to find these programme structures and routines reassuringly predictable. In GIR, the children noted there was a clear routine and expectation around reading volume and validation.

> They gave us like a booklet that said Reading Road Map on it and it was like a map and there was all like the different genres of the books so you could tick off the books and you could count how many you've done [...] Yeah. There were a lot of books, I think 35.
>
> But for every book that you read you get two achievement points, for every completed book review you get two, so, all in all, if you do a book review and read the book you get four achievement points for it.
>
> *(GIR Children's Focus Group)*

In addition to the structures of programmes, children expressed pride in continued involvement in programmes and also commented that the experience of participation was a refreshing break from school routines, for instance 'It's a really nice change of pace, so usually at school we wouldn't do something this regular and this fun' (PSC Children's Focus Group). Such insights illuminate why some programmes also aimed to effect whole-school change.

Whole-school change

Not all of the programmes worked at the school level, for instance, DL worked more individually with children and families and WBD worked nationally but with and through local links. For those that did work at school level, their expectations around whole-school change were evident, they sought to empower schools and teachers and to showcase ways in which teachers might develop their own practice in order to engage children in positive reading and writing experiences. Whilst this code was specific to those who worked in school contexts, it was frequently articulated by programme staff as an aim and expectation of their work.

> I've tried to step aside and get my class teachers to show how they use drama. Because again I just don't want my expertise or my identity as a drama specialist to get in the way of teachers believing that they can use this practice.
>
> *(PSC Interview 1, Practitioner)*

> We're hoping to work with subject leaders to broaden their, maybe their approaches or their understanding to approaches to creating writing. So, using some of the Ministry of Stories methodology to see how that can support them to lead English and specifically creative writing in their schools.
>
> *(MoS Interview 1, Programme staff)*

The focus on teacher professional development and co-creation of resources also highlighted the programmes' commitment to lasting and sustainable change. Rather than relying on short-term interventions they were conscious that more significant partnership working was needed to effect long-term impact on children's volitional reading and writing.

Conclusion

To conclude, across the programmes, it was acknowledged that children's access to, as well as engagement in, volitional reading and writing for enjoyment was largely inequitably distributed and experienced. The passion and drive to make a dent on this inequity was strongly voiced across programme leads, volunteers and teacher stakeholders, reflecting programme expectations. Stakeholders were involved in various ways to evaluate the extent to which children experienced the programmes in ways that were intended and whilst programme leads were mindful of potential limitations of evaluation practices, they sought ways to monitor the authentic impact of their work, through planned and unplanned activities, from different perspectives and over time.

Thus, a core expectation of programme work was to develop understanding of where support to access and experience enjoyment of reading and writing is most needed, and to give non-judgemental encouragement and attention to participating children. Programmes located their work in diverse ways and contexts, physically on doorsteps, in schools or libraries, in and out of school time, their work was both aligned to and explicitly outside of curricular framing and they worked at developing their understanding of the unique contribution of their programmes to the children and young people.

Across the codes and data from the six programmes, it was clear that focused attention to children was a key shared expectation and driver for their work. They expected to and arguably did build trusting relationships and safe spaces to explore ideas and make 'mistakes' and in some cases facilitated consistent relationships over extended periods of time with children and adults. This personal and tailored focus was emphasised in various ways to encourage teachers, volunteers and parents to listen to children – to really notice what they perhaps had not had time to previously – and for children to talk and listen to each other's ideas and insights. Such an approach arguably served to validate children's identities and contributions, and to spark creativity, by recognising the multifaceted frames of reading and writing and by offering opportunities for children to see themselves as engaged and successful readers and writers.

9

THE PROGRAMMES AND THEIR COMMUNITIES

Introduction

This chapter shares the findings from data collection with the six programmes, Doorstep Library (DL), Get Islington Reading (GIR), Literacy Pirates (LP), World Book Day (WBD), Ministry of Stories (MoS) and the Primary Shakespeare Company (PSC). Initially, the codes and sub-codes relating to 'community' are shared, and then each of these is explored with qualitative examples from the programmes' documentation, observations of their work in action, multiple interviews with programme staff and focus groups with a range of adults (e.g. volunteers, creatives) and children, gathered over the period of the Literacy Special Initiative.

The activity system element 'community' relates to the engagement and relationships between the people and organisations that were part of the programmes. It refers to members of the community who were internal and external to the programmes, including education managers, programme delivery staff, volunteers, school staff, parents/family and children. Two main codes were identified, 'membership' and 'community creation as a value'. The 'membership' sub-codes were 'diversity and expertise', 'historical and local relationships' and 'needs analysis'. The 'community creation as a value' sub-codes identified were 'creating inclusive communities' and 'creating communities as legacy' (see Table 9.1).

Membership

The overarching code of 'membership' identified the varied range of the staff, volunteers, creatives and external local partners involved in the construction, delivery and evaluation of the programmes. Analysis of the data showed that an important strength of the programmes was the diversity of the programme members and their specific expertise and knowledge. The programmes were often effectively attuned to local networks and were able to draw on previous partnerships with individuals and organisations and they carefully planned ways to build new relationships to strengthen

DOI: 10.4324/9781003532606-13

TABLE 9.1 Definitions of codes in the 'community' category

Membership	The range of people involved in the programme's community and the organisational structures deployed to manage them.
Diversity and expertise	The breadth of expertise involved in the community delivering the programme.
Historical and local relationships	Ways of working which build on local and historical relationships.
Needs analysis	The attention paid to understanding the needs, interests and current practices of the target community of children, young people and parents.
Community creation as a value	Commitment to ways of working that build communities of connection around the programmes and reading and writing for pleasure.
Creating inclusive communities	Strategies deployed to draw children and children, and children and adults together into a wider programme community.
Creating communities as a legacy	Strategies and intentions that focus on seeking to foster and sustain a sense of community locally.

their work. All these choices were driven by well-developed understanding of the needs, interests and current practices of the groups they were seeking to support. New programmes and established programmes developing new ways of working, or working in new areas, used different approaches to develop this understanding. These tended to be iterative and reflective, involving a range of stakeholder voices and means of communication over time.

Diversity and expertise

The membership sub-code 'diversity and expertise' surfaced the different strengths and contributions from teachers, volunteers and paid programme staff through to the programme communities. In the MoS, PSC and GIR programmes, teachers were involved in the planning and development of the initiative in their schools and as part of stakeholder groups. In LP and DL, teachers used their knowledge of the programme and the children they worked with to refer and connect children with these charities' opportunities. For WBD's new initiative, a group of teachers from six schools were able 'to test and develop the quality assurance framework, education materials and one pound book criteria' (WBD Programme documentation).

Volunteers were central to the day-to-day delivery of three of the programmes. Reading and writing supporters and mentors worked with the young people in schools (MoS), in their local communities (DL) and in an after-school centre/pirate ship (LP). The volunteers were mostly local, often bringing skills from roles in education and creative industries. They responded to adverts or were recruited from the business world as part of a commitment to corporate social responsibility initiatives.

The volunteers became 'loyal and regular' and many of them showed 'strong commitment' to the programme (LP Interview 1, Programme staff). Several of the education managers noted that the adults involved, whether paid or volunteers, valued the opportunity to participate in the programme offer and benefited as learners themselves. Each programme drew on a varied range of people and organisations in response to the different nature of their work. This encompassed paid programme education managers and core programme staff, including composers, actors, musicians, writers, playwrights, puppeteers, ex-teachers and arts practitioners. In addition, some programmes involved older children working with younger ones (MoS). Local connections were important to each programme, so many included a wider group of local authority personnel, for example public librarians, as well as other members of the local community in designing or publicising their work, including, for instance, the Mayor of Islington (GIR). In addition, the programmes had different degrees of involvement from supporters, individuals, donors, corporates, Trusts and Foundations, and public relations teams.

The programmes intentionally sought to capitalise upon the expertise and experience of their networks and wider community. They drew on experts from different sectoral spaces, including libraries and the arts, who provided, in some cases, specific professional skills and experience such as musicians, dramatists (PSC) and authors (GIR). The lead organisations also included other community members in specific organisational structures, for example a 'strategic advisory group, a board of trustees, an education forum' (WBD Programme documentation), these mostly pertained to the charities or organisations themselves, and were also applied, though not always specifically, to the Mercers' Company's funded programmes.

The variety of skills and networks within the programme communities enabled the young people to encounter a range of individuals with different roles, work and life experiences. As one education manager noted, they sought to ensure the children experienced as much diversity as possible:

> The children go with a different volunteer every week, we definitely think there's a benefit to the children meeting someone new every week ... we want them to see lots of people mirrored so we have set targets around non-white crew mates and also male crew mates because basically white women dominate volunteering otherwise.
>
> *(LP Interview 1, Programme staff)*

The expertise of the other adults involved in the programmes encompassed the skills to give one-to-one attention to the children; for example, 'actually your role is to be there for those three or four children' (LP Visit 2 Interview 3, Practitioner), in order to sensitively support and encourage children's journeys as readers and writers. This focus on supportive child-led interaction was a core expectation of all programmes (see Chapter 8) and whether the adults involved were artists or volunteers, it was seen to be something that could be developed through training:

> The expectation isn't they are writers or that they've got lots of experience of working with young people. Actually, it's that they have the interests, the skill and commitment around the mentoring. So can they make really accurate good listeners to give people their undivided attention. Those are the things that we're really looking for.
>
> *(MoS Interview 2, Programme staff)*

Supporting adults often described themselves as 'relentlessly positive' (LP Interview 1, Programme staff), and also highlighted the sensitivity that they needed to motivate children who might come to a session with varying levels of confidence and enthusiasm. In addition, the adults' expertise included the skills of modelling reading and writing practices for parents and children, in ways that were both accessible and informed. This was seen as an important way of supporting and changing the children's initial often less than positive relationships to reading and writing. In some observed sessions, the supporting adults narrated and modelled their own thought processes as readers and writers to facilitate children's thinking and nurture a sense of community.

The children's focus groups indicated that the young people too were aware of the diverse expertise of the adults working with them, noting, 'next time when we practice, they're going to bring in some like music people, was it like a French horn ...?' (PSC Children's Focus Group 2) and they recognised and appreciated their skills: 'They're really intelligent, they're really fast, they take their time sometimes and they just bring amazing books like every day' (DL Children's Focus Group 2). In these ways, the intentional staffing based on diversity and expertise made an important positive contribution to children's experiences of reading and writing in the programmes.

Historical and local relationships, and understanding needs

The two further sub-codes under 'membership', 'historical and local relationships' and 'needs analysis', are presented together in this section. Most of the programmes, in developing their work for the Literacy Special Initiative, sought to build on previously established contacts and historical relationships with schools, libraries and others in the target community, which are likely to have enabled a shared commitment to the enterprise. As programme development took place in the context of the COVID-19 pandemic, these longer-term local relationships enhanced the speed of planning and the capacity to cope with the challenges:

> Both of us have been involved in a council initiative called Islington Reads, which was set up after a Fairness Commission about 12 years ago ... so there was already capacity to do joined up partnership work around reading for pleasure.
>
> *(GIR Teacher/Volunteer Focus Group)*

Whether capitalising on their local knowledge or developing new knowledge, programmes built their work around geographic hubs, partly in response to the Mercers' Company criteria for the Literacy Special Initiative. This variously enabled the programmes to link to other local initiatives, draw in a group of primaries and their feeder secondary schools, and work with local school groups or federations. In gathering schools together in a local area, some programmes found already established helpful relationships between English subject leaders and teachers: 'Because a lot of the schools know each other already there's quite a strong sense of partnership between them. So, it feels like we're not starting from scratch in building those relationships and that's a positive' (MoS Interview 2, Programme staff). In addition, some programmes offered open access community programmes and actively wanted a cross-section of children attending. A commitment to place-based delivery and local community expertise was evident in programmes whose centres were physically situated within particular boroughs and with an extended history of working in these, but was also established in new ways of working, such as through GIR.

CASE STUDY: A PLACE-BASED APPROACH – THE ROLE OF 'COMMUNITY' IN GET ISLINGTON READING

Community was key to GIR in its work supporting children's reading for pleasure as they moved from primary to secondary schools. Leaders described GIR as 'place-based', identifying specific local needs through a stakeholder steering group which included the public library and school improvement service, planning and adapting the programme together. Programme activities took place in different community locations, such as a theatre in education experience in Islington central library, an interactive poetry reading from a local author in the library performance space, and a school-based author-led writing workshop.

Schools were supported to identify their own priorities, and plan with GIR and local authors using audits and workshops. Rather than prescribing a way of working, GIR created a 'menu' of support such as author visits or bespoke library collections. It highlighted local initiatives and services and encouraged children to use the library as a social space. All activities fostered a sense of community by talking with children about their own interests and experiences. GIR further ensured that children's voices were central to creating a reading for pleasure community by involving a focus group of young people in devising an interests-led online reading adventure, promoted across the borough. In addition, it set up school opportunities for talking about favourite texts, sharing reviews and identified bespoke library book packages to meet the children's needs.

Each of the programmes conducted some form of community needs analysis to understand the environment in which they were working. This enabled some to plan and shape their work responsively to specific needs (of children, teachers and parents) and in the light of local expertise (in terms of volunteers or the community offer for instance). In other programmes, the focus was at the level of the school and involved clarifying the children's, teachers', school's needs and then acting flexibly and responsively, often co-designing the work with the adults involved. For many of the programmes, there was a process of negotiation between teachers, schools and librarians' expectations, their own perceived needs, and the skill set and expertise of the programme team:

> It's slightly different to a lot of engagement in projects where you're going in with a training offer, or going in with, you've got a product already. It genuinely is a conversation at the beginning and that was really working in terms of getting them on side, because you're not telling them what to do. You're asking how can we work together?
>
> *(WBD Interview 2, Programme staff)*

Helping teachers to identify an area of need (personal or school-wide) through self-reflection using an audit and/or through related continuing professional development, enabled programmes to encourage practitioners' participation in the shaping of their own development (e.g. GIR, MoS). Additionally, recognition of staff skills and the need to build from these were commonly referred to, for example 'my whole remit is to work with teachers and how they teach writing as we know this is a centre of so much expertise' (PSC Interview 1, Programme staff). Programme work on forging or building on local relationships and ensuring programmes were developed to respond to specific community needs clearly contributed to the success of the programmes and helped to create inclusive communities.

Community creation as a value

Community creation emerged in the data analysis to be a core value held by all members of the programme teams from leaders to volunteers and so formed an overarching code. The value or aspiration for the programmes is discussed below in combination with the sub-code 'creating inclusive communities', which relates to data around the specific actions undertaken to enact this value.

Creating inclusive communities

The programmes worked to develop a sense of community on the regular occasions that the diverse membership gathered in classrooms, homes, training spaces and/or libraries and in the more transient context of theatrical performances or end of programme celebration events. Community creation was frequently expressed both as a goal and a core value by programme staff. This involved commitment to working to develop communities of connection around the programmes themselves and around reading and writing, and often reflected the programme staff's understanding of reading and writing as social practices. 'These resources will be based on educational research findings and support schools in embedding reading for pleasure pedagogies and in creating vibrant communities of readers' (WBD, Programme documentation).

In response to a parallel understanding of writing as a social, not just a solitary act, MoS identified 'creating communities of writers' as a core aim in its documentation and in interviews. This was also observed in action, through the use for instance of a co-created shared 'story contract' which was modelled in the classroom and reflected respect for all writers' ideas (MoS Observation Visit 1). 'So, what we're trying to do is create communities of young people, or communities of adults sometimes, of writers who work and support each other together' (MoS Interview 1, Programme staff). Across programmes, in some instances personal relationships made with volunteers reinforced this sense of community connections: 'I had two kids, every week they ... and apparently, they still ask about me ... just sometimes you make a real connection and that's very heart-warming' (DL Interview 3, Volunteer).

Whilst voicing the construction of community as a valued goal, staff recognised the contextual challenges involved, for example one volunteer noted that whilst he preferred to work in a circle, a more communal approach, the expectation in the classroom was to work at tables and he found that 'really difficult and limiting' and that 'it impacted negatively on the children's writing' (Teacher/Volunteer Focus Group). There were also reported challenges in building communities through online activities during COVID-19: '[W]e've got to find a way to get that sense of community back into the project' (PSC Interview 1, Programme staff).

The strategies used to develop these inclusive communities of readers or writers oriented around developing relationships, as well as a high degree of social interaction and support for one another. This attention to the inclusion of all involved was also noted in the MoS's collaborative planning and reviewing meeting observed, with the sixth formers who were volunteering being integrated into the work with ease and treated as equal members (MoS, Observation Visit 2). Also, on the part of WBD there was an awareness of the need to include all teaching staff in sharing their reading identities, in order to 'normalise different routes into reading' (WBD, Observation Visit 2) and thus support all young readers.

The programmes often planned for interaction. Young people worked in groups and supported each other, they were invited to respond to each other's writing in supportive and caring ways, and were encouraged to converse about their reading. The relational context in which most of the programmes worked, and the environments created in public libraries, classrooms and after-school clubs, were commonly documented as enabling and relaxed. In these a sense of kinship, connection and comfort was often commented upon and observed:

> We ended up doing a lot of co-rehearsal where instead of just running through the play every time we rehearsed, they would go off into little groups and support each other and encourage each other and performing speaking and listening. Or in their writing … reading through each other's writing and suggesting, editing and there just became this really nice positive progression that happened where the children were not afraid to read their writing. I had so many more children happy to read their writing out and so many more children proud of what they'd done, because I think they'd been able to talk through it with some people they felt comfortable with.
>
> *(Teacher/Volunteer Focus Group)*

This perception that the young people valued the opportunity to connect with others around the literacy activities offered by programmes was borne out in the focus group interviews. Fun was frequently mentioned, as well as friends and a sense of a bond with others. Although these positive feelings were not always explicitly linked to reading or writing, they are likely to have been associated with it:

> I think the best experience is that we were bonding with our friends.
>
> *(MoS Children's Focus Group 1)*

> I think the best part of it was the actual writing the chapter one, like all together and just putting in everyone's ideas.
>
> *(MoS Children's Focus Group 1)*

The children also contrasted their experience of the programmes with school contexts: 'The crewmates here, they help us more and they make things more fun, yeah, and in school it's a bit different, because they don't really like to joke around' (LP Children's Focus Group 1). A highly positive and affirmative attitude on the part of all adults to the children and young people was frequently referred to and was consistently observed. Peer feedback was also seen to serve the purpose of encouraging the young writers:

> Children read their writing aloud – they read together and talk of 'making sense of the writing together'. They correct as they go, and the crew mate says 'What do we need to do here?' There is a sense of shared ownership in the writing. What do we need here. … In the final plenary the children have chosen their sentence and it is on the screen in front of them. They read their sentences aloud and are praised by everyone – the children all enjoy the session, no one leaves or doesn't engage. At the end the crew mates and children all give 'shout outs' – they talk of people who've helped them.
>
> *(LP Observation 1)*

The focus groups from all the programmes indicated that such positive encouragement was noticed and valued by the young people, for instance, 'Say, we were scared to do something, they would like encourage us to do it and help us do it better' (PSC Children's Focus Group 1). Additionally, observations evidenced these relaxed relational connections, for example in observing one group of young people and a mentor writing, a strong sense of fraternity was evident with intense conversations about writing, and considerable affirmative feedback, for example 'withholding information is powerful – good job', alongside low-key chatty discussions about books they had read and the book their teacher was reading to them (MoS Observation 2).

This appreciation of the children and their work is likely to have supported their confidence and assurance as readers and writers. It will also have helped build connections and a sense of an inclusive community. Significantly, many of the young people voiced the view that the adults on the programmes were listening to them, were connected to them as people, not particularly as 'pupils' perhaps, and had faith in them and trusted them. This was also noted in comments by volunteers and was highly evident in observations:

> The volunteers … they tell us, do you need help, and if we answer with a, yes, they'll read it out to us, which will make us feel kind of special because we're having help, and they take their time to help us.
>
> *(LP Children's Focus Group 2)*

> I think a successful session from me is one where I feel like there's children can see their own involvement in what we've created. And that they're very invested in the development of the piece. So, I think … what I always hope to achieve … is that they leave the lesson feeling invigorated, feeling listened to. Also feeling like we are working on something as a whole team, that I'm not telling them what to do, that we're kind of co-creating together, but that they feel that with the other children in their class as well.
>
> *(PSC Visit 2, Practitioner interview)*

Programmes frequently sought opportunities to share the young people's work publicly, in class, in assemblies and on screen, for instance, 'We had our names up on the screen for all the schools to celebrate like all of us that we've read the books' (GIR Children's Focus Group 1). This sharing was part of an established routine, 'There's a slideshow in the morning every Monday and some of the best reviews are put there, so we read them out' (GIR, Librarian Interview 2). The children also noticed this routine and hoped it would encourage other readers, 'like they see a review on the slideshow and ... another student might like how it was structured so they might want to go and read the same book' (GIR Children's Focus Group 1).

With those programmes that involved some kind of final celebration or event, opportunities were seized to widen the community of appreciation. On these occasions, parents were often involved, the red carpet was literally rolled out (PSC) and a broader sense of community was sought. Although such celebrations may be transient in nature, the approach was recognised by volunteers as of value: 'There's an audience. I think that's a very special part where their imagination and their work is celebrated, all without the pressure of a grade' (Volunteer Focus Group). There was also a sense that at this moment, the young people were members of the wider school and local community. Moreover, the efforts and contributions made by different individuals and schools were received respectfully and appreciatively. Everyone was rooting for each other:

> They love seeing the other schools' performances. They're always really gracious as well. It's really interesting, I've never had an experience where you've had sort of sense of competitiveness. It's always just everybody's really wowed by what everybody else is doing.
>
> *(PSC Interview, Practitioner)*

Recognition of this wider community engagement was often mentioned by adults involved in the programmes as something they focused on:

> The last thing is about engaging with our local community, and that could be about the school community more broadly, so how do peers celebrate the work that young people are creating in school, or what's the relationship with the teachers in the school, or the relationship with parents when we're sharing or presenting work.
>
> *(MoS Interview 1, Programme staff)*

Less high-profile connections to parents in order to widen the community were also common. These included involving parents in weekly meetings with the same pairs of volunteers (DL), sending books and activities home themed around interests for children and adults (GIR), and producing resources to support family interaction around texts (WBD). These connections to homes helped to widen the reach of the programmes and appeared to boost the confidence and engagement of parents with reading and writing for pleasure activities.

In addition, teaching links were made to the children's own out-of-school activities, such as attending the mosque or being a scout, and spreading the word through grassroots football, rugby, netball, athletics and gymnastics clubs, so taking reading out of the school reading space into the community (WBD Observation 2). As one volunteer noted, 'we looked at the book to start with and they chose their own women who had inspired them from their community, from people in the public eye [for their writing topic]' (Teachers/Volunteers Focus Group). Another programme planned a parental engagement campaign, to 'reinforce that messaging so it's coming through school and the local supermarket and it's just part and parcel of what it means to live in Islington and to be part of that community' (GIR Interview 2, Programme staff).

CASE STUDY: CREATING A COMMUNITY ON THE DOORSTEP WITH DOORSTEP LIBRARY

Doorstep Library's work was based in the community, reading with children in their homes. Through weekly visits, DL had a unique opportunity to connect families with other local support organisations, recognising that fostering 'a happier less stressful life' could mean that 'parents can take time to relax and reading is more likely' (DL Interview 1, Programme staff). DL included siblings and parents in the visits wherever possible, rather than only working one-to-one, nurturing a community of reading within the household. Volunteers worked hard to get to know each family and child's needs and interests and responsively adapted the books they brought to share, as well as the information and wider support connections they offered. This involved sensitively building relationships and actively working to be inclusive 'we don't want to be official visitors coming with clipboards or anything like that. That's obviously what we want to avoid' (DL Interview 3, Programme staff). Volunteers were passionate about offering positive reading opportunities to targeted areas and the potential long-term benefits for children, families and communities, working to leave a legacy in homes so parents could 'see how simple and enjoyable it is just to pick up a story and read with your children'. DL staff also sought to broker connections for parents in response to need, 'to make sure that each family is supported by their local community' (DL Interview 1, Programme staff).

Creating communities as a legacy

Under the overarching code 'creating communities as a value', the other code which was less frequently mentioned was 'creating communities as a legacy'. Several programme staff expressed a desire for some form of community legacy in the context of families, schools or more widely. The programmes recognised that creating communities not only helped with the delivery of their activities, but also helped to ensure future activities could take place. This recognition meant that the programmes dedicated time to building relationships with a wide web of individuals connected to their work or the sites where they offered their programmes, and over time, the potential for legacy emerged through reach too:

> It's [information about the initiative] gone out to the siblings, it's gone out to the extended family, it's gone out to all the teachers, it's gone to the governors and when you start to build all that together, the councillors and the mayor and

> directors, chief exec, you actually build, they'll do something probably at the school improvement English leads meeting and it just keeps rippling and that's what you want.
>
> *(GIR Interview, Librarian)*

Some of the programmes' vision extended to the long-term potential community consequences of their literacy focused work. 'We don't see ourselves as providing a service to these schools, we see ourselves as establishing a network of increasingly like-minded educators' (PSC Interview 2, Programme staff). One education manager noted that they not only sought to build classroom writing communities but also aimed to create something wider and potentially longer lasting, that was expressed as 'building communities in the borough – enabling better communication and relationships between schools and parents and other organisations'. They also described this as 'trying to do something a little bit more holistic in terms of our work in the borough and the community of that borough' (MoS Interview 3, Programme staff).

Conclusion

The wide range of people and organisations involved in the individual programmes comprised a talented community. Whilst the size of these communities varied across the six programmes, the breadth and diversity of expertise of community members was a notable strength. None of the programmes operated in isolation, all sought out a diverse range of local partners with capability to work towards their aims. In this respect the programmes were outward-looking, they positioned themselves as enabling learning organisations and did not see themselves as the privileged holders of knowledge or expertise in this space. Rather they worked to develop and build on historic partnerships with colleagues from schools, libraries and the wider arts and cultural sector. Several of them also involved local volunteers who themselves worked in different sectors.

In different ways, all the programmes sought to understand the needs of their community. Those working directly or indirectly with schools, found ways to identify the needs of specific groups of children and teachers, or sought to establish an understanding of the wider context nationally or locally, in order to tailor their programme plans. This resulted in most cases in programmes being shaped in culturally responsive ways for the young people and their parents. Those involved in the programmes frequently voiced their desire to create communities around the work; it was a core value. The societal and educational challenges involved were widely recognised, yet the core members of the programme teams remained determined to build communities and micro-communities, collectives of readers and writers.

A range of strategies were used, consciously and unconsciously, to develop communities of connection and engagement in classrooms, after-school clubs, homes and libraries. In many cases the sense of community established may have been transient, nonetheless it was seen to involve positive relationships, a high degree of social interaction and very supportive affirmative attitudes which honoured the children's interests and celebrated their choices as readers and writers. Communities of appreciation and support existed, and opportunities were persistently taken to celebrate the children's achievements. The young people perceived that the programmes afforded them the opportunity to make relational connections with each other, bonds even, and also commented upon the positive connections with the adults involved, whom they believed listened to them, respected their choices and valued their ideas. A sense of a genuinely level playing field which was inclusive of all was evident in their comments and those of the volunteers and practitioners. This appeared to have helped shape a sense of pride, belonging and commitment on the part of all involved. Additionally, for some programmes, a desire to create a more sustained community legacy, both in the immediate context and in the wider local community, was noted.

10

THE ROLES OF THOSE IN THE PROGRAMMES

Introduction

This chapter shares the findings from data collection with the six programmes, Doorstep Library (DL), Get Islington Reading (GIR), Literacy Pirates (LP), World Book Day (WBD), Ministry of Stories (MoS) and the Primary Shakespeare Company (PSC). Initially, the codes and sub-codes relating to 'roles' are shared, and then each of these is explored with qualitative examples from the programmes' documentation, observations of their work in action, multiple interviews with programme staff and focus groups with a range of adults (e.g. volunteers, creatives) and children, gathered over the period of the Literacy Special Initiative.

The third of the four elements within the activity system, 'roles', relate to the responsibilities and tasks of different members of the various programmes, such as education managers, delivery staff, volunteers, school staff, parents, families and children – before, during and after the programme. Two main codes were identified: 'management/strategic steering' which derived from the processes and organisation of each programme and included the sub-codes recruitment and training, partnerships and evaluation processes; and 'supporting adults' which arose from the responsibilities and interactions of programme staff and volunteers. The sub-codes identified within supporting adults included 'flexibility and autonomy' and 'values' (see Table 10.1).

Management/strategic steering

The first broad code that emerged when investigating roles in the programme was 'management/ strategic steering'. This code related to planning, decision making, organisation and ways of working developed by the leadership and management of each programme. Some commonalities were found that enhanced their programmes and enabled them to more effectively support children's reading and writing for pleasure. Management and strategic steering was broken down into three sub-codes, recruitment and training, partnership, and evaluation.

DOI: 10.4324/9781003532606-14

TABLE 10.1 Definitions of codes within the 'roles' category

Management/strategic steering	Tasks involved in the overall establishment and running of the programmes. Leadership and organisation of partners and supporting adults.
Recruitment and training	How participants and organisations are identified and recruited to join the programme.
Partnerships	Ways of working based on history, relationships, open communication.
Evaluation	How evaluation is organised by programme leaders and what this involves, formative, iterative and summative.
Supporting adults	The adults who work directly with the children in the programmes and their roles in the programmes, including teachers, librarians, authors, other creative experts, lead facilitators, mentors, volunteers.
Flexibility and autonomy	The relative importance and balance between flexibility and prescription experienced in these roles.
Values	How supporting adults' roles are framed by the programme's values and ethos.

Recruitment and training

An essential role in programme management was recruitment and training of volunteers or other staff involved in implementation, and recruitment of schools or families and children to participate in the programmes. Extensive and understandable amounts of care were taken when recruiting and training supporting adults to ensure they would be able to appropriately support children, so measures were established to 'quality assure' this role:

> Potential volunteers first have to attend an information briefing to ensure they fully understand the commitment and then are invited to apply. They are interviewed, have Enhanced DBS checks and references taken up. Following a day's training delivered in-house, they are paired with an experienced volunteer and have to undertake three trial sessions before they are recruited.
>
> *(DL Application)*

The programmes also recruited volunteers with particular soft skills and dispositions, such as communication and empathy, and, in the case of LP, the ability to link to the wider community:

> We do recruit for ethos and fit before skills because we think we can train a lot of skills We're trying to bring a diverse group of people into the organisation who have got lots of lovely and different perspectives as well as experiences.
>
> *(LP Interview 1, Programme staff)*

Specific expertise such as that needed to lead drama workshops was an important factor in one programme's recruitment process:

> We have a core of practitioners who have been with us pretty much from the beginning and we initially recruited ... so we knew the quality of their work intimately. To expand that pool ... we'd go and observe them [prospective practitioners] leading, you know, if they were working on another programme we would go into schools and watch them.
>
> *(PSC Interview 2, Programme staff)*

While the diverse range of expertise was valued and capitalised upon, the programmes also offered their arts partners, teachers and volunteers, induction, training and/or support as appropriate to their roles to enrich their knowledge and skills, including 'things like behaviour management, safeguarding refreshers ... based around what people say they need some support with' (MoS Interview 1, Programme staff). Others also gave examples of training focusing on planning ways to work with the children:

> We've done practitioner training already this year ... we meet with our 25 or so freelance directors. We take them through what schools will be doing. We take them through our ethos and ways to work. We bring in professionals to upskill our [arts] practitioners ... Then we do days of insets with the teachers too. We take them through the expectations of the programme and through some group planning together of things that they might do.
>
> *(PSC Interview 1, Programme staff)*

The programmes established their expectations and the commitment of all involved in their accompanying paperwork and through engaging senior leaders in meetings. In this way they helped schools, where applicable, to understand what they could offer and how to make best use of this. One effective strategy for the PSC involved practitioners with whom they had previously worked sharing their experiences with newly recruited teachers during programme training. The teachers also reported that reading the 'framework of expectations' document before the training 'really helps give you a sense of what's expected' (PSC Interview 3, Programme staff).

As WBD wanted to work with teachers to develop new resources, it adopted an open approach to recruiting a range of participants including new teachers as well as those who were more experienced. For all the programmes working directly with schools, recruitment relied on local knowledge, historical relationships and programme partnerships. Recruitment was targeted towards schools that were known to the programme to demonstrate indicators of disadvantage or were recommended to the programme by trusted partners. A noticeable thread running through all of the programmes' recruitment strategies was drawing on a range of other sources of information and organisations and trusting others to direct them. For example, where referral of individual children to programmes was needed, schools were used as reliable partners:

> We think that teachers help us get to the kids who need it most. If it was just families finding the centre then ... we'd only be including families with the time and capacity to do that. So, we get schools to choose them, for falling behind and having fewer opportunities.
>
> *(LP Interview 2, Programme staff)*

DL combined local knowledge and partnerships with other organisations to support them in targeting locations from which to recruit families, and it also considered the safety of these locations for its volunteers:

> We've turned some estates down because we didn't feel that our volunteers would be safe ... Sometimes speaking to the Safer Neighbourhood teams, we try and make sure we've got those connections as well. And just finding out from other local service providers what's it really like once you're on the estates.
>
> *(DL Interview 2, Programme staff)*

These examples from the data offer some insight into the care and attention given to reaching and working with the children in most need of support to enjoy reading and writing. This care extended to ensuring that all programme members, volunteers and schools were in tune with the programme goals and everyone involved was safe and heard.

Partnership and evaluation

Partnership was also key to all the programmes for purposes beyond recruitment, whether forging new collaborations or drawing on existing relationships. These were sometimes at the level of organisations or between individuals involved in programme delivery. In all instances, sensitive cooperation and flexibility seemed to be key in planning and delivering the programmes in partnership. The programme leaders offered examples of developing their work to respond to the time constraints of partner organisations whilst still meeting their own goals, and they took time to really listen and adapt approaches. For example, MoS planned sessions with the teachers to meet the needs of the children, building on what they were told about the children's starting points: 'Pupils have missed out on a lot during KS1. The teachers would like them to have confidence in their creativity and support with structuring their thinking. They are strong on sentence starters but struggle with past tense' (MoS Observation 1). Whilst GIR brought the librarians, teachers and authors together, and offered twilight sessions that created 'a better [mutual] understanding' and a 'platform to explore' programmes and plan collaboratively (GIR Interview 3, Programme staff). The change in emphasis from normal relationships between schools and the library was described as 'not so much of a support role to schools ... it's much more, "What are we doing together?" and delivering it' (GIR Interview 3, Programme staff). Programme sessions were also used to reinforce the expectations of the partnership, such as in a PSC online session with teachers where the team set out the plan for visits but also set the tone and built relationships to support programme delivery:

> There is laughter, enjoyment and talk and in the first break it's impossible to tell which teacher is from which school, as they all mix together. This continues into the planning session where teachers are mixed up on different tables.
>
> *(PSC Observation 1)*

As discussed in Chapter 9 on the programmes and their communities, partner organisations were used to identify and connect with children and families, helping with knowledge of the local area and gaps in reach and provision. These partnerships required trusting relationships in which the lead organisations knew when to delegate tasks and were open to different perspectives to guide their work. Teachers also put trust in the expertise of the organisations they were working with:

> You do take a step back as class teacher and leader of the programme within your school. Because they are the professionals within the theatre with the lighting, the sound and getting everybody into position ... that was a huge relief actually because they obviously do it so much better and then we were able to learn from them.
>
> *(PSC Visit 2, Teacher interview)*

Commitment and the ability to lead others were also elements of the different partnerships. One organisation described their work as helping English leaders to bring about a 'cultural shift' in their schools (MoS Interview 1, Programme staff) and others also placed trust in their school partners and delivery staff to lead changes to reading and writing practices: 'Each school will nominate ambassadors to lead the programme ... These teachers will be responsible for coordinating audits, attending training, championing initiatives and running school specific programmes in the second and third year of the programme' (GIR Programme documentation).

Effective leadership between the organisations and their different partners relied on excellent communication and commitment, 'having a very proactive lead, within the school or setting, who wants to make it happen as well and is making time for this and is giving it some priority' (GIR Interview 3, Programme staff). To work with and respond to different perspectives, valuing the expertise of multiple partners, the organisations demonstrated a focus on negotiation, leading and maintaining an overview whilst being flexible enough to listen and adapt. These interactions were described by more than one organisation as 'conversations'.

In on-the-ground delivery, most of the organisations' leaders viewed their role as facilitators who were continuing to learn. They offered structured resources, plans and ways of working that could facilitate changes in practice in schools, and shape activities in programme sessions, and these were negotiated and adapted responsively by and with the supporting adults:

> So, the school lead in each case is responsible for developing that whole school reading culture. The way that they do that is entirely dependent on their context, and we're shaping that through providing them with research and a support network and ideas and activities and best practice type things in the engagements that we have with them.
>
> *(GIR Interview 2, Programme staff)*

The value placed on collaboration and partnership also influenced the programmes' different approaches to evaluation. Commonly, across all of the six programmes evaluation was viewed as collaborative and multi-focused, this included attending to the impact on the participating pupils, taking an overview of programme development, and monitoring the work of individual volunteers. Predominantly the programmes were working on ways to track the impact of their work on the children, whether through observations and ongoing tracking from volunteers and teachers, and/or through surveys and focus groups.

CASE STUDY: WORLD BOOK DAY, ESTABLISHING NEW ROLES TOGETHER

Establishing non-hierarchical roles was crucial to WBD's work for the Literacy Special Initiative. As it worked with teachers to explore and create new resources to extend reading for pleasure practices beyond an annual school WBD event, it needed successful dialogue and collaboration to meet its aims. Openness and flexibility characterised the way that this organisation established roles and responsibilities. Early in the process WBD staff met with participants to negotiate roles rather than setting out a series of prescribed expectations:

> While we need to get to a place where there's a coherent WBD stance that's taken in all of their recommendations and expertise, we're never looking for them to come together in a way that is a World Book Day way of doing things.
>
> *(WBD Interview 1, Programme staff)*

Whilst making its goals clear, how WBD worked with teachers was established through interaction and conversation: 'You're not telling them what to do. You're asking how can we work together?' (WBD Interview 2, Programme staff). The discussion and resource creation activities were collaborative meetings, including more and less experienced English leaders and valuing everyone's contributions. A teacher new to leading English in school who was part of the programme reported that they gained 'ideas that I have never thought of' that 'moulded the kind of literacy lead that I've become' (WBD Interview 3, Teacher).

This inclusive approach enabled all involved to feel trusted and to share their honest opinions which allowed the organisation to develop resources that would ultimately be positively received by its intended teacher audience.

Supporting adults

The second main code within 'roles' was supporting adults. These adults were crucial to the work of all the programmes and included volunteers, teachers and creative practitioners of various kinds. The data showed that the way in which all these adults worked was characterised by some level of flexibility and autonomy underpinned by a shared understanding of programme values. These two sub-themes are explored below.

Flexibility and autonomy

Adults involved in delivering the programme in all instances worked within an overarching structure and set of expectations which nonetheless left each individual with flexibility to adapt their approach to the needs of the children and the context of their work: 'They're trusted to do what's right for their setting rather than a one size fits all' (GIR Visit 1, Interview, Programme staff). The programmes saw their role as ensuring supporting adults had relevant guidance and training and freedom to interact accordingly:

> There are a couple of resources in the crew mate handbook to help them come up with the kinds of questions that they might want to ask about reading, but particularly when they've been coming for a while they're just reading and talking to the child about reading, they know the kinds of questions to ask.
>
> *(LP Interview 2, Programme staff)*

Supporting adults also commented about the autonomy they experienced and that they could make decisions based on their knowledge of children and families. This involved, for instance, changing and adapting activities responsively and selecting texts based on children's interests: 'The sessions are quite free in what happens in them. There's not a specific format. It's not about you must play these games, or you must read this particular book' (DL Visit 2 Observation).

These adults understood that they could and indeed should be flexible and change how they worked with children based on listening to and observing them and also perceived that their sensitive adaptations and tuning in to the children, including by celebrating children's reading and writing, was different from the experience of adults working with children in school:

> I think it's about following the child, I feel, just giving that child the voice and even if it's totally random and different from last week, you've just got to go with it.
>
> *(Teacher/Volunteer Focus Group)*

> Part of what we do is trying to be doing the thought process again that you wouldn't have time necessarily for in a school, to think about, OK, if they like that ... oh, they might like the next one, and having the time and thought to do that.
>
> *(Teacher/Volunteer Focus Group)*

The supporting adults, therefore, often expressed values framed in contrast to or as complementary to those perceived to be central to education currently, namely attainment and the standards agenda:

> Whilst we know that those skills are fundamental to children accessing books and also that we know that they need to write and using text as an example is helpful, actually that's not the purpose of what we're trying to achieve.
>
> *(WBD Interview 2, Programme staff)*

> We haven't got the pressures that they have at school to reach targets and get to certain levels. We can just solely focus on enjoying a book and sharing a book with the children and with the families.
>
> *(Teacher/Volunteer Focus Group)*

Some staff, working in out-of-school contexts, had found ways to address some of the limitations of schooled literacy, by recognising the pressures the young people face in school and providing consistent positive feedback to support the young people when they tried reading and writing activities. Being able to provide this authentic positive feedback involved being flexible when children's engagement with activities might have deviated from the original instructions, valuing instead that the children participated:

> So we, if a young pirate, and sometimes they do, they write something about Pokémon that makes absolutely no sense and perhaps isn't quite anywhere near the brief that we would have hoped, but their faces are beaming and it's going to be celebrated and supported and enjoyed and promoted in the same way and that's quite a niche part of the programme, but it is quite important.
>
> *(Teacher/Volunteer Focus Group)*

> Crew mates interact with the children, they read and appreciate their work and provide the encouragement for them to complete their writing. The session leader calls them incredible writers who deserve to be published.
>
> *(LP Observation 2)*

This supportive way of recognising and affirming all children's achievements in a highly explicit manner was also observed in programme visits and was identified as a key feature of all the five programmes working directly with the children.

Values

The final sub-code related to supporting adults was 'values'. Interestingly, the programme planning and delivery teams across the six programmes held several key values in common, in relation to their work around reading and writing for pleasure. Frequently, they voiced the priority they gave to social justice and to addressing inequities through their work with children and families, especially those who might be experiencing different challenges socially and economically. For example, by highlighting how they considered different parental circumstances:

> Not all of our parents can speak English, so let's make sure that feels good and not all of our parents have good mobility, so how are we making sure that they can come to that? Not all of our parents work, so how do we make sure … it runs through everything and I think it comes through strongly actually, even into the volunteering. In training, the first question you ask them when they settle (I remember it was very specifically trained to me years ago) that you don't say, 'at work', you say, give me an example from your day or something that you do.
>
> *(LP Interview 2, Programme staff)*

The supporting adults' values rested on a shared view that engaging children in reading and writing for pleasure was the key to helping them gain confidence, motivating them to enjoy reading and writing, and do more of it, ultimately improving their wellbeing and progress towards academic goals as a result of enhanced literacy skills.

Involving and empowering children and young people as individuals was another core strand reflected in the voices of staff working in the various programmes. In the five programmes that worked face to face with children (as well as in online contexts) this was worked towards through building relationships, attending to children's interests as readers and writers, valuing their ideas and enabling them to express themselves in various ways related to volitional reading and writing. These people were determined not only to listen to children and support them as readers or writers, but to respect their unique contributions – whatever their nature. They positioned the children as readers and writers: 'I think that's what the sessions do for them, is that they are not doing writing, they are writers' (MoS Interview 3, Programme staff). An awareness of the need to nurture the children's confidence in their reading and writing was evident in the responses of the supporting adults. This was regardless of whether they were facilitators, creative practitioners who were paid or the volunteers within the programmes. This was also consistently observed in action. Consequently, the young people's work was very frequently celebrated:

> So, the whole thing is that you always get celebrated, you always get your work published and that's a key part of what we do.
>
> *(Teacher/Volunteer Focus Group)*

> I would say I'm there to really encourage their own ideas, for them to feel okay about expressing their own ideas even if they're different from other people's and, yeah, to celebrate what they bring and make them feel confident as much as I can in their own abilities as writers.
>
> *(Teacher/Volunteer Focus Group)*

> We see the things that those children create are not an imitation, they're not a poor imitation of an adult art form, they are within their own terms, they are a valid piece of art to us.
>
> *(PSC Interview 1, Programme staff)*

The values expressed by the programme teams influenced specific ways of working that facilitated the young people's agency and recognised them as individuals with something valuable and interesting to share. Adults were encouraged to listen to children and follow their lead, as well as reflect upon and share their own experiences as authentic role models:

> Questions, listening, listening is the most important thing ... it's absolutely placing the young person and their ideas central, and their role is to support, nurture, encourage; not to impose.
>
> *(MoS Interview 1, Programme staff)*

> I actually think it's the personal experience more that comes into it, they like having a human who, that makes mistakes and things ... we get crew mates to share 'Oh at work I struggled with this'.
>
> *(LP Interview 2, Programme staff)*

The supporting adults also frequently referred to their role as bringing fun, energy and enthusiasm and consistently giving positive encouragement. One explained: 'There's this thing about entering a safe space and they see somebody else have a go at something, take a risk' (Teachers/Volunteers Focus Group).

Others also worked to make learning more meaningful by linking to children's interests and home experiences. The adults' values and affirmative ways of working were recognised by the children who emphasised that they felt supported to try because they trusted the adults would help and appreciate their attempts. They also noted that the adults responded to their individual needs and interests:

> If you wanted to be better, like be the best you, I suggest coming here because there's always going to be someone or a few people who is there for you, they're going to help you and one of the most important things, if you're stuck they'll always be there to tell you it's OK to be stuck, you can just try again, because from a mistake you learn the answer.
>
> *(LP Children's Focus Group 2)*

> I really like Doorstep Library because, they straight away realise if you're not interested in a book, they ask you and see if you want to change the book if you don't really like it or if you don't like your experience.
>
> *(DL Children's Focus Group 1)*

In addition to the positive, nurturing relationships created, teachers, children and volunteers explained that the supportive adults encouraged high expectations in the children's reading and writing practices. The subtle blend of encouraging and celebrating whilst still enabling children to develop new skills and challenge themselves in their reading and writing connected to the aspirational values held by the supporting adults for the children with whom they worked: 'Okay, so when they come ... since they're the experts, they like make our lines better and that's the part that I, it makes me enjoy it more because it's like more exciting lines' (PSC Children's Focus Group 1).

Another key value of the supporting adults was building trust through relationships. This emerged as a key theme within focus group discussions with the adults involved in the programmes, whether teachers, volunteers or practitioners. A key component of these supportive relationships involved the adults building respectful relationships with children and, in some programmes, families, for example asking about their views on the books that were being shared and accepting that as volunteers they would not judge 'if the child has a tantrum in the middle of a session and they have to stop it short' (DL Interview 1, Programme staff). For WBD staff who worked with adults not children for this programme, they also wanted to create trusting relationships where teachers influenced their work:

> I was keen that they were given that opportunity to feed back to me honestly about what they were seeing in our practice as well. And again, that was a trust building exercise and I am genuinely interested in what they've got to say.
>
> *(WBD Interview 1, Programme staff)*

The shared values of the supporting adults were noticeable as they shaped the everyday interaction and enactment of the programmes. Nearly all the adults in the data collection appeared to share a deep understanding of the potential of children's volitional reading and writing to positively influence their self-confidence, social engagement and wellbeing, motivation to learn and ultimate academic skills. The supporting adults' interactions were driven by believing that 'switched off' children could be enticed and supported to develop a love of reading and writing with ultimate positive benefits for their academic outcomes and more. They clearly understood that this involved sharing the pleasure in reading and responding sensitively to empower individuals by adapting and refining programme approaches in the moment.

Conclusion

Analysis of the roles within the programmes and how these were implemented reveals several common approaches. The programmes built their capacity by drawing on existing partnerships and forging new ones with other local organisations. This enabled them to access specific local knowledge about target groups and resources. Whilst the programmes took the lead, they established mechanisms for frequent and genuine consultation and negotiation with their partners, whether in steering the whole programme, identifying and recruiting child participants, or in planning together with schools or other organisations to deliver their programme. They trusted the expertise of their partners and delegated responsibility accordingly. Teachers also trusted in the expertise of the programmes and benefited from the opportunity to learn from them and the different approaches they deployed. The process of the partner organisations working together was one of dialogue and collaboration.

Programme leaders ensured that evaluation was built in at multiple levels, including supporting adults tracking and reporting on children and families' engagement, steering group monitoring of programme implementation, ongoing dialogue and feedback, and qualitative and quantitative research at the end of programmes. The priority for monitoring was children's engagement and the quality of the interactions between adults and children, rather than skills-focused outcomes. Programme management also involved recruiting supporting adults with appropriate soft-skills and real commitment to the role as well as specific professional experience and expertise where needed. To ensure that these crucial members of staff upheld the programme values, recruitment involved trial periods of working, skills focused training, observation in role, recommendations from partner organisations and targeting specific groups.

Enabling children to enjoy reading and writing was essential to each programme, and this involved building a shared ethos around celebrating every contribution made by a child. Some supporting adults drew on expertise in creative fields to motivate and engage children but all adults, in the face-to-face work documented and observed, sensitively observed and adapted their support to meet the needs of individual children. Supporting adults worked within structured guidelines that created a familiar routine, but each programme allowed them flexibility within these to follow the children's lead and to share something of themselves as adult readers and writers. All programmes encouraged adults to link their work to children's interests and home experiences, some also worked to recruit supporting adults from diverse groups within their community. There was strong agreement that these adults had the time, space and freedom to pursue ways of working that they perceived were different from the literacy experiences in schools, such as through varied stimuli and formats for writing or discussing and finding new texts and authors to enthuse a child. Supporting adults emphasised that they were free from assessment expectations which allowed them to celebrate all children's contributions without focusing on how to improve. Nonetheless, programme volunteers conveyed high expectations to individual children in terms of what they could achieve and offered positive support.

Perhaps most noticeably, the programmes shared key values which informed the way they worked with partner organisations and supporting adults, as well as who was recruited and how they enacted their roles with children. These were consistently reflected in all elements of the data collection with all stakeholders, so they seemed to represent the reality of the programmes. They included: building respectful trusting relationships with children, families and supporting adults, listening to children and responding to their individual needs and interests, understanding volitional reading and writing practices as contributing to social justice, providing safe spaces to 'take risks' and offering relentless positivity, energy and enthusiasm.

11

THE PROGRAMMES' RESOURCES

Introduction

This chapter shares the findings from data collection with the six programmes, Doorstep Library (DL), Get Islington Reading (GIR), Literacy Pirates (LP), World Book Day (WBD), Ministry of Stories (MoS) and the Primary Shakespeare Company (PSC). Initially, the codes and sub-codes relating to 'resources' are shared, and then each of these is explored with qualitative examples from the programmes' documentation, observations of their work in action, multiple interviews with programme staff and focus groups with a range of adults (e.g. volunteers, creatives) and children, gathered over the period of the Literacy Special Initiative.

The activity system element *resources* focuses on understanding the ways in which specific tools and/or physical tangible objects were used by the programmes to support their aims as well as the adults' use of interactions and language. This latter consideration of language as a resource stems from activity theory which highlights the use of language to mediate the understanding of different participants in each activity system. Consequently, the data collected related to two main codes tangible resources and intangible resources (see Table 11.1)

Tangible resources

Tangible resources included a range of items, including, for example, books, plays, stimuli for writing (e.g. objects and images), programme documentation and environments. Some programmes provided tangible objects including book tokens and stationery for the children, whilst other programmes provided lesson plans and web resources for practitioners or parents. Tangible resources also related to the outcome of the various programmes, many of which held an end-of-programme event to celebrate children's work, and the learning environments created by the programmes, either the physical space/s or through virtual and/or online spaces. The three sub-codes of tangible resources were identified, namely artefacts, place, space and environment, and practical objects.

DOI: 10.4324/9781003532606-15

TABLE 11.1 Definitions of codes in the 'resources' category

Tangible resources	
Artefacts	Final outcomes from the programme which may have been kept by participants/programmes and referred back to. This included book anthologies, published books, films/film clips and applications (Apps).
Place, space, environment	Where places and spaces were important to the activity taking place within programmes. This could be a physical and/or online space. Some programmes moved their activity into online spaces during the time of the COVID-19 pandemic.
Practical objects	Objects that were directly used within the programme. This might include lesson plans for practitioners, a plastic stool, books given to children.
Intangible resources	
Interaction	The ways in which adults communicated with children and/or the way children communicated with each other in the course of reading and writing-focused activities.
Signposting	Where additional information was either given or suggested to practitioners. The flagging of additional and/or supporting services, including community groups and/or library services.
Choice and interest	The ways in which choice and interest of practitioners and/or children directly impacted on their engagement with the programme.

Artefacts

This sub-code refers to potential outcomes from the programmes that were created and may have been kept by participants and/or the programmes and referred back to at a later date, for example, anthologies, published books, films, film clips, applications and so forth. One purpose of these artefacts was to celebrate children's work with others:

> The real-life tangible products that the children get and that can then be celebrated, so a book and a film, apps and it's their work is now out in the world and that we can celebrate that with their parents and with the teachers, schools and the wider public.
>
> *(LP Interview 1, Programme staff)*

A number of programmes, including MoS, LP and PSC, mentioned child-led artefacts as a key outcome of their interventions, and all programmes highlighted the role artefacts played in demonstrating children's engagement with reading and writing. These artefacts were at times collaborative, with children drawing attention to how everyone's ideas and work was included in the final anthology, whilst at other times children's artefacts were individual, as in MoS the children had their own notebooks for use in sessions and in GIR children were given miniature blank books to turn into their personal poetry collection. These small books become cherished memorabilia held onto by children long after the programme had finished (GIR Interview 1, Programme staff).

In addition to the production of artefacts being used to celebrate and engage children in reading and writing, artefacts from previous programmes were also used to encourage and inspire children at the start of the programmes. For some children the desired outputs, such as a theatre production, were hard to imagine, so in such instances, teachers planned to provide children with insights into the final outputs in the form of documentation of previous years' accomplishments:

> They couldn't quite imagine it because it wasn't an experience they'd ever had until they had it. ... It would almost be really good this year if I showed my class this year the photographs from last year's cohort in the theatre.
>
> *(PSC Visit 2, Teacher interview)*

The programme staff stressed the importance of applying a professional standard to artefacts designed for an audience to enjoy. These artefacts were created either by working with professionals or through high production values of the published outputs and/or celebrations. These artefacts were afforded considerable weight and recognised as a way to show respect to young writers:

> We always work towards some sort of purposeful outcome. So, it might be a publication, we might publish a book or an anthology or some poetry, or it could be a performance or a reading or a presentation, but there's always that sense of working with purpose towards an outcome that has real value. And we try and present young people's work to professional standards, we think their writing deserves to be treated in that way as much as any other writers. So, the production values that go into presenting young people's work are really high, and we treat it very seriously, with a lot of care and with a lot of respect.
>
> *(MoS, Interview 1, Programme staff)*

A notable feature of the artefacts created and used was the variety of creative approaches employed. End products frequently referenced included films, an opera, Apps, anthologies, podcasts, celebration events and festivals, each drawing on different approaches to reading and writing and the expertise of authors, dramatists, musicians and so forth:

> So, I worked with an after-school club of year 6s who had some challenges in literacy and we created a poetry book of their poems and then the other programme was with year 6s in a school and we made a book, an actual story about Mayan culture and Mayan civilisation.
>
> *(Teachers/Volunteers Focus Group)*

> Children work with the composer, the director and the writer to produce the lyrics of the opera. Each participating class works on a different section of the piece and at the end of term, at the festival performance, each class performs their section, so the piece becomes a complete opera.
>
> *(PSC Interview 1, Programme staff)*

In addition to creative, tangible outputs, the children involved in GIR frequently referenced the certificates they could receive for engaging in the Summer Reading Challenge and the Reading Road Map (GIR Children's Focus Group 2). Although these certificates were not produced or created by the children, they were still seen as tangible markers of the children's engagement with a reading programme and of importance to the young people based on the frequency of their reference. Overall, artefacts, whether created or received, were used to celebrate and recognise children's achievements in the programme as well as offering important reference points and purposes for their volitional reading and writing. Artefacts were used in tandem with programme choices of place, space and environment to enthuse and motivate children.

Place, space and environment

The second sub-code under tangible resources was place, space and environment. The use of the environment was important to all programmes, whether it was through the rearrangement of library spaces, or the creation of inspiring spaces where reading and writing took place. Therefore, this sub-code arises from references made to places and spaces as being important to the literacy activity taking place. These could be a physical and/or online space, the latter became particularly significant during the Literacy Special Initiative given that some programmes moved their activity into online spaces during the time of the COVID-19 pandemic. This sub-code is exemplified through the words of two adults who comment on the apparent impact and importance of space on the reading and writing activities taking place:

> Okay, so you'd walk into a beautiful pirate ship, huge rooms ... there's a tunnel, a secret tunnel for the children to go through for their entrance into the learning part of the ship. There are books everywhere, so you see there's lovely shelves of books and the resources, such thoughtful resources all around the theme of pirates and the nautical theme.
>
> *(LP Interview 1, Programme staff)*

> We've created a really beautiful space [in the garden area], we've created drop-off points around the school where children can just sit on the sofa and pick up a book and that's where it started and then it's developed into a really strong pupil voice in our school around reading, what they want to read, what they're enjoying, what they're recommending to each other and we've seen particularly, we've seen a really big shift actually in terms of children's engagement.
>
> *(Teachers/Volunteers Focus Group)*

For children, being in different places and spaces was often interpreted as an exciting break from the norm. This sentiment was reinforced when the different place offered larger spatial scales or more homely comforts than those available in classrooms:

> I like the outdoor library because if, let's say, you're bored at playtime then you can just go in there. It's like a really comfy space, there's lots of pillows and there's benches and there's a whole cupboard full of books and it's really nice

> and the indoor library, it's decorated nice and it has lots of good books and that's why we enjoy it.
>
> *(GIR Children's Focus Group 2)*

Additionally, the children associated these changes in environments as enabling them to engage more positively with reading and writing. One child, highlighting the impact of a writing event in a new environment, noted 'It helped me because, as you might say, when we went to the Spotlight place, I was writing a lot, so I think it was because of the Gorsefield trip' (MoS Children's Focus Group 2). The environment also played a role in conveying expectations of the programmes as something different. The places and spaces were designed to share positive and inspirational messages about the ways in which reading and writing were framed there. Adults too remarked upon these spaces, for example, the pirate ship setting was seen as 'pretty cool' by an adult and helped, she believed, to create a sense of excitement for volunteers (LP Visit 2 Interview 3, Practitioner). Children who attended LP were also aware of the unique layout of their space and proactively sought out the researcher's opinion on it.

CHILD: I thought you might ask if this place is made out of fantasy.
RESEARCHER: Well, it's quite an exciting building.
CHILD: And plus, pirates are my favourite*(LP Children's Focus Group 2)*

Whilst some programmes created new spaces within existing environments, for example in a school hall or classroom, other programmes were inviting children into out-of-school spaces. One programme, DL, inhabited a space within or just outside children's homes, this environment was considered to be significant and at times 'neither home nor school' (Teacher/Volunteer Focus Group). The delivery of sessions inside children's homes offered volunteers a holistic and rich understanding of the children in their family's environment (DL Interview 1, Programme staff). The case study of PSC highlights how one programme drew on artefacts and the environment to engage children and support their teachers.

CASE STUDY: TANGIBLE RESOURCES – PRIMARY SHAKESPEARE COMPANY

The PSC works with children and teachers to create a final theatre piece in collaboration with a number of schools. Informed by their classwork and watching the touring production of a play, children work with the composer, the director and the writer to produce the lyrics of the opera. Each participating class works on a different section of the piece and at the end of term at the festival performance, each class performs their section, so the piece becomes a complete opera. Photographs of the opera became valued artefacts.

A notable element relating to the artefacts code was the creative range that PSC employed to engage the children in creating different sorts of texts, such as songs, as well as artefacts not conventionally associated with reading and writing, such as costumes and props. The range of creative activities the children were involved in as a result was seen by teachers as allowing the young people to learn more about each other and themselves (PSC Visit 2 Observation).

The value of the practical objects and resources was dependent on how well the design of the objects seemed to support the needs of children, teachers and practitioners. For instance, teachers involved in PSC commented on the quality of documents on their website and how these were particularly suited to time-poor teachers:

> You can see the thought and intelligence behind it, the actual work that's gone into it ... the way the lessons were planned and put on the website and we were able to access them ... they were sequenced, lesson one, and then below that the resources for lesson one ... those plans, because they were so well done, they were so easy to use.
>
> *(PSC Visit 2 Interview, Teacher)*

Importantly, the environments employed in programme activities were flexible and regularly adapted. Similarly, practical objects drawn upon in programme delivery were regularly re-considered and developed further.

Practical objects

There was some degree of overlap between the sub-codes of 'practical objects' and artefacts, so the decision was made to refer to artefacts as those items that were outcomes of the programme, whilst practical objects were designated as part of the ongoing delivery of the programmes. Examples of practical objects referenced by programmes and/or through documentation included, digital reading challenges, reading audits, maps and passports, book collections, book clubs/reading clubs.

Books were an obvious practical object for reading and writing interventions, and a number of programmes gifted books to their participants as well as providing opportunities to borrow or access books in sessions:

> The library staff then come to the front and remind children they can join the library for free and come after school or at the weekend with friends and that there will be boxes of experiments they can borrow too. Children are given Reading Sparks bags with free books to take home.
>
> *(GIR Observation 1)*

> We offer every child and young person – from 0 to 18 – the opportunity to discover the power of reading for pleasure by giving them the opportunity to have a book of their own.
>
> *(WBD Programme documentation)*

The use of book gifting as a strategy was expanded, in some instances, to include those connected to the children in the programmes. So, parents also received books as well as activities related to them. This expansion enabled families to engage with each other around these materials:

> I mean obviously the approach was also like a family reading approach. There was a book for the children, a book for the adults and then there were some

> activities around that and they were themed around interests. And so that seemed to be good, seemed to be positive.
>
> *(GIR Interview 2, Programme staff)*

Additionally, staff working with the programmes were keen to ensure that they had a robust overview of their resources and that they were suitable, which led to regular reviewing and revising of resources and was frequently mentioned. Programmes viewed their resource provision and gifting as a matter of social justice, and many staff saw it as their role to remove economic barriers that might impact on children's ability to access quality texts:

> It still completely flabbergasts me how many families just have no books at all, it's just not something that's in any way thought of as important or valued or seen as a source of pleasure and that, I think, is a massive thing. Just to turn up with books and be passionate about books, or even online to be surrounded by books, and just show that passion and transmit that fun is a huge starting point. Then the relationship comes I think.
>
> *(Teachers/Volunteers Focus Group)*

Practical objects also took the form of school-based resources for practitioners and parents, and included lesson plans written by teachers, continuing professional development resources and online resources through website access. As a member of the PSC noted, 'We provide daily plans in literacy over 5 weeks to meet the year group learning objectives. We also provide full term plans for numeracy, science, art, DT' (PSC Interview 2, Programme staff).

There was also an interest in creating resources that were suitable in a wide range of settings. Programmes sought to design resources that were accessible, and flexible enough to work with reluctant readers as well as those who are more assured and also sought to create resources that could support parents:

> So definitely school resources to be used in school, but ... we're also introducing something called Share a Story Corner, which is quite sweet. But essentially, it's about developing confidence with parents who've got very young children and don't really see the point of reading with them.
>
> *(WBD Interview 1, Programme staff)*

One programme made good use of a practical stool which was frequently noted as being an important part of the DL experience. Volunteers described the stool as a symbolic marker of the session:

> Volunteers work in pairs, carrying a backpack full of books and small stools to sit on. We have little plastic stools that we take out which volunteers use on doorsteps while the children use them, but the volunteers carry them, bring them along so that the children can sit on them on their doorsteps. Or sometimes when we are invited into a home even then the children really like them because it's kind of, their story stool. It sets up the scene.
>
> *(DL Interview 1, Programme staff)*

This simple object, in common with the more elaborate learning environments noted under 'place, spaces, environment', signalled a specific opportunity for volitional reading focused on the child, thus highlighting that this time was special and for them. The programmes' tangible resources were often used in this way as markers to denote difference, and to frame the reading and writing opportunities as invitational and somewhat novel experiences. This sense of fun, freedom and difference was also supported by characteristics of the intangible resources employed by the programmes.

Intangible resources

Intangible resources related to specific interactions and the language used as part of programme activities, and referred to additional support offered, for example signposting parents to services in the community or connecting participants with community library services. The sub-codes identified under intangible resources were interaction, signposting, and choice and interest.

Interaction

There were multiple examples of interaction taking place across programmes, between facilitators, creatives, teachers, volunteers and the children, as well as between children. This code was most frequently recorded through the observations, closely followed by volunteers' and teachers' comments during the focus group discussions. As reflected in the sub-code 'place, space and environment', engagement and the nature of interaction in these spaces was important, as the routines and environment mediated the children's experiences of reading and writing:

> And we'll do about 45 minutes of reading and each week they can pick a book that they like, there's a library at the ship and then we'll do reading out loud. It could be doing voices, acting and taking turn reading pages, for example, and then we'll move on to the creative writing part.
>
> *(Teachers/Volunteers Focus Group)*

This interaction sub-code also refers to the ways in which adults engaged with children. There are overlaps here with the code of 'interactions' within the activity theory element 'expectations'. However, the subtle but critical difference is that interaction in this element refers to the more dynamic connection and association with reading and writing:

> We share the books with the children and we involve the parents and it's so nice to see them enjoying the books. It doesn't matter what level their reading is at, if they can't read the books that they want to read, then we'll read to them ... It's a family of four boys and he's the first at the door wanting to choose his books and he reads to me more now, I used to read to him and now he joins in and is also choosing different books because his reading has developed and he can read a bit more now.
>
> *(Teachers/Volunteers Focus Group)*

A crucial aspect of these interactions was that they were responsive to the needs of the children, several programmes mentioned they worked to balance giving children attention when they want it, but giving them space too. Whatever the length or depth of these interactions, the adults commonly focused on providing encouragement and appreciation of the children's efforts in reading and writing, seeing them as accomplished readers and writers from the outset. Interactions were often focused on creating safe opportunities for children to be creative, with practitioners being involved as role models, reassuring children that their contributions would be accepted and evidencing this (MoS Observation 2):

> I think you also just get to model being excited about reading and that bleeds into not just that child, but the little child who hasn't started reading yet and the family, and you show how easy it is to pick up a book and just have fun.
>
> *(Teachers/Volunteers Focus Group)*

This idea of modelling behaviours also followed through to the ways in which programmes enabled children to engage with each other in positive ways when reading or writing was the focus of the interaction:

> Children read their writing aloud – they read together and talk of 'making sense of the writing together'. They correct as they go, and the crew mate says 'What do I need to do here?' There is a sense of shared ownership in the writing.
>
> *(LP Observation 1)*

The supporting adults in programmes were often observed to reflect on their own personal experiences as readers and writers and share these with the children, as well as participate alongside the children modelling enthusiasm for reading and writing. The intentionality of these responsive, supportive interactions with children appeared to be pivotal to the success of the programmes' work and the, at times, focused and at other times energetic engagement of the children as readers and writers. This linked to the supporting adults' understanding of flexibility and adaptability as part of their role. Supporting adult interactions also involved signposting for children and adults.

Signposting

The second sub-code within the wider code of intangible resources was signposting. This was more frequently mentioned in the interviews with programme staff and refers to instances where additional information was either given or suggested by practitioners, for example, the flagging of supporting services, including community groups and library services.

Two programmes in particular, GIR and DL, talked the most about the importance of signposting to other existing organisations or structures, for instance 'So, if there's brilliant things happening in the libraries, we want to make sure that the schools know about it' (GIR Interview 1, Programme staff) and 'We signpost them to other services, we want them to feel like they're connected together with the community as well' (DL Interview 1, Programme staff). The process of signposting was often strategic, with programmes using knowledge of local services and families to ensure the value of the information provided. This played a vital role in contributing to the development of positive and supportive relationships with families, with these two programmes linking families with other reading initiatives like WBD and local services or activities.

However, signposting was also noted in other programmes and involved personal recommendations, such as volunteers passing on book recommendations to children or staff at WBD flagging up other literacy organisations' resources. It was also sometimes specific to parental support for reading, writing or curriculum topics related to the programme, for instance 'We provide resources for parents in terms of read around, here's some other things on that subject, here's some places to go, here's some things to do' (PSC Interview 1, Programme staff). The signposting of resources to families became an important part for many programmes during the early stage of the COVID-19 pandemic, using newsletters not only to practically share activities but also to keep in touch, to maintain relationships already developed. Signposting was approached with sensitivity and respect, presenting choices available to adults and children, in common with programme activities.

Choice and interest

Whilst 'choice and interest' as a sub-code did not fit neatly into the 'intangible resources' code and shared some overlap with coding in the 'expectations' category, it was still felt to be an additional resource in its own right; for example, one outcome of 'choice and interest' might be a specific book chosen by a child:

> So, we know that it's about, at a broad level, it's about children choosing to read. Some level of volition of reading, some level of choice over what it is they're reading, and the point of the £1 books is that children have the opportunity to go and choose something that they want to read.
>
> *(WBD Interview 1, Programme staff)*

Children very frequently noted that they enjoyed being able to routinely access and choose from a range of texts in their programmes, including LP, GIR and DL, for instance 'So, there's different books and there's a big library and you pick whatever books' (LP Children's Focus Group 2). Teachers too recognised the power of choice: 'Being able to choose books for themselves not only seemed to increase their interest in reading, but also seemed to augment their identity as readers, with children taking pride in making and sharing their choices' (WBD Visit Interview, Teacher).

However, sometimes children had to navigate sharing resources, 'My least favourite part of Pirates is sometimes when you go to the book corner, you want to pick one of the books, after someone comes bustling in and picks the books' (LP Children's Focus Group 2) and expressed a degree of dissatisfaction with the books available, 'Sometimes they bring the same books that I read it over and over again and sometimes I have to remind them that I've already read this book' (DL Children's Focus Group 2) and 'I wasn't really as impressed with some of the selection this year, because of the fact that it just, some of them are like a primary school book still' (GIR Children's Focus Group 2). These opinions further reinforced how important choice and interest were to children's continued engagement and highlighted that they had come to value and anticipate these opportunities offered by the programmes. Selection of texts was only one way of providing for interest and choice. In addition to children's choice over reading materials or book selection, programmes also regularly afforded children agency and choice and agency in writing and in multiple other ways:

> At the end of that session, they see their very own choice of words put into a song, which they then have to stand up and sing, and so they see the entire thing from birth to result and there's a performative element. So, they get a great feeling of their own agency by then singing the song which has the words that they have chosen themselves.
>
> *(Teachers/Volunteers Focus Group)*

Essentially, all of the programme expectations were underpinned by the principles of choice and interest for reading and writing and these aims shaped the development of their work.

Conclusion

All six programmes incorporated both tangible and intangible resources into their programmes which often prompted positive interest and engagement in reading and writing. Crucial to a number of programmes was the role of artefacts, which became part of the legacy of many, with all programmes considering the need for high production values of the published outputs and the importance of creating appropriate time and space for child-led artefacts. For all programmes this celebration of children's work was considered fundamental in reinforcing the young people's engagement with reading and writing.

The tangible environment was key to many programmes. Several of them paid attention to the physical environments in which they worked, with some programmes inviting children into specially designed literacy spaces, some developing creative and immersive environments in schools, and others visiting homes with props and books to denote reading time. GIR operated in multiple environments, connecting children and young people to the local public library, the school library, their classrooms and the wider school environments. These diverse spaces and places played a role in children's reading and writing engagement. Physical books and texts within programmes were either bought and gifted to supplement engagement with reading and/or used as a thread within the programme. Using resources in this way was felt to lead to positive relationships around or with reading and writing, as well as removing potential economic barriers to accessing quality texts.

The intangible but crucial resource of interaction was also significant across programmes, carefully developed to support positive reading and writing experiences. Interaction as a resource involved orchestrating different types of interactions within programme activities and environments focused on engaging and enthusing the young participants, it was contingent upon sensitive, responsive adult interactions supporting the children's participation in different ways at different times. With some similarities to interaction, signposting within programmes to different organisations was also an important resource, including linking children and families to other literacy organisations, public libraries, the Schools Library Service, theatre groups and community groups. Signposting was designed to support children's engagement in reading and writing, or to improve family circumstances to create time and space for reading and writing. Signposting was therefore aligned with the responsive, relational nature that underpinned programme interactions. Similarly, embedding choice and interest and framing principles for the books and texts within programme activities was also about responding to individuals. This thoughtful deployment of resources fostered children's agency within the often-connected reading and writing activities and led to book talk, discussion and dialogue. Overall, the intentional, sensitive development and application of resources, tangible and intangible, across all the programmes encouraged children's choices, fired their imaginations and led to a noticeable and positive development in young people's confidence in reading and writing.

PART IV

Considering Implications for Professional Practice

12

THE READING AND WRITING FOR PLEASURE FRAMEWORK FOR PRACTICE

Introduction

This chapter explains the Reading and Writing for Pleasure Framework for Practice, which provides a research-informed basis for developing practice that nurtures young people's volitional engagement in reading and writing. The Framework for Practice was created from the consistent findings emerging from synthesis of the reviews of the global research literature about evidenced approaches to nurturing reading and writing for pleasure (explored in Part II), and the empirical research conducted with the six literacy programmes under the Literacy Special Initiative (explored in Part III). This chapter offers an in-depth discussion of the organisational characteristics of the literacy programmes participating in this initiative with the intention that these common elements might also provide important considerations for other literacy charities and organisations as well as schools. The other inter-related elements of the Framework are then summarised in the chapter before being exemplified in practice from different contexts in Chapter 13. The current chapter concludes with a set of recommendations for all those who wish to foster children's volitional engagement as readers and writers, and suggests ways of using the Framework to evaluate and inform organisational development and strategy, as well as pedagogy and provision.

The Reading and Writing for Pleasure Framework for Practice (see Figure 12.1) indicates that a rich combination of individually and socially oriented approaches is optimal, mediated through the responsive involvement of adults. It highlights the child-led autonomy-focused nature of this work, and the ways that relaxed interactions around texts forge social and relational connections of value between readers and/or writers. Text access and dedicated time and space are essential as these enable the dynamic individual-social combination to function successfully. Surrounding these key approaches to motivating children and young people's volitional reading and writing are the shared values and organisational characteristics found to shape and support such work.

DOI: 10.4324/9781003532606-17

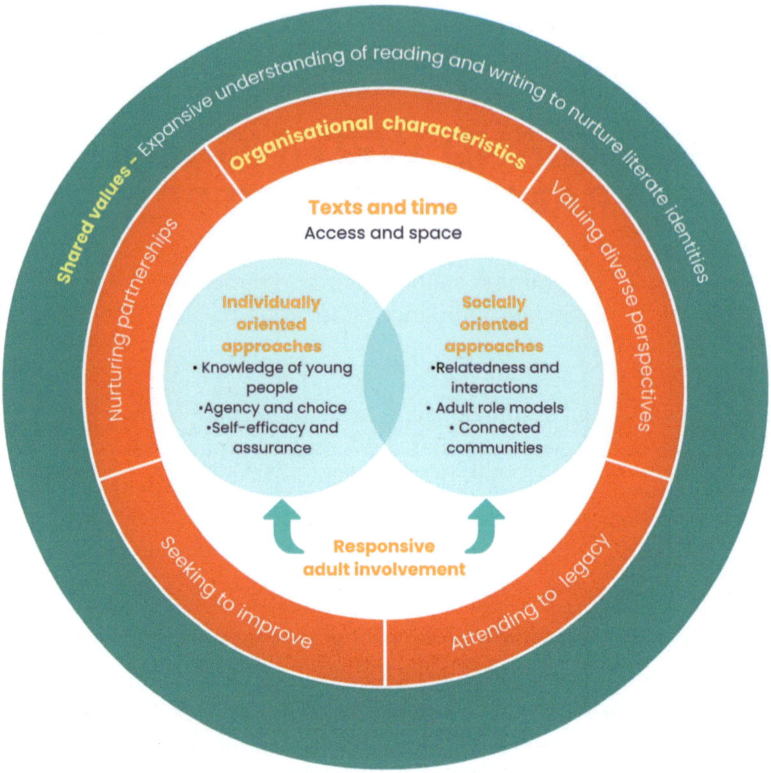

FIGURE 12.1 The Reading and Writing for Pleasure Framework for Practice

Shared values and organisational characteristics

In the Literacy Special Initiative, despite the six programmes' obvious and intentional differences in where, with whom and how they worked to engage children and young people in reading and writing for pleasure, the research team were able to discern commonly shared values and four enabling organisational characteristics from the data collected about the programmes. Whilst some research has examined the work of literacy charities' initiatives with a view to considering their efficacy and optimal functioning (e.g. de Bondt et al., 2020; Galea et al., 2024), due to a lack of resources, literacy charities are often obliged to undertake their own in-house evaluations. Furthermore, even when these are outsourced, there is rarely time to turn the resultant reports into academic peer-reviewed publications. Thus, research focused on the shared values and structural features of charitable literacy programmes and equivalent initiatives led by schools appears to be somewhat absent in the research literature.

So, the shared values and organisational characteristics are derived from this study of the six programmes alone and are not developed from a synergy between the research literature and the empirical data, in this way they stand in contrast to the remaining elements of the Reading and Writing for Pleasure Framework for Practice. Nonetheless, and critically, these enabling features underpinned the programmes' approaches to nurturing children's enjoyment and engagement as readers and writers.

To different degrees, and in different ways, these values and characteristics underpinned the organisations' holistic and relational approach towards nurturing children's enjoyment and engagement in reading and writing and were pivotal in enabling and supporting them to achieve their aims. The next section describes the two outer layers of the Framework, the shared values, and then the organisational characteristics, including nurturing partnerships, valuing diverse perspectives, seeking to improve and attending to legacy, are considered.

Shared values

The outer ring of the Reading and Writing for Pleasure Framework for Practice denotes the shared values and perceptions of reading and writing for pleasure that underpinned the literacy programmes in this research. These are likely to also be important for schools and other groups and organisations working in this field. All the six literacy programmes' practices and approaches were underpinned by commonly held 'expansive' understandings of reading and writing. In other words, they recognised the importance of children's affective, creative, behavioural and social engagement as readers and writers, for their identities, social relationships and wellbeing, as well as for their cognitive engagement and academic progress. The programmes' conceptions, often linked to addressing disadvantage, were not limited by a focus on curriculum goals for reading and writing, but they did not ignore or eschew these. All the programmes recognised and valued the need for the development of children's skills in reading and writing. However, their pre-eminent intentions in this Literacy Special Initiative were to facilitate highly engaging and motivating literacy experiences that sought to develop the young people's positive sense of self as readers and/or writers.

The predominant shared values voiced as desires and evidenced in action included prioritising social justice and addressing inequities through their work. They did this by involving and empowering children and young people as individuals, enabling them to see themselves as readers and writers and experience success in this regard with the aim of improving their educational opportunities, engagement and subsequent life chances. Their shared values also included a commitment to building respectful trusting relationships with children, families and supporting adults, listening to children and responding to their individual needs and interests, providing safe spaces to 'take risks', to interact with one another and by offering positive feedback, energy and enthusiasm. Similarly, programme members agreed that families should be consulted, supported and accepted without judgement. The various individuals involved in programmes, whether as providers or recipients of their diverse activities, commented on the reliability and trust that was cultivated through this ethos.

The shared values of addressing inequities, empowering children, building open relationships, providing safe and interactive spaces to take risks and accepting families without judgement, were understood and applied by members of each programme team, including volunteers and paid staff at all levels. Individuals were able to talk about what it means to be a reader and writer and were focused on the impact for young people which they believed could be realised through nurturing a sense of belonging, community and relentlessly positive experiences within their programmes. These deeply held and commonly articulated core values led to the approaches explained in the inner layers of the Framework, such as creating and providing positive experiences of reading and writing for the young, ensuring interactions were non-judgemental, nurturing and kind, and offering children agency over their reading and writing choices.

In a school context, shared values and a vision for developing children as volitional readers and writers, within and beyond school, is equally important. Open discussion among the staff team about what these values might be, linked to an understanding of the evidence base, has already been seen to lead to shifts in whole-school reading cultures documented by educators involved in the Open University's Reading Schools Programme: Building a Culture of Reading (The Open University Reading for Pleasure, 2025). The importance of creating a shared staff understanding of the what and why of any initiative before embarking on the how is also endorsed in the Education Endowment Foundation's cycle for school improvement (Sharples et al., 2024). This can be achieved in diverse ways, but is likely to include practical opportunities for adults in staff meetings, and continuing professional development to discuss their experiences and identities as readers and writers, space to explore the research documenting the benefits of valuing children's volitional reading and writing, and time to co-create an action plan for the whole school staff and each class. This would need to encompass clear attention to tracking the impact on children and young people's engagement, enjoyment and confidence as well as their skills. International evidence indicates, as discussed in Chapter 1, that there is a strong relationship between literacy motivation and attainment, between the will and the skill.

The six charity literacy programmes not only coalesced around their shared values and intent to nurture reading and writing for pleasure, but also included these values in the procedural aspects of their work, such as planning, policies and training. Perhaps more powerfully still, these values were evident in the commitment, intention and lived daily interactions of the programme members, ensuring that the principles were more influential than mere stated aims. Whilst not all members of the programmes were driven by research in this area, significantly, the research literature also shows that children's literate identities play a key role in their wider sense of self, and their motivation and desire to read or write for pleasure (see Chapter 4). Thus, the research literature and the evidence from the programmes reinforce the shaping influence of developing shared values within staff teams focused on enhancing young people's confidence and motivation, and subsequent educational engagement, through expansive understandings of reading and writing for pleasure. In this way, the community, programme or school can support children by understanding that they are working to enable the young people to see themselves as readers and writers, not simply pupils 'doing' reading and writing.

Organisational characteristics

The four organisational characteristics in the Reading and Writing for Pleasure Framework for Practice also underpinned the work of the literacy programmes and offer points of reflection for those in other educational contexts. The first of these was nurturing partnerships.

Nurturing partnerships

Cultivating relationships was an important and reciprocal element in developing the programmes' understanding of local and individual needs. By working at a community level (rather than necessarily only in a given local community), the programmes understood the specific context of their stakeholders and often sought out partnership level relationships to enhance their offer. In addition, the ability to tailor interactions and/or resources to local need, created interest in the work, and often attracted the attention of locally based volunteers and employers. The programmes all created processes to develop their understandings of the needs of the individuals and communities with whom they worked. Doing so enabled them to responsively interact and offer tailored support, thereby establishing genuine connections with their stakeholders. Establishing connections pivoted around creating, sharing and consistently reflecting upon expectations, whether with staff, teachers, volunteers or children, regarding how programmes would operate and their core values.

When working collaboratively with partner organisations, programmes demonstrated a markedly open ethos, seeking to listen to stakeholders' views to understand programme interaction and build forwards. This listening stance and commitment ensured that the organisations were both trusted and valued as active partners sharing the common goal of developing young people's pleasurable engagement as agentic readers and writers. Schools might also prioritise creating open-minded collaborative partnership working when applying the Framework, for example regularly meeting with library colleagues, school advisors, local literacy charities, parents and children to plan enhanced reading and/or writing for pleasure provision together. Collaboration within schools, between schools and across year groups will also be important in developing autonomy-oriented work that nurtures volitional readers and writers.

Valuing diverse perspectives

Supporting diversity through experience with a range of people trying a range of activities, and hearing new ideas was evidenced as important in all programmes, and involved them in seeking to ensure that no one voice dominated approaches or perspectives. This diversity was embedded in activities, often as a springboard for further interaction and development. Each programme's consultative approach to programme design also extended to positioning individuals as the 'more knowledgeable other' – in some cases this was the child, for instance by enabling them to share which types of books or writing they wanted to engage with. Additionally, volunteers were encouraged to share their own literacy experiences and identities to support children's understanding of what it takes to become an experienced reader and writer. These approaches and the role modelling involved, which was not always explicitly planned, but emerged in interaction, may encompass a more child-led or equal status relationship than is usual in literacy and other areas of the curriculum, but could readily be applied in sessions and activities focused on reading and writing for pleasure in school. Indeed, programmes frequently drew attention to supporting adults and their role in enacting the core values of programmes through the ways in which they interacted with children and young children. These interactions hinged upon positive, respectful and trusting relationships, where children were listened to, heard and their views and needs were honoured and responded to accordingly.

Similarly, creatives were encouraged to utilise their unique skills, approaches and expertise so that teachers and children could experience literacy through a different lens. Programmes were mindful of where expertise and proficiency lay and worked to find ways to harness these skills. For example, some practitioners involved with previous programme cohorts were invited to design and author resources for others, whilst others were invited to talk to new practitioners as part of training sessions. In school, sensitive deployment of adults based on expertise and experience to support volitional literacy engagement might include capitalising on the wider staff skill set, drawing in other staff beyond the literacy leadership team and external adults with interests in drama and creative activities, and experience of literacy in different formats (e.g. rap, song, gaming, BookTok). For example, by establishing regular Mystery Readers (in which parents, office and kitchen staff as well as community members read to a class), schools could tap into the diverse expertise and personal passions of members of their wider community, enabling them to share and showcase their own interests with different groups or classes. Likewise local writers, journalists from local newspapers, editors of magazines or such in the local community might visit to share their skills, passions and ways of working.

Seeking to improve

In recognising what they learned from others, the organisations consistently positioned themselves as learning organisations. This was evident both when working with internal staff and when working externally with partners, volunteers and children. In and through their programmes, the staff worked hard to develop their understanding of the young people and of ways to nurture reading and writing for pleasure and, in so doing, they sought to improve their offer. Most programmes were resolute that they embraced a position outside of, and different to, school assessment criteria and, as such, they deliberately sought to create non-judgemental spaces to foster enjoyment for participating children, teachers and families. Whilst this might feel a challenge for schools, work with teachers has shown that it is possible to create dedicated time in the school day, when the focus is on nurturing enjoyment. In communities where volitional reading and writing are foregrounded, children often spontaneously seize additional opportunities on the playground, in the corridors, at break and at lunchtimes to read and write, sometimes alone, but frequently through and with others (Coakley-Fields, 2019; Cremin, 2017; Cremin et al., 2014, 2024; Ivey and Johnston, 2015; Moses and Kelly, 2018; Myhill et al., 2023).

As learning organisations, the programmes each used different tools to understand the value of their work, informally through ongoing interaction at the close of sessions, and more formally through evaluations, surveys and audits, that in many cases included seeking children's perspectives. In school, surveys, focus groups, informal observations and conversations with children and staff are also important to monitor the progress and impact of approaches to developing young people's engagement as readers and writers. Ongoing formative assessment, particular of the less engaged, can enable educators to understand and document subtle shifts in their literacy identities and build on these. The programmes regularly reflected on the appropriacy and efficacy of their training for volunteers and used review groups and annual appraisals of the impact of their programmes, all of which can be mirrored in schools by including reading and writing for pleasure in school improvement plans, ongoing monitoring and continuing professional development schedules. The programmes were felt to be in a constant state of evolution and committed to improving, refining and developing the ways in which they engaged with different levels of stakeholders. These activities were firmly rooted in ensuring that children were the key beneficiaries of their work, with the quality of the interactions between adults and with children viewed as crucial to their success. In schools, setting clear success criteria that focus on nurturing more positive attitudes to and engagement in reading and writing, and that encompass attention to volitional reading and writing beyond the school gates, can help staff teams review the efficacy of their work and refine and adapt their provision accordingly.

Attending to legacy

All of the six programmes were keen that their interactions should have some legacy or lasting impact. Those involved shared a commitment to developing children's attitudes and pleasurable engagement in literacy, and as noted earlier, many saw this as a core value, every child's right and a matter of social justice. This attention to legacy was concerned with ensuring that young people were given opportunities to develop their attitudes towards, and engagement with, literacy over the long term, well beyond the immediate work of the programmes. In some cases, this involved connecting children and families to other partner organisations and working with teachers and librarians to enhance their practice. Similarly, in school this might include working towards a school-wide vision of the long-term goals. In addition, it could encompass connecting children with services that support volitional reading and writing outside school and in holiday periods such as local libraries and charitable programmes, as well as supporting families with reading and writing, for instance through offering book swaps, reading cafes or themed writing workshops for parents and children. It could also involve sharing information across transitions between year groups and key stages, so that staff can build on an understanding of children's motivations, identities and interests as readers and writers.

Involvement in the programmes was seen to impact in various ways on most of those involved. For many volunteers there was a desire to redress inequities and to give back to their local communities and a sense of communal engagement in the work of the programme. For the creatives involved there were other benefits in terms of sharing the love of their craft and seeking to instil that in the children and in some cases, other practitioners. Equally, school staff who are involved in planned volitional reading and writing opportunities are likely to grow in confidence in this space and experience the satisfaction of their own and the children's engagement and motivation. For the writing-focused programmes, having a performance or creating a tangible output like a published book or film in itself created a legacy. This benefited the current cohort and served as an invitation to new cohorts. Schools, too, may wish to create a range of outputs, such as newspapers, podcasts, magazines, anthologies, performances, public debates or films, enabling the young to experience real purposes and audiences which can serve as a focal point and celebration of their pleasurable and focused engagement in and enjoyment of reading and writing.

Ultimately, all programmes intended that their approaches would lead to lasting change in the ways children and adults viewed writing and reading and saw themselves as readers and writers. This is a powerful goal with equivalent significance to primary schools, who may not feel they can expend time on developing readers and writers due to the pressure to deliver the curriculum and ensure targets are met. They may even feel obliged to accept narrow conceptions of literacy and as a consequence may not question what counts as reading and writing in their contexts. Schools can become constrained by national tests, seeing high standards in these as their corporate goal without a wider vision of the communal enterprise of education, and recognition of the role that reading and writing for pleasure can play in redressing social and economic inequalities.

Moving inwards from the two outer circles of the Framework for Practice, the core of the Framework is now considered. This encompasses not only the text access, time and space that the research literature and the data from the programmes highlighted, but also the individually and socially oriented approaches as well as the crucial role of the responsively involved adult. These elements do not, even implicitly, denote routines, separate practices or activities but are closely inter-related elements of the whole Framework. An educator could not, for example, just offer children the time and space to write, even if the young people had chosen their focus and expect to successfully nurture their pleasurable engagement. The elements of the Framework operate dynamically and in complex combination. An exploration of the way in which organisations and schools realise these elements in and through their practice is offered in Chapter 13.

Texts, time and space

The importance of texts and time for nurturing children and young people's engagement in reading and writing was highlighted in the literature and the empirical study. Both evidence that accessing texts and having time and space to engage with them are key to reading and writing for pleasure. The importance of providing myriad opportunities for children to choose from a rich range of diverse texts is clear. This would include regular sharing, browsing, recommending, gifting and lending texts as well as enabling text ownership. Children are more motivated when the texts available are culturally relevant and connected to their lives and interests.

When time is set aside – at home, in school, in a library, or as part of wider community events – and opportunities are offered to 'just' read and write, children are enabled to exercise their agency and make choices as readers and writers. They begin to expect, depend upon and look forward to this time which benefits from a carefully curated balance of familiar routine and flexibility, accommodating both extended periods of quiet, immersed engagement in reading and composing texts, and vibrant interactions with others about these. Engaging with time to read and write is enhanced by relaxed adult support and feedback. In reading, this would involve, for instance, adults creating a balance between offering a range of appropriate text recommendations and stepping back to let children make the final decision. In writing, this would encompass adults offering the freedom for children to choose writing topics or modes that are meaningful to them, and giving positive feedback, supporting children's intrinsic motivation and engagement as writers.

The combined findings also point to the value of physically inviting and relationally informal environments which are often learner shaped and owned. These would include classroom, library and out of school spaces, as well as curated, safe, digital environments. Environmental spaces that are perceived to be safe, social and non-judgemental support young people to take risks as writers and to engage more deeply as readers, alone and through interaction with others.

Individually oriented approaches

At the centre of the Framework for Practice are individually oriented approaches. These are supported by access to texts and time and work in tandem with socially oriented approaches. They are a key feature evident in the research literature and the programmes' approaches. Individually oriented approaches comprise three strands, developing knowledge of the young people, and nurturing their autonomy and agency as well as their self-efficacy and assurance as readers and writers. These strands emphasise the volitional nature of reading and writing for pleasure.

Adults foregrounding the voices of children and young people and seeking to understand their unique interests, lives and literate identities is evident in both the research and the work of the programmes. This knowledge is developed through prioritising adult–child relationships and interactions and offering opportunities that enable children to share something of themselves and their own personal, cultural and literary experiences. When their views about reading and writing practices are sought, heard, respected and, most significantly, acted upon, this widens young people's rights as readers and writers and enhances their involvement. When adults plan structured opportunities that are responsive to children's needs and interests as readers and writers, this impacts positively on their identities and motivation.

Nurturing young people's agency and choice as readers and writers is motivating and supports the development of positive literacy identities. Both the programmes and the research literature show that child-led text choice and access to personally relevant reading material that responds to individual and collective interests is vital. Enabling the young to discriminate and make wise choices as readers matters. Young writers too are motivated by being supported to exercise their authorial agency, write for personal and authentic real-world purposes, choose their topics and modes of writing, experience the use and value of writing, and draw upon their lives and experiences of multimodal texts to express themselves. Adults who focus on supporting the development of children's agency and choice may also advance discussions with them around what counts as reading and writing, its relevance in their students' lives and their rights as readers and writers.

Fostering young people's sense of self-efficacy and assurance as readers and writers is also seen to be crucial. Mutually reinforcing relationships exist between competence and motivation, and both studies in this area and the evidence from the programmes show that supportive environments, constructive feedback and responsively structured, yet informal, literacy opportunities foster children's sense of self-efficacy as readers and writers. This can be enhanced through reading and writing support, ideas generation and reassurance in the face of challenges. Drawing on personalised understandings of individual learners, adults build children's perceived competence and confidence in one-to-one and group conversations and persistently celebrate their contributions, imaginative engagement and other successes.

Socially oriented approaches

Socially oriented approaches to reading and writing for pleasure are at the heart of the programmes' practice and are extensively evidenced in the research reviewed. These are facilitated by responsive adult involvement, and underpinned by social interaction, relatedness and role modelling. They can enable the development of connected communities of readers and writers.

Social interactions around reading and writing that value children's interests and views and foster relational connections enable them to feel recognised and accepted as readers and writers. This can be intensely satisfying and motivating. Studies indicate, and the programmes evidence, that non-hierarchical, trusting relationships influence and can even undo young people's assumptions or negative attitudes towards reading and writing. Such relationships are facilitated by conversational exchanges and spontaneous interactions around texts that are being written and read. Often, these are centred around young people's ideas and led by them, enabling individuals to make choices about how they participate and their reading and writing foci. Informal peer support, playful activities, and reassuring structures around volitional reading and writing that prioritise equality of participation and develop mutual respect, set the foundation for such interaction.

Adult role models demonstrate their personal engagement as readers and writers and thus encourage young people to read and write for pleasure. Both the research and the programmes indicate that some adults share and reflect upon their literacy experiences and in the process enhance the authenticity, real-world relevance and pleasure to be found in reading and writing. Positioned as fellow readers and writers, these adults may voice their personal and emotional response to texts, write alongside children and express their own compositional challenges and satisfactions. They invite the young people to do the same and sensitively build on their responses.

The creation of connected communities of readers and writers shapes young people's literate identities and their desire to engage in reading and writing. Strongly evidenced in the programmes and increasingly documented in research, these communities connect children and their families, educators, school and public librarians, volunteers, authors, professional writers and other creative partners in diverse clusters and affinity groups. Operating in different spaces, offline and on, such connected communities not only widen young people's literacy networks but can increase their awareness of and pleasure in the communal, collective and relational experience of being a reader and a writer.

Responsive adult involvement

Attuned and responsive adult involvement mediates and motivates young people's engagement as readers and writers, individually and collectively. The combined evidence indicates that adults who develop children's reading and writing for pleasure nurture connections and relatedness, engage affectively, and, through their behaviour, show that they are interested in and appreciate the young people's perspectives. Their personal involvement may include support for text selection, affirmative feedback and guidance when encountering challenges, and the tailored provision of opportunities for children to be inspired by books read aloud, by recommendations, and by participation in informal interchanges around children's texts – written or read. They may also offer space to consider the experience of being a reader and a writer, sharing their own experiences and enabling children and young people to talk honestly about what they have enjoyed or found difficult.

Being a role model is important, but more than this, responsive adults listen, engage and adapt their practice, both in the moment and over the longer term through planning different approaches based on knowledge of the children with whom they work. For literacy programmes and charities, this may be a normal part of their approach, but for any educator, it can present a challenge when working with whole classes. Focusing on paying particular attention to smaller numbers of children, and the least engaged readers and writers, can make this both feasible and more impactful. By noticing these children's interests and offering new reading or writing opportunities, seeking out their views and heeding these, whilst offering space to read and write together can make a powerful change to how these young people perceive themselves and how much they want to be involved. Part of the role of the responsively involved adult is to make time to notice children's engagement in a range of contexts and develop practices that capitalise on their positive literacy identity enactments, however fleeting. For instance, spotting a child drawing cartoons with a friend, laughing in response to humorous poetry, lingering at a display of graphic novels, could become a stepping stone towards reading or writing for pleasure. Developing whole-school understanding of the highly significant role of adults in understanding, reflecting and adapting their provision in response to such evidence, combined with wider knowledge of the child as a literacy learner is crucial. Ring-fencing time and senior leadership endorsement for such formative assessment of readers' engagement will support teachers to take on this important role.

Recommendations and implications

Reading and writing for pleasure urgently require a higher profile in education, both to raise attainment and achievement and to increase children's engagement as motivated and socially engaged readers and writers. The Framework for Practice, developed from the Special Initiative funded by the Mercers' Company, offers a strongly research-informed basis for practice in all contexts where the aim is to develop young people's volitional reading and writing – these include homes, schools, public and school libraries, charitable programmes, online literacy spaces and local communities.

The Framework for Practice reveals that effective approaches for nurturing reading and writing for pleasure are framed by expansive understandings of literacy, which recognise young people as readers and writers, not pupils 'doing reading and writing', and which focus on them personally. The values-driven programmes, whose work is not defined by curriculum expectations, clearly evidence this egalitarian emphasis on children as experts, the staff and volunteers involved respect the young people's views, ideas and uphold their rights as readers and writers.

Access to diverse, relevant texts and dedicated time underpin the optimal individually and socially oriented approaches to reading and writing for pleasure which are mediated through responsive adult involvement. Individually, in the sense that they are learner-centred, autonomy-focused and sensitive to young people's own interests, literate identities and wider cultural practices. Socially, in the sense that they include rich opportunities for informal interaction around texts that are inclusive, non-hierarchical, involve adult role models, and nurture the creation of positive connections and communities of readers and writers. These approaches reflect relational pedagogy in action.

Literacy organisations and schools, teachers, student teachers and librarians can make use of the Reading and Writing for Pleasure Framework for Practice to affirm and celebrate, question and challenge their practice, and in the light of this, identify priorities for development. Additionally, the Framework offers an opportunity to develop a shared vocabulary with volunteers, partners, stakeholders, funders, governors and trustees and to demonstrate to these and other colleagues, the value of current practice, and the potential for enrichment in order to maximise impact on young people as readers and writers.

It is thus recommended that within and across organisations committed to enriching young readers and writers, the adults involved are supported to:

1. Review their practice to develop positive literate identities for all children, consider their long-term aims and the partnerships that could support these.
2. Widen their conceptions of literacy and reader and writer identities.
3. Ensure that young people have access to a rich choice of texts and dedicated time and space to read and write primarily for enjoyment.
4. Invite and respond to young people's views about reading and writing for pleasure, developing their agency and supporting their self-efficacy as readers and writers.
5. Embed opportunities for relaxed and supportive social interaction around reading and writing for pleasure, and authentically model their own pleasurable engagement and challenges.
6. Develop nurturing relational practices that construct connected communities of readers and writers.

Ways forward for working with the recommendations and the Framework for Practice might include working with staff in organisations to examine one or more element. A strategic focus on the development of reading and writing for pleasure within an organisation could involve discussing and establishing shared values using the recommendations, the case studies of practice woven through Part III and in Chapter 13, and considering evidence from the literature in Part II to identify a long-term vision and specific aims for developing children's engagement in context, incorporating the views of multiple stakeholders. Organisational characteristics may not previously have been considered in relation to volitional reading and writing, and opportunities to develop cultures of connection and sustainable legacies with communities and families may be needed. Schools might also review how they can attend to diverse voices when planning activities and providing texts for reading and writing.

Where the focus might more usefully be on pedagogy, the Reading and Writing for Pleasure Framework offers a tool for reflection and evaluation, identifying what could be strengthened, for example by exploring how staff currently deploy individual approaches to understand children's needs and interests as readers and writers, and other ways this might be leveraged, as well as how this knowledge could be used to inform and enrich practice. Perhaps social strategies are already established in terms of programme or classroom opportunities, but attention could turn to building connected communities of readers and writers within and beyond the whole school or programme. Additionally, the Framework for Practice could be used as a stimulus for continuing professional development, practitioner research, stakeholder consultation or policy development in diverse contexts.

Conclusion

The Reading and Writing for Pleasure Framework for Practice was developed from synergies between the research literature and the data collected from the research study of six literacy programmes run by London-based charities. It provides a strongly evidence-based summary to support school and programme development. The Framework highlights the overarching shared values deployed by the programmes, namely social justice, agency and choice, empowering children, avoiding judgement, establishing trusting relationships around reading and writing, and fostering belonging and community. Key enabling organisational characteristics of the programmes that were found to support this work included nurturing partnerships, valuing diverse perspectives, seeking to improve and attending to legacy.

The inter-related pedagogical elements of the Framework include the significance of access to culturally relevant, diverse and engaging texts, and dedicated time and space with which to engage with them in relaxed social spaces, free from curriculum demands or other extrinsic expectations. Individually oriented approaches are central and incorporate the need for practitioners to build practice around knowledge of young people's interests and experiences, providing agency and choice of texts, of writing themes, activities, collaboration and more. Supporting children's self-efficacy and assurance is an essential part of individual approaches, through valuing children's efforts, opinions and ideas about reading and writing and offering encouraging, positive feedback.

Socially oriented approaches are an equally important part of the Framework and involve building relatedness and interactions around reading and writing activities and preferences. Adult role models contribute by talking about their own experiences of reading and writing, working with and alongside children to generate ideas and compose, and by sharing reading recommendations and reflections. Regular social engagement between adults and children around informal, child-led reading and writing can support the development of connected communities, with peers and other adults who reciprocally nurture a culture of volitional reading and writing. The role of responsive adult involvement is core to all these pedagogical elements, noticing and adapting interaction and activities in the short term and offering planned opportunities in the longer term to enable all children to develop positive reader and writer identities.

Schools and literacy programmes can review and develop their approaches to reading and writing for pleasure using the Framework for Practice elements and the six recommendations. The following chapter provides a range of case studies of these elements in diverse contexts to further facilitate application of the Framework.

References

Coakley-Fields, M.R. (2019) 'Inclusive talk: Weaving fiction discussions across the school day, *The Reading Teacher*, 72(6), pp. 721–729.

Cremin, T. (2017) 'Apprentice story writers: Exploring young children's print awareness and agency in early story authoring', in Cremin, T., Flewitt, R., Mardell, B. and Swann, J. (eds), *Storytelling in Early Childhood: Enriching Language, Literacy, and Classroom Culture*, London and New York: Routledge, pp. 67–84.

Cremin, T., Hendry, H., Rodriguez Leon, L. and Hulston, S.J. (2024) 'Informal book talk: Digging beneath the surface', *English 3–13*, 52(7), pp. 930–945.

Cremin, T., Mottram, M., Collins, F.M., Powell, S. and Safford, K. (2014) *Building Communities of Engaged Readers: Reading for Pleasure*, Abingdon: Routledge.

de Bondt, M., Willenberg, I.A. and Bus, A.G. (2020) 'Do book giveaway programs promote the home literacy environment and children's literacy-related behaviour and skills?', *Review of Educational Research*, 90(3), pp. 349–375.

Galea, C., Robidoux, S., Salins, A., Noble, C. and McArthur, G. (2024) 'The impact of shared book reading on children and families: A study of Dolly Parton's imagination library in Tamworth, Australia', *Journal of Research in Childhood Education*, pp. 1–30.

Ivey, G. and Johnston, P. (2015) 'Engaged reading as a collaborative transformative practice', *Journal of Literacy Research*, 47(3), pp. 297–327.

Moses, L. and Kelly, L.B. (2018) '"We're a little loud. That's because we like to read!": Developing positive views of reading in a diverse, urban first grade', *Journal of Early Childhood Literacy*, 18(3), pp. 307–337.

Myhill, D., Cremin, T. and Oliver, L. (2023) 'The impact of a changed writing environment on students' motivation to write', *Frontiers in Psychology*, 14, 1212940.

The Open University Reading for Pleasure (2025) Reading Schools Programme 2025–26. https://ourfp.org/schools-teachers/reading-schools-programme-2025-26/.

Sharples, J., Eaton, J. and Boughelaf, J. (2024) *A School's Guide to Implementation*, London: Education Endowment Foundation.

13

APPLYING THE READING AND WRITING FOR PLEASURE FRAMEWORK FOR PRACTICE

Introduction

This chapter explores ways to apply the Reading and Writing for Pleasure Framework in the context of schools and organisations, examining strategies that make use of the recommendations noted at the close of Chapter 12. The aim of the chapter is to support educators to reflect upon how the Framework might relate to their own circumstances by providing examples of practice from diverse schools and organisations. Although the Framework is derived from synergies in effective approaches to supporting children's enjoyment and engagement of reading *and* writing, the organisations in the study, and most of the research literature, had a clear focus on reading *or* writing. In school practice too, it is more common, and arguably more likely to have impact, for school staff to concentrate on developing approaches to reading *or* writing at any one time, and a focus on readers is likely to afford benefits for the young people as writers and vice versa (Graham et al., 2018). Consequently, the chapter shares case studies of the Framework applied to the work of charitable literacy programmes and schools, centred on developing first reading for pleasure and then writing for pleasure, with a final school case study that combines approaches to both. Reflecting on these case studies may enable practitioners to notice aspects which are well developed or would benefit from more attention in their own organisation, and to identify possible strategies for change.

Initially, the chapter shares practical examples of applying the Framework to work on reading for pleasure, beginning with a brief reflection on recent activities and research conducted by the Open University team. Then organisational case studies from the charitable literacy programme, Doorstep Library, and from Lydgate Infant School in Sheffield are presented. These examples are followed by using the Framework to examine writing for pleasure approaches in case studies from the charitable literacy programme, Ministry of Stories, and from Elmhurst Primary School in London. The Elmhurst case study attends to both reading and writing for pleasure provision and practice, seen though the Framework's lens. Each case study, which was co-constructed with those involved, exemplifies the core aspects of the Framework: texts and

DOI: 10.4324/9781003532606-18

time, individually oriented approaches and socially oriented approaches. The integral, essential role of responsive adults and the underlying shared values which staff hold are also explored.

Since developing the Framework, the research of the Open University Reading for Pleasure team has identified many instances of specific elements of the Framework in action, for example, in the practices of student teachers and class teachers in the early years. In addition, we have been prompted by the Framework to notice how the Student Teacher Reading for Pleasure Ambassadors scheme which we run enables the trainee teachers to fulfil the role of the responsive adult during their initial training in school. In this scheme, led jointly by the Open University and the UK Literacy Association, volunteer student teachers, still in their training from across the UK, are supported to promote reading for pleasure with their pre-service teacher peers and to enrich their own provision while on teaching practice. In research with the Ambassadors, many shared how they quickly tuned into children's reading interests and offered tailored recommendations. They also shared instances of following the children's lead to talk about a friendship theme emerging from a read aloud and sensitively adjusting their reader-to-reader interactions by attuning their responses (Hendry et al., 2025). Many also highlighted socially engaging strategies such as Diversity Cafes and Relax and Read Book Clubs, online and off, that they have organised with their peers in order to rekindle a love of literature. Additionally, in a study of informal book talk, observations with four teachers working with 5–7-year-olds showed how one primary practitioner used free reading time to take an individual approach by giving undivided attention to a particular child, ensuring they experienced agency and choice through selecting a book to share, controlling the page turning and leading the interaction with their teacher (Cremin et al., 2024). Both these studies reveal far more about the reading in these different contexts but offer simple examples that illustrate elements of the Framework are already in action in the work of practitioners across the country. These can be strengthened and developed to include an intentional, organisation-wide approach as explored in the following case studies.

DOORSTEP LIBRARY

Doorstep Library recruits and trains Home Reading Volunteers to read weekly with children and parents/carers in their homes or on their doorstep in targeted under-resourced areas in London. Their work is concentrated in areas where opportunities for reading are restricted – there may be limited access to books in the home, or language barriers may be preventing parents or carers from being able to provide additional reading support to the children in their care.

During their visits, the volunteers read stories, lend books and connect families to their local community. Volunteers work in pairs, carrying a backpack full of books and small stools to sit on. They visit each family once a week during term-time, read stories with the children on the doorstep or in the home, and lend them books to exchange when they return the following week. They also run online reading sessions with families they cannot reach in person. The reading time in homes is informal and social, siblings often read side to side and take turns reading with the volunteers. They choose a book to share from the volunteer's backpack and can stop and try other books during the session. The emphasis is on fun and motivating children to read by following their interests.

Shared values

From the chief executive officer to the committed volunteer team there is a passionate, shared understanding of reading for pleasure as a vital foundation to children's education and future life chances, a strong sense of social justice underpins the charity's provision. The work of the team is jointly focused on enabling access to texts, and empowering families to see the value in reading at home and to access community support relevant to their needs. They understand that families challenged by money worries, or issues related to health and housing, need help to address these before they can relax and read with their children. These shared values are established in recruitment and training, but also regularly revisited in team debriefs and meetings.

Texts and time

At the heart of Doorstep Library's approach is bringing texts and time to families. Through weekly scheduled visits, the volunteers establish a routine for reading with children and parents/carers, so this becomes uninterrupted time in which the volunteers model enjoying sharing texts together. The focused time for reading might be on the doorstep away from the hubbub of the home, or on the sofa, wherever is more comfortable for the children and family. The children keep a book to read and exchange it each visit, so all the children have books at home that can be regularly swapped and updated. The texts on offer change every week, and the volunteers' expertise involves tuning into individual children's responses and interests to bring a bespoke selection of texts to their door.

Individually oriented approaches

The individually oriented approach of offering texts that will engage children to read for whom reading is not a regular habit, involves volunteers taking the time to get to know the children. Through trial and error, sharing books and noticing children's level of engagement as well as chatting as they read, reflecting aloud on their own thoughts and asking open questions that stimulate chat, the volunteers find out more about the children they are working with, often visiting over months or even years. From this informal reader to reader interaction, they provide a choice of tempting texts. These personalised text recommendations are designed to capture and sustain children's attention and motivation to read. Children's agency and choice is also built into each session as siblings get their own choices of texts from the backpack and after each visit the volunteers reflect on the discussion and plan what to take along to engage the children next time, based on what the children have asked for or enjoyed. Volunteers support the children's self-efficacy and assurance by valuing their ideas and conversations around the books, helping them with their reading skills as well as reading to them and finding texts that they can gradually read more confidently.

Socially oriented approaches

The visits from the volunteers are inherently socially oriented, involving relaxed interactions and building genuine relationships with children and families, volunteers share their own responses to the content of the texts and encourage the children to do likewise. In this way, the volunteers provide reading role models for the children as well as their parents and carers. They encourage parents to get involved in the reading sessions and take an active interest in their children's education but also take time to support and signpost families to what is on offer in their community in terms of events and facilities, helping them gain access to everything from libraries to reading clubs, youth centres, grants, days out, courses, talks and workshops.

Responsive adult involvement

Volunteers at Doorstep Library fulfil the role of 'responsive adults' by ensuring that they talk about their love of reading, they demonstrate this through enthusiasm for the books that are offered. They encourage discussion about books within families, so that siblings and parents may discuss books outside of the volunteer sessions. They also encourage and value children's own perspectives on what they read through book-prompted conversations and encourage them to explore their own opinions through open questioning. The children report feeling valued and supported, they are in their own environment and over time build a bond with the volunteers. Where children are reluctant to read and lacking in confidence, the volunteers will simply read to them and encourage them to discuss the books, with no pressure on the child to read aloud. They build confidence by showing the children that it is okay to not understand something, or that even adults make mistakes when reading.

Whilst Doorstep Library aims to support reading enjoyment in the home and so works closely with parents and carers, there are many parallels with the approaches taken in a school context. In home or school settings it is vital to create informal and relaxed socially oriented approaches, as well as tuning in to children's individual interests and fostering positive views of themselves as readers, through opportunities to choose texts and lead the interaction. These elements are clearly shown in the approaches taken by Lydgate Infant School.

LYDGATE INFANT SCHOOL

Lydgate is an award-winning four-form entry infant school in Sheffield with around 360 children on roll. Twenty-seven different languages are spoken by pupils and diversity is celebrated and valued. The school has been consistently rated good by Ofsted and was most recently commended for its focus on inspiring and exciting children through reading. The school's KS1 Reading, Writing and Maths outcomes in 2023 were significantly above the national average. The school won the HarperCollins, Open University, United Kingdom Literacy Association Reading for Pleasure Whole School Award in 2024 for its work on the social reading environment and reading aloud. Lydgate Infant School completed the first year of whole-school development 'Reading Schools' Programme: Building a Culture of Reading with the Open University (2022–2023) and worked on the next stage through the 'Strengthening and Sustaining' Programme follow-on year (2023–2024). This case study of its provision draws on the evidence submitted for the award and other examples of practice shared through the Open University Reading for Pleasure website, as well as a close working relationship with the school.

Shared values

The teachers in this infant school consider they are in a privileged position to develop the young people's reading skills and to foster their love of reading. They aim to operate explicitly as reading role models and want all pupils to feel that they are part of the whole-school reading community. The schools is proud to be a multilingual school, and reading in all the children's heritage languages is valued and encouraged. The staff are committed to growing their knowledge of children's texts and constantly seek to enrich their reading for pleasure pedagogy with the shared goal that all children will leave the school as keen readers, who read frequently for their own purposes.

Texts and time

To ensure that the teachers in the school have relevant knowledge of texts to engage and recommend to children, the English leaders, Vikki Varley and Daisy Whitehead, involve the staff in ongoing events and challenges to boost their knowledge of contemporary children's literature. There is a long-term commitment to staff development including time for book recommendations in staff briefings, a regular staff book club, book blankets around different themes to spark discussion and highlight new texts, personal challenges such as shadowing book awards, attending conferences and visiting the Schools Library Service (SLS) book collection. An updated and inviting selection of texts are available in each classroom, using money raised from book fairs, a small, dedicated budget, and SLS borrowing. Time for reading aloud is a key strategy to involve all children in reading for pleasure, with a dedicated weekly storytime assembly and daily reading aloud sessions as well as timetabled reading sessions where children can choose to read independently and with friends.

Individually oriented approaches

Staff create and share reading rivers of their own reading with children and vice versa to gain knowledge of them as readers, this knowledge feeds into the book collections in the classroom, enabling adults to be responsive to children's interests in their choice of texts to read aloud and to recommended. Reading rivers are visual posters of different types of reading that the child or adult engages with, for their own purposes, online and off, over the course of a day, a weekend or more. Photos, drawings and cut outs of reading material are often used to share the range of everyday transient reading encountered, such as road signs, cereal packets, take away menus, etc., as well as more extended reading in other forms, such as books, magazines and so forth.

Using knowledge from the shared reading rivers and discussion about them, staff offer children a choice of texts in reading aloud, where they can vote for the text they want to hear and exert their agency, and multilingual storytelling activities are used to connect to children's home and family backgrounds. These connections then feed into the social experiences of reading in the school as staff and children know each other as readers and recognise that all individual responses to reading are valued. Vikki has introduced further personalisation to entice children who are not choosing to read for pleasure. She invited some of these less engaged readers to choose books they would like to add to their personalised book boxes, by browsing and discussing texts laid out as a book blanket. Agency and choice are further fostered by agreeing the 'rules' around these boxes. The child can choose which order to read the books they have placed in them, to re-read them, discard them, or substitute them from the class library during relaxed reading time. Their self-efficacy and self-assurance are nurtured though this and the opportunity to informally share their book with the class teacher or friends. Vikki considers that this approach models ways of engaging with texts and ignites individual children's interest in reading, as well as supporting them socially.

All classes have timetabled sessions dedicated to free-choice reading. For example, each day after lunch in Vikki's class there is 15–20 minutes of dedicated 'Relaxed Reading Time' where all children choose their own texts and choose who to read with. Vikki comments: '[T]his is a crucial space for building reader-relationships. It's an opportunity for talking informally about reading habits and preferences, and a time where children see me read my own text choices. It's also the most pleasurable and treasured part of our day.'

Socially oriented approaches

Working with visiting authors, and discussing staff and children's views about texts through the Spark! and Sheffield book awards showcases adults as reading role models with their own preferences and interests and supports the development of connections across the school community of readers. This involves thought and preparation from the school staff, for example maximising the impact of author visits by sharing texts, exploring themes and creating opportunities for children to respond to the texts creatively, including immersive activities, writing and storyboarding, before an author visits. This whole-school approach to exploring new authors creates shared excitement, relational connections and joint knowledge for book chats. Vikki explains that after engaging with a visiting author, changes to children's reading habits are noticeable, they became more social, bringing copies of books from home and being more interested in other similar books. The conversations and shared experiences translate into home reading enthusiasm, showing the power of social connections to motivate readers (and, as the Framework also highlights, writers).

Socially oriented approaches are also built into school organisation and environments. There is a system of older children reading to younger pupils, and an outdoor reading area to choose and chat in, promoting reader to reader relationships and informal opportunities during playtimes. Regular reading displays are used to encourage casual book talk around the school about what different classes are reading, and different perspectives on shared texts. By modelling informal book talk naturally through interactions, responsive trusted adults provide children who have previously not been engaged in choosing to read with the language and confidence to initiate book talk with others.

Responsive adult involvement

As part of the whole-school commitment to developing reading for pleasure, all staff completed a grid drawing on the work of Moss (2000) focused on children who can read and do, who can read but don't, who can't read and don't, and who can't read but try/do have a love of reading. This is used as part of the transition conversations with new teachers as children move between classes, and to their next school. It offers the teachers a head start on who may need additional support to enrich their engagement in reading as they change classes and it allows teachers to learn about and then plan their response to support children's emerging identities as readers.

Staff at Lydgate also aim to nurture reader to reader connections by sharing their authentic reading lives, including the challenges. Daisy, for example, leaves a text (a book, magazine or even the puzzle off a cereal packet) on her chair each morning, sparking interest and chatter when the children find the text. Texts brought in from home too are valued, for example by making a time for children to share them as a book recommendation or through read aloud. Children are also encouraged to leave sticky notes on books they have read as another way of communicating their responses with others and weekly school library visits provide an additional opportunity for conversations and home book borrowing. Classrooms have a 'Familiar Read Box' to ensure that children who are less confident readers can find and enjoy texts that are already familiar to them through read aloud.

Books available for independent reading time are not grouped by reading skill: all children have access to all texts and in reading time, due to its relaxed nature, children often share and support each other in reading words and pictures in texts. Teachers with good subject knowledge of children's texts and of each reader are on hand to make recommendations to those who find choosing challenging. Staff make use of opportunities to position children in situations where they are the 'expert' in order to help build their self-efficacy as readers, for example reading to a younger child in school (after practising so that they feel confident) or being a library monitor. Lydgate staff are currently working with Dr Sabine Little from the University of Sheffield to build a multilingual library so that children can read texts in their heritage languages in school and at home, which is another important element of building their self-efficacy and sense of self as readers through working with responsively involved and attentive adults.

In common with Lydgate's focus on building self-efficacy in and through reading for pleasure, supporting children and young people's enjoyment in writing and helping them to perceive themselves as writers are core elements of the work of the charity Ministry of Stories. Like the individual and social approaches taken to encourage children to choose to read at Lydgate, the responsive adults at the heart of Ministry's work value and champion the children's writing using open-ended creative approaches that nurture individual self-efficacy and connect children within a community of writers. Their programmes complement and enhance the work of schools and offer many transferable approaches from which other programmes and schools can learn.

MINISTRY OF STORIES

Ministry of Stories is committed to helping children and young people develop their writing and to helping teachers (primary and secondary) inspire their students to write. The charity runs a range of programmes including, for example, free community writing opportunities (from their Hoxton Street Monster Supplies shop and dedicated writing centre base in Hackney), and workshops and programmes of sustained engagement in schools. In the Literacy Special Initiative, they worked with a group of 11 primary schools in the London Borough of Tower Hamlets seeking to inspire, enthuse and support students writing for pleasure. During this programme, the team worked to understand each school's needs, challenges and curriculum, then in response developed and delivered writer-led bespoke units of work in the schools. These units of work encompassed, for instance, a focus on 'Recipe of me' with poetry workshops, performance poetry as part of a topic on the Romans, and producing newspaper reports about environmental responsibility. All these school-based projects enjoyed creative twists to surprise and engage students. The projects involved workshops for pupils, practical teacher continuing professional development, support for leadership and a celebratory event. Sometimes volunteer writing mentors also joined the writer-led work with classes of children.

Shared values

The charity, which was founded in 2010, works in some of the most disadvantaged areas of London. It has established and sustains a strong set of values for both adults and children: namely respect, courage and imagination. Applied to writing they highlight respecting each individual writer, their ideas and all forms of writing, the courage to be different and to listen to and learn from others and honouring the power and potential of the imagination. These values underpin policy, practice and relationships, and are evident within the organisation's structure, training for writing facilitators, volunteers and writing mentors, and in their work with teachers and young people. The organisation's additional, but perhaps more implicit goal, is to build communities of writers.

Texts and time

Projects are typically delivered weekly over the course of a school term, and considerable time in a unit is dedicated to writing. This is facilitated in short, structured opportunities, enabling children to add to their evolving compositions, and through longer stretches of time which have the potential to develop every child's engagement and investment in the experience and the work. Those who are less assured as writers are trusted and supported to develop their voice, in part through the expectation of making a contribution to the agreed end-of-unit publication. This enhances the purposeful nature of the writing which has a real-world audience beyond the child writers. Through the writing workshop time, which is both structured yet somewhat informal in nature, writing facilitators and volunteers are able to learn more about the children's personal interests and purposes for writing and whilst common themes are chosen, as in a poetry focus for example, considerable choice and agency is woven through, and children choose a poetic form or free verse to suit their content.

Individually oriented approaches

The professional artist-practitioners who lead the sessions for Ministry of Stories are learner-led in their approach, they listen to and respect the children's ideas, however unusual, and offer considerable support to help them both generate ideas and select from them. The children are encouraged to be playful, to rely on their own ideas and resources, and starter prompts, drama games and a range of activities are offered to help. The artist-practitioners focus on valuing the young people as individuals and meeting them where they are, as well as validating them as writers in each session and over time. They give sensitive and affirmative feedback that seeks to retain and develop each writer's sense of self-efficacy as a creative individual. The children's authorial agency is not only seen in the extent to which the young people can direct and shape their writing, but also in the sense that each piece of writing belongs to them as writers – no one else is in a position to make decisions about it. Personal ownership of their compositions is asserted at all times. These individually oriented approaches also encompass celebratory opportunities at the end of the unit when the young writers share and publish their writing.

Socially oriented approaches

The safe spaces to write created by the artists-practitioners include both time for individual, semi-silent writing and for high levels of interaction, for instance when the young people are generating ideas or discussing a chosen extract of their work with peers or volunteers. These interactions are somewhat non-hierarchical in nature and provide opportunities for young people to participate freely in the conversational ethos of Ministry of Stories writing classrooms alongside their peers and the adults. The adults in the room often position themselves as fellow writers, and refer to their own writing lives, interests and practices. As role models they are able to offer an insider's perspective on the writing process, and many evidence their own engagement in recreational writing, which serves to build connections between children and adults as writers. By invoking various low-key routines, using particular artefacts (e.g. Ministry journals and collectively generated 'story contracts' unique to each class), offering ongoing relaxed interaction and evidencing their shared values in action, Ministry practitioners create a writing community during their sessions. Final celebrations of the published writing serve to reinforce this, and offer a sense of shared achievement.

Responsively involved adults

Personal relational connections are evident between artist-practitioners, volunteers and children. Ministry of Stories adults listen carefully to the young people's emerging compositions and show highly personal positive and authentic engagement. They demonstrate that they are genuinely interested in and value the young people and their ideas as writers. Regular opportunities are built in for children to comment on each other's writing and praise is persistently offered. Alongside positioning the children as writers, this enables even the least experienced authors to take responsibility and ownership of their writing, which helps to build their confidence. Where barriers do exist, adults work hard to overcome or remove these, by, for example, scribing for a child whose ideas are moving quicker than their physical writing. Adults seek to meet the writers where they are on any given day, in any given session, accepting and building from their own starting points to build their self-efficacy and confidence.

Key to the work of Ministry of Stories are the opportunities for writing individually, and using short writing provocations to build confidence, alongside lively discussions, activities and writer role-models designed to fire imagination and support children in generating ideas. These common strands are also visible in the following case study of Elmhurst School, as are the engaging influence of author involvement and creative outputs. This school has carefully developed its approaches to both reading and writing for pleasure and this final case study provides an example of the way in which it threads this through staff development, teaching approaches and resourcing to provide a multi-layered and impactful approach to fostering a love of reading and writing in young people.

ELMHURST PRIMARY SCHOOL

Elmhurst is an award-winning four-form entry primary school in Newham, London. In 2019, Elmhurst won the Harper Collins, Open University, UKLA Reading for Pleasure Award, in 2023 it was awarded the UKLA Literacy School of the Year and in 2024, the Open University/UKLA Reading for Pleasure Quality Mark (Platinum – the highest level). The description of the provision noted below draws on the school's submissions for these awards, observations in context as well as a close working relationship with the school and its involvement in Open University research studies. The school is a member of the New Vision Multi-Academy Trust with four other local schools and leads the New Vision English Hub for the Department for Education in England. Elmhurst Primary is located in an area of high deprivation. With a student population of more than 1,000 in 2025, more than 95 per cent speak English as a second language and 23.3 per cent are eligible for Free School Meals, a proxy in England for less economically advantaged children. The school's motto, 'Little seeds, big dreams', is evident in the high-profile focus on staff development to offer a rich and evidence-based curriculum. Constant reviewing of provision is the norm and the commitment of staff to the young people's education tailored to the diverse local community is apparent. In national assessments, the school scores highly (in the 95th percentile for combined Reading, Writing and Maths at the expected standard, 2024) and the English inspectorate, Ofsted, graded the school as Outstanding in 2021. Drawing on the school's work it is possible to see how both reading and writing for pleasure are developed.

Shared values

The school reports that over the last seven years it has undertaken a comprehensive review and transformation of its literacy curriculum. Although its results on national tests were high (infant and primary), staff were concerned that the young people were merely producing what they were told to do within literacy lessons, and were not developing independence, nor were they fully able to use their 'skills and value their own voices, passions, traditions and funds of knowledge both within the classroom, across the school, and throughout the community'. The school's focus, as Katharine Young, Head of School, notes, is now based not just on teaching reading, writing and oracy, but on 'developing readers, writers and orators who have the skills and choose to use them for their own purposes'.

Texts and time

Recognising that a consistent supply of high-quality texts is essential for nurturing a rich literacy culture, Elmhurst invests thousands of pounds annually to purchase books, with student input and book shopping helping to guide sections and ensure a relevant collection. Children also select the books from the library for their class book corners every term. Child and teacher surveys indicate this involvement heightens their enthusiasm for reading, fosters discussions and gives teachers insights into student preferences. Termly visits to the public library are organised, and drawing on ongoing research (CLPE, 2018, 2019, 2020, 2021, 2022, 2023, 2024), new purchases focus on texts that reflect the school intake and children's diverse realities, interests, as well as popular genres. The school environment foregrounds reading and writing, with corridor and classroom displays alike sharing publications from children and professional writers.

Dedicated timetabled time is set aside for choice-led recreational reading in school, alone and with others, and children hear texts read aloud daily in class and in many assemblies and are encouraged to talk about them informally. Weekly school library visits and regular Battle of the Books sessions offer further opportunities that support children's reading for pleasure, which surveys suggest is high. Staff knowledge of children's texts is foregrounded, many teachers attend regular book groups, and the school has set up a teacher-writing group to allow staff to develop their own writer identities and skills. Some members participate in shortlisting and longlisting for the UKLA Awards. New staff receive training in text knowledge and use, and in supporting the development of young writers.

Concomitantly, staff dedicate time and space to analyse quality texts in genre-focused English lessons and offer daily independent writing time. This comprises approximately 15 minutes of teacher input, 30–45 minutes of writing and conferencing time and 10–15 minutes of class reviewing time. Additionally, all children have 'Personal Writing Project' books in which they can pursue any writing endeavour they wish. One lesson each fortnight is dedicated to this and support is offered, children can, and many do, continue them in their own time or in class when they have finished the day's work. They are expected to publish at least one piece of writing each half-term from their personal project work and this is celebrated.

Individually oriented approaches

Staff are supported to continually develop their knowledge of individual readers and writers, to meet children where they are in their reading journeys and pay particular attention to those who are less skilled or engaged. Each term, teachers focus on three students to cultivate more positive reading and/or writing identities, with feedback from these children regularly indicating progress in various ways. Termly reading surveys are undertaken and children discuss their habits and set targets with teachers. Discussions about children's literate identities are part of class handovers, as this ensures teachers start each year with comprehensive understandings of readers' tastes, interests and their class's collective preferences. Children have autonomy to select books that interest them, are involved in choosing book corner selections and school library borrowing rates are high.

In order to support the development of volitional writers, and in recognition of the cognitively demanding nature of writing, staff seek to understand each child's own writing voice and interests and allow children to draw on their own passions by writing about any topic of their choice within the genre being taught, as well as working on their personal writing project. Staff teach children about the different purposes of writing (e.g. to entertain, inform, reflect, make a record, persuade) and adopt a mastery focused approach to writing, teaching in small, distinct mini-lessons to allow all writers to find success and keep up. Equally, starting with the viewpoint of celebrating what the children can do and have done, allows children to feel successful, before teachers then push them towards next steps and improvements. In the genre-framed lessons children also choose their own audiences/outcome for their writing. Each class agrees on a class publishing goal and many children also have a personal publishing goal. The English leader, Sam Creighton, reports that this provides real motivation for the children and shows them the power of their own writing. It is also likely to nurture their self-efficacy and assurance as writers as their work is being read by more than their teachers and peers. Examples include children selling social-political poetry to the local community to raise money for charity, receiving feedback on their short stories from published writers (including Philip Reeve, Katya Balen and Jennifer Killick), having their explanation texts on display in the public library and sending persuasive letters to recipients of their choice (from their parents to the prime minister). Even the youngest children in Reception are afforded volition in their writing, for example writing cards to their parents/carers, addressing the envelopes and walking to the post box so they could see the journey of their writing from idea to audience, and writing books about things they love, recording these and sharing them with their parents.

Socially oriented approaches

Socially oriented approaches are underpinned by interaction and role modelling, both of which are evident at Elmhurst, and these can enable the development of connected communities of readers and writers. The school's approach to developing readers, writers and orators is underpinned by a conceptualisation of reading and writing as both individual and social activities. Multiple opportunities are afforded the young people to discuss and debate the texts they are reading and/or composing in English lessons, and to engage in spontaneous interactions around their own compositions as well as their self-chosen books.

Teachers explicitly model their own genuine engagement in reading and writing. As readers, they share their reading lives and layered responses to texts and many staff also have their own personal collections of books in their classrooms for loan. All teachers write model texts prior to each class writing project, allowing them to talk to the children from experience and also pre-empting any issues they might face. Additionally, staff write alongside children in the workshop-style lessons, positioning themselves as fellow writers who are inside the writing process, able to express their own challenges and to offer advice from a place of knowledge and experience. Staff invite the children to do likewise, to share their work in pairs, groups or with the whole class from the author's chair in order to receive constructive feedback based on their self-identified issues/struggles.

The emphasis on children as authors is clear, and children create their own 'publishing houses' to produce independent pieces of writing that are separate from their class projects. They often write these collaboratively and help to revise and edit each other's manuscripts. A sense of classroom reading and writing communities is evident in many classes and the school has a strong reading and writing for pleasure ethos and culture, with authors visiting regularly and opportunities for children to engage in a range of reading communities – their class reading community, smaller communities of like-minded readers (e.g. in lower and upper school book clubs) and the school-wide reading community. The school provides systems of both monitoring and support to ensure a basic standard of provision in these areas. Such expectations include identifying children for reading engagement interventions each term, daily story time, daily independent reading time, daily writing time, daily time to share writing with peers, book corners in every class, weekly informal book chats and visits to the school library, among other measures.

Responsive adult involvement

Staff deliberately work to foster reader and writing connections with their class. Regarding reading, they do this through a relaxed daily story time and through getting to know the children as readers, making tailored book recommendations to them, and sharing their own reading lives and preferences with them. Regarding writing, these connections are fostered by the teachers writing and sharing their own texts, as well as giving advice and feedback from the vantage point of a fellow writer and writing mentor. Fundamentally, their responses are conversational; Elmhurst staff know from experience that the time and space to informally, passionately and authentically talk about reading and writing is key to success.

Staff also strongly believe that children must be empowered and enabled to use their own voices and critical capacities, rather than being taught and trained to think and write in certain ways. The discussion-based approach to reading lessons and the high priority given to informal book talk (both within the curriculum and through the school day) teaches children that their own interpretations are not only valid, but valued. They do not come to school to be told what a book is about, they come to share their thoughts with teachers and peers and to help each other come to new and shared understandings. This is equally important in writing, children are given the opportunity to write about whatever topic they want within that unit's focus genre. This is further reinforced by their personal project writing, and by the time assigned to writing, which is indicative of the value afforded it by staff. All of the above approaches go a long way to fostering positive reading and writing identities in the children.

Conclusion

The case studies shared in this chapter further illustrate that the Reading and Writing for Pleasure Framework for Practice is not a programme or a single solution to engaging children in reading and writing. In fact, there are many ways in which organisations and practitioners can provide individually oriented and socially oriented approaches that nurture agency, choice, self-efficacy and assurance, as well as the connections, relatedness and role models that influence positive reader and writer identities.

The different organisations and practitioners whose work has been shared in this chapter take multi-layered approaches, understood and lived by all those involved in the school or literacy programme, and these drive the decisions and interaction within them. Approaches are designed to be inherently flexible and responsive to the needs and interests of the children and young people who they aim to support, and reflexivity and continued improvement is built into this work. The individually and socially oriented approaches are not complicated or necessarily expensive, but they take time, planning and commitment to embed. They need and benefit from being iteratively reviewed to identify the impact on children as readers and writers, and to find ways to engage any young people as yet still on the periphery of the literacy communities created. The Reading and Writing for Pleasure Framework for Practice can be used to reflect upon and review how the various elements are developed and sustained in each unique context and as a prompt to plan together for this important undertaking-that of nurturing young readers and writers.

References

CLPE (2018) Reflecting Realities: Survey of Ethnic Representation within UK Children's Literature 2017, London: CLPE.

CLPE (2019) Reflecting Realities: Survey of Ethnic Representation within UK Children's Literature 2018, London: CLPE.

CLPE (2020) Reflecting Realities: Survey of Ethnic Representation within UK Children's Literature 2019, London: CLPE.

CLPE (2021) Reflecting Realities: Survey of Ethnic Representation within UK Children's Literature (November 2021), London: CLPE.

CLPE (2022) Reflecting Realities: Survey of Ethnic Representation within UK Children's Literature 2017–2022, London: CLPE.

CLPE (2023) Reflecting Realities: Survey of Ethnic Representation within UK Children's Literature 2022, London: CLPE.

CLPE (2024) Reflecting Realities: Survey of Ethnic Representation within UK Children's Literature 2023, London: CLPE.

Cremin, T., Hendry, H., Rodriguez-Leon, L. and Hulston, S.J. (2024) 'Informal book talk: Digging beneath the surface', *Education 3–13*, 52(7), pp. 930–945.

Graham, S., Liu, K., Aitken, A., Ng, C., Bartlett, B., Harris, K.R. and Holzapel, J. (2018) 'Effectiveness of literacy programs: Balancing reading and writing instruction: A meta-analysis', *Reading Research Quarterly*, 53(3), pp. 279–304.

Hendry, H., Cremin, T. and Harrison, A. (2025) 'Developing pre-service teachers' pedagogical content knowledge for reading for pleasure: What is missing? what next?', *Education Science*, 15(5), p. 588. https://doi.org/10.3390/educsci15050588

Moss, G. (2000) 'Raising boys' attainment in reading: Some principles for intervention', *Reading*, 34(3), pp. 101–106.

CONCLUSION

Forging Social and Relational Ways Forward

Introduction

The Literacy Special Initiative focused on children and young people's reading and writing for pleasure (2020–2023) and afforded a rich opportunity for six London-based programmes to enrich and develop their provision for young people as readers and writers. Additionally, it enabled the Open University research team to review the relevant literatures, document and analyse the principles and practices of these programmes, and synthesise the resultant insights, creating the Framework for Practice. This provides a research-informed basis for developing the individual, social and relational practice that nurture volitionally engaged young readers and writers.

This final chapter summarises the insights from the work and explores potential ways forward. Initially, it revisits the team's insights regarding the remit of the Literacy Special Initiative, garnered through the extensive literature reviews, the data collection and identified synergies. It also highlights the limitations of the work undertaken. The chapter then turns to consider the tensions and challenges that exist for researchers, for teachers and for literacy charities working to develop children's volitional engagement as readers and writers. In particular, what counts as reading and writing are considered and the demands involved in balancing the teaching of literacy skills and fostering the will to engage as readers and writers. Additionally, the challenge of documenting and interpreting children's literacy identity journeys in an era dominated by data-fication and limited notions of literacy are discussed. Next, gaps revealed in the research are considered and recommendations made for future studies.

The chapter also offers new insights into the relational nature of approaches that foster children's volitional engagement as readers and writers, connecting these to the Framework for Practice. Finally, it is argued that to nurture children and young people's deep engagement in reading and writing and foster their desire to engage volitionally in these literacy practices within and beyond school, wide professional understanding of the empirical research base is needed, alongside urgent collective action from policy makers, literacy organisations, parents, schools and teachers. Suggestions are offered in this regard.

DOI: 10.4324/9781003532606-19

Responding to the remit of the Literacy Special Initiative

The research undertaken within the Literacy Special Initiative responded to the remit set by the Mercers' Company which was to establish the approaches that seemed to be effective in inspiring and encouraging children and young people to read and write for pleasure. This remit did not require the research team to evaluate the impact of individual programmes and so the Framework stems from synergies between the collective approaches documented and analysed and the research literature in the field. A further challenge lies in the nature of the research available. Whilst many studies identify factors related to children and young people's engagement in reading and writing, such as texts and particular pedagogical approaches, relatively few attend to the consequences for young people's engagement in reading and writing activities or track differences over sustained periods of time. Even fewer consider children's literate identities in the round as readers, writers and oral communicators. This represented a challenge from the outset, and as argued later, more work is needed that seeks to track the flow on from classrooms to volitional reading and writing at home, although as we acknowledge, this is not a simple task.

It is also acknowledged that the two separate reviews that were thematically analysed and combined, focused mainly, but not exclusively, on studies involving 5–13-year-olds from 2000–2023. These reviews indicated that the evidence is uneven; there are far fewer studies which attend to children's volitional engagement in writing, this has not been extensively examined in research. Furthermore, the studies included, drawn from cognitive psychology and education, predominantly examine practice in classrooms as there is less research that focuses on volitional reading or writing in libraries, in children's lives at home, online, or in the community, and the peer-reviewed evidence base around reading and writing for pleasure initiatives within charitable literacy organisations is also small. Notwithstanding these limitations, synergies were able to be identified within and across the two separate reviews and the empirical data about approaches that nurture children and young people's engagement in reading and writing for pleasure.

Multiple factors shape children's lived experience of reading and writing, influencing whether they choose to read and write volitionally in their own time. Accordingly, the work draws attention to the significance of developing young people's literate identities since young people with a positive sense of self as readers and writers enjoy and engage in reading and writing more frequently than their less assured peers. So building positive literacy histories and positioning children as readers and writers matters. These positive identities are fostered by offering considerable text access, time and space to read, share and compose texts that respond to their personal interests, and serve children's social purposes alongside authentic reasons to write for real audiences.

Synergies were identified around individually oriented approaches. In essence, these approaches encompassed teachers' knowledge of children as readers and writers, nurturing and respecting agency and choice as well as the development of their self-efficacy and assurance as literate individuals. The adults facilitating these learner-centred, autonomy supportive approaches not only work to get to know the children individually as readers and writers, but listen to and respect their thoughts about texts, and their voices as writers. In addition, they actively seek the young people's views about volitional reading and writing, honour these and tailor their practice in response. This enhances the children's involvement and rights as volitional readers and writers.

The socially oriented approaches identified included the provision of multiple opportunities for supported social interaction, and relaxed conversational engagement around texts in non-assessed contexts. These were also linked to hearing, critiquing and discussing texts, to the generation of ideas for writing, and sharing compositions, such informal interactions appear to socially motivate young readers and writers. The evidence also suggests that adults are involved as fellow readers and writers, role-modelling their engagement and building relational connections that nurture young people's dispositions, desires and literate identities. Through positioning reading and writing for pleasure as communal, collective and relational practices, educators who are responsively involved work to create networks and connected communities that can sustain reading and writing for pleasure. The interdependent approaches these adults deploy are shaped by a broad and expansive understanding of the nature of reading and writing.

What counts as reading and writing

What counts as reading and writing, let alone what counts as engaging in these activities for pleasure, is complex and multi-faceted, shaped by each child, each text and the wider social context. For many educators, notions of reading and writing have become constrained. Indeed, as noted in the Introduction, the current performative agenda evident in Western countries places high value on raising standards, testing and grades, and consequently reading and writing are predominantly conceptualised, taught and tested as a set of assessable skills. Such narrow conceptualisations are seen in policy documentation and curricula, framed by autonomous notions of literacy (Street, 1998), rather than broader ideological models which recognise the shaping influence of texts and contexts. Autonomous conceptualisations take no account of difference and fail to recognise the uniqueness of each learner, they thus pay limited or no attention to the significance of supporting children to become genuinely engaged self-directed readers and writers. National assessment frameworks, which are also underpinned by such autonomous models, have unintended consequences, and prompt teachers to prioritise the assessed product of children's individual literate engagement. Consequently, less attention is afforded the process, young people's motivation and attitudes to reading and writing, and their emerging literate identities. This has repercussions for children's literacy self-efficacy, and is likely to impact negatively on their cognitive, social, affective and behavioural engagement in reading and writing.

In many countries, there is considerable pressure on teachers to profile phonics, comprehension, grammar and punctuation, to 'deliver' the prescribed curriculum and ensure that their country's required standards are reached. Whilst curriculum and skills teaching are necessary, when compliance and conformity hold sway and children's progress is assessed by limited attainment goals, then educators can feel their hands are tied and their freedom to develop autonomy-focused literacy practices is constrained (Frankel and Fields, 2019; Wyse and Hacking, 2024). Additionally, even in contexts where reading and writing for pleasure are recognised and seen to count, the concepts themselves can cause confusion, whilst the former is extensively used, it has multiple interpretations, and the latter is rarely encountered in educational contexts worldwide. Increased conceptual clarity is needed in order that governments, teachers, schools, charities and families can come together around the shared goal of developing young people's desire to read and write and to make meaning from and through texts, finding pleasure and satisfaction in the process.

Balancing motivation and proficiency

Even when professionals recognise that the will to read and the skills of reading operate reciprocally (Troyer et al., 2019) and that young writers' motivation is linked to their writing performance (Graham et al., 2017), balancing curriculum provision represents a genuine challenge. Tensions between the performative and volitional agendas persist through schooling. They are evident in the early years of primary school when, in England for instance, the systematic synthetics phonics agenda tends to dominate (Wyse and Bradbury, 2022) and they are sustained by ongoing assessment of individuals' literacy skills, both in school focused and national tests. Annual assessments of children's literacy competence and the information passed on to new teachers foreground young people's skills and scores, and seldom pay any attention to their attitudes, dispositions, preferences and emerging identities as readers and writers. Consequently, very young people who are somewhat detached from the experience, who have low levels of literacy self-efficacy and who have yet to find the intrinsic value of reading and writing, may find themselves obliged to attend additional skill-based intervention classes in the following year. Such attendance may reduce their access to more agentic, relaxed literacy experiences that could serve to mitigate their disengagement (Hempel-Jorgensen et al., 2018).

Nonetheless, the curriculum can encompass both literacy skills teaching and the enablement of young people's autonomy as readers and writers. Arguably, the former is teacher-directed, shaped, owned and individually focused, whilst the latter is more learner-directed, shaped and owned and is both individually and socially focused. As the Literacy Special Initiative has shown, research into children's identities in reading and writing communities highlights the mutually reinforcing relationship between children's personal and collective literacy identities. However, in data-driven education systems, young people's literacy journeys with their attendant targets and success criteria are conceived of and assessed individually. Additionally, schools can become satisfied with achieving short-term aims, for instance enabling more children to reach their country's expected standard, a minimum entitlement, and may not explicitly be aiming to develop readers and writers for life, their maximum entitlement.

Documenting children's volitional reading and writing

Difficulties also exist for educators and researchers in seeking to measure or 'assess' children's pleasurable engagement and volition as readers and writers, especially given the fluid nature of their literacy identities which shift in response to text and context. This challenge is evidenced in the reading research literature, which, with regard to documenting relationships between readers' engagement and myriad associated benefits, is predominantly quantitative in nature. While such studies are valuable, and different measures are used to report on trends and relationships between variables, self-reported reading frequency is most commonly used as a measure of volitional reading. Yet, as this book has established, what counts as reading for pleasure is far more layered than simply the time spent engaging in it. Furthermore, the findings of these studies are nuanced and the associations between readers' reported engagement, their skills and wellbeing for example, are also mediated by age, socioeconomic and cultural factors as well as reading materials. This complexity needs to be recognised and generalisations avoided.

Influenced by limited notions of literacy (Street, 1998) and the increased 'datafication' of education (Selwyn, 2015), teachers as well as researchers can develop an over-reliance on numbers to characterise young people's literacy development, foregrounding reading ages and test scores for instance to measure 'success'. For third-sector organisations too, reductionist notions of literacy education have been influential and shaped their provision; they often feel obliged to 'prove' that their projects have impacted positively on young people's literacy attainment. Additionally, both charities and teachers, at least in England, are working in a culture which has normalised randomised control trials as the route to measure the effectiveness of literacy interventions. These too have created challenges (Koutsouris and Norwich, 2018); randomised control trials cannot account for contextual factors, such as school assessment regimes, national expectations about literacy standards, students' characteristics and teacher effectiveness. Yet, as research shows, these and other contextual factors shape teachers' and students' identities and engagement as readers and writers (Hempel Jorgensen et al., 2018; Woodard, 2017).

Nonetheless, it appears the profession is expected to adopt this 'what works' mindset which tends to eschew complexity and sidelines the significance of readers' and writers' identities and their social, affective and relational nature. The profession's increasing dependence on numerical data also means that in those schools wanting to develop children's volitional engagement in literacy, an over-reliance on attitudinal surveys may develop, with little recognition that social desirability bias will inflate the young people's responses, and limited use of wider tools to gain a more rounded picture. Alternative ways to document children's journeys as readers and writers deserve to more be widely known and new approaches developed, particularly for disengaged students, whose sense of self-efficacy, autonomy and relatedness needs to be discerned in order for attuned and responsive support to be provided. Enhanced professional noticing is essential (Simpson et al., 2020) and ways of 'doing data differently' (Burnett et al., 2021) urgently need to become more mainstream, allowing the fluidity and complexity of children's literate identities to be better understood. These may also 'help pave the way for re-positioning teachers as the experts on and chief investigators of their practice' (Burnett et al., 2021, p. 15). Involving educators in collaborative research–practice partnerships represents a mutually beneficial way forward in understanding children's literacy journeys, co-designing research (McGeown et al., 2023), and co-constructing what counts as literacy beyond school (Cremin et al., 2012).

Qualitative studies are well positioned to document children's lived experience as readers and writers, particularly in the light of wider recognition of the social aspects of young people's literacy engagement. Such studies can also discern individual differences and the ways in which different texts and contexts shape their volitional reading and writing. Nonetheless, challenges also abound for qualitative researchers. It is demanding to capture the complexity of children's experience of being readers and writers in their own spaces and places. Being able to observe what happens as they engage in and across different domains – in schools, homes and local communities both on and offline – is not only time-consuming and expensive, it can present practical and ethical dilemmas. Young people's conceptions of reading and writing frame their responses and influence what they choose, or not, to share about what they read and write, where and with whom. Since children's volitional engagement in literacy is shaped by different settings and institutionally framed notions of what it means to be a reader and writer, understanding the wider context of influence is essential.

Historically, such socio-cultural work has tended to be school-based, but studies examining the ecology of young people's reading habits beyond the classroom are growing (e.g. Jerasa and Boffone, 2021; Reddan et al., 2024) and new methodologies are emerging that involve children as co-participant researchers (e.g. Loh, 2024; McGeown et al. 2020). In the former study, Loh's (2024) teenage participants documented their print and digital reading on a smartphone app and then took part in photo-elicitation interviews. In the latter study, the researchers trained primary aged learners to interview their peers about what they read and why. Both studies repositioned the young people through their roles as mobile ethnographers and interviewers and sought to shift the power imbalances between adults and children in the process. As Webber et al (2024) argue, such approaches have real potential to gain insiders' perspectives and discern what volitional reading, and also potentially writing, comprises in the lives and worlds of young people today.

Research lacunae and area for future investigation

In terms of research lacunae, there is a relative dearth of international research which explicitly examines the notion of volitional writing and approaches to nurturing this, both within and beyond classrooms. Whilst there are studies which consider children's and teachers' identities as writers (as seen in Chapters 4 and 7), more research is needed that focuses exclusively on the environmental conditions and pedagogical practices that encourage and empower young people to write volitionally. One reason to explain the scant number of empirical studies which directly address writing for enjoyment is that the focus of attention in research has been on the writing, not the writer. Studies predominantly examine the writing skills to be taught (e.g. grammar, vocabulary) the quality of the written product, and attend to instructional practices and interventions which may lead to stronger written outcomes. Whilst the significance of motivation in writing is acknowledged, it has not been prioritised internationally in research, policy or practice. Arguably more recreational reading is normalised and accepted within wider society, whereas leisure writing is not, it is commonly seen as the preserve of professional writers. This has consequences for teachers', children's and young people's perceptions of writing, such that personal and online writing practices (e.g. diary writing and fan fiction) may not be recognised or nurtured in school. There is clearly more to be understood about young writers as authors in these and many other compositional spaces, their intentions, desires and the environmental conditions which support their volitional engagement.

Additionally, studies which examine approaches that might motivate children to read represent a far smaller body of work than those devoted to the development of young readers' proficiency. Research that examines reading and writing skill development and attendant instruction dominates the field. Even when examining practices widely perceived as supportive of reading for pleasure, such as reading aloud for example, researchers have primarily examined the consequences for children's oral language acquisition and comprehension. Perceiving the practice of read-aloud and reading time mainly through the lens of associated literacy benefits constrains understanding of their contribution to children's desire to read. However, young people's affective engagement and the nature of interaction during reading aloud has been documented and some studies are now more explicitly tracking the flow on into independent reading (e.g. Batini and De Carlo, 2025). This example is indicative of an emerging trend in studies of reading for pleasure, and one that is to be welcomed; more overt attention is beginning to be paid to the shaping influence of classroom practice on young people's self-directed reading beyond school.

Nonetheless, tracking the contribution of diverse practices in different contexts to children's reading and writing habits, and to the nature and depth of their social, affective, behavioural and cognitive engagement, is a nuanced undertaking. As argued earlier, it is likely to be enriched by researchers and educators working in partnership, increased professional noticing and the involvement of the young people themselves as co-participants on the journey. Whilst, as Oxley and McGeown (2023) argue, the conceptualisation of effectiveness is an area for future research into reading for pleasure practices, attention also needs to be paid to text and context, since the efficacy of any pedagogic practice is always context and text dependent. It is not, for example, whether children are offered time to 'just' write, but the approach taken in this time, the ways in which children are positioned by others and position themselves during it that shapes their engagement, both within the experience and potentially later when they may choose to revisit their composition or create another.

Furthermore, studies of writing have historically tended to focus on motivation as 'an internal characteristic of an individual' (Myhill et al., 2023, p. 14), but writing is a social act of meaning making and is always situated in particular contexts of use. As Wigfield and Koenka (2020) observe, more attention needs to be paid to the teaching and learning context, the environments in which young people's sense of themselves as writers are shaped and formed. Such research could help develop new understandings of young writers' engagement, both their potential pleasure in the experience and in writing for pleasure in their own time. Knowing more about the nature of young people's leisure time writing practices and their engagement in writing as design, both on and offline, could also help to broaden practitioners' understanding of the ways in which children's written texts communicate meaning, and how these practices contribute to their identities as writers.

The Literacy Special Initiative also highlighted other areas that would merit further exploration. These include research that explicitly examines the nature and characteristics of social motivation, the value of belonging to communities of engaged readers and writers and the support that membership of such reading and writing networks offers. Additionally, since 'experience in reading is intrinsically bound to experience in writing' (Parry and Taylor, 2018, p. 109), new research which explores the reading–writing connection and their interplay would be valuable. Holistic research that pays attention to the intertwined physical, social, material and affective aspects of volitional reading and writing would enable educators to develop a more rounded picture of children's literate identities with potentially positive consequences for curriculum and pedagogy.

Moreover, more longitudinal studies are needed, specifically discerning if and in what ways enjoyable literacy experiences in school, in home and in extracurricular third sector initiatives lead to a proclivity to read or write for pleasure and sustain young people's identities as readers and writers across a life course. Two such studies pave the way. The first (Zare et al., 2023) indicates that for their adult undergraduate participants, childhood memories of reading enjoyment were positively linked to later print exposure and their adult inclination to read for pleasure. Nonetheless, studies with a wider range of participants would be valuable. The second (Mackey, 2025), whilst noting that lifelong reading journeys are fluid and idiosyncratic, explores how teachers might help young people develop a meta-awareness of their preferences and priorities as readers and begin to be cognisant of potential social support structures for use in later life. Finally, new empirical studies that enrich understanding of the intersecting identities, subjectivities and complexities of young people's volitional reading and writing practices within and well beyond school could help educators recognise and build upon these individual and social practices.

Exploring social and relational pedagogies

This work has revealed the growing number of studies which examine interactions around reading and writing for pleasure and the value and nature of these. Whilst Chapter 5 foregrounded studies of social interaction, the other three chapters in Part II also included evidence from research highlighting the ways in which low-key interactions around texts can enable young people to develop social and relational connections of value between readers and writers.

Socio-cultural researchers have investigated children's literacy interactions and social networks as a way of understanding their individual and communal experiences of being readers and writers. Some of this work has involved observing interactions in the playground and the wider community (e.g. Cummings et al., 2018; Maybin, 2013), but predominantly this has involved classroom-based observational work (e.g. Coakley-Fields, 2019; Cremin et al., 2024; Dyson, 1993, 2009; Ivey and Johnston 2015, 2023; Rowe et al., 2022). The studies noted have all illuminated a high degree of relaxed interaction between peers, and between children and adults around texts being read or written. The interchanges described in these, and many other papers, are not moments of instruction (although lessons may have been learned), they are moments of relational connection. Sometimes intense and sometimes relaxed, shared engagements with texts can create moments of pleasure that surface fleetingly, often linked to previous encounters and potentially feeding future ones. When these moments involve teachers and young people, as fellow readers/writers authentically sharing their text to life connections and authorial challenges, they represent examples of 'presence' in teaching and learning. According to Rodgers and Raider-Roth (2006, p. 284) this emerges in interaction 'when one comes to see the other and allows one's self to be seen'. Examining this concept empirically, Roefs et al (2021, p. 19) evidence presence as a relational connection that is experienced when a student's individuality becomes visible, and they suggest it manifestly involves 'experiencing togetherness'. Such affective and personally engaging shared encounters are also aligned to what Burnett and Merchant (2018, p. 63) describe as 'enchantment – an affect generated in the relations between readers, texts and things'. They argue that by focusing on enchantment, a more inclusive notion of reading for pleasure is created, one that encompasses the multitude of everyday digital practices in which children and adults engage. We recognise and value this notion and suggest it can also be applied to many of the relaxed relational and affective encounters documented in studies that we reviewed of print texts.

This enchantment is not just evident however in moments of spontaneous conversational text connections, reading, and indeed writing, are physical and affective experiences which involve the whole body and even when the activity is undertaken alone, research suggests that young people are often aware of the proximity of others in the vicinity (Kuzmičová et al., 2018). Children frequently choose to sit with friends in relaxed reading time, or when working on their own personal writing projects, positioned to interact and to connect should they choose to do so. The structured informality of these contexts, the reciprocal relationships evidenced, and the practices associated with them also resonate with conceptualisations of 'pedagogies of relation' (Aspelin, 2014; Ljungblad, 2021). Research into relational pedagogy asserts that it represents another way of seeing education, one that recognises humans as social and collective beings and re-orients the focus 'from individuals, groups and their practices onto relationships' (Ljungblad, 2021, p. 863). Essentially, reading and writing for pleasure are agentic acts of making meaning which develop in part through relational connections – connections with oneself, with texts, with others and with one's understanding of the world.

In the context of formal literacy instruction however, young people, particularly those who are less assured as readers and writers, are likely to perceive they are reading or writing under the teacher's direction, and at the teacher's behest. They may be required to read aloud or answer questions about their teacher's chosen text and may be expected to include the features of the set genre in their composition. Such teaching is not only necessary, it is also likely to be appropriately focused on the individual and assessed individually. However, approaches that nurture reading and writing for pleasure are markedly more informal, autonomy-focused, social and learner-directed. They respond to the young people's own goals and interests, and enable them to exert their rights as readers and writers, for example choosing what to read or write, where, and with whom – if anyone – they might share the experience.

Whilst these two agendas are not diametrically opposed, the subtle distinctions between them are salient, particularly with regard to the tenor and tone of the environment as this will shape the possible social interactions and relational connections. Arguably, autonomy-focused literacy environments in school are far more relaxed, informal and low-key than instructionally focused environments. Informality is also inherent in relational pedagogy and can, as Hickey and Riddle (2022, p. 789) argue, 'reconfigure the relational interface'. The structured informality evident in many of the classrooms in the research reviewed, attest to educators' expertise in establishing relaxed literacy cultures and rich opportunities for building relationships around texts which, studies suggest, tend to be relatively non-hierarchical, typified by reciprocity, mutual respect and close bonds. Such relationships were evidenced in the work of the programmes too, they commonly created a strong sense of environmental informality, despite offering clearly structured provision.

Whilst no known studies examine volitional reading or writing though the lens of pedagogies of relation, we suggest that these autonomy-focused literacy practices are effectively nurtured by relational pedagogies. Within such framing, priority is not given to children's skills, progression or next steps as readers or writers, rather, personal attention is afforded each child and respectful relationships built that value, appreciate and respect their interests, experiences and literate identities. Adults offer inclusive and thus socially-just reading and writing opportunities in which young people can participate and interact with others informally and on their own terms. This approach is not intended to replace skills teaching, curriculum goals or teacher-led lessons, instead we argue that, in school contexts, the balance between relational reading and writing and teacher-directed lessons should be reviewed, with time and attention afforded both.

The evidence base indicates that creating spaces for engagement within a community of readers and writers in school is supportive, particularly when educators and role models show close attention to the children's emerging identities and adapt and attune their practice in response. This can help to develop relational connections around reading and writing that are affectively engaging and highly motivating.

Collaborative ways forward

In order to halt the persistent international decline in children and young people's attitudes to and enjoyment of reading and writing, professional understanding of the empirical research base is needed, alongside urgent collective action from policy makers, literacy organisations, schools, teachers and parents. Collaborative ways forward that capitalise upon the expertise of diverse organisations have the potential to help turn the tide and enable all children and young people to become motivated and engaged readers and writers.

In the UK, multiple third-sector literacy organisations exist, offering programmes that support young people, locally and nationally, in homes and foster homes, in hospitals, libraries, clubs, faith spaces, online and many other contexts. Arguably, however, third-sector literacy expertise is somewhat under-recognised by mainstream education, positioned as a 'nice to have' if finance allows or deployed to offer disengaged and often disadvantaged youngsters additional support to 'catch up' academically. Furthermore, scarce resources can make literacy charities, particularly small ones, feel obliged to offer short-term projects that aim to show measurable results within tight time frames. Schools and local councils, pressured by the standards agenda, tend to demand evidence of increased literacy proficiency in order to fund such initiatives. For the third sector to foreground reading and writing for pleasure provision represents a potential risk, requires a measure of faith and considerable commitment to the enterprise. This challenge is exacerbated in England by persistent cuts in education, the arts and cultural sector, and the decline in local library services, and it creates unnecessary competition between third-sector literacy organisations.

Yet as the research within the Literacy Special Initiative has shown, the third-sector colleagues who worked in the six programmes, the staff, creative practitioners, volunteers, public librarians and members of the community make a rich contribution to young people's pleasurable engagement in literacy. The programmes all nurtured local partnerships, listened to and valued the perspectives and expertise of others, and operated as learning organisations. The education profession, policy makers, funding bodies and researchers have a great deal to learn from their ways of working. The third sector offers a rich reservoir of expertise and talent that needs to be more widely accessed and shared. Learning from and partnering with third-sector literacy organisations in sustained place-based work that is adapted according to context and connects to libraries, local businesses and communities, offers the potential to increase young people's engagement as readers and writers. We need to move beyond deploying the same blunt educational instruments of curriculum, interventions and testing that have not addressed (and have possibly increased) children's disengagement in reading and writing, especially for the very children who need it most. Professional networks which value teacher autonomy and seek to widen their knowledge and practice in these areas are also valuable. We see this in the ongoing commitment that teachers in the UK make to lead or join the annual 100-plus Open University/United Kingdom Literacy Association Teacher Reading Groups which have been supported nationally, but led locally, since 2017. Expanding these to involve more librarians and third-sector volunteers, as well as bookshop owners and interested others, represents another way forward to connect, share and develop expertise to support young people as readers. Growing national networks of teacher writing groups also has potential, as the US National Writing Project has shown.

To address the challenge of young people's deep disengagement in reading and writing, differently configured pathways to partnerships between homes, schools and third-sector organisations deserve to be explored. These could support the development of the 'funds of courage' needed to nurture socially-just reading (and writing) for pleasure practices (Kucirkova and Cremin, 2024). Operating across sectors, practitioners of all kinds, through recognising the vulnerability and resilience involved, can build forwards by connecting, conversing and envisioning potentialities. Taking the time to broker local partnerships and build collegiality and trust to nurture everyone's professional learning, may also encourage the co-presence of teachers and arts partners in classrooms and open up consideration of their relational pedagogies in action. If these partnerships develop in-depth knowledge of groups of literacy learners and then draw on the Framework for Practice to plan co-constructed and highly attuned responses, this could prove fruitful. Such responses will involve prioritising young people's rights as readers and writers, aligning the work to their interests and contemporary literacy practices, and enabling them to shape the journey alongside the cross-sectoral groups of adults involved.

Multi-agency approaches and collaborative ways forward have the potential to re-affirm that developing children's reading and writing for pleasure is not a package that can be bought off the shelf, nor a set of routines to deploy at home, in school or community initiatives. Rather, as our research within the Literacy Special Initiative has shown, to motivate children as readers and writers, autonomy-focused practices that are both individually and socially oriented are needed, mediated through the responsive involvement of highly engaged adults. Text access, time and space enable this dynamic combination to operate successfully and can help create connected communities of readers and writers. Through forging social and relational ways forward, children and young people's deep engagement in and enjoyment of reading and writing can be nurtured.

References

Aspelin, J. (2014) 'Beyond individualised teaching', *Education Inquiry*, 5(2), 23926.

Batini, F. and De Carlo, M.E. (2025) 'Shared reading aloud as a practice to promote equity: Review, method, and evidence-based research', in Cremin, T. and McGeown, S. (eds), *Reading for Pleasure: International Perspectives from Research*, London: Routledge, pp. 125–137.

Burnett, C. and Merchant, G. (2018) 'Affective encounters: Enchantment and the possibility of reading for pleasure', *Literacy*, 52(2), pp. 62–69.

Burnett, C., Merchant, G. and Guest, I. (2021) 'Destabilising data: The use of creative data visualisation to generate professional dialogue', *British Educational Research Journal*, 47(1), pp. 105–127.

Coakley-Fields, M.R. (2019) 'Inclusive talk: Weaving fiction discussions across the school day', *The Reading Teacher*, 72(6), pp. 721–729.

Cremin, T., Mottram, M., Collins, F., Powell, S. and Drury, R. (2012) 'Building communities: Teachers researching literacy lives', *Improving Schools*, 15(2), pp. 101–115.

Cremin, T., Hendry, H., Rodriguez Leon, L., and Hulston, S.J. (2024) 'Informal book talk: Digging beneath the surface', *English 3–13, 52*(7), pp. 930–945.

Cummings, S., McLaughlin, T. and Finch, B. (2018) 'Examining preadolescent children's engagement in out-of-school literacy and exploring opportunities for supporting literacy development', *Australian Journal of Language and Literacy*, 41, pp. 103–116.

Dyson, A.H. (1993) *Social Worlds of Children's Learning to Write in an Urban Primary School*, New York: Teachers' College Press.

Dyson, A.H. (2009) 'Writing in childhood worlds', in Beard, R., Myhill, D., Riley, J. and Nystrand, M. (eds), *The SAGE Handbook of Writing Development*, London: SAGE, pp. 232–245.

Frankel, K.K. and Fields, S.S. (2019) 'Disrupting storylines: A case study of one adolescent's identity, agency, and positioning during literacy tutoring', *Literacy Research and Instruction*, 58(3), pp. 142–163.

Graham, S., Kiuhara, S.A., Harris, K.R. and Fishman, E.J. (2017) 'The relationship among strategic writing behaviour, writing motivation, and writing performance with young, developing writers', *Elementary School Journal*, 118(1), pp. 82–104.

Hempel-Jorgensen, A., Cremin, T., Harris, D. and Chamberlain, L. (2018) 'Pedagogy for reading for pleasure in low socio-economic primary schools: Beyond "pedagogy of poverty"?', *Literacy*, 52(2), pp. 86–94.

Hickey, A. and Riddle, S. (2022) 'Relational pedagogy and the role of informality in renegotiating learning and teaching encounters', *Pedagogy, Culture and Society*, 30(5), pp. 787–799.

Ivey, G. and Johnston, P. (2015) 'Engaged reading as a collaborative transformative practice', *Journal of Literacy Research*, 47(3), pp. 297–327.

Ivey, G. and Johnston, P. (2023) *Teens Choosing to Read: Fostering Social, Emotional, and Intellectual Growth Through Books*, New York: Teachers College Press.

Jerasa, S. and Boffone, T. (2021) 'BookTok 101: TikTok, digital literacies, and out-of-school reading practices', *Journal of Adolescent and Adult Literature*, 65(3), pp. 219–226.

Koutsouris, G. and Norwich, B. (2018) 'What exactly do RCT findings tell us in education research?', *British Educational Research Journal*, 44(6), pp. 939–959.

Kucirkova, N. and Cremin, T. (2024) 'Funds of courage: Advancing social justice in children's reading for pleasure', *Cambridge Journal of Education*, 54(4) pp. 437–454.

Kuzmičová, A., Dias, P., Vogrinčič Čepič, A., Albrechtslund, A.-M.B., Casado, A., Kotrla Topić, M., Mínguez López, X., Nilsson, S.K. and Teixeira-Botelho, I. (2018) 'Reading and company: Embodiment and social space in silent reading practices', *Literacy*, 52(2), pp. 70–77.

Ljungblad, A.L. (2021) 'Pedagogical Relational Teachership (PeRT): A multi-relational perspective', *International Journal of Inclusive Education*, 25(7), pp. 860–876.

Loh, C.E. (2024) 'What makes adolescents want to read? Examining adolescents' contemporary print and new media (fiction) leisure reading through mobile ethnography', *Language and Education*, 38(4), pp. 596–616.

Mackey, M. (2025) 'Lifelong reading journeys', in Cremin, T. and McGeown, S. (eds), *Reading for Pleasure: International Perspectives*, London and New York: Routledge, pp. 170–185.

Maybin, J. (2013) 'What counts as reading? PIRLS, EastEnders and The Man on the Flying Trapeze', *Literacy*, 47(2), pp. 59–66.

McGeown, S., Oxley, E., Ricketts J. and Shapiro, S. (2023) 'Working at the intersection of research and practice: The love to read project', *International Journal of Educational Research*, 117, pp. 102–134

McGeown, S., Bonsall, J., Andries, V., Howarth, D. and Wilkinson, K. (2020) 'Understanding reading motivation across different text types: Qualitative insights from children', *Journal of Research in Reading*, 43(4), pp 597–608.

Myhill, D., Cremin, T. and Oliver, L. (2023) 'The impact of changed writing environment on students' motivation to write', *Frontiers in Psychology*, 14.

Oxley, E. and McGeown, S. (2023) 'Reading for pleasure practices in school: Children's perspectives and experiences', *Educational Research*, 65(3), pp. 375–391.

Parry, B. and Taylor, L. (2018) 'Readers in the round: Children's holistic engagements with texts', *Literacy*, 52(2), pp. 103–110.

Reddan, B., Rutherford, L., Schoonens, A. and Dezuanni, M. (2024) *Social Reading Cultures on BookTube, Bookstagram, and BookTok*, London: Routledge.

Rodgers, C.R. and Raider-Roth, M.B. (2006) 'Presence in teaching', *Teachers, Teaching, Theory Practice*, 12, pp. 265–287.

Roefs, E., Leeman, Y., Oosterheert, I. and Meijer, P. (2021) 'Teachers' experiences of presence in their daily educational practice', *Education Sciences*, 11, 48.

Rowe, D.W., Shimizu, A.Y. and Davis, Z.G. (2022) 'Essential practices for engaging young children as writers: Lessons from expert early writing teachers', *The Reading Teacher*, 75(4), pp. 485–494.

Selwyn, N. (2015) 'Data entry: Towards the critical study of digital data and education', *Learning, Media and Technology*, 40(1), pp. 64–82.

Simpson, A., Pomerantz, F., Kaufman, D. and Ellis, S. (2020) *Developing Habits of Noticing in Literacy and Language Classrooms: Research and Practice Across Professional Cultures*, Sydney: Routledge.

Street, B. (1998) 'New literacies in theory and practice: What are the implications for language in education?', *Linguistics and Education*, 10(1), pp. 1–24.

Troyer, M., Kim, S.J., Hale, E., Wantchekon, K.A. and Armstrong, C. (2019) 'Relations among intrinsic and extrinsic reading motivation, reading amount, and comprehension: A conceptual replication', *Reading and Writing*, 32(5), pp. 1197–1218.

Webber, C., Wilkinson, K., Duncan, L.G. and McGeown, S. (2024) 'Adolescents' perspectives on the barriers to reading for pleasure', *Literacy*, 58(2), pp. 204–215.
Wigfield, A. and Koenka, A.C. (2020) 'Where do we go from here in academic motivation theory and research? Some reflections and recommendations for future work', *Contemporary Educational Psychology*, 61, Article 101872.
Woodard, R.L. (2017) 'An elementary teacher legitimising students' writerly identities while authenticating her own', in Cremin, T. and Locke, T. (eds), *Writer identity and the Teaching and Learning of Writing*, London: Routledge, pp. 115–131.
Wyse, D. and Bradbury, A. (2022) 'Reading wars or reading reconciliation? A critical examination of robust research evidence, curriculum policy and teachers' practices for teaching phonics and reading', *Review of Education*, 10(1), e3314.
Wyse, D. and Hacking, C. (2024) *The Balancing Act: An Evidence-Based Approach to Teaching Phonics Reading and Writing*, London: Routledge.
Zare, M., Kozak, S., Rodrigues, M.L. and Martin-Chang, S. (2023) 'The roots of reading for pleasure: Recollections of reading and current habits', *Literacy*, 57(3), pp. 262–274.

INDEX

Note: Page numbers in *italics* refer to figures.